MODERN HUMANITIES RESEARCH ASSOCIATION
CRITICAL TEXTS
VOLUME 68

LIFE AND DEATH ON THE PLANTATIONS
SELECTED JESUIT LETTERS FROM THE CARIBBEAN

LIFE AND DEATH ON THE PLANTATIONS

Selected Jesuit Letters from the Caribbean

EDITED AND TRANSLATED BY
MICHAEL HARRIGAN

Modern Humanities Research Association
Critical Texts 68
2021

Published by

The Modern Humanities Research Association
Salisbury House
Station Road
Cambridge CB1 2LA
United Kingdom

© *Modern Humanities Research Association 2021*

First published 2021

ISBN 978-1-78188-901-5

CONTENTS

ACKNOWLEDGEMENTS

I wish to express my gratitude to the Society for Early Modern French Studies for the award of an Amy Wygant Research Bursary in 2018, which facilitated the consultation of archival sources. I am also grateful to the staff of the Archives françaises de la Compagnie de Jésus (Societas Iesu) (AFSI), Vanves; Bibliothèque Mazarine (BM), Paris; Médiathèque de Carcassonne Agglo (MdC), and Archives départementales de l'Aude, Carcassonne; and Archivum Romanum Societatis Iesu (ARSI), Rome, for facilitating consultation of manuscripts. The Archives départementales du Cher (AdC), Bourges, and Médiathèque Albert-Camus, Issoudun, as well as MdC and ARSI, also generously sent digital facsimiles of manuscripts. My thanks to Claire White and Gerard Lowe for advice throughout the writing and production of this edition, to Julia Prest for commenting on the Introduction, and to Leah Morin for copy-editing. Particular thanks are also due to Constanza, Francis, Daniel, L. A., and Edie Harrigan.

ABBREVIATIONS

AdC   Archives départementales du Cher, Bourges
AFSI   Archives françaises de la Compagnie de Jésus (Societas Iesu), Vanves
ARSI   Archivum Romanum Societatis Iesu, Rome
BM   Bibliothèque Mazarine, Paris
GBro   Fonds Brotier
MdC   Collections of Médiathèque de Carcassonne Agglo/Bibliothèque
        Intercommunale de Conservation de Carcassonne Agglo, Carcassonne

INTRODUCTION

The events which led to the papal approval of the Society of Jesus (Societas Iesu) as a religious order in 1540, and its rapid growth from the sixteenth century onwards, have been well documented.[1] The Society expanded in a matter of decades from a group of students in Paris centred around the Basque former soldier Ignatius of Loyola (1491–1556) to a global network dedicated to spreading the Word throughout Europe, the Americas, Asia, and Africa.

Papal bulls in 1540 and 1550 shaped the tasks of the Society, as did its *Constitutions*, the body of rules attributed in large part to Ignatius of Loyola himself; the Society was to be explicitly missionary in its function and organization, with its duties including catechizing, administering the sacraments, and further charitable works.[2] Members were distinguished into categories, or *grades*. The period of novitiate, before taking initial vows, was of two years' duration. Scholastics and *coadiutores* — *coadiutores* were either unordained members who performed temporal offices, or ordained members who carried out minor spiritual offices — were bound by three vows: of poverty, chastity, and obedience.[3] Fully *professed* Jesuits were ordained priests who would take a fourth vow, to obey the instructions of the pope to 'go anywhere His Holiness will order [...] for the sake of matters pertaining to the worship of God and the good of the Christian religion'.[4]

The Jesuit approach, working *ad maiorem Dei gloriam* ('for the greater glory of God'), was remarkably dynamic. The Jesuits would quickly gain unrivalled importance in the education of continental Europe's Catholic population. Yet it is their missionary initiatives outside Europe which would come to be considered emblematic of their mobility in the early modern era. Francis Xavier (1506–1552), one of Ignatius's original companions, undertook a voyage of proselytization from 1540, which brought him as far as India and Japan before his death en route to China. Jesuits such as the Italian Matteo Ricci (1552–1610) were active in China from the late sixteenth century on — in the case of Ricci,

---

[1] See notably John W. O'Malley, *The First Jesuits* (Cambridge, MA: Harvard University Press, 1993); J. W. O'Malley, *Saints or Devils Incarnate? Studies in Jesuit History* (Leiden; Boston: Brill, 2013).

[2] For an introduction to the functions and development of the Society of Jesus, see O'Malley, *Saints or Devils*; on the sacraments, p. 42.

[3] See Wiktor Gramatowski, *Jesuit Glossary*, trans. by Camilla Russell (Rome: ARSI, 1992), p. 8.

[4] *The Constitutions of the Society of Jesus and their Complementary Norms* [*Constitutions and Norms*], trans. by Carl J. Moell and others (Saint Louis, MO: Institute of Jesuit Sources, 1996), Chapter 1, [7] 5, p. 25.

at the imperial court — and worked towards making Christian dogma (as well as European science) comprehensible in a challenging linguistic context. In Paraguay, Jesuits would organize large communities of the Amerindian Guaraní peoples into settlements known as *reducciones*. Such initiatives inspired regular criticism amongst European observers; the Jesuits' reputed willingness to accept theological compromises in Asia was at the root of the bitter Chinese Rites controversy (*Querelle des rites chinois*) from the seventeenth century, while Voltaire's eighteenth-century account of the *reducciones* is emblematic of contemporary European suspicion of their governance of these settlements.[5]

The global reach of the Society of Jesus was facilitated by its organized, hierarchical structure. Headed by a superior general elected for life and based in Rome, the Society divided its missions into assistancies, which were in turn divided into provinces, each governed by a *provincial*. The French Assistancy (*Assistentia Galliae*) was made up of five provinces by the seventeenth century: France, Aquitaine, Lyon, Toulouse, and Champagne. Epistolary communication between members of the Society was essential for the exchange of information within this dynamic network. Such correspondence had been visualized as integral to the Society from its very beginnings. The *Constitutions* give the following instructions:

> At the beginning of every four-month period, those under a provincial who is over various houses or colleges should write a letter containing only matters of edification in the vernacular language of the province, as well as another of the same tenor in Latin. They should send the provincial two copies of each, so that he can send one copy of the Latin and the vernacular to the general, along with a letter of his own stating anything noteworthy or edifying that was not mentioned by the individuals, and can have the second recopied as often as is needed to inform the others of his own province.[6]

Letters also had the important function of spreading news about the progress of the Jesuit missions around the world amongst readers in early modern Europe, and both informed and edified. In their printed form, the *Lettres édifiantes et curieuses* would be an important source of information about the cultures outside Europe in the early modern period. They would be published in French from 1703 to 1776 in thirty-four volumes, and relay information about such missions as those to Canada, South America, the Middle East, and India, and the famous mission to China.[7]

The present edition consists in the transcription and translation of a selection of letters which were sent from the Caribbean by two *professed* Jesuit

---

[5]   Voltaire (François-Marie Arouet), *Candide, ou l'optimisme* (1759), in *Romans et contes*, ed. by René Groos (Paris: Gallimard, 1954), pp. 149–237 (pp. 179–82).

[6]   *Constitutions and Norms*, p. 336.

[7]   *Lettres édifiantes et curieuses*, 34 vols (Paris: Nicolas Le Clerc, 1703–76).

missionaries, manuscript copies/the original of which are now housed in archives in France. The first of these missionaries, Jean Mongin (1637–1698), wrote from Martinique and Saint Kitts in the late 1670s and early 1680s.

Mongin was born in Carcassonne on 14 February 1637, and joined the Society of Jesus on 1 April 1655, pronouncing his fourth vow at Perpignan on 15 August 1671.[8] His *Indipeta* — a letter in which Jesuits expressed their views on the destination they would be best suited to — is held by the Archivum Romanum Societatis Iesu [ARSI], Rome. In this letter, dated 20 August 1662, Mongin expresses a preference for being sent to Asia (the letter also reveals that Mongin was his mother's 'only son').[9] Mongin also reveals in his account of the voyage to the colonies that he had spent time as a missionary in Roussillon before leaving for the Caribbean: enough time to have received a nickname from the 'good people' concerning the Huguenots he had converted.[10]

The vessel on which Mongin sailed left France on 12 December 1675, during the Franco-Dutch War (1672–78). He writes that he brought his own 'navigational instruments' with him. With a fellow Jesuit, Father Bonnal, he disembarked at Fort Saint-Pierre in Martinique on 7 February 1676. Mongin's *Journal* reveals that there were four other Jesuits there at the time, one of whom was the superior general of all the islands, and who had previously spent 'thirty-seven years in the dreadful travails of Canada' ('trente-sept ans dans les horribles fatigues du Canada'). In a telling illustration of the state of the mission, Mongin adds that another missionary had been buried 'two days previously', and 'two or three' others had recently departed 'to try and have their health restored in France'.[11] He writes from Saint Kitts that he began the mission to the slaves there in August 1680.[12] Bernard David writes that Mongin would ultimately return to France in 1684; he died in Tournon on 26 June 1698.[13]

The final letter reproduced here was written by another French Jesuit named Claude Breban (also spelled as *Brebant* or *Bréban*). Breban was born in Issoudun

---

[8] Biographical information from Bernard David, *Dictionnaire biographique de la Martinique (1635–1848)*, 3 vols (Fort-de-France: Société d'histoire de la Martinique, 1984), I: *Le Clergé, 1635–1715*, p. 176. See ARSI, Gall. 11, I, fols 134–35; Tolos. 13, fol. 131, n. 5; my thanks to Sergio Palagiano (ARSI) for confirming Mongin's biographical information and furnishing archival references relating to Mongin.

[9] Jean Mongin, Letter to Giovanni Paolo Oliva, 20 August 1662, ARSI, *Indipetae*, xxvi, no. 59. See also Amélie Vantard, 'Les Vocations pour les missions *ad gentes* (France 1650–1750)' (doctoral thesis, Université du Maine, 2010), pp. 88–89, 286, 293 n. 170.

[10] 'J'eusse bien souhaité qu'on m'eût pu donner un nom plus conforme à ma profession, tel qu'était celui qu'il plaisait aux bonnes gens de me donner dans le Roussillon, à l'occasion des Huguenots dont je recevais la profession', *Journal*, MdC, MS 73, fol. 20ᵛ.

[11] Mongin writes that the poor state of the ship on which he sailed was commented on at La Rochelle; *Journal*, MdC, MS 73, fol. 9ʳ; on the instruments, fol. 20ᵛ; on the state of the mission, fol. 28ʳ.

[12] Mongin, Letter of 1682, AFSI, GBro185, fol. 11ʳ.

[13] David, p. 176; ARSI, Tolos. 13, fol. 268.

on 10 August 1695, the son of a merchant, François; the surname is spelled 'Brebant' on the baptismal act.[14] He entered the Society of Jesus in Paris on 11 November 1713, professing his fourth vow on 2 February 1731. A number of minor publications from the 1720s have been attributed to him.[15] He died as a missionary in Saint-Domingue on 24 August 1735.[16]

Note on Text

A total of five letters in French have been transcribed or partly transcribed in this edition, each one accompanied by a translation into English, and with contextual notes in the translations. Copies of three of Mongin's letters are transcribed in their entirety (italics indicate a title in the following manuscripts):

> **Letter 1**: Letter from Martinique, September 1676, Carcassonne, Collections of Médiathèque de Carcassonne Agglo/Bibliothèque Intercommunale de Conservation de Carcassonne Agglo [MdC], MS 73 [former code Ma 82] (inv. 2459–47), fols 32^r–41^r.[17]
>
> **Letter 2**: *Copy of the Letter Written by Reverend Father Jean Mongin to Reverend Father Antoine Pagez, Provincial of the Society of Jesus for the Province of Toulouse, from the Island of Martinique*, 10 May 1679, Paris, Bibliothèque Mazarine [BM], Ant MS 9, fols 23^r–39^v.[18]
>
> **Letter 3**: *Copy of the Letter of Father Jean Mongin, Missionary to the Americas, to a Person of Quality of Languedoc, Written on the Island of Saint Christopher in the Month of May 1682*, Vanves, Archives françaises de la Compagnie de Jésus (Societas Iesu) [AFSI], Fonds Brotier [GBro] 185, fols 1^r–49^v.[19]

---

[14] My thanks to the staff of the Médiathèque Albert-Camus, Issoudun, for sending a digital reproduction of Breban's baptismal act of 11 August 1695.

[15] Carlos Sommervogel, *Bibliothèque de la Compagnie de Jésus*, 3rd edn, 11 vols (Brussels: Oscar Schepens; Paris: Alphonse Picard, 1890–1932), II (1891), article 'Breban, Claude', p. 107.

[16] ARSI, Franc. 20, fol. 63^v, n. 6, fol. 266; Gall. 20, fols 230–30^v. My thanks to Sergio Palagiano (ARSI) for forwarding this biographical detail about Breban and references. For biographical detail, see also Nicole Dyonet, 'Le Père Bréban, missionnaire berrichon à Saint-Domingue: lettre inédite de janvier 1732', *Bulletin du Centre d'histoire des espaces atlantiques*, 8 (1997), 103–30 (103–04), and Jean-Yves Ribault, 'Témoins de l'esclavage à Saint-Domingue: les lettres de deux jésuites berrichons, les PP. Margat et Bréban', *Cahiers d'archéologie et d'histoire du Berry*, 143 (September 2000), 27–36 (29).

[17] Marcel Chatillon, in his edition of Mongin's letters, writes that this letter is addressed to the Jesuit provincial of Toulouse; *L'Évangélisation des esclaves au XVIIe siècle*, ed. by Marcel Chatillon, *Bulletin de la Société d'histoire de la Guadeloupe*, 61–62 (3rd and 4th trimesters 1984), p. 6. Although there is no title to the manuscript letter, Mongin's reference to having been sent to Le Carbet by the addressee makes this likely; MdC, MS 73, fol. 32^r.

[18] *Copie de la lettre du R. P. Jean Mongin, écritte au R. P. Antoine Pagez provincial de la Compagnie de Jésus en la province de Toulouse, de l'isle de la Martinique le 10e may 1679*, BM, Ant MS 9, fols 23^r–39^v.

[19] *Copie de la lettre du père Jean Mongin missionnaire de l'Amérique, à une personne de condition de Languedoc, écrite de l'isle de Sainct Christophle au mois de may 1682*, AFSI, GBro185, 1^r–49^v.

An alternative version of Mongin's Letter 3 exists, which is partly transcribed in this book:

> **Letter 4 [Extract]:** *Seventh Letter to a Languedocian Gentleman, Containing the Relation of the Mission to the Black Slaves, from Saint Christopher Island*, MdC, MS 73, fols 79^r–119^v [title page on fol. 79^r, letter begins fol. 80^r]. Fols 79^r–84^r are transcribed in this edition.[20]

The initial section (fols 80^r–84^r) of Letter 4 (MdC, MS 73, fols 79^r–119^v), differs substantially from the beginning (fols 1^r–9^r) of Letter 3 (AFSI, GBro185, fols 1^r–49^v). From Letter 4, fol. 84^r onwards, the differences are far less substantial. For reasons of space, the significant disparities from this point on between Letters 3 and 4 have been indicated in footnotes to the transcription of Letter 3.

The fifth letter in this edition, that sent from Saint-Domingue by Claude Breban, has been transcribed and translated in its totality:

> **Letter 5:** Letter [to Breban's brother] from Cap-Français, Saint-Domingue, 19 January 1732, Bourges, Archives départementales du Cher [AdC], 2F 788.[21]

Those of Mongin's letters held in Carcassonne transcribed wholly and partly in this book are part of a total of seven letters transcribed in MS 73, which are attributed to Mongin.[22] Fols 1^r–31^r consist in Mongin's incomplete account of the voyage which originally brought him to Martinique, and which is signed with the date of 15 July 1676. Folio 1^r is numbered both p. 7 (seemingly the pagination of the first letter) and p. 13 (this latter pagination runs, with gaps, through the manuscript), implying that the manuscript is missing at least six initial folios. This first letter has been referred to in this edition as the *Journal*; it has not been translated into English, although a transcription in French was published in 1962.[23] Despite the absence of its initial pages, certain details in this letter show it was intended for reading by a French Languedocian gentleman; there is a reference to the recipient's 'château', to the 'nearby' birthplace of the renowned Jesuit Jean-François Régis (1597–1640), and a final address to 'Monsieur'.[24]

The third letter in MdC, MS 73 (fols 43^r–49^v; title page 43^r, letter begins

---

[20] *Septième lettre à un gentilhomme du Languedoc contenant la relation de la mission des nègres, de l'isle Saint Cristofe*, MdC, MS 73, fols 79^r–119^v.

[21] Breban's letter begins: 'Au Cap Français, île et côte de Saint-Domingue, le 19 de janvier 1732', AdC, 2F 788. Letter begins with fol. 2^r.

[22] The manuscript was consulted for this edition at the Archives départementales de l'Aude in 2018. MS 73 is listed as 'Lettres du P. Mongin, jésuite, missionnaire, contenant ses relations sur la mission de la Martinique', in *Catalogue général des manuscrits des bibliothèques publiques de France*, XIII (Paris: Plon, Nourrit et Cie, 1891), p. 197.

[23] Jean Mangin [=Mongin], 'Journal d'un voyage à la Martinique en 1676', repr. by Jacques Petitjean-Roget, *Annales des Antilles*, 10 (1962), 35–58.

[24] *Journal*, MdC, MS 73, fols 1^r, 6^r, 31^r. Régis was born in Foncouverte, Bas-Languedoc. Guillaume Daubenton, *La Vie du bienheureux Jean-François Régis* (Paris: Nicolas Le Clerc, 1716), p. 2.

fol. 44^r) is an account of the French attack on a Dutch fleet at Tobago, sent to a 'Languedocian gentleman' and dated 26 March 1677.[25] Since the author of this letter had recently arrived in the colonies — he writes that the vessel which had brought him to Martinique had arrived in La Rochelle the previous year — and refers both to himself as a 'missionary' and to having previously sent an account of his voyage to the recipient, it should be expected to be Mongin. An illegible signature follows the letter, which appears to be in another hand, and possibly unconnected to the letter.

The fourth letter in MdC, MS 73 (fols 51^r–68^r; title page 51^r, letter begins fol. 52^r) is dated 29 December 1678 and is preceded by a title page which reads *Quatrième lettre au R. P. provincial des jésuites de la province de Thoulouse contenant la relation de la mission de la Martinique*. It is an alternative version of the letter sent by Mongin to Antoine Pagez on 10 May 1679 (BM, Ant MS 9), which is reproduced in the present volume (as Letter 2). There are significant differences between both letters, and the principal variations have been indicated in the notes to Letter 2 in the present edition. In the BM, Ant MS 9 version, Mongin states that he had remembered that he 'had not sent' Letter 2, only four months after writing it, which may go some way to explaining the discrepancies between the dates.

The fifth letter in MdC, MS 73 (fols 71^r–73^v), is dated 15 January 1679 and describes the reception of the Count d'Estrées after a victorious French assault on Tobago, with a series of *devises* and *madrigaux allégoriques*. This letter is followed, in turn, by a sixth, dated 3 March 1681, addressed to a Father de Fontenay, 'professor of mathematics at the Collège de Clermont in Paris', which consists for the most part in observations of a comet visible between 1680 and 1681.[26]

The text of the MdC manuscript has been manipulated to some degree over time. Certain names have been crossed out, as have religious titles; for example 'votre révérence voulut' has become 'vous voulûtes' (fol. 52^r). Nearly a page of text (fols 66^r–66^v) has been covered over by a replacement text. This has been glued over the original, and makes reading the original impossible. The pagination indicates that there are occasional folios missing from MS 73; along with the initial folios, those missing include three between current fols 115^v and 116^r, and an uncertain number from fol. 119^v onwards. There are also a number of pages in MS 73 on which material unrelated to the missions figures;

---

[25] *Troisième lettre à un gentilhomme du Languedoc contenant l'attaque et l'embrasement des vaisseaux holandois à l'isle de Tabac faite par Mr le Comte d'Estrée*, MdC, MS 73, fols 43^r–49^v.
[26] The letter is preceded by the title page: *Sixième lettre au R. Père de Fontenai professeur de matématique au Collège de Clairmont à Paris; observations de la comète de 1681 et 82 faites dans l'isle de St Cristofe* [modified to *St Christofle*], MdC, MS 73, fols 75^r–78^v (title page, fol. 75^r; letter begins fol. 76^r). The content of the letter indicates the correct dates are 1680–81 (fol. 77^r).

signatures have been practised, and there are a certain number of doodles, while the repeated mentions of dates from 1724 to 1730 hint at the years in which these texts were copied.

Copies of part of Mongin's correspondence were published by Marcel Chatillon in 1984, accompanied by a useful introduction.[27] These transcriptions call for revision, however. Amongst the letters reproduced in his edition, Chatillon claims to have transcribed the totality of the 1682 seventh letter in MdC, MS 73 and the initial, widely differing first part of AFSI, GBro185. However, in the present edition the totality of the more complete AFSI letter has instead been transcribed, as Letter 3, and translated. The beginning of the MdC, MS 73 version has then been transcribed — as Letter 4 [Extract] — and translated, and significant divergences from fol. 84^r onwards in this letter have been indicated in notes to Letter 3 (the transcription of AFSI, GBro185). Comparison of Chatillon's transcription of AFSI, GBro185 with a nineteenth-century transcription of the same letter (AFSI, GBro102) suggests that he used this later transcription for his edition. This has led him to duplicate the regular textual variations which were introduced in the later copy (AFSI, GBro102), and make his transcription an occasionally unreliable source. One example of an error which results is Chatillon's transcription of the number of enslaved people who 'know the principles of faith well' ('savent bien les principes de la foi') as 511, the figure given on p. 97 of AFSI, GBro102. However, the number actually reads 971 in both AFSI, GBro185 and MdC, MS 73. In turn, Chatillon has himself on occasion mistranscribed the later AFSI, GBro102 copy of Mongin's letter; for example, in a description of the size of armies in Africa, he erroneously transcribes 'dix [mille]' as 'six [mille]'.[28] Chatillon has also blended (and therefore incorrectly attributed) some content of the variants of Mongin's letters,[29] and omitted short sections of text.[30]

Claude Breban's letter from Saint-Domingue (Letter 5) has previously been transcribed and published in French by Nicole Dyonet in a 1997 article.[31] Dyonet's transcription contains few errors (amongst the rare mistranscriptions is an overestimation of the time given to slaves to cultivate their own gardens).[32] It should be pointed out that there appear to be two versions of Dyonet's article available; that housed in the Bibliothèque nationale de France (BnF 8-G-23098),

---

[27] For Chatillon, see this Introduction, n. 17.

[28] AFSI, GBro102, p. 42; Chatillon, p. 129; AFSI, GBro185, fol. 3^v.

[29] Compare the text from 'que si on revient plus souvent de cette mission' to 'craignent dans cette mission' in MdC, MS 73, fols 66^r–66^v, which appears in Chatillon, pp. 68–69 (i.e. attributed to BM, Ant MS 9), and the paragraph from 'Après avoir expliqué' to 'dans la seule île de la Martinique', in AFSI, GBro185, fols 9^r–9^v, but which appears in Chatillon, p. 78 (i.e. attributed to MdC, MS 73).

[30] Omissions include MdC, MS 73, fol. 87^r from 'comme on a vu' to 'grandes ferveurs'.

[31] For Dyonet, see this Introduction, n. 16.

[32] AdC, 2F 788, fols 16^r, 17^r.

for example, only contains a truncated transcription of Breban's letter.

Both Mongin and Breban are noteworthy for their testimony concerning the population of the colonies and, in particular, the enslaved. Mongin illustrates the sources of information about Atlantic slavery that were available during the late seventeenth century. He used information from recognized descriptions of Africa such as d'Avity's *Description générale de l'Afrique*.[33] He knew (and criticized) then-recent work such as the Dominican Jean-Baptiste Du Tertre's monumental *Histoire générale des Antilles*, the most important work on the early French Caribbean colonies, as well as another *Histoire* attributed to a Huguenot named Charles de Rochefort whom Du Tertre accused of plagiarizing him.[34] Mongin appears to have read such fundamental analyses of slavery as that in Luis de Molina's late sixteenth-century *De iustitia et iure*.[35] He was at least aware of the existence of the 1627 *De instauranda Aethiopum salute*, written by Alonso de Sandoval (1576–1652), a Jesuit missionary to the black slaves of Cartagena, Colombia.[36] In his 1682 letter, Mongin states that the care of all the slaves of his quarter had been given to him, making him an unrivalled source of information about enslaved people in the seventeenth-century French colonies.

Mongin's and Breban's letters are also notable for their relatively intimate perspective. Mongin's reference in his 1682 letter to the reaction to one of his previous letters shows that he was engaged in correspondence with the unnamed 'Languedocian gentleman'.[37] Jean-Yves Ribault has noted that Breban's form of address to his brother indicates that he too was a priest.[38] In writing to friends/patrons, or a family member, Mongin and Breban complement the formalized correspondence widely distributed within Jesuit networks.

A number of interventions in MdC, MS 73 could be interpreted as indicating that the letters copied therein were intended for publication at some point. Interventions include the crossing out of names which nonetheless remain visible to readers of the manuscript, occasional instructions for opening new paragraphs, and, on one folio, the appearance of the term 'L'Imprimeur

[33] Pierre d'Avity, *Description générale de l'Afrique* (Paris: C. Sonnius, 1637).
[34] Jean-Baptiste Du Tertre, *Histoire générale des isles de Saint-Christophe, de la Guadeloupe, de la Martinique et autres dans l'Amérique* (Paris: Jacques and Emmanuel Langlois, 1654); 2nd edn published as *Histoire générale des Antilles habitées par les François*, 4 vols (Paris: Thomas Jolly, 1667–71); Charles de Rochefort, *Histoire naturelle et morale des îles Antilles de l'Amérique* (Rotterdam: A. Leers, 1658); 2nd edn (Rotterdam: A. Leers, 1665).
[35] Luis de Molina, *De iustitia et iure*, 6 vols (Mainz: Nicolaus Heyll, sumptibus Haered. Joh. Godefredi Schönwederi, 1659). Compare for example Molina, *De iustitia et iure*, I, col. 174 (on the source of slaves) with Mongin, AFSI, GBro185, fol. 3ᵛ.
[36] Alonso de Sandoval, *De instauranda Aethiopum salute* (Seville: Francisco de Lira, 1627), repr. as *De instauranda Aethiopum salute: el mundo de la esclavitud negra en America*, ed. by Angel Valtierra (Bogotá: Empresa nacional de publicaciones, 1956).
[37] AFSI, GBro185, fol. 1ʳ.
[38] Ribault, p. 29.

au lecteur' ('The printer to the reader').[39] What will at least be clear in the letters reproduced in the present edition is the role of epistolary networks in transmitting knowledge that would later be qualified as geographical, cultural, and 'ethnographical'.[40] While Mongin and Breban furnished first-hand information about the colonies to their correspondents, they also actively sought information about the peoples of Africa, from sources that varied from authoritative texts, to the testimony of other ecclesiastics, to — with debatable success — the African slaves in their charge. As their correspondence also makes clear, they were themselves aware of the unreliability of contemporary Europeans' knowledge about African societies.

The Early Plantation Context

These letters were written in quite distinct geographical and demographic contexts: Mongin's from Martinique, and then from Saint Kitts, in the 1670s and 1680s, and Breban's from Saint-Domingue in 1732. The French, as with the English, had settled on Saint Kitts in the mid-1620s, and the French colonized Martinique and Guadeloupe in the middle of the following decade. The French colonies in the Antilles were administered by the Compagnie des Indes occidentales from 1664, before coming under royal administration in 1674.[41] There was a *gouverneur général des îles*: during Mongin's sojourn Jean-Charles de Baas-Castelmore (whose intervention Mongin describes in his first letter), who occupied the role from 1669 to 1677, and Charles Courbon, Comte de Blénac, from 1677 to 1690.[42]

At the time of Mongin's arrival in the Caribbean, Martinique was the focus of French settlement. With the capital at Fort Saint-Pierre, it was the seat of the governor general, the *intendant* (a high-ranking administrator answerable to the king), and the fleet.[43] Mongin characterizes its population as diverse. There was a large population of free colonists of European, mainly French, origin, who were Catholic for the most part, with some Protestant and Jewish settlers. The majority was made up of enslaved Africans, with the Amerindian population in 'very small number', having been relegated to Dominica.[44]

The French and English shared the island of Saint Kitts, with the English

---

[39] MdC, MS 73, fol. 75^r, bottom right-hand corner.

[40] On missionary accounts as ethnography, see for example *The Indigenous People of the Caribbean*, ed. by Samuel Meredith Wilson (Gainesville: University of Florida Press, 1997).

[41] Louis-Élie Moreau de Saint-Méry, *Loix et constitutions des colonies françoises de l'Amérique sous le vent*, 6 vols (Paris: Quillau; Lambert, 1784–90), I, 283.

[42] James Pritchard, *In Search of Empire: The French in the Americas, 1670–1730* (Cambridge: Cambridge University Press, 2004), p. 432.

[43] AFSI, GBro185, fol. 49^r.

[44] BM, Ant MS 9, fols 23^v, 24^r.

colony in the centre separating the French possessions into western and eastern parts. It was an uneasy coexistence, and there were tensions between both colonies. A Jesuit named Jean de La Mousse, who was a missionary in mainland South America, visited the island in late 1688 and was impressed by its prosperity. He noted that 'there is hardly one inch of the land which is not cultivated', that 'everyone has horses' of which 'a great number could be seen at the doors of churches', and with women 'always on horseback, as are the men'.[45] The two-storey Jesuit house was built of 'extremely thick dressed stone, with supports to protect it from hurricanes', there was a hall decorated with 'fine geographical maps with gold borders, and armchairs of excellent material'. There was a sugar mill, a refinery, and a 'great number of slaves who are very well instructed and good Christians'. It was not to last, however. La Mousse was to learn that the Jesuits had lost 'absolutely everything: house, church, chapel, library, furniture, slaves, livestock' when the English later invaded the colony.[46] The French colony on Saint Kitts would be definitively taken by the English at the turn of the 1700s.

The most significant destination for French settlement in the Caribbean during the eighteenth century would be the western third of Hispaniola, Saint-Domingue, which had become a French colony in 1665. Initial settlement was sporadic, and for much of its early decades — and at the time Mongin was in the Antilles — Saint-Domingue was characterized mainly as the home of freebooters and hunters of feral livestock. The colony was the seat of the *gouverneur général des îles sous le vent* from 1714.[47] Much larger than Martinique or Saint Kitts, its distinctly 'rugged' mountainous contours, John D. Garrigus observes, were amongst the factors which continued to make it a frontier colony for much of the eighteenth century.[48] At the time of Breban's arrival in Saint-Domingue, however, it was undergoing the great expansion that would make it the most prosperous of the French colonies.

The expansion in Saint-Domingue was due to the production of cash crops, which had also been the focus of agricultural production on Martinique and Saint Kitts that Mongin describes. Martinique in the 1670s was principally a sugar colony, and the Jesuit vividly describes the importance of the crop in the locality in Saint Kitts in which he was based during the early 1680s.[49]

[45] Jean de La Mousse, *Relation du voyage du père Jean de La Mousse, de Cayenne aux îles de l'Amérique, et des îles à Cayenne, et ses missions à Tullery, dans la terre-ferme de l'Amérique, les années 1688, 1689, 1690, 1691, extraite de quelques-unes de ses lettres,* in Les Indiens de la Sinnamary: journal du père Jean de La Mousse en Guyane (1684–1691), ed. by Gérard Collomb (Paris: Chandeigne, 2006), pp. 155–204 (pp. 163–64).

[46] La Mousse, pp. 164–67.

[47] Moreau de Saint-Méry, *Loix et constitutions,* II, ix; Pritchard, p. 433.

[48] John D. Garrigus, *Before Haiti: Race and Citizenship in French Saint-Domingue* (New York; Basingstoke: Palgrave Macmillan, 2006), pp. 23–30.

[49] AFSI, GBro185, fol. 9ᵛ.

Of Saint-Domingue, Stewart R. King notes that well-watered, fertile, flat land around Cap-Français led 'by [the mid-eighteenth century] to most of the suitable land in the North [being] [...] under sugar cultivation'.[50] Breban, himself writing from Cap-Français, testifies to precisely this process, and to the vast numbers of enslaved people who were required at the various stages of sugar production.[51] The intensive production of indigo, in turn, is also mentioned by Breban (in fact, according to Burnard and Garrigus, the smaller size of indigo 'works' meant they considerably 'outnumbered sugar mills' in Saint-Domingue 'up to the mid-eighteenth century').[52] Tobacco had been of considerable importance during the early settlement of the Antilles, but its production in Saint-Domingue is also alluded to by Breban, who mentions its frequent consumption by both enslaved people and white Creoles.[53] In an important manuscript depiction of Saint-Domingue written around the time of Breban's letter, his fellow Jesuit Jean-Baptiste Le Pers, who spent over a quarter of a century in the colony, left his own reflection on the product. Le Pers's claim that 'the tobacco of Saint-Domingue is the most esteemed of all the Caribbean islands for smoking, and that of Havana for taking through the nose' might be compared with Breban's own observations of tobacco consumption in the colonies.[54]

These were, as such, colonies dependent on intensive forms of labour. In the early decades of the colonies, this took the form of indentured labour: poor Europeans known as *engagés* were recruited in Europe to work for a colonial master for a fixed period (a period of three years in the French colonies). In the case of the French Antilles in 1687, Philip D. Curtin has highlighted that the high proportion of recently arrived *engagés* amongst the white population in the French Antilles (Curtin gives a figure of 42%) gives an 'imperfect but impressive suggestion of the many thousands who must have been imported but soon died'.[55] White indentured labourers were also employed during the settlement of Saint-Domingue, and Alexandre Oexmelin's vivid contemporary

---

[50] Stewart R. King, *Blue Coat or Powdered Wig: Free People of Color in Pre-Revolutionary Saint Domingue* (Athens, GA; London: University of Georgia Press, 2001), pp. 21–28.

[51] AdC, 2F 788, fol. 9^v.

[52] Trevor Burnard and John Garrigus, *The Plantation Machine: Atlantic Capitalism in French Saint-Domingue and British Jamaica* (Philadelphia: University of Pennsylvania Press, 2016), p. 34.

[53] AdC, 2F 788, fols 22^v–23^r.

[54] Jean-Baptiste Le Pers, *Le Portrait ou miroir de Saint-Domingue*, AFSI, GBro188 (1726? see fol. 22^r), later ed. and modified by Pierre-François-Xavier de Charlevoix, in *Histoire de l'isle Espagnole ou de Saint-Domingue*, 2 vols (Paris: Jacques Guerin, 1730–31), compare II, 501–06; 'le tabac de Saint-Domingue est le plus estimé de toutes les Antilles pour fumer, et celui de La Havane à prendre par le nez'. AFSI, GBro188, fol. 10^r.

[55] Philip D. Curtin, *The Rise and Fall of the Plantation Complex: Essays in Atlantic History*, 2nd edn (Cambridge: Cambridge University Press, 1998), p. 84.

account of Caribbean piracy illustrates the kind of mistreatment they continued to endure.[56] However, Mongin, by the time of his 1682 letter, is illustrative in considering the period of indentured labour as the time of 'our first French' settlers ('nos premiers Français').[57] The Antilles had by then become fully fledged slave societies.

Population estimates of the French colonies hint at the dynamics within such societies. For 1687 (the earliest date she lists) Sue Peabody gives a figure of 4976 whites and 11,092 slaves in Martinique, and of 3153 whites and 4470 slaves in Saint Kitts, with a small population of 'free coloureds' in each of these colonies discussed by Mongin. For Saint-Domingue in 1730–31 she gives a figure of 10,449 whites to 79,545 slaves, and 2456 'free coloureds'; here, the disproportion between slaves and white settlers would grow ever wider in the following decades, even as the number of free coloureds became more significant.[58] Although not to the same degree, in Martinique throughout the eighteenth century (the French colony on Saint Kitts had fallen to the English), the disproportion between enslaved people and the minority of white settlers would also become more marked, even as the population of free coloureds grew continuously; a similar trend took place in Guadeloupe. In each of these colonies, free populations were dependent on the labour of a population of slaves that was numerically superior (to the greatest degree in Saint-Domingue on the eve of the French Revolution). In an illustration of contemporary perspectives, it may be noted that Breban estimated that there were 'at least twenty blacks for one white' in the French American colonies.[59]

The origins of those who came to inhabit the islands also instruct us about the social environments in which Mongin and Breban were immersed. Garrigus notes that 'in the Lesser Antilles, the enslaved population was mostly island-born by the middle of the eighteenth century', but that in Saint-Domingue 'African-born slaves nearly always outnumbered' Creole slaves.[60] At the time of Breban's arrival in Saint-Domingue, the Bight of Benin was, Burnard and Garrigus write, the 'prime zone for captives arriving in Saint-Domingue'.[61] A number of scholars have also theorized that, at this time, Saint-Domingue was at a stage which predated strict colour-based divisions which would be imposed later in the eighteenth century.[62] Nonetheless, Saint-Domingue was a slave

---

[56] Alexandre Oexmelin (Exquemelin), *Histoire des avanturiers*, 2 vols (Paris: Jacques Le Febvre, 1686), repr. as *Histoire des avanturiers flibustiers*, 2 vols (Paris: Jacques Le Febvre, 1699).

[57] AFSI, GBro185, fol. 2[v].

[58] Sue Peabody, '"A Dangerous Zeal": Catholic Missions to Slaves in the French Antilles, 1635–1800', *French Historical Studies*, 25.1 (winter 2002), 53–90 (75).

[59] AdC, 2F 788, fols 2[v]–3[r].

[60] Garrigus, p. 33.

[61] Burnard and Garrigus give a figure of 45% from the 'Benin area' from 1713 to 42 (p. 110).

[62] See for example Garrigus, p. 11.

society, and to such an extent that the titles of white settlers depended on the number of slaves they owned, according to Le Pers. He states that one became *Monsieur* with 'four or five slaves', beyond which one could 'aspire' to the title of *Messire*.[63] As Le Pers put it, someone with no slaves was a 'poor planter' ('pauvre habitant'), even with significant land; with up to twelve slaves one was a 'modest planter' ('petit habitant'), 'middling' ('médiocre') from twelve to twenty-five, and more than twenty-five a 'rich planter' ('riche habitant'); a slave would bring 'fifty *écus*' every year to a master.[64] Indeed Le Pers claimed that he had seen slaves being sold for 'up to 1200 francs'.[65]

Mongin had arrived on the islands nearly a decade before the 1685 *Code Noir*, which codified colonial legislation, and his letters prefigure many of the concerns illustrated in this edict. In its 1685 form, the *Code Noir* was concerned with ensuring Catholic orthodoxy, as well as public order, the nourishment and clothing of slaves, and their punishment in case of theft, violence, or escape. It specified, for example, that all the slaves 'in [the king's] islands' must be given a Catholic baptism (Article 2), enjoined the king's subjects to 'observe Sundays and feast days', forbidding them to work their slaves on such days (Article 6), and also prohibiting priests from carrying out marriages between slaves without the consent of their masters (Article 11). It also imposed heavy fines on free men who had fathered children with enslaved women, unless these men were to marry — and thereby free — the women (Article 9).[66] Much of this legislation crystallized either previous legislation (such as prohibiting the putting to work of enslaved people on Sundays or feast days), or commonly understood practice, which might in turn be based on ancient jurisprudence or religious precepts.[67] Precepts were not always adhered to; in his 1682 letter, Mongin laments the impediments to marrying slaves caused by the 'custom of the land' ('coutume du pays'), which disregarded what he called 'the ancient laws' ('les lois anciennes').[68]

Mongin and Breban's awareness of the deprivation and violence of life in enslavement will be evident in their testimony. They both refer to the great hardship in which enslaved people lived, and even hint that theft in these circumstances was excusable. Mongin describes the forms of severe violence

---

[63] Le Pers, AFSI, GBro188, fol. 28ʳ.

[64] Le Pers, AFSI, GBro188, fol. 37ᵛ.

[65] 'j'en ay vu vendre jusqu'à douze cents francs', Le Pers, AFSI, GBro188, fol. 58ᵛ.

[66] *Le Code Noir; ou, édit du roy servant de règlement pour le gouvernement et l'administration de justice et la police des isles françoises de l'Amérique, & pour la discipline et le commerce des nègres et esclaves dans ledit pays, donné à Versailles au mois de mars 1685* (Paris: Veuve Saugrain, 1718).

[67] *Arrêt du Conseil de la Martinique, [...] qui défend absolument d'exiger aucun travail des esclaves les jours de dimanches et de fêtes*, 7 October 1652, in Moreau de Saint-Méry, *Loix et constitutions*, I, 73.

[68] AFSI, GBro185, fol. 18ʳ.

to which slaves were exposed. Amongst these, for female slaves, was the risk of sexual exploitation; Mongin is unhesitant in his condemnation of this insidious violence, and he describes visiting the (presumably white) overseers, or *commandeurs*, of Saint Kitts in an attempt to limit their exploitation of the female slaves under their supervision. However, he also considered certain slaveowners to be somewhat benevolent towards their slaves. A further strand in the thinking of these French observers conditioned how they viewed enslaved people on the temporal as well as spiritual planes. As members of the Society of Jesus, they saw African populations as members of their flock or potential converts, and looking after their spiritual needs as their primary role in the colonies.

Spirituality on the Islands

The Society of Jesus established a mission in the French Caribbean from the early years of the foundation of the colony on Martinique.[69] By 1679, there were *residences* in the French colonies in Cayenne, Saint Kitts, Guadeloupe, and Martinique, which were classified as 'missiones ultramarinae communes omnibus Provinciis Galliae'.[70] By the mid-eighteenth century, there were also missions to Grenada, Kourou, Sinnamare, and Ouyapoc. Whereas the French possessions on Saint Kitts had passed to the English at the beginning of the same century, there was now a residence in Saint-Domingue.[71] A 1685 memoir illustrates the conditions around the time of Mongin's mission in the Antilles. It notes that in Martinique there were 'eighteen churches or chapels served by eleven Jesuit Fathers, seven Jacobins, and five Capuchins', in Saint Kitts there were 'six churches and a chapel, served by four Jesuits, two Capuchins, two Carmelites, and a secular priest'. With the exception of the Jesuits, who 'live[d] in an exemplary fashion', the memoir also states that the clergy 'either neglect their parochial duties, or are involved in constant disputes amongst themselves'.[72] Mongin's dedication to his own duties will be clear from his

---

[69] See Jacques Bouton, *Relation de l'establissement des François depuis l'an 1635 en l'isle de la Martinique* (Paris: Sébastien Cramoisy, 1640).

[70] Filippo Buonanni [?], *Catalogus provinciarum Societatis Iesu* (Rome: Typis Ignatii de Lazariis, 1679), non-paginated.

[71] Augustino Hingerle, *Catalogus provinciarum, collegiorum, residentiarum, seminariorum, et missionum, universae Societatis Iesu anni 1750* (Tyrnava: Society of Jesus, 1750), p. 52.

[72] 'il y a à la Martinique dix-huit églises ou chapelles desservies par onze pères jésuites, sept jacobins, et cinq capucins, [...] à Saint-Christophe, six églises et une chapelle desservies par quatre jésuites, deux capucins, deux carmes, et un prêtre séculier. [...] La plupart de ces religieux hors les jésuites qui vivent exemplairement et sont d'un grand secours à cette colonie, ou négligent leurs fonctions de curés, ou vivent entre eux en des contestations perpétuelles.' *Mémoire sur l'establissement d'un évesché aux isles d'Amérique*, 19 May 1685, Aix-en-Provence, Archives nationales d'outre-mer, C8 B1 (63), non-paginated (fol. 2^r of 2).

correspondence; at least in the Carcassonne version (dated 1678) of his letter to the Jesuit provincial of Toulouse, the coexistence of the missionary orders is depicted positively.[73]

In Saint-Domingue, the Jesuits replaced the Capuchins in the north of the colony from 1704–05, and by the mid-1740s they were responsible for nineteen parishes in a considerable area of land.[74] The Dominicans were the other significant missionary order in Saint-Domingue, and were granted the status of missionaries to the west and the south of the colony, in the 1720s.[75] The Jesuits were expelled from Saint-Domingue in 1763, due to a combination of financial mismanagement, pressure from the Paris Parlement, and the hostility of colonists, as Peabody points out.[76] From this point onwards, secular clergy ('prêtres séculiers') took over the mission until 1768, at which point it reverted to the Capuchins.[77] There was a chronic shortage of priests for the parishes around Cap-Français, according to the Jesuit Jean-Baptiste Margat de Tilly, writing in 1743. In an observation that reflects Breban's own fate, Margat called Saint-Domingue a land that 'devours its inhabitants', exemplified by the fact that 'fifty-six Jesuits had died since the foundation of the mission' forty years earlier.[78]

The Jesuits also played a role in the education of the young of the colonies (as they did with such success in Europe); indeed, Jean de La Mousse had heard that the Jesuits were instrumental in theatre performances, both by female boarders at the Ursuline convent and by their own male students, in late seventeenth-century Martinique.[79] It was the spirituality of the colonial populations that was the principal preoccupation of Jesuits such as Mongin and Breban. The first of Mongin's letters reproduced in this volume illustrates a preoccupation with the spiritual orthodoxy of the white settler population, whereas the letters that follow are concerned with the spirituality of the large population of slaves of African origin. By the time of Breban's mission a half-century later, the far larger slave population in Saint-Domingue could be compared, as Le Pers put it, to 'the magnet which attracts missionaries here'.[80]

[73] MdC, MS 73, fol. 62ʳ; Mongin refers to being 'perturbed' by 'the lives of [his] companions' in BM, Ant MS 9, fol. 38ᵛ and MdC, MS 73, fol. 68ʳ.
[74] Jean-Baptiste Margat de Tilly, Letter of 20 July 1743, *Lettres édifiantes et curieuses*, VII (Paris: J.-G. Merigot le jeune, 1781), pp. 185–255 (pp. 186–90).
[75] Moreau de Saint-Méry, *Description topographique, physique, civile, politique et historique de la partie française de l'isle Saint-Domingue*, 2 vols (Philadelphia: Chez l'auteur, 1797–98), II, 336.
[76] Peabody, pp. 80–83.
[77] Moreau de Saint-Méry, *Description*, I, 107.
[78] Margat, p. 233.
[79] La Mousse, pp. 162–63.
[80] 'comme la pierre d'aimant qui y attire des missionnaires', Le Pers, AFSI, GBro188, fol. 119ʳ.

We can gain some insight into the energy and approaches of the Society of Jesus in the French Caribbean from the 1655 account of Pierre Pelleprat, who was praised as a pioneer by Mongin in his 1679 letter from Martinique.[81] Pelleprat described Jesuit attempts to convert Amerindian and African populations, with a 'separate catechism' on feast days and Sundays, reading them the 'principles of faith' while they were at work, and 'even translating the *Pater*, the *Ave*, the *Credo*, and the Commandments'. Amerindians and Africans might be 'assembled' in churches 'an hour before daybreak, notably during feasts and Sundays during Lent'. They might be preached to during their labours at night, 'in the fields during the day', and they might even be stopped on their way if they encountered a Jesuit, who would 'say something salutary to them, or have them pray to God', so that many would 'make the sign of the cross, when they encounter our Fathers'.[82]

However, the islands had acquired a reputation for tolerance of heresy during the seventeenth century, which is also reflected in Mongin's correspondence. The Dominican Du Tertre gives some insight into the reasons for this in his *Histoire générale des Antilles*. In a volume published in 1671, he wrote that 'many people who [were] zealous about the spiritual welfare of the Antilles' had complained about the 'spiritual disorders that, it is claimed, have infiltrated these islands' since they had come under the control of the Compagnie des Indes occidentales. Du Tertre transcribed a letter that he had been sent by an ecclesiastic, which addressed five sorts of 'disorders'. The first two were that Jews and Protestants were permitted to be planters (*habitants*), and that Protestants made no effort to prepare slaves for baptism or the 'other sacraments of the Church'. In response to the second 'disorder', the author of the letter suggested that Protestants 'should be deprived of the right to possess slaves, given that this permission is only given by a special dispensation to the Catholics who inhabit the islands, for this instruction, and the conversion to the faith [of slaves]'. His last three objections were that Protestants were not far off 'practising their false religion' in the colonial environment (they might 'sing their psalms out loud' in the vessels of the Compagnie), they held high office 'in the militia, as in trade', and on a part of Guadeloupe where there were 'neither priests, nor churches' their slaves 'live[d] and die[d]' without 'receiving' God. Du Tertre responded to this in a nuanced fashion, claiming that the 'zeal' of missionaries had prevented the worst excesses of the 'heretics'. However, Du Tertre acknowledged that Protestants did have privileged roles in 'the distribution of merchandise', as the Compagnie's 'unique aim was commerce', and as France's ports were 'full of Huguenot captains, pilots, and merchants' with skills in 'navigation' and

---

[81] BM, Ant MS 9, fol. 38^r.

[82] Pierre Pelleprat (1609–1667), *Relation des missions des pères de la Compagnie de Jésus* (Paris: Sébastien Cramoisy, 1655), Part 1: *Des isles de l'Amérique*, pp. 58–60.

commerce.[83] This was the backdrop to Mongin's arrival in the Caribbean, and to the first of his letters (1676) transcribed in the present volume. As this letter makes clear, Mongin arrived on Martinique at a time when Protestantism was still a concern; there were communities of Huguenots at Le Carbet and Saint-Pierre which, in the Jesuit's eyes, were socially problematic.[84]

The transforming context in which Breban arrived in Saint-Domingue, a half-century later, is illustrated once more by Le Pers. At this stage, Protestantism was no longer a concern, but the difficulty was rather with a planter population that was simply irreligious, and whose God was Mammon.[85] Le Pers depicted religion on 'Saint-Domingue and the islands in general' as Catholic but 'with a few differences' ('à quelques différences près'). 'As with the Calvinists', there were no bishops, and 'the clergy [was] only made up of monks, the same as it is among the Abyssinians'. He noted that confirmation was not practised, as was the case with 'Lutherans' (the French Caribbean colonies were not organized into dioceses at this stage, so there was no bishop to confirm Catholics). Ultimately he saw the Church as 'acephalous, without authority, jurisdiction, revenue, order, or discipline, and so such poor Christians are to be seen nowhere else'.[86]

While the institutional framework had been lacking from the beginnings of the colonies, Le Pers described a context which was new for missionaries, with the influx into Saint-Domingue of large populations of African slaves from diverse ethnic and linguistic groups. There were, he wrote, 'slaves from more than fifty different nations' from Africa, including 'Aradas' (Ardra), who 'lived in the centre of Guinea' and accounted for a quarter of all slaves, Congo, who 'were barely less numerous', and smaller populations of other African peoples.[87] He classified the African slaves transported to the French colonies into three 'principal nations': the Congo, the Senegalese, and the Ardra. He saw all of them as essentially 'without religion', although some Congo had what he called 'a little trace [teinture] of Christianity' given that their own kings were Christian, with the Portuguese being 'well established along their coast'. Some of the Senegalese, he noted, were Muslim and were circumcised, while the Ardra and 'an infinite number of other nations' were 'engulfed in the darkness of the crudest idolatry'. However, he added that all these Africans 'embraced'

[83] Du Tertre, *Histoire générale des Antilles*, III (1671), 312–17.

[84] See Jacques Petitjean-Roget, 'Les Protestants à la Martinique sous l'ancien régime', *Revue d'histoire des colonies*, 42.147 (1955), 220–65; MdC, MS 73, fol. 37[r].

[85] Le Pers, AFSI, GBro188, fol. 42[v].

[86] 'L'Église y est acéphale, sans autorité, sans juridiction, sans revenus, sans ordre, sans discipline. Aussi ne voit-on nulle part d'aussi pauvres chrétiens.' Le Pers, AFSI, GBro188, fol. 50[v].

[87] 'Après eux viennent les Sénégalais, les Mines, les Ibo ou Timbo, les Mandingues, les Naga, les Bambara, les Poulos et autres.' Le Pers, AFSI, GBro188, fol. 65[r]–65[v].

Christianity and demanded baptism 'with insistence'.[88] It was a phenomenon that was observed in a similar context by Breban, as it had been by Mongin in the Lesser Antilles fifty years previously.[89]

As Mongin illustrates to a striking degree, preparing neophytes for the sacraments was a major preoccupation for Jesuits in the Caribbean as it was elsewhere. There are seven sacraments in Catholicism: baptism, confirmation, Eucharist, penance, marriage, anointing the sick, and Holy Orders. In the strategies he used, Mongin was following a Jesuit tradition exemplified by José de Acosta (1540–1600), whose six-book work on the strategies for converting the Amerindians had been published nearly a century previously.[90] Acosta's fifth book dealt with catechism, and his sixth with the administration of the sacraments.[91] His concerns included what should be known by an Amerindian *in extremo mortis* before he or she could be baptized, or the 'remedies' (*remedia*) against idolatry.[92] He counselled the 'necessity of a catechism' in the vernacular, of two sorts: a brief one that might even be memorized by Amerindians, and a further one that developed its points in more detail. His book on the sacraments dealt with such concerns as what was necessary for baptism (*voluntas*, *fides*, *poenitentia*, or *intention*, *faith*, and *penitence*). Those who sought baptism should 'ask and insist' ('petant et instent'), and it was a 'custom' in the Church to 'ask [the aspirant] three times' if he or she wanted to be baptized.[93] For Acosta, the 'baptism' of African slaves brought from Cape Verde, who 'in a ship or on the shore' had been 'sprinkled with water' by a 'cleric or soldier', exemplified the abuse of the sacrament.[94] Communion was to be 'principally' administered upon danger of death, and every year on Easter Sunday.[95] While confession was a 'necessity', in the context of the Spanish possessions the problem of language came up; Acosta also considered hearing confessions in Amerindian languages to be a 'necessity'. It would otherwise require a 'third witness' which might skew the 'sincerity' of the confession. In any case, the confessor's 'zeal' might make up for an imperfect knowledge of the penitent's language.[96] The aspects of marriage that occupied Acosta's attention included the troubling issue of virginity being considered a flaw, the closer degrees of consanguinity in which

---

[88] Le Pers, AFSI, GBro188, fol. 81ʳ–81ᵛ.

[89] On this 'receptivity to baptism' see also Peabody, p. 63.

[90] José de Acosta, *De procuranda Indorum salute* (1588), bilingual Latin-Spanish edn, ed. by L. Pereña and others, 2 vols (Madrid: Consejo Superior de Investigaciones Cientificas, 1984–87).

[91] Liber V, *De Catechismo et catechizando ratione*, in Acosta, *De procuranda*, II, 175–353; Liber VI, *De sacramentis Indiis administrandis*, in Acosta, *De procuranda*, II, 355–493.

[92] Acosta, *De procuranda*, II, 242–47, 258–71.

[93] On catechism, Acosta, *De procuranda*, II, 290–93; on baptism, p. 362.

[94] 'multis simul a clerico aut milite quopiam aqua aspergebantur'. Acosta, *De procuranda*, II, 368.

[95] Acosta, *De procuranda*, II, 388.

[96] Acosta, *De procuranda*, II, 430–33.

marriage was permitted, or what should be done about marriages contracted before a neophyte became Christian (the convert should separate from a spouse who was an impediment to his or her new faith).[97]

Not all of these difficulties were to be experienced — or at least to the same degree — in the French colonies, with a numerically inferior Amerindian population relegated far from the centres of French settlement after several decades of colonization. The questions of language were of quite a different nature, given that the French colonies imported African populations from very different linguistic groups. On Martinique, Mongin considered one of the advantages of the Caribbean missions to be precisely that the time-consuming learning of new languages was unnecessary, given that slaves generally learned enough French 'to understand us and to be understood'.[98] He was also positive, in his letter from Saint Kitts, about the religious instruction of slaves through nascent Creole, or what he called 'a sort of French jargon'.[99] However, Breban's less optimistic depiction of the difficulties in administering the sacraments to African slaves reflects a perspective that recurs in Catholic missionary accounts (accounts of a wide diversity of cultures). Baptism, Eucharist, marriage, and penance inspired distinct challenges for missionaries administering to both African-born and Creole slaves in the Caribbean.

Baptism was generally administered to slaves in ceremonies at which large numbers attended, across the French Caribbean. In 1655, Pelleprat wrote that baptism was administered 'four times a year' by the Jesuits, and estimated at six hundred the number of adults and children who received it annually.[100] On Saint Kitts, Mongin baptized groups of neophytes at such times as the morning of Easter Saturday (he writes it was the 'day and time indicated by the Church' for the sacrament), on the following Tuesday, or just after the Sunday after that, Quasimodo Sunday, and still others at Pentecost.[101] A decade after Breban's letter, in Saint-Domingue, Margat claimed that Boutin was following the 'former custom of the Church' in usually only baptizing adults on two occasions in the year at Cap-Français, which were 'Holy Saturday and the eve of Pentecost', and which might leave him baptizing about 'two or three hundred adults'. Margat also claimed that it was Boutin who instigated a specific Mass for the slaves on Cap-Français, which would be said after the parish High Mass, in which he would 'explain the Gospel [...] in their manner' and end with catechism.[102]

---

[97] On virginity, Acosta, *De procuranda*, II, 464; on consanguinity, p. 468; on marriages before conversion, pp. 474–77.

[98] BM, Ant MS 9, fol. 27ᵛ.

[99] AFSI, GBro185, fol. 8ʳ.

[100] Pelleprat, Part 1: *Des isles de l'Amérique*, p. 57.

[101] AFSI, GBro185, fol. 26ʳ.

[102] 'Il se conformait pour le baptême des adultes à l'ancienne coutume de l'Église.' Margat, pp. 242–43.

The slaves' own solicitation for baptism noted by Mongin and Breban entailed certain challenges. According to Le Pers, slaves in Saint-Domingue sometimes 'so bothered' missionaries that they were baptized only one year after their arrival in the colonies, instead of the three years which they usually needed to be 'capable of receiving it'.[103] The difficulties centred rather on the fact that those to be baptized needed to be instructed beforehand. The 'intention, faith, and penitence' that concerned Acosta were of concern to Mongin too. From Saint Kitts, Mongin explained that of these 'dispositions' that were prerequisites to the sacrament, the latter two were particularly challenging: faith because of what he called the 'ignorance' of slaves, and repentance because of their immorality.[104] Le Pers is again instructive about Saint-Domingue; he wrote that it was not the belief in God that was an impediment, as 'the idea of [a] Divinity is naturally engraved in our souls, and His image impressed upon [empreinte dans] all creatures'. However, 'grace should assist nature' to avoid falling into error.[105] Indeed, Le Pers considered that if 'the knowledge of the mystery of the very Holy Trinity [was] necessary for salvation' then many slaves who 'had passed their entire lives in [the French] colonies should not be baptized, not even at death'.[106] Breban's reflection on the 'entire years' needed to prepare slaves for baptism is reflective of the difficulties facing the missionary in Saint-Domingue at this stage.[107]

Confession, through the intermediary of a priest, was necessary for penitence. Mongin writes that the confessions of white and black people took place on Saint Kitts during different periods around Easter; the whites first, and black slaves afterwards, because of the great number of the latter and the time it took to confess them.[108] Breban's testimony about confession is particularly interesting, for both linguistic and spiritual reasons, as it includes a transcription of a sample confession of a slave. As will be seen, Breban's reactions to what he heard at the confessional were varied; he praised the honesty of slaves, condemned their thefts — tellingly, because such thefts exposed them to punishment by their masters — and noted their sexual promiscuity with sadness, all the more so because of what it revealed about the sexual exploitation of female slaves by French settlers.[109]

Confession, as Mongin illustrates so strikingly, was also the prelude to the Eucharist, which was, in principle, to be received by all at Easter (from which the expression *faire ses pâques* derives). On Saint Kitts as described by Mongin,

---

[103] Le Pers, AFSI, GBro188, fol. 122^r.
[104] AFSI, GBro185, fol. 17^r.
[105] Le Pers, AFSI, GBro188, fols 81^r–82^v.
[106] Le Pers, AFSI, GBro188, fol. 86^r.
[107] AdC, 2F 788, fol. 19^r.
[108] AFSI, GBro185, fol. 26^v.
[109] AdC, 2F 788, fols 20^r–22^v.

black slaves received the Eucharist later than whites for the reasons mentioned above. Frequent Communion was encouraged in the Jesuit tradition; Ignatius of Loyola advocated Communion 'at least once a year', and preferably 'every eight days' (i.e. weekly).[110] Once more, European Catholic practice encountered significant challenges in the colonies. In Breban's view, Communion was even more fraught than baptism, and he testifies to the care that had to be taken before admitting neophytes to what he called 'our most holy mysteries'.[111] Many slaves, Le Pers wrote, 'did not receive Communion [*ne communient point*] their entire lives' because they did not understand the significance of the 'sacred bread', while the 'knowledge [*science*] that very many slaves ha[d] of religion consists in the knowledge that there is a God, a paradise, [and] a hell'.[112]

The sacrament of marriage inspired a different set of challenges when it came to the enslaved. Unsurprisingly, both Mongin and Breban were saddened by extramarital relations. Mongin actively attempted to put an end to these through uniting slaves in marriage. His letter from Saint Kitts is telling about the difficulties this inspired, not least among the slaves themselves whom he characterized as unwilling to abandon their own sexual promiscuity. In a slave society, there were further difficulties centring on proprietorship. As was noted earlier, Article 11 of the *Code Noir* made the consent of masters necessary for the marriage of slaves. For Mongin, writing several years before its promulgation, it was rather the 'custom of the land' that was an impediment to marriage between slaves of different masters, and in opposition to the 'ancient laws' which made slaves 'independent' of their masters in this domain. Nearly a half-century later in Saint-Domingue, Le Pers noted the impossible bind that slaves were placed in, in relation to marriage; the 'law of the prince' said that a slave needed a master's permission to marry, but a master 'forbade any alliance outside of his property' (like Mongin, Le Pers noted that there might well not be a person of the opposite sex to marry amongst the one master's slaves, not to mention the issue of a slave's own preference).[113]

It is Mongin's letter from Saint Kitts that also strikingly illustrates the missionary strategies of the Catholic Reformation. Along with veneration for the seven sacraments, Jesuit spirituality also followed Ignatius's promotion of such contested practices as the veneration of relics, the earning of indulgences, and even the use of candles.[114] The active place that such practices held in the

---

[110] Ignatius of Loyola, *Exercitia spiritualia S. P. Ignatii Loyolae cum sensu eoremdem explanato, a P. Ignatio Diertins S. I. Editio quinta* (Antwerp: Henrici Thieullier, 1696), p. 311.
[111] AdC, 2F 788, fol. 19ᵛ.
[112] Le Pers, AFSI, GBro188, fols 86ᵛ–87ʳ.
[113] Le Pers, AFSI, GBro188, fol. 88ʳ. Le Pers used the term *atelier*, which usually refers to a workshop.
[114] 'laudare praeterea reliquias, venerationem et invocationem Sanctorum, item stationes, peregrinationesque pias; indulgentias, jubilaea, candelas in templis accendi solitas, et

late 1600s Catholicism practiced by colonists and slaves — to varying degrees — will be clear in Mongin's correspondence. The same ecclesiastic describes a document he had created, which he called a 'catalogue', in which he evaluated and classified the spiritual progress of the many slaves. He admired the piety of slaves seeking to earn indulgences, and distributed 'blessed medals' to those who could not benefit from such indulgences immediately, for logistical reasons.[115] Mongin mentions that his zealous predecessor in his Saint Kitts mission used 'devotional gifts, such as images, medals and rosaries' to attract slaves, and gives a vivid account of his own use of 'fine devotional presents' to reward the progress of his neophytes.[116] He imported devotional images, and testifies to the profound effects these might have on spectators, white and black, and, conversely, to the unwanted humour they also provoked amongst certain slaves.[117]

Both Mongin and Breban, like many other missionaries to the Caribbean, characterize the slave population as marked, for the most part, by their piety.[118] Their letters also illustrate that there were exceptions, most notably through lack of respect for moral interdicts, particularly fornication. There was a further area which troubled missionaries to the early modern Caribbean, to different degrees. Like Acosta, Mongin was also concerned with unorthodox spiritualities, which explains his concern in his 1682 letter with what he called the 'sorcerers' on Saint Kitts. This letter distinguishes between healers using natural remedies, *devins*, healers using spells, and poisoners. Relatively unconcerned with the first sort, Mongin saw the remaining three as problematic: the *devins* principally because of the social disruption they caused, and healers through spells because of their spiritual unorthodoxy. He had some faith in the abilities of poisoners to cause harm to their fellow slaves, for example by the administration of 'herbs' that would cause their victims to waste away.[119] Fifty years later in Saint-Domingue, Breban thought that there were few 'true sorcerers', but he was convinced of the existence of poisoners amongst the slave population, who were capable of causing significant casualties amongst their brethren.[120] Le Pers also described how many slaves of African origin were 'involved with spells' ('se mêlent de sortilèges'), with belief in their power shared by the slave population,

---

reliqua hujusmodi pietatis ac devotionis nostrae adminicula'. Ignatius of Loyola, *Exercitia*, p. 312.

[115] AFSI, GBro185, fols 31^v–32^r.

[116] AFSI, GBro185, fols 10^v, 42^v.

[117] AFSI, GBro185, fol. 39^r.

[118] On the piety and detachment of a Christian slave on his deathbed see also Le Pers, AFSI, GBro188, fols 90^v–91^r. Le Pers, who found that the salvation of slaves faced 'great difficulties', was 'reassured' by Psalm 36 (35): 'homines et jumenta salvabis domine, judicia Dei abyssus multa' [*sic*]. AFSI, GBro188, fol. 87^v.

[119] AFSI, GBro185, fols 39^v–42^r.

[120] AdC, 2F 788, fols 24^r–25^r.

and with many among them even 'wearing something blessed' ('quelque chose de bénit') on their person to protect against harm.[121] The use of poison by slaves has been explored in studies by Burnard and Garrigus, and by Diana Paton, the latter of whom postulates that 'the end of witchcraft prosecutions in France was precipitated by the Parisian "affair of the poisons" of 1676–82', and notes an 'increasing separation of the idea of poisoning from the idea of witchcraft'.[122] Mongin's letters date from precisely these years, and, when compared with Breban's, illustrate the degree to which these missionaries, at least, had faith in the potential of witchcraft to cause harm, or drew distinctions between witchcraft and more direct forms of poisoning.

The Jesuits and Transatlantic Slavery

Mongin and Breban's perspectives on slavery were shaped by their position as members of an international missionary order. They were influenced by early modern intellectual responses to slavery and the slave trade as it took on radically transformed configurations in Africa and the Americas. The Society of Jesus had its own authorities on the morality of the trade in African slaves. In turn, the order responded in distinct manners to practices of slavery in the Caribbean.

Classic studies such as David Brion Davis's *The Problem of Slavery in Western Culture* and Georges Scelle's earlier study provide thorough overviews of the range of Jesuit responses to Atlantic slavery and the slave trade.[123] As such, the following pages will be limited to discussions of the themes and authorities most clearly reflected in Mongin's and Breban's letters. Western European thinking about slavery in the early modern period drew from the classics, from the Old and New Testaments, from canon law, and Roman jurisprudence. Jesuit thought about slavery was formed in such an international context, yet the Society of Jesus also made key contributions to the theorization of slavery, and its legitimacy, particularly concerning its transatlantic forms.

The writings of the Dominican Domingo de Soto in the mid-1550s illustrate the range of authorities on which early modern theorists drew, as well as showing that the African slave trade, even at this point, gave rise to a new set

---

[121] Le Pers, AFSI, GBro188, fols 83^v–84^r. 'Bénit' has been modified to 'béni' in the manuscript.

[122] Burnard and Garrigus, pp. 101–36; Diana Paton, 'Witchcraft, Poison, Law, and Atlantic Slavery', *William and Mary Quarterly*, 69.2 (2012), 235–64 (241–42).

[123] Amongst studies of Jesuit responses to slavery see Georges Scelle, *La Traite négrière aux Indes de Castille: contrats et traités d'assiento*, 2 vols (Paris: Librairie de la Société du Recueil J.-B. Sirey et du Journal du Palais, L. Larose & L. Tenin, 1906), I, 710–20; David Brion Davis, *The Problem of Slavery in Western Culture* (Ithaca, NY: Cornell University Press, 1966), pp. 187–94.

of interrogations. Soto tackled the question of whether one man could be the *dominus* of another.[124] The question arose because 'all men were born free [*liberi*] according to natural law', but jurisprudence (Justinian's *Institutes*) and Aristotle (in his *Politics*) admitted slavery.[125] Soto concluded that Aristotle's 'natural slavery', which gave those of superior intellect (*ingenium*) dominion over their inferiors, was of mutual benefit, and was justified. Soto did not consider that Aristotelian natural slavery gave masters the right to treat such slaves as property — for it was a *mutually* profitable relationship — and still less did he consider it a motive for the invasion of the lands of those who might 'appear to be slaves'.[126] There could also be 'legal' forms of slavery, in two manners. The first consisted in those who were in need submitting to voluntary enslavement in return for a *pretium*. Soto saw this as 'licit', as it consisted in accepting the loss of liberty in return for sustaining one's life, and he noted that Leviticus 25 had even approved of necessitous parents selling their children. The second form of legal slavery consisted in a prisoner of war accepting servitude rather than being put to death.

Soto viewed this through the Thomist perspective. Nature was corrupted after the original sin, and so slavery which would have been 'against [pre-lapsarian] nature' now existed, and punished 'men' who were no longer virtuous. Soto wrote that Christ might well have liberated Christians from the 'law of sin and death' ('Christus enim liberos à lege non tantùm peccati & mortis fecit'), but not from the law of nations ('ius gentium'). This law of nations was so-called because 'everyone could understand it through natural reason'.[127]

Even in the 1550s, there was one aspect which was problematic for Soto: the European trade in Africa or, as Soto wrote, of the 'Ethiopians' ('Aethiopes'). Soto considered that impoverished African parents selling children fell into the category of legal slavery. However, Soto also noted that 'certain people affirmed' that Africans were sold to the Portuguese through being 'seduced' by 'deceit and artifice' ('fraude & dolo'), attracted by 'pretty things' ('iocalibus'), and even 'forced [...], embarked, and sold'. 'If this were true', Soto continued, then those who 'seized', 'bought', or 'possessed' such slaves should free them. For, he wrote, if one could not with justice keep property without 'just title', then one would be far more obliged to 'free a man who had been born free and was unjustly

---

[124] Domingo de Soto, *De iustitia et iure libri decem* (Salamanca: [n. pub.], 1556), in bilingual Latin–Spanish facsimile edn, ed. by Venancio Diego Carro, trans. by Marcelino González Ordóñez, 5 vols (Madrid: Instituto de Estudios políticos, 1968), II, Book 4, Question 2, Article 2, pp. 288–91.

[125] Aristotle, *Politics*, bilingual Greek–English edn, trans. by H. Rackham (Cambridge, MA: Harvard University Press, 1959); *Institutes* [usual translation]: *D. Justiniani Institutionum libri quatuor*, bilingual Latin–English edn, trans. by George Harris as *The Four Books of Justinian's Institutions*, 3rd edn (Oxford: Collingwood, Newman and Baxter, 1811).

[126] Soto, Book 4, p. 290.

[127] 'proptereà quod ratio naturalis omnes gentes illud ius docuit'. Soto, Book 4, pp. 290–91.

enslaved'. He also saw the 'pretext' of a buyer alleging he would convert a slave to Christianity as an 'injury' to the faith, which instead had to be 'taught' to non-believers, who should be 'persuaded' of its truth.[128]

The fundamental importance of the Jesuit Luis de Molina (1535–1600) to early modern thinking about slavery has been widely acknowledged, and his influence is clear in Mongin's writings.[129] The first volume of Molina's *De iustitia et iure* contains an extensive analysis of questions concerning the legitimacy of slavery, which includes a novel exploration of the Portuguese trade in slaves in Africa and its legitimacy (*disputationes* 34 and 35), and whether one could possess and trade such slaves (*disputatio* 36).[130]

Molina also distinguished between the Aristotelian model of slaves of inferior intellect who should serve those with superior faculties, and prisoners of war enslaved through 'legal and civil' slavery.[131] He found further justifications for slavery in the 'doctors of civil and canon law', and in Scripture: in Leviticus 25, and in the letters of Paul.[132] *Disputatio* 33 examines the titles of *dominium*. The first of these is *just war* in which a captive during a conflict might have his death sentence commuted to perpetual slavery, and the second that of committing a crime ('propter delictum'). The third was through sale and purchase, as described in the Old Testament. One might sell oneself, according to Roman law, under six conditions (for example, providing that such a person was not a minor), while parents also had the right to sell their own children into slavery. The fourth title was 'through birth' ('nativitatis conditio'), of being born to a slave woman ('ancilla').[133]

Molina's *disputatio* 34 is a significant reflection on the Portuguese trade in slaves in Africa, and the role of the 'law of war' in this. Molina considered that the Portuguese themselves acquired slaves through sale ('emptio'), rather than themselves engaging in warfare. He depicted Africa as divided up into small kingships, which made war on one another, leading to the enslavement of Africans. Slaves were also sold on to merchants known as 'Tangosmaos'. Africans might also be enslaved for committing crimes, but in these regions even minor thefts — of hens, for example — might be punished by capital punishment or by slavery. A son might be enslaved for a minor theft, and a

[128] Soto, Book 4, p. 289.
[129] See for example Frank Bartholemew Costello, *The Political Philosophy of Luis de Molina, S. J. (1535–1600)* (Rome: Institutum Historicum; Spokane, WA: Gonzaga University Press, 1974), pp. 163–98; Jesús María García Añoveros, 'Luis de Molina y la esclavitud de los negros africanos en el siglo XVI. Principios doctrinales y conclusiones', *Revista de Indias*, 60.219 (2000), 307–29.
[130] Molina, *De iustitia et iure*, I, cols 157–214.
[131] Molina, *De iustitia et iure*, I, col. 158.
[132] For example I Timothy 6; I Corinthians 7; Ephesians 6; Colossians 3 and 4. Molina, *De iustitia et iure*, I, col. 158.
[133] Molina, *De iustitia et iure*, I, cols 160–67.

father's crimes might be punished by his descendants being condemned to death or enslaved. An 'angered' prince could 'easily' order the condemnation of a subject.[134]

It will be clear that Molina saw many aspects of enslavement in Africa as problematic, and he identified cases of unjust servitude in Angola which would be referred to by Mongin in his own correspondence. Molina claimed that, were a subject to remove a feather from the king of Angola's peacocks, he and his family would be severely punished and could be enslaved, and that similar punishments awaited those who touched the gourds suspended on palm trees to collect sap. The children of a deceased debtor could be captured. Molina explicitly qualified certain forms of enslavement as 'suspicious' ('quae sane negotiatione valde est suspecta'). Fathers could have their sons or wives enslaved for 'minor causes', and one's 'son or daughter' could be exchanged for 'small bells' or a 'mirror'.[135]

Molina's *disputatio* 35 focused precisely on the legitimacy of Portuguese slavers in Africa. He saw wars between Africans as typically unjust, the punishments that would send someone into slavery in Africa as disproportionate (for adultery, for example), and he noted that innocents might be unjustly punished with enslavement for the crimes of others (such as the innocent sons of criminal fathers).[136] Portuguese slavers 'did not [themselves] care about the title' of the many slaves they bought.[137] Molina's conclusion was that, in these contexts, the trade in slaves should be avoided where the legitimacy of a title was uncertain. Buyers should make enquiries about how slaves had been procured, and, where an enslavement proved unjust, then freedom should be restored.[138]

A not dissimilar vision of Africa informs Tomas Sánchez's (1550–1610) discussion of the legitimacy of the Portuguese trade in African slaves. He listed the titles by which one might be justly enslaved (*dubium* III) before assessing the degree to which African slavery could be justified using these criteria (*dubium* IV). While the 'titles' of those enslaved in a just war were amongst those that were accepted, others were more problematic.[139] Africans might be 'hunted as wild beasts', sold by parents motivated by anger, or punished by slavery because

---

[134] Molina, *De iustitia et iure*, I, cols 168–69.

[135] Molina, *De iustitia et iure*, I, cols 174–75; on Angola, compare with Mongin, AFSI, GBro185, fol. 3^v.

[136] Molina, *De iustitia et iure*, I, cols 181, 190.

[137] Molina, *De iustitia et iure*, I, col. 169.

[138] Molina, *De iustitia et iure*, I, cols 181–82; 'raroque erit crimen patris, quod servitute filiorum juste possit puniri', col. 181.

[139] Tomas Sánchez, *Consilia; seu, Opuscula moralia* (Cologne: Sumptibus Stephani Breyelii & Haered. Bernardi Gualteri, 1640), pp. 4–7. See also Russell Parsons Jameson, *Montesquieu et l'esclavage* (Paris: Hachette, 1911), pp. 124–25; John T. Noonan, Jr, *A Church that Can and Cannot Change: The Development of Catholic Moral Teaching* (Notre Dame, IN: University of Notre Dame Press, 2005), pp. 82–83.

of 'tyrannical' laws. Because Africans were 'simple' ('rudes'), they might not 'understand the slavery' they were being sold into, might be married and thus 'could not sell themselves' ('non se possunt vendere'), or be sold by fraud into slavery. There were further doubts centring on issues of possession: on what one should do in the event of doubts about the just possession of an object.[140]

Sánchez concluded that taking Africans from their lands in these conditions was tainted with mortal sin. Those who bought slaves 'in great number' from traders in African slaves might commit mortal sin by not establishing that these slaves 'had been justly captured'. Whosoever bought 'one or another slave' from such merchants was obliged to investigate if he had been 'justly captured'; not so a buyer further down the chain, for whom due investigation would be impossible. Whoever bought in good faith would not be obliged to free a slave if doubts surfaced afterwards. However, whoever bought in bad faith committed mortal sin and should free the slave.[141]

From these perspectives, it will be clear that, long before Mongin's arrival in the Caribbean, the circumstances in which Africans were thought to have been enslaved inspired questions concerning specific forms of slavery, rather than its legitimacy per se. Indeed, in 1627, the Jesuit Sandoval acknowledged that a 'great controversy' existed amongst the learned concerning the 'justification' of the Atlantic slave trade.[142] Sandoval left the resolution of this to 'doctores' such as Molina, referring to his *disputationes* 34 and 35 discussed above. Sandoval also included a letter from Luis Brandon, rector of the Jesuit college in Luanda, in which Brandon replied to Sandoval's question of whether the slaves who were sent to the Americas had been 'justly enslaved' ('bien cautivos'). Brandon reminded Sandoval that the Portuguese Mesa da Consciência, and the bishops of the Portuguese possessions on the African coast, had not objected to the practice. The question centred on whether the slaves had been bought in good faith or not, and here Brandon referred Sandoval to Sánchez's exoneration of such buyers. Brandon added a further caveat to investigating the conditions in which slaves had been captured, for he wrote that slaves would inevitably say they had been unjustly captured, whether this were the case or not. Even if, he continued, there might be some slaves who had been unjustly enslaved amongst the 'ten or twelve thousand blacks who left this port [Luanda] every year', one could never know if this was the case with certainty. Not embarking the 'many souls' who would be saved when amongst Christians because of a few who had been 'unjustly captured, without knowing which ones they are', did not seem 'adequate service to God'.[143]

[140] Sánchez, *Consilia*, I, 5–6.
[141] Sánchez, *Consilia*, I, 6–7. See also Davis, p. 190.
[142] Sandoval, Book 1, Chapter 17: *De la esclavitud de estos negros de Guinea y demás puertos, hablando en general*, pp. 97–104 (p. 97).
[143] Sandoval, pp. 97–99.

However, the depiction of African slavery that Sandoval gleaned from the witnesses he interrogated was at odds with Brandon's optimistic view. Sandoval learned that, from Luanda, African agents called *pumberos* went deep inland to slave markets in which they obtained slaves from merchants who had themselves travelled 'more than two or three hundred leagues'. The *pumberos* brought back the severed hands of those slaves who had died along the way.[144] He learned that in the ports of Guinea, the Portuguese traded goods such as wine, which their agents exchanged for slaves inland. In the lands of the Serer and Wolofs, criminals and prisoners of war were traded; Sandoval, however, considered the wars generally unjustified, and the crimes, which included 'adultery, homicide, and theft', were judged in public and punished by 'execution or captivity'. The slaving expeditions inland might capture large numbers of Africans, surprised while they slept.[145] Sandoval also relayed the testimony of a captain of a slave vessel which had been shipwrecked, and out of which, he reported, only thirty of the nine hundred slaves onboard had survived. This captain stated that the reason he had so many slaves in the first place was that two 'powerful kings' in Africa were at war, and each asked the Europeans for assistance, each accompanying their request with a gift of slaves. The 'abundant' harvest of slaves after the war, along with those who had originally been sent, led to a 'great number' being embarked for Cartagena.[146]

Sandoval is also exceptional for relating the perspectives of those who witnessed the trade; some suffered qualms of conscience, having witnessed the illegitimate enslavement of Africans, and others were proud of their profits. One clergyman refuted Molina in a clumsy manner ('bajamente'), while claiming that all the inhabitants of Guinea were nothing more than the slaves of their monarch.[147] Sandoval had even been approached by two slave traders who wanted to know if 'the way their slaves were enslaved was licit'. One stated that he 'went to Angola for slaves, with great effort, expenses, and dangers along the way', and asked if he might 'justify this captivity because of the labour, expense, and danger that [he] underwent in coming and going there'. The parallel with which Sandoval replied angered one of the traders; he suggested that the merchant go to an ecclesiastical establishment in Cartagena named San Francisco, that he remove its great lantern and take it home with him, and, when brought before the judicial authorities, that he explain that, rather than stealing the lantern, he had simply taken it to 'compensate his labour in going from one place to another'.[148]

---

[144] Sandoval, pp. 100–01.
[145] Sandoval, pp. 100–02.
[146] Sandoval, p. 100.
[147] Sandoval, pp. 103–04.
[148] 'para satisfacer con ella el trabajo que había pasado en ir de aquí allá por ella'. Sandoval, pp. 99–100.

The works of Soto, and of the Jesuits Molina and Sánchez, illustrate how African forms of slavery presented theologians based in Europe with a novel set of moral difficulties. While Aristotle was amongst the authorities on whom they drew, they were not describing 'natural' slavery, and their concern was rather with the validity of legal forms of slavery, according to the *ius gentium*: whether owners had 'just title', to use Soto's term. They considered that Africans might be 'seduced' or forced into slavery (Soto), or enslaved as a result of conflict that was unjust, or through disproportionate punishments (Molina). One had to ensure oneself that enslavement was indeed just, or risk committing mortal sin. Sandoval, in the Spanish Americas, testifies first-hand to the various reactions this inspired amongst those implicated in the trade. A further, frequently invoked justification for slavery was that it allowed heathens to achieve salvation through conversion to Christianity; while Soto refused this, its justification is strikingly illustrated in Brandon's letter to Sandoval.

Sandoval was influential not just within his own order, but on the Consejo de Indias, the council for the Spanish Americas, as Scelle has indicated.[149] How such depictions of African slavery impacted on French thought about slavery can be seen in a 1698 discussion of the morality of the practice of slavery (a *cas de conscience*) by the influential Dominican Germain Fromageau.[150] Fromageau evaluated two opposing points of view, the first that of opponents of slavery because it was 'not permitted to buy something [*une chose*] that one knew to be stolen', such as Africans who were 'taken away by force', something that was 'well known' ('public'). Amongst the principal elements of the opposing point of view, which saw such enslavement as 'advantageous' for Africans, were the better treatment they would supposedly receive from Christians, notably with their baptism, and that their African monarch 'tolerated this trade' ('souffre ce commerce').

The terms of Fromageau's response will be familiar in the light of the preceding pages. He replied that, while servitude was said to be 'contrary to nature', it had been introduced by the *ius gentium*, and this allowed a victor in a 'just war' to enslave a defeated enemy (his source was Justinian's *Institutes*). Slavery was permitted in the Old Testament, and in the New Testament Paul 'exhorted slaves to obey their masters' in a well-known passage (Ephesians 6. 5). As Fromageau summed it up, 'in brief, divine and human law allow slavery [*permettent les esclaves*].' The problem was not the trade in slaves, but precisely

---

[149] Scelle, I, 718–19. See also Davis (p. 191) on the 1685 ruling of the 'Spanish Council of the Indies' which, he claims, '[defended] [...] the legitimacy of the African trade' based on Jesuit authors including Sandoval.

[150] Germain Fromageau and Adrien Augustin de Bussy de Lamet, *Le Dictionnaire des cas de conscience*, 2 vols (Paris: J.-B. Coignard, 1733), I, article 'Esclaves', pp. 1437–44. See Michael Harrigan, *Frontiers of Servitude: Slavery in Narratives of the Early French Atlantic* (Manchester: Manchester University Press, 2018), pp. 59–61.

the ways Africans entered slavery. The three ways one could be enslaved, 'through war, punishment, and sale', were problematic in Africa, as wars were unjust, punishments unmerited, and those selling themselves or their children 'did not understand the slavery they were entering'. Fromageau, basing himself on Molina's *disputatio* 35 amongst other theological sources, reasoned that, when slaves were considered like 'the other goods that a man possesses', then it was an 'injustice to buy slaves from those who did not possess them legitimately [*à juste titre*]', or when 'one doubted that they [had been] acquired legitimately'. Significantly, Molina and Sánchez (and Antonino Diana) were the sources referred to by Fromageau for the argument that the 'trade in slaves in Guinea, in Ethiopia, and in other infidel lands is ordinarily unjust, so that merchants who buy or sell slaves there commit mortal sin, and must free them'.[151]

In his account of his years in the French Caribbean at the turn of the eighteenth century, the Dominican Jean-Baptiste Labat gave a striking illustration of the implications of Fromageau's judgement *in situ*. Labat summed up the 'four sorts of people who were sold to the companies or other merchants' as 'miscreants, and generally all those who have merited death or another punishment', 'prisoners of war' (for Labat, these wars had as their aim the rounding up of people to be enslaved), slaves of monarchs, and the fourth sort, the 'greatest number', those who were stolen ('que l'on dérobe'), 'men, women, and children'. Labat followed this by summing up three 'cas de conscience' in the Sorbonne: (1) if merchants or agents could 'buy slaves they knew to be stolen, given that what seems a disorder to us is a received custom amongst these people, and authorized by their kings'; (2) if planters could buy slaves 'without instructing themselves about whether they had been stolen or sold for a legitimate reason'; (3) the 'reparations' once it was known kidnapped slaves had been bought. It can be seen that there is some disparity between Labat's three-point summary and Fromageau's printed formulation. However, how the judgement in the Sorbonne was considered on the islands is clear, from Labat's account:

> The way these three articles were decided by one of our [own] clerics was not received in the islands. It was found to have insurmountable difficulties, and our planters said that the doctors who had been consulted had neither a plantation in the islands nor a stake [*intérêt*] in the companies, and that they would have decided otherwise had they been in one of these two situations.[152]

[151] Fromageau and Lamet, pp. 1437–44. Antonino Diana (1585–1663) categorized slaves into war captives, criminals, and those who had sold themselves; while he discussed themes of actuality such as the limits to the punishment of slaves, or the need for a master's consent to marriage, his discussion of the African slave trade is notably minimal. Diana, *Summa Diana* (Antwerp: apud Hieronymum & Ioannem Bapt. Verdussen, 1656), pp. 181–87, 'servi possunt puniri à Dominis, sed non poenis atrocibus' (p. 186). Diana is limited to one interrogation about the African trade: 'an sit licita emptio mancipiorum fieri solita ab aliquibus in Angola, Guinea, & viridi Promontorio?' (p. 182).

[152] Jean-Baptiste Labat, *Nouveau voyage aux isles de l'Amérique*, 6 vols (Paris: Guillaume

Some parallels can be established between Mongin's and Breban's testimonies and how the Jesuits thought of slavery elsewhere in the Americas. Dauril Alden, for example, qualifies the Portuguese Jesuit response as generally accepting the use of slaves, while condemning excessive punishments; however, Alden also identifies isolated, more overt, critiques which might even be sanctioned by a critic being sent back from the colonies.[153] David G. Sweet sees an evolution in Latin American perspectives by the beginning of the eighteenth century, by which time efforts to 'legitimize slavery' had died away, and Jesuit commentaries were limited to attempting to ensure that 'slave-owners should try to observe the minimal requirements of decency in their exploitation of the slaves'.[154] Le Pers, that long-standing witness to slavery in Saint-Domingue, wrote that the African slave trade was 'tolerated rather than permitted [*moins permis que toléré*] by the Church, and only with the purpose of the eternal salvation of these poor unfortunates [*pauvres misérables*]'.[155]

With a half-century between them, Mongin's and Breban's testimonies illustrate a range of responses. They saw the societies of the west coast of Africa as chaotic, and the source of slaves rounded up under conditions that were morally problematic (Mongin apparently referring to Molina's depiction of Africa). Mongin, for example, considered that, while slaves might be prisoners of war, Africans could be enslaved for minor infractions, or even despite having committed no infraction at all.[156] He sums up the early theological disputes concerning the legitimacy of slavery as permitting 'legitimate servitude', through 'birth, criminal conviction, or the law of war', but surmises that 'most authors' thought that African practices of enslavement were nonetheless problematic (and Molina must be assumed to be amongst those from the 'universities of Portugal' he mentions).[157] Mongin explicitly declares that Europeans bought and transported slaves without concerning themselves with the legality of the purchase.[158] He indicates that it could be somewhat uncertain on what basis slavery was 'established' in the French colonies ('by the king's declaration, or by tolerance and established use').[159]

Mongin claimed that French slavers were comparatively benevolent, and

---

Cavelier and P.-F. Giffard, 1722), IV, 116–20.

[153] Dauril Alden, *The Making of an Enterprise: The Society of Jesus in Portugal, its Empire, and Beyond 1540–1750* (Stanford, CA: Stanford University Press, 1996), pp. 502–12. On a Father Leite's refusal to 'confess anyone, even a Jesuit, who made use of slaves', see Alden, p. 509.

[154] David G. Sweet, 'Black Robes and "Black Destiny": Jesuit Views of African Slavery in 17th-Century Latin America', *Revista de Historia de América*, 86 (July–December 1978), 87–133 (126).

[155] Le Pers, AFSI, GBro188, fol. 58[r].

[156] AFSI, GBro185, fol. 3[v].

[157] MdC, MS 73, fol. 81[v].

[158] AFSI, GBro185, fol. 4[r].

[159] AFSI, GBro185, fol. 3[r].

French practices legally well regulated.[160] However, he was, like Breban, acutely conscious that slaves were mistreated, as has been seen earlier. In practice, their order accepted the use of slaves. The Jesuits owned plantations, such as the substantial one at Terrier-Rouge in the north of Saint-Domingue; Breban's discreet pride concerning the slaves on such plantations illustrates how the perception that they were relatively well treated could then help justify their use.[161]

One further illustration of how the Jesuits considered the treatment of slaves may be seen in the 1729 withdrawal of a certain number of feast days (with papal permission) by the superior of the Jesuit missions in Saint-Domingue. This was because such feast days were considered to be misused by the slave and white population, and one aspect of this misuse was the 'cruelty' of only leaving these days to slaves 'to procure food for themselves'.[162] Such an initiative hints that Catholicism was more than a simple tool for 'collusion' between missionaries and planters in the exploitation of slaves, as some critical approaches would have it (such approaches may be nuanced by what Peabody has demonstrated about the distinct practices of religious orders).[163] There might very well be such collusion in practice; the Dominican Labat, who was both missionary and planter, is a striking example. However, the difficulties surrounding the Christianization of slaves demonstrate that Catholicism was not simply one more strand in colonial governance. This has been discussed elsewhere in more detail, but Le Pers, once more, gives us some idea of how this was experienced around the time of Breban.[164] Le Pers refuted the idea that baptized slaves should be freed, by referring to 'the example of the first Christians' and of Saint Paul.[165] 'Jesus Christ', he wrote, 'left in their entirety the different conditions established amongst men, and of which God His Father is the author.'[166] Tellingly, he also criticized certain masters who 'claimed through a horrible blasphemy that religion spoils their slaves, in that it mitigates their authority over them, and that the slave through his baptism enters into a sort of society and equality [*contracte une espèce de société et d'égalité*] with his master'.[167] What such planters were concerned about was a phenomenon that was both social and religious, and stemmed from belonging and exclusion. Slaves might well be excluded on the social plane, but baptism instead included them, at

---

[160] MdC, MS 73, fol. 82[r].

[161] Moreau de Saint-Méry, *Description*, I, 157; AdC, 2F 788, fols 7[r], 17[r].

[162] P. L. Larcher, 14 November 1729, and Rochalard, 14 October 1730, reproduced in Moreau de Saint-Méry, *Loix et constitutions*, III, 274–77.

[163] See Doris L. Garraway, *The Libertine Colony: Creolization in the Early French Caribbean* (Durham, NC; London: Duke University Press, 2005), p. 159; Peabody, pp. 68–71.

[164] Harrigan, *Frontiers of Servitude*, pp. 141–47.

[165] Le Pers, AFSI, GBro188, fol. 85[v].

[166] Le Pers, AFSI, GBro188, fol. 86[r].

[167] Le Pers, AFSI, GBro188, fol. 85[r].

a time when religious belonging was itself a major — perhaps, the major — component in social cohesion. As Mongin's 1682 letter illustrates so clearly, forms of social exclusion might continue to exist within a spiritual community composed of people sharing a faith.

The present edition will illustrate further aspects of Jesuit perspectives on the treatment of slaves. Members of the order, as Peabody has noted, were involved in many 'conflicts with colonial authorities', which might even be considered subversive of the civil order; as she points out, in Saint-Domingue this even stretched to giving a decent burial to a female slave who had been executed.[168] Mongin's correspondence indicates the many areas of the lives of slaves in which Jesuit missionaries intervened. His 1682 Fonds Brotier letter gives us a glimpse of some such areas which ran counter to the interests of planters, with him attempting to have those who punished excessively brought to justice; he also intervened so as to mitigate the punishment of two slaves who had been sentenced to death.[169] If the Carcassonne copy of his 1682 letter is to be believed, it was a further set of challenges that led the missionaries of other orders to leave the care of slaves to the Jesuits, who were conversely motivated by the difficulties of the mission to the slaves.[170]

Note on Transcription

Spelling, use of accents, and capitalization have been modernized in all letters, and their titles, in the transcriptions. Antiquated terminology in French has not been modified. Early modern conventions on the use of *avoir* with certain verbs ('qui ont passé' where modern use would expect 'qui sont passés', for example) have not been modified, but modern conventions for agreements of past participles have been adopted.[171] Modern conventions regarding elision have been adopted ('jusques à' to 'jusqu'à', etc.).[172] Obvious errors or inconsistencies in transcription have been corrected, or indicated when informative about context.

Punctuation has been modernized. With the MdC manuscript, this has mainly entailed replacing semi-colons with commas or full stops. With the BM manuscript, excessive commas have been removed, and colons and semi-colons replaced. With AFSI, GBro185, commas have been replaced with full stops where necessary; in Breban's letter, commas/semi-colons have been similarly replaced.

---

[168] Peabody, p. 83. On the burial by Boutin 'avec une espèce de solennité', see *Extrait de la lettre du ministre aux administrateurs*, 22 October 1737, in Moreau de Saint-Méry, *Loix et constitutions*, III, 485. See Peabody, p. 79.

[169] AFSI, GBro185, fols 47ʳ–48ʳ.

[170] MdC, MS 73, fol. 83ᵛ.

[171] AFSI, GBro185, fol. 2ᵛ.

[172] AFSI, GBro185, fol. 6ᵛ.

A number of question marks have been added. I have nonetheless minimized interference with punctuation, except where comprehension would be difficult. In the manuscripts, quotations are not distinguished from the rest of the text in AFSI, GBro185, and large text is used for quotations in Latin in BM, Ant MS 9. Quotations are indicated (with some exceptions) by underlining in MdC, MS 73, as with Breban's letter from AdC, 2F 788. In the transcriptions from the manuscripts in this volume, I have indicated quotations through underlining when this has been used in a manuscript, and have adopted italics otherwise. In the BM version of Mongin's 1679 letter (Letter 2 in this book), and the longer AFSI, GBro185 version of that of 1682 (Letter 3 in this book), only the most significant variants which appear in the Carcassonne copies of each have been transcribed. A more restricted number of variants in the Carcassonne copies of each letter have been indicated/translated in the notes to Translations 2 and 3.

Note on Translation

The translation of early modern terms describing non-European peoples has entailed challenging choices. In the case of slaves of African origin or heritage, in particular, terminology is associated with sociocultural, as well as what is now called 'ethnic', connotations. On the one hand, mitigating this terminology may be said to soften the vocabulary characteristic of the early colonies. On the other, seeking to use anachronistic terminology in English would risk creating associations with other historical contexts for English-speaking readers.

The term *nègre* encapsulated both skin colour and unfree status, though it could also be used on the less frequent occasions when an author referred to freed black (as opposed to 'free coloured') slaves.[173] In a 1680 polemical text, the English minister Morgan Godwyn wrote that 'these two words, *Negro* and *Slave*, [were] by custom grown homogenous and convertible'.[174] Nonetheless, for the reasons described in the previous paragraph, the former term has been avoided as a translation of the term *nègre*, and the following conventions have been used instead. When the term *nègre* clearly refers to enslaved individuals, either in Africa or in the Caribbean, the term 'slave' or 'black slave' is used. 'African' has generally been chosen when the person described is clearly African rather than *Creole*, or when an author is reflecting on the African context. I have preferred 'black' when the author is reflecting on skin colour, or making a comparison with *blancs*, or 'whites'.

To ensure as accurate a reflection of context as possible, a gender-inclusive vocabulary has not been adopted when such a step would not reflect an author's perspective. In Breban's discussion of contemporary debates about the

---

[173] On the evolution of such terminology see King, pp. 9, 158–64; Garrigus, pp. 8, 168.
[174] Morgan Godwyn, *The Negro's and Indian's Advocate: Suing for their Admission to the Church* (London: Printed for the author, 1680), p. 36.

physiognomy of Africans, for example, I have translated *savants* as 'learned men'.[175] All translations into English of biblical verses in this book, when directly quoted, are taken from the Douay-Rheims Bible; I have modernized the spelling of such translations.[176]

---

[175] AdC, 2F 788, fol. 5ᵛ.
[176] *The Holy Bible Faithfully Translated into English out of the Authentical Latin* [Old Testament], 2nd edn, 2 vols (Rouen: J. Cousturier, 1635); *The New Testament of Jesus Christ, Translated Faithfully into English* (Rheims: J. Fogny, 1582). Each edition shall be referred to by its respective publication date in footnotes.

LETTER 1

Carcassonne,
MdC, MS 73, fols 32^r–41^r.

This manuscript has undergone a number of alterations, particularly of the names of people mentioned within. The original text before alterations remains visible for the most part, and has been modernized and transcribed below, with footnotes indicating significant modifications. However, where obvious errors have been rectified on the manuscript, the correction has been transcribed.

[**32^r**] Martinique 7bre 1676,[1]

M. R. P.[2]

J'ai commencé depuis 15 jours de jouir de quelque relâche, et j'en profite pour écrire à V.R. plus amplement[3] que je n'ai fait par le passé; on a voulu que je lui[4] fisse savoir plus en détail les conversions de quelques hérétiques, lesquelles ont ici fait quelque bruit, et sont mêlées avec quelques incidents considérables quelque temps après que V.R. [m'eut?][5] envoyé au Carbet m'informant de quelques paroissiens sur les besoins spirituels de la paroisse, j'en appris un, et qui consistait dans la mauvaise conduite de la femme d'un marchand appelé M. N. mais j'en trouvai le remède bien difficile quand on m'ajouta que toute cette maison était calviniste; néanmoins voyant qu'il fallait l'appliquer[6] à la cause du mal, je résolus de travailler à leur conversion; pour cet effet j'eus deux conférences avec le mari dont ayant reconnu l'inutilité je quittai pour un temps de les continuer. Je n'avais pas plus d'espérance de la conversion de la femme parce que la prudence me rendait[7] inaccessible, tant à cause de sa[8] réputation, que pour le danger de faire soupçonner mon dessein; mais Dieu

---

[1] '4' appears to have been inserted before '7bre'.
[2] 'M. R. P.' has been altered to 'Mr.'.
[3] Altered to 'pour vous écrire plus amplement'.
[4] 'lui' has been crossed out and replaced by 'vous'.
[5] 'V.R.' and the auxiliary verb which follows have been crossed out, and 'je fus' inserted.
[6] 'l'appliquer' replaced by 'aller'.
[7] 'me rendait' altered to 'me la rendait'.
[8] Originally 'sa'; modified, possibly to 'la'.

TRANSLATION 1

Carcassonne,
MdC, MS 73, fols 32^r–41^{r}.[1]

Martinique, September 1676,

Dear Reverend Father,

For about fifteen days I have begun to have some respite, and I am making use of it to write to Your Reverence in greater length than I have done in the past. It was desired that I let you know in more detail about the conversions of a number of heretics which have been much talked about here, and which took place in quite noteworthy circumstances. Some time after Your Reverence sent [me] to Le Carbet, when asking several parishioners about the spiritual needs of the parish, I learned of one, which was the bad conduct of the wife of a merchant named Mr X., but I knew the cure would be very difficult when I was also told that the whole household was Calvinist. Nonetheless, seeing that the remedy had to be applied to the cause of the problem, I resolved to work towards their conversion. For this purpose I had two discussions with the husband, and recognizing that it was pointless, I left them for a time. I had no more hope for the conversion of the wife, because prudence made [her] inaccessible [to me], as much because of her reputation as because of the danger of my plan being suspected, but God soon enabled me to overcome these difficulties. One day,

---

[1]   On the Jesuit provincial of Toulouse as the addressee of this letter, see Introduction, n. 17.

m'aplanit bientôt ces difficultés. Un jour qu'elle me vit sortir du presbytère elle m'alla couper chemin au milieu de la place pour me parler de quelque affaire qui regardait la cure⁹ sur quoi lui ayant répondu en peu de mots, je lui en dis quelqu'un sur sa religion, d'abord elle témoigna y avoir une grande [32ᵛ] attache, et elle avoua enfin que la seule crainte de son mari l'y retenait, après quoi je me retirai lui disant que cet aveu me donnait de grandes espérances de son salut, et qu'on pourrait trouver un tempérament à la faveur duquel elle pourrait être catholique sans avoir la crainte qui l'en empêchait. Les causes que j'ai déjà dites m'empêchèrent de prolonger, et de réitérer cet entretien; et je priai les personnes les plus graves et les plus propres pour cette affaire, de l'achever aussi bien qu'elle avait été commencée, leur disant les raisons pourquoi je ne pouvais la continuer; c'était les dames de Gourcelas, et de Loubière avec Mlle de Saint-Pierre¹⁰ dont le mérite est universellement reconnu. Ces trois illustres veuves embrassèrent cette affaire de tout leur cœur, et pour cet effet renouèrent avec Mlle N. une amitié dont sa mauvaise conduite l'avait rendue indigne auparavant.

Elles lui dirent donc de ma part que si elle n'avait point assez de générosité pour vaincre la crainte de son mari,¹¹ elle pouvait secrètement abjurer l'hérésie, et recevoir les sacrements, et qu'elle pouvait dans le reste dissimuler, d'autant plus facilement, que dans ce pays, il n'y avait ni prêche ni cène, que fort peu de catholiques y peuvent garder l'abstinence des jours maigres, et que sa maison était tellement disposée qu'elle pouvait ouïr la messe de sa chambre; outre que ces préceptes de l'Église ne l'obligeaient point dans le péril d'être abandonnée de son mari, qui est son unique appui.

Ces dames lui représentèrent toutes ces choses avec tant de zèle, et répondirent si bien à toutes ses difficultés qu'elles la laissa remplies d'une douce espérance de voir en bref¹² cette conversion, leur disant pour conclusion qu'elle leur demandait trois jours pour y penser.

[33ʳ] C'était la veille de la Pentecôte, et le mardi suivant elle me rencontra pour me prier de ne m'écarter pas le lendemain, à cause de quelque affaire importante où l'on ne pouvait se passer de moi. Je lui demandai quelque éclaircissement sur ce point; elle me répondit que je n'en avais pas besoin, et que je ne pouvais ignorer la parole qu'elle avait donnée; qu'en un mot elle voulait faire abjuration de l'hérésie. Ces paroles dites avec une fermeté extraordinaire me causèrent une des plus sensibles consolations que j'aie eues à ma vie. Je lui répondis qu'elle savait bien que les dames étaient à la campagne; elle me répliqua qu'elle les allait faire avertir, et que s'il fallait elle irait elle-même.

---

⁹ 'qui regardait la cure' crossed out.
¹⁰ All three surnames have been crossed out and each replaced with 'N.' 'Loubière' is spelled 'L'obiere' throughout the manuscript text.
¹¹ 'la crainte de son mari' altered to 'la crainte qu'elle avait de son mari'.
¹² 'en bref' replaced with 'bientôt'.

after she had seen me coming out of the presbytery, she came to talk to me about some little matter concerning it, and our paths crossed in the square. Having answered her succinctly on the matter, I then spoke to her about her religion. She seemed greatly attached to it at first, but in the end, she admitted that it was only her fear of her husband that retained her. After this, I went on my way, saying to her that her admission gave me great hope for her salvation, and that a solution could be found through which she could be Catholic without being held back by fear. I was prevented by the causes I have already mentioned from prolonging and renewing this conversation, and I requested several people who are most serious, and most suitable for such an affair, to conclude it as successfully as it had been started. I told them the reasons that prevented me from continuing it. [These people] were Madame de Gourcelas and Madame de Loubière with Mademoiselle de Saint-Pierre, whose merit is recognized by everyone.[2] These three illustrious widows took on this affair wholeheartedly, and for this purpose they resumed a friendship with Mademoiselle X. of which her bad conduct had previously made her unworthy.[3]

They said to her, then, on my behalf that if she did not have enough generosity of spirit to conquer her fear of her husband, she could abjure heresy in secret, and receive the sacraments, that with regard to the rest she could dissimulate all the more easily because in this land there is neither place of worship nor Communion [for Protestants], that few Catholics can keep abstinence on fasting days, and that the position of her house was such that she could hear the Mass from her room. Aside from this, the precepts of the Church did not bind her when she was in danger of being abandoned by her husband, who is her only support.

These ladies exposed all these things to her with so much zeal, and replied so well to all her objections that she left them filled with a sweet hope of soon seeing this conversion. She said to them in conclusion that she asked them for three days to think about it.

It was the eve of Pentecost, and the following Tuesday she met with me and requested me not to go very far away the following day, because of an important matter for which I was needed.[4] I asked her for some enlightenment on this point, and she replied that I had no need of it, and that I could not be unaware that she had given her word: that, in a nutshell, she wanted to abjure her heresy. These words, pronounced with extraordinary firmness, gave me one of the deepest consolations I have ever felt in my life. I replied to her that she was well aware that the ladies were in the countryside. She replied in turn that she was going to have them called for, and that if she had to, she would go there herself.

[2] Mery Rools, Sieur de Gourcelas, was the brother of the Sieur de Loubière (or *Loubières*), according to Pierre Régis Dessalles. The widows Gourcelas and Loubières are mentioned in requests for exemptions on the *capitation*, or tax paid on slaves, in 1673–74 (Madame de Gourcelas) and 1683 (Madame de Loubières). Adrien Dessalles, *Histoire générale des Antilles*, 5 vols [vol. 3 written by Pierre Régis Dessalles] (Paris: France, 1847), III, 40, 179.
[3] 'Mademoiselle X.' was the wife of 'Mr X.'. 'Mademoiselle' might refer to married non-noble women, as well as unmarried women.
[4] Pentecost Sunday falls seven weeks after Easter Sunday. In the following paragraphs Mongin mentions both Trinity Sunday, which falls one week after Pentecost, and Corpus Christi, on the Thursday following Trinity Sunday.

Jamais je ne vis un tel empressement; néanmoins il fallut attendre malgré elle jusqu'au samedi veille de la très Sainte Trinité. Je reçus alors sa profession de foi selon les formes de l'Église chez Mme de Gourcelas,[13] mais ce ne fut qu'après lui avoir inculqué[14] en présence de ces trois dames qui étaient les seuls témoins qu'elle avait voulus, qu'il y allait de sa vie si elle ne prétendait faire qu'une grimace, et si elle ne voulait vivre, et mourir dans la foi qu'elle allait embrasser; après quoi elle n'aurait plus la liberté dont elle jouissait encore. Elle me répondit qu'elle savait tout cela, et termina toutes les assurances de sa sincérité par la prestation du serment à l'accoutumée. Ensuite ces dames lui ayant fait plusieurs caresses elles prirent le soin de continuer son instruction qu'elles n'avaient faite auparavant que sur les choses les plus nécessaires; alors on la disposa à la confession, et la communion selon ce que j'en marquais à ces dames, qui à son égard me déchargeaient de tous les soins dont elles étaient capables. Je pris celui de lui administrer les sacrements trois jours après dans la chapelle de [33ᵛ] l'habitation de Mlle de Saint-Pierre,[15] laquelle y assista avec bien de la consolation. Ensuite j'obtins de la néophyte qu'elle se confesserait tous les mois au curé ordinaire du Carbet qui venait alors reprendre son poste. Pendant que j'avais travaillé à la conversion de Mlle N. je n'avais pas oublié celle de sa bonne mère Mme Peré,[16] c'est une veuve d'environ[17] 50 ans dont l'habitation est dans le même quartier. J'en souhaitais d'autant plus la conversion, que je la voyais fort malade, et que son exemple entraînerait le reste de sa famille composée de six personnes sans compter Mlle N. mais j'y trouvais un obstacle qui était un refus d'une chose, qui lui était très importante, et que je ne pouvais lui accorder en conscience quoiqu'elle me la demandât fort instamment.

Cette raison ruinant mon espérance, me fit différer pendant deux mois à voir Mme Peré[18] jusqu'à ce qu'enfin la conversion de sa fille diminua ma défiance. Je lui fis demander si elle agréerait ma visite, et il me fut répondu que oui. Je la commençai par adoucir son esprit aigri, et Dieu me fit la grâce d'y réussir si bien qu'ayant voulu ensuite lui dire adieu, et imiter la feinte que notre Seigneur pratiqua pour se faire retenir par ses disciples à Emmaüs, elle me fit aussi de pareilles instances aux leurs, pour m'arrêter se plaignant fort honnêtement de la brièveté de ma visite, alors je profitai de cette bonne disposition, et je lui découvris le dessein qui [34ʳ] m'avait amené là, mais je n'en pus tirer si ce n'est qu'elle était trop âgée pour changer de religion; surtout disait-elle n'ayant pas sujet de douter de la sienne, ce qu'elle tâchait même de prouver le moins mal qu'il se pût.[19]

---

[13] 'Gourcelas' replaced with 'N.'.
[14] 'inculqué' crossed out and replaced with 'dit'.
[15] 'Saint-Pierre' replaced with 'N.'.
[16] 'Peré' replaced with 'N.'.
[17] Modified to read 'une veuve âgée d'environ'.
[18] 'Peré' replaced with 'N.'.
[19] 'il se pût' has been modified to 'il se peut'.

I had never before seen such haste. Nevertheless, she had to wait, in spite of her wishes, until the following Saturday, which was the eve of Trinity Sunday. I then received her profession of faith according to the formula of the Church, at Madame de Gourcelas's house, but this was only after — and in the presence of these three ladies who were the only witnesses she wanted — inculcating in her that her life was at stake if she was only pretending, and if she did not want to live and die in the faith that she was going to embrace, and that after this she would no longer have the freedom that she currently enjoyed. She replied to me that she knew all this, and she ended all these assurances of her sincerity by the customary swearing of the oath.

Next, these ladies, having been extremely kind to her, took the trouble of continuing her instruction, which they had previously only done concerning the most necessary things. Then she was prepared for confession and Communion according to the instructions I gave these ladies, who relieved me of all the duties, in relation to her, of which they were capable. I looked after that of administering the sacraments to her three days afterwards in the chapel of the plantation of Mademoiselle de Saint-Pierre, who attended with much consolation. I then obtained of the neophyte that she would confess every month to the usual curate of Le Carbet, who had just returned to his post. While I had been working on the conversion of Mademoiselle X., I had not forgotten that of her worthy mother, Madame Peré, a widow of about fifty, whose plantation is in the same area. I was all the more desirous of her conversion because I saw that she was very sick, and that her example would bring the rest of her family — which was composed of six people without counting Mademoiselle X. — with her. However, I discovered an obstacle, which was the refusal of one thing which was very important to her, and that I could not, in conscience, grant her, even though she asked me with great insistence.

As my hopes were dashed for this reason, I put off seeing Madame Peré for two months, until the conversion of her daughter made me less wary. I sent her a request to accept my visit, and I received a positive reply. I began by softening her embittered spirit, and God granted me the grace of succeeding so well that, going to say goodbye to her, and imitating the ruse that Our Lord used so that His disciples would keep Him with them at Emmaus,[5] she begged me, as they did, to stay, reproaching me the brevity of my visit in a very civil manner. So I took advantage of this willingness, and I uncovered to her the motive that had brought me there, but I could get nothing from her except that she was too old to change religion, *especially*, she said, *as she had no reason to doubt her own*, which she even tried to prove in the least bad of ways.

---

[5] A reference to Luke 24. 28–29.

Je ne perdis pourtant pas espérance, et ayant recommandé l'affaire à Dieu, il me fit la grâce de m'accorder cette conversion, et celle de tout le reste de la famille; cette bonne femme se contenta pour lors de m'en donner parole, disant qu'elle ne pouvait l'exécuter dans le logis dont elle était alors locataire, parce qu'une huguenote qui en est la propriétaire l'obsédait éternellement. Ce fut la cause que je m'employai avec diligence pour lui trouver une autre maison à louage. J'y réussis, mais comme on faisait le transport de la famille, je fus rappelé à mon premier poste du Fort Saint-Pierre pour y aller prêcher l'octave du Saint-Sacrement où ayant tout communiqué au R. P. de La Pierre,[20] qui après quelque indisposition s'en retournait à ce quartier dont il avait soin, il acheva heureusement ce qui manquait à cette conversion, reçût sa profession de foi et lui administra les sacrements, et ouït sa confession générale, dont ensuite il nous porta la nouvelle au fort. Peu de jours après le reste de la famille fit la même chose dans la paroisse, le plus petit garçon qui est de neuf à dix ans servait à la grand-messe avec la petite soutane rouge, et un fort beau surplis que sa sœur lui avait fait; il n'est pas possible de croire la joie que cela causait à tous les catholiques.

[34ᵛ] Cependant la conversion de Mlle N. était encore cachée à cause de son mari dont on craignait avec raison la violence. Il en avait néanmoins des conjectures assez fortes, et on croyait qu'il voulait l'ignorer tant qu'il pourrait, pour n'être obligé de la maltraiter par la complaisance extrême qu'il a pour ses frères en Christ.[21] Quoi qu'il en fût, on jugea qu'il fallait enfin le lui faire savoir au plus tôt, et que l'expédient le plus sûr pour prévenir ses emportements était de le lui faire déclarer par M. le Général qui seul pouvait à même temps lui recommander efficacement la modération.

Je fus chargé d'en prier M. le Général, lequel aussitôt que je me fus acquitté de ma commission, manda le Sieur N. mais M. de La Herpinière qui portait cet ordre au Carbet y trouva les affaires fort malheureusement changées à son arrivée. Voici la cause de ce funeste changement. Ce fut en ce même temps qu'un zélé mais indiscret[22] prit la résolution de parler à M. N. de la conversion de sa femme, se faisant fort d'empêcher par le pouvoir qu'il prétendait avoir [sur][23] son esprit, les désordres qu'on appréhendait de cette déclaration. Il communiqua sa pensée aux dames, qui firent en vain tous leurs efforts pour l'en dissuader lui prédisant toutes les suites, et lui assurant qu'il n'y avait nul moyen que celui d'y employer M. de Baas Lieutenant Général.

---

[20] 'où ayant tout communiqué au' crossed out and replaced with 'et le'.
[21] 'ses frères en Christ' replaced with 'ses confrères'.
[22] 'mais indiscret' crossed out.
[23] 'sur' is an insertion.

However, I did not lose hope, and, having recommended the matter to God, through His grace He granted me this conversion and that of all the rest of her family. At that point, this worthy woman settled for giving me her word, saying that she could not undertake it in her abode as she was merely a tenant, and was constantly pestered by the owner, a Huguenot woman. Because of this, I diligently went about finding her another house to rent. I succeeded in doing so, but, as the family were moving, I was called back to my initial post in Fort Saint-Pierre to preach the Octave of Corpus Christi.[6] There, I explained everything to Reverend Father de La Pierre who, after illness, was going back to the quarter which was under his care. He successfully finished what was lacking from this conversion, received her profession of faith and administered the sacraments to her, and heard her general confession.[7] He then brought the news of this to us at the Fort. A few days later the rest of the family did the same thing in the parish. The smallest boy who is nine or ten years old served at High Mass wearing the short red cassock, and a lovely surplice that his sister had made for him. The joy that this caused all the Catholics was unbelievable.

However, the conversion of Mademoiselle X. was still secret because of her husband, whose ire was rightly feared. Nonetheless, there were strong enough clues, and it was thought that he wanted to ignore it as long as he could, so that he would not be obliged to mistreat her, given how he indulges the wishes of his brothers in Christ. In any case, it was judged necessary to let him know about it without delay, and that the surest expedient to prevent his rage was to have the General — who alone could at the same time effectively advise him moderation — declare it to him.[8]

I was given the task of requesting this of the General who, as soon as I had carried out my task, sent for Mr X. However, Mr de La Herpinière, who brought this order to Le Carbet, found upon his arrival that things had changed in a most unhappy way.[9] The cause of this unhappy change was as follows. It was at this time that an indiscreet zealot resolved to speak to Mr X. about his wife's conversion; he claimed that he could prevent the trouble that it was feared this declaration would cause, because of the sway he claimed to have over him. He made his thoughts known to the ladies, and they in vain made every effort to dissuade him from it, forewarning him of the consequences, and assuring him that there was no other means but to employ Mr de Baas, the Lieutenant General.

---

[6] *Octave*: period of eight days after certain liturgical feast days, or celebration on the eighth day following such feast days.
[7] Moshe Sluhovsky distinguishes between 'traditional confession, which took place once or twice a year and [...] offered pardon for specific sinful acts', and the general confession, a 'Jesuit practice, [which] regarded confession [...] as a method of self-examination'. Sluhovsky, *Believe not Every Spirit: Possession, Mysticism, and Discernment in Early Modern Catholicism* (Chicago: University of Chicago Press, 2007), p. 266.
[8] *The General*: Jean-Charles de Baas-Castlemore (d. 1677), governor general from 1669 to 1677.
[9] La Herpinière, or L'Herpinière. The nephew of Baas, and a Protestant, according to Gérard Lafleur, 'Les Hollandais et les Antilles françaises', in *Entre calvinistes et catholiques: les relations religieuses entre la France et les Pays-Bas du Nord (XVIᵉ–XVIIIᵉ siècles)*, ed. by Yves Krumenacker (Rennes: Presses universitaires de Rennes, 2010), pp. 113–33 (p. 124).

Nonobstant tout cela son zèle le fit passer outre. Il alla parler comme il l'avait projeté à M. N. Aussitôt celui-ci s'emporta furieusement, protesta [35ʳ] qu'il ne verrait jamais sa femme, qu'il l'allait abandonner, et après avoir dit cent autres choses qui marquaient un prodigieux égarement d'esprit il sortit de chez lui, et la nuit suivante alla coucher ailleurs, et selon quelques-uns, dans un canot qui était à la rade, se plaignant avec extravagance de ceux qui avaient travaillé à la réduction de sa femme.

Cette jeune créole qui était alors absente de sa maison n'eut pas plutôt appris la rage de son mari qu'elle y accourt tout alarmée, lui assure qu'elle se repent, qu'elle ne veut jamais aller à l'église, que dans sa profession elle avait été violentée, et séduite par les dames; ce qu'elle reprocha ensuite à Mme de Loubière[24] qui était accourue à ce bruit, et laquelle n'y reçut de cet homme et de cette femme qu'un traitement le plus indigne qu'on pourrait faire à une servante.

Voilà l'état où était cette affaire lorsque M. de La Herpinière arriva du Fort-Royal au Carbet pour appeler M. N. de la part de M. le Général qui voulait comme j'ai dit lui donner le premier la nouvelle de la conversion de sa femme avec quelque avis; mais cette apostasie ayant rompu toutes nos mesures, il en fallut prendre d'autres pour réparer ce malheur. On dit aussitôt qu'il fallait surseoir l'exécution de la commission qu'avait donnée M. de Baas, et lui faire savoir le changement des affaires. Cependant la légèreté scandaleuse de cette femme ayant éclaté servait d'entretien à tous les quartiers de l'île; elle diminuait la joie des [35ᵛ] catholiques qui par quelque soupçon avaient eu connaissance de sa conversion. Elle affligeait, et étonnait également les personnes dont Dieu s'était servi pour cette bonne œuvre, qui se souvenaient de l'empressement que la convertie avait témoigné, et pour avoir la liberté de se déclarer, et pour se faire toujours instruire, étant devenue pour cet effet inséparable de Mlle de Saint-Pierre[25] que j'avais chargée de ce soin pour les raisons déjà dites, et qui m'en écrivait de temps en temps les choses les plus édifiantes du monde.

Mais la plus affligée de tous fut la bonne Mme Peré;[26] elle était fort malade, et ayant appris cette triste nouvelle, *qu'on me porte à l'église* dit-elle, *la mère ne doit pas mourir qu'après avoir réparé le scandale de la fille.* Elle n'avait pas encore été à la messe, et n'avait fait sa profession que dans le lit où elle est détenue depuis un an; comme son mal augmentait alors, je ne fus pas d'avis qu'on condescendît à sa dévotion, qu'après que le médecin eut jugé qu'on le pouvait sans péril; ce fut donc la première fête, qu'on la porta à la messe dans un hamac;[27] elle y reçut les sacrements, et comme c'était le jour de l'Assomption de Notre-Dame, il y avait

---

[24] 'Loubière' replaced with 'N.'.
[25] 'Saint-Pierre' replaced with 'S. P.'.
[26] 'Peré' replaced with 'N. sa mère'.
[27] 'ou lit de coton' has been added after 'hamac'.

Notwithstanding all of this, his zeal drove him on and he went to speak to Mr X. as he had planned to. Straightaway Mr X. flew into a furious rage, and swore that he would never see his wife again, and that he was going to abandon her, and, after saying a hundred other things that showed that he was beside himself to an extraordinary degree, he left his house. He spent the following night elsewhere and, according to some, in a canoe in the bay, protesting vehemently about those who had worked towards the submission of his wife.

This young Creole woman, who was away from the house at this time, had no sooner learned of her husband's rage than she ran back home, greatly alarmed. She assured him that she had repented, that she never wanted to go to the church, that she had been put under pressure in her profession [of faith], and had been won over by the ladies; she then reproached Madame de Loubière, who had come running when she heard, for this. The latter received from this man and woman nothing but the most shameful treatment one might give a servant.

This was the state of affairs when Mr de La Herpinière arrived in Le Carbet from Fort-Royal to call Mr X. on behalf of the General, who wanted, as I have said, to be the first to give him the news of the conversion of his wife, and some advice with it. Our efforts had, however, been frustrated by this apostasy, and we had to take other measures to remedy the evil. Immediately, it was said that the execution of Mr de Baas's commission had to be put off, and he had to be notified of the change in circumstances. However, the scandalous irreverence of this woman was out in the open and was being talked about all over the island. It diminished the joy of the Catholics who had suspected something and had come to know of the conversion. It distressed and astonished in equal measure those people whom God had employed for this good work, and who remembered the eagerness the convert had shown. Eager to assert her faith and to receive constant instruction, she had become inseparable from Mademoiselle de Saint-Pierre, whom I had entrusted with this task for the reasons already discussed, and who from time to time would write the most edifying things in the world about her to me.

But the most distressed of all was good Madame Peré; she was extremely ill, and, having learned this sad news, said: 'Let me be brought to the church. A mother should not die before righting her daughter's wrong.' She had not yet attended Mass, and had only made her profession in the bed where she had been lying for a year. As her sickness was worsening at that time, I was not of the opinion that we should consent to her devotion until after the doctor had judged that we could without danger. So, on [her] first feast-day she was carried to the Mass in a hammock. There she received the sacraments, and as it was the feast of the Assumption of Our Lady there was an exceptionally

une foule extraordinaire qui environna la malade pour lui témoigner l'extrême joie qu'ils avaient de sa conversion, pendant qu'elle détestait l'inconstance de sa fille, et qu'elle protestait que ce [36ʳ] malheur tempérait beaucoup la satisfaction qu'elle avait de se voir enfin au pied des autels pour y réitérer publiquement l'abjuration qu'elle avait déjà faite en particulier; elle ajoutait qu'après Dieu elle devait sa conversion à la Sainte Vierge, parce que pendant le temps de son hérésie elle n'avait pas manqué de l'invoquer. Elle dit toutes ces choses avec tant de force, et avec tant de dévotion qu'elle tirait les larmes aux catholiques surtout quand ils la considéraient environnée de sa famille qui avait suivi son exemple. Ceux qui rapportèrent cela aux absents disaient que Mme Peré²⁸ avait prêché ce jour-là; ensuite on la rapporta dans son logis qui est à demi-lieue de la paroisse.

Pendant qu'elle faisait ainsi pénitence publique pour une faute qu'elle n'avait pas faite, je pensais à en faire faire autant, mais d'une autre manière, à celle qui était la coupable, et à ses complices. Je ne voulus pas d'abord la mettre en justice conformément à l'ordonnance du roi contre les relaps, mais comme il était évident à tout le monde que sa faute n'était qu'un effet des menaces de son mari, je pris le parti de recourir encore à M. le Général pour lui rendre raison à même temps de ce qu'on n'avait pas exécuté l'ordre dont j'ai parlé; Mme de Loubière eut heureusement la même pensée, et après qu'elle eut prié Mlle Saint-Pierre, et M. Peltier²⁹ capitaine du quartier de la vouloir accompagner jusqu'au Fort-Royal [36ᵛ] pour cette affaire qu'elle faisait sienne, elle me fit pareillement la même prière disant qu'il n'y avait personne qui pût mieux justifier que moi la conduite qu'on avait tenue dans cette conversion.

Je me mis donc dans cette compagnie par l'avis de nos pères; nous fîmes heureusement le voyage pendant lequel Mme de Loubière³⁰ me protesta plusieurs fois que c'était le seul intérêt de Dieu, et nullement le sien qui lui faisait aller porter sa plainte à M. de Baas contre M. N. et sa femme; qu'elle savait bien distinguer l'injure de Dieu de la sienne, et qu'elle serait assez satisfaite pourvu que la religion le fût par la punition, ou par la seconde conversion de cette relapse. C'était cette dernière chose que nous prétendions, et que nous espérions de voir assurément aussitôt que le Sieur N. aurait été obligé par M. de Baas de laisser sa femme dans la liberté de conscience.

Nous exposâmes donc à M. le Général la conduite que nous avions gardée dans cette affaire, l'empressement de cette femme pour sa profession, la déclaration que je lui avais faite auparavant, de l'ordonnance du roi contre les relaps; la nécessité de faire en secret cette abjuration, attendu l'impossibilité d'obtenir jamais le consentement du mari; le scandale de cette apostasie, les

---

²⁸ 'Peré' replaced with 'N.'.
²⁹ 'Loubière' replaced with 'L.', 'Saint-Pierre' with 'S.P.', and 'Peltier' with 'P.'. The manuscript reads 'Mlle Saint-Pierre' (and not 'Mlle de Saint-Pierre') here.
³⁰ 'Loubière' replaced with 'L.' in this and subsequent mentions in this letter.

large crowd which surrounded the patient to bear witness to their extreme joy in her conversion. She, meanwhile, expressed her disapproval of her daughter's inconstancy, protesting that this scandal considerably tempered the satisfaction she had in seeing herself at the foot of the altar at last, so as to reiterate in public the abjuration she had already made in private. She added that, after God, she owed her conversion to the Holy Virgin, because during the time of her heresy she had invoked her ceaselessly. She said all of these things with so much force, and so much devotion, that she brought tears to the eyes of the Catholics, especially when they looked upon her, surrounded by her family who had followed her example. The witnesses who described this to those who were absent said that Madame Peré had preached on this day. She was then brought back to her house, which is a half league[10] away from the parish church.

While she was making public penitence in this way for a wrong she had not committed, I was thinking of having the guilty party do so herself, with her accomplices, but in another way. I did not want to have her at once[11] prosecuted under the king's ordinance against the relapsed,[12] but, as it was clear to everybody that her sin was only due to her husband's threats, I decided to have recourse once more to the General, to explain to him that the order which I have mentioned had not been carried out. Fortunately Madame de Loubière had the same thought, and, after she had asked Mademoiselle Saint-Pierre and Mr Peltier, the captain of the quarter, to be kind enough to accompany her to Fort-Royal for this matter, which she took on personally, she also asked me to do the same. She said that there was nobody who could justify our behaviour in this conversion better than I could.

I went along with this group, following the advice of our Fathers. We successfully made the voyage, during which Madame de Loubière declared to me many times that it was for God alone, and not her own interest, that she went to accuse Mr X. and his wife before Mr de Baas, that she was well aware of the difference between an injury to God and one done to herself, and that she would be satisfied enough once religion was also satisfied, by the punishment or the second conversion of this lapsed Catholic. It was the latter that we wished for, and that we assuredly expected to see as soon as Mr de Baas obliged Mr X. to leave his wife her freedom of conscience.

We described to the General our conduct in this affair, the eagerness of this woman for her profession, the declaration that I had made beforehand of the king's ordinance against lapsed [Catholics], the need to make this abjuration in secret given the impossibility of ever obtaining the husband's consent,

---

[10] The *lieue* (league) varied according to region; the *lieue commune* of France is listed as 4.45 km in Horace Doursther, *Dictionnaire universel des poids et mesures anciens et modernes* (Brussels: Hayet, 1840), p. 210.

[11] 'D'abord': 'at once' or 'first'. The context implies the former.

[12] A *Déclaration du roi contre les relaps* of April 1663 forbade subjects who had abjured Protestantism from reconverting from Catholicism. There were further measures in the years before the 1685 Revocation of the Edict of Nantes.

excuses ridicules de cette relapse sur les prétendues violences dont elle chargeait les dames, les emportements de son mari, le traitement qu'ils avaient fait à Mme de Loubière, et enfin l'empressement des autres huguenots du Carbet pour faire continuer [37ʳ] ce désordre par leurs conseils: après quoi je tirai de ma poche la profession de foi de cette femme, signée de sa main, et accompagnée de l'attestation de tous ceux qui y avaient assisté, et qui à même temps l'avaient signée; à quoi nous ajoutâmes pour empêcher qu'on ne la désespérât pas, que la faute n'était qu'une faute d'infirmité, et celle du mari de malice.

M. le Général après nous avoir écoutés avec une bonté admirable donna d'abord là où nous voulûmes; il manda les deux accusés avec tous les autres huguenots du Carbet, donnant ordre à M. Peltier[31] de leur intimer celui-là, et de les embarquer tous à même temps. Tout cela fut exécuté avec la même promptitude, car quoique nous fussions de retour au Carbet, le lendemain à midi, le même jour on remplit un canot de ces gens pour les transmettre au Fort-Royal. C'était pour eux un orage qu'ils avaient voulu conjurer, car comme les plus coupables, et les plus mutins nous avaient vus auparavant mettre sur mer, le reproche que leur conscience leur faisait, leur fit juger qu'ils étaient le sujet de notre voyage; ils s'étaient aussitôt assemblés dans une gargote avec ceux du Fort Saint-Pierre, et là cette Église réformée, parmi les pots, et les verres délibéra sur ce qu'elle avait à faire pour parer au coup qui la menaçait. Elle députa M. Bourgeois le médecin[32] ayant cru sur sa parole qu'il avait grand crédit auprès de M. de Baas (lequel pourtant m'a dit qu'il était sur le point de le chasser de l'île). Cet habile [37ᵛ] s'acquitta de sa commission avec tant de précipitation qu'il abandonna un malade de la première qualité pour faire ce voyage, dont il ne rapporta aucun fruit, quoiqu'à son retour il se vantât d'avoir eu une conférence de deux heures avec M. le Général.

Cependant le canot de ses confrères arriva au Fort-Royal avec sa garnison;[33] aussitôt le Sieur N. fut mis dans le cachot, et sa femme avec le reste de sa compagnie citée par-devant M. de Baas, lequel ménagea cette affaire de la manière la plus sage, et la plus efficace du monde. Il dit d'abord à Mlle N. qu'il l'avait appelée pour savoir d'elle quelle était sa religion, laissant entièrement à sa volonté de se déclarer sur ce point, et ne prétendant nullement de la violenter (ce qu'il disait pour aller au-devant des plaintes même injustes des calvinistes, et les empêcher d'attribuer à la force cette seconde conversion). Elle répondit qu'elle avait fait profession de la foi catholique apostolique et romaine. M. de Baas répliqua qu'il empêcherait absolument qu'on lui fît aucune violence pour la quitter, ou pour la suivre.

Je la veux suivre, dit-elle, *toute ma vie*.

---

[31] 'Peltier' replaced with 'P.'.
[32] 'M. Bourgeois le médecin' replaced with 'le Sieur B.'.
[33] 'garnison' replaced with 'charge'.

the scandal of this apostasy, the ridiculous excuses of this lapsed Catholic concerning the supposed force she accused the ladies of, the rage of her husband, the way they had treated Madame de Loubière, and finally the readiness of the other Huguenots of Le Carbet to maintain this unrest collectively.[13] After this I took the woman's profession of faith, which she had signed with her own hand, out of my bag. It was accompanied by the attestation of all those who had attended, and who had all signed it at the same time. To prevent her being excessively tormented, we added that her sin was only one of weakness, but that of her husband was a sin of malice.

After the General had listened to us, with admirable kindness, he at once[14] did what we wanted; he sent for the two accused along with all the other Huguenots of Le Carbet, ordering Mr Peltier to convey the order to them, and to embark all of them at the same time. All of this was carried out with the same promptness, for, although we were back in Le Carbet at midday the next day, the same day a canoe was filled with these people to transport them to Fort-Royal. They would have preferred to quell this storm, for, since the most guilty and most mutinous had previously seen us putting out to sea, the reproach of their conscience made them suspect that our voyage was due to them. They had straightaway gathered in a cheap tavern with those of Fort Saint-Pierre, and there this Reformed Church, amongst the pots and the glasses, deliberated about what it could do to ward off the threat. They deputed Mr Bourgeois, the physician, believing his assurances that he had great credit with Mr de Baas (Mr de Baas told me, however, that he was on the point of expelling him from the island). This fine negotiator carried out his commission with so much precipitation that he abandoned a patient of the highest rank to make this voyage, from which he brought back no fruit, despite bragging on his return that he had had a discussion with the General for two hours.

Meanwhile his confreres' canoe arrived at Fort-Royal with its consignment. Straightaway Mr X. was put in a cell, and his wife was summoned with the others before Mr de Baas. He handled this matter in the wisest and most skilful way one could. He said, first, to Mademoiselle X. that he had called her so that she could tell him of which religion she was, and that he left it entirely up to her to reveal this, and that he did not intend to use violence upon her (which he said to anticipate any complaints — even unjust — by the Calvinists, and to prevent them from attributing this second conversion to force). She replied that she had made profession of the Catholic, apostolic, and Roman faith. Mr de Baas replied that he would absolutely prevent anyone from using any force on her to make her leave it, or to follow it. 'I want to follow it', she said, 'for my whole life.'

'Then you are now no longer free', retorted the General, 'and after the

[13] Here, the 'conseils' of the Huguenots can be interpreted either as advice or as a collective assembly.
[14] 'D'abord': as with n. 11, 'at once' implied by context.

Vous n'êtes donc plus libre maintenant, repartit M. le Général, *et après la déclaration que vous venez de me faire, je vous en fais une autre, qui est qu'il n'y va pas moins*[34] *que de la corde (que vous aviez déjà méritée) si vous apostasiez une seconde fois.*

Ensuite il lui dit des choses fortes pour l'exhorter à la constance, et pour lui représenter sa faute [38ʳ] passée; après quoi il[35] s'adressa aux autres huguenots qui n'étaient que des magasiniers[36] qu'il traita en faquins; mais l'infortuné mari fut le plus grand objet de sa juste colère. Il le fit tirer du cachot pour lui venir rendre compte de tout ce qui s'était passé, et après l'avoir traité de la manière qu'il méritait, il lui ordonna deux choses, la première d'aller chez Mme de Loubière lui demander pardon avec sa femme de l'outrage qu'ils lui avaient fait; la deuxième de laisser entièrement cette convertie dans une parfaite liberté de faire les fonctions de la religion catholique; sur quoi il écrivit un billet pour prier le curé de l'avertir si elle manquait à ce devoir.

Ces deux ordres ont été fort bien exécutés; depuis ce temps-là elle a reçu les sacrements, et elle ne manque pas de se trouver à l'église pour tous les actes de piété pour lesquels on s'y assemble. Je lui parlai dernièrement, et je ne la quittai qu'après l'avoir vue bien pleurer pour sa faute; mais ce qui édifie bien tout le monde, et que les huguenots mêmes ne nient pas, est la réforme admirable de ses mœurs, qui consiste principalement dans la grande modestie pour ses habits, et dans sa grande retraite pour les visites des hommes; jusque-là que dernièrement un homme de la première qualité la poursuivant jusque dans sa chambre avec la même liberté qu'avant sa conversion, elle sauta par la fenêtre, ne pouvant autrement le fuir. Elle a fait plusieurs choses [38ᵛ] semblables qui étonnent ceux qui l'ont connue avant qu'elle fût catholique, de manière qu'un huguenot parlant de ce changement, disait il y a quelques jours que s'il se mariait il voudrait que sa femme fût de notre religion. Mais afin qu'elle soit maintenant plus constante qu'elle ne l'avait été, je l'ai réconciliée avec quelque peine avec les dames qui avaient travaillé à son instruction; afin qu'elles continuent cet acte de charité.

Pendant que la fille répare ainsi sa faute, la mère est bien éloignée d'en commettre une semblable; sa maladie qui s'augmente toujours lui fournit une belle occasion d'édifier tous les catholiques dont les principaux l'honorent souvent de leurs visites; ils en sortent d'ordinaire tous charmés des beaux sentiments de piété qui paraissent dans ses discours principalement sur le sujet de sa conversion. Un honnête homme lui dit dernièrement[37] qu'il allait chez elle comme à l'école, et en effet il ne faut que la voir, et que l'entendre pour apprendre à bien souffrir, et à bien mourir.[38]

---

[34] 'de' has been inserted before 'moins'.
[35] 'il' replaces the erroneous 'elle' here.
[36] 'magasiniers' has been replaced with 'marchands'.
[37] 'dernièrement' replaced with 'un jour'.
[38] In this paragraph, 'répare' has been changed in the manuscript to 'réparait', 'est bien'

declaration that you have just made to me, I will now make you another one, which is that the rope (which you have already merited) is the price you will pay if you commit apostasy a second time.'

He then spoke to her very forcefully to exhort her to constancy, and to represent her past sin to her, after which he addressed the other Huguenots, who were mere merchants, and whom he regarded as wretches. But the unfortunate husband was the principal target of his just anger. He had him taken from his cell to come before him and give an account of everything that had occurred, and after speaking to him in the manner he deserved, he ordered him to do two things. The first was to go to Madame de Loubière's house and, with his wife, to ask her pardon for their affront to her. The second was that he leave the convert complete freedom to practise Catholicism, at which point he wrote a letter requesting that the priest alert him if she did not fulfil her duties.

These two orders were carried out very successfully. Since then she has received the sacraments, and she is present, without fail, at the church for all the acts of piety for which we gather. I spoke to her recently, and I did not leave her until I had seen her weep bitterly for her sin; but what really edifies everybody, and what even the Huguenots do not deny, is the admirable way she has reformed her morals. This consists principally in her great modesty in dress, and in her great reserve with regard to visits by men, and to such an extent that recently, when a man of highest rank pursued her into her room with the same liberty as before her conversion, she jumped out of the window as she was unable to escape him otherwise. She has done many similar things which astonish those who knew her before she became a Catholic, so much so that a Huguenot who was talking about this transformation said, a few days ago, that if he were to marry he would like his wife to be of our religion. However, so that she will now be more constant, I reconciled her — with some trouble — with the ladies who had worked on instructing her, so that they will continue this act of charity.

While the daughter was thus repairing her fault, the mother was very far from committing a similar one. Her sickness, which was constantly worsening, gave her a good opportunity to edify all the Catholics. Some, of the highest rank, often honoured her with their visits, and they usually left quite charmed by the wonderful sentiments of piety in her conversation, principally with regard to the subject of her conversion. A respectable man said to her not long ago that he went to her house as if it were a school, and, indeed, you only had[15] to look at her, and listen to her, to learn how to suffer well and to die well.

---

[15] The manuscript has undergone a number of modifications which may make the awareness of Madame Peré's death more explicit. In addition the first line of the text that follows the transcription of her letter, and which confirms her death, may have been added later. See notes to transcription in French.

Dernièrement[39] elle envoya cette lettre à son gendre pour le prier de la venir voir:

Monsieur

Étant ce que je vous suis, et sur le point d'aller rendre compte à Dieu, j'avais souhaité de vous la grâce d'oublier ce qui s'est passé entre nous deux et celle de venir avec votre femme me fermer les yeux. Je vous sais bon gré de ce que vous [39r] ne m'avez pas tout refusé, et que de ces trois faveurs vous m'en avez accordé deux; mais la tendresse que j'ai pour vous ne me permet pas de dissimuler que le refus de la troisième qui est votre visite, m'a été bien sensible, et quoique vous me priviez d'une des plus grandes consolations que je désirais avoir en mourant, toutefois mon intérêt seul ne me la faisait pas souhaiter, puisqu'il y va, et de votre honneur, et de votre salut. Car vous ne trouvez personne ni parmi les honnêtes gens, ni parmi[40] ceux de votre religion qui ne juge votre procédé à mon égard contraire et à votre honneur, et à l'Évangile que vous faites profession de lire plus souvent que nous. Cependant ne croyez pas que j'en aie du ressentiment dans l'état où je suis, je tâche de m'en consoler en embrassant mon crucifix avec lequel j'apprends peu à peu à me passer de tout, et à prier Dieu pour ceux qui disent qu'ils me pardonnent, à même temps qu'ils refusent pour toujours de me voir. Du moins Mlle N.[41] contribue beaucoup par sa présence à ma consolation, et de mon côté je ne manquerai pas jusqu'au dernier soupir à lui inculquer le respect, et l'amour qu'elle vous doit; ce que je fais avec d'autant plus de soin que je connais par votre dernière lettre que vous en avez reçu quelque nouveau déplaisir que vous appelez sa fâcheuse révolte, car je crois que vous avez trop de jugement pour qualifier de ce nom sa conversion à notre sainte foi, outre que vous n'aurez pas sitôt oublié, que vous avez avoué en bonne compagnie qu'après sa conversion [39v] vous remarquâtes dans sa conduite une réforme qui vous donnait bien de la joie, et si elle ne continue peut-être pas, vos confrères aussi bien que les catholiques disent que vous ne vous en devez prendre qu'à un homme de votre religion. Quoi qu'il en soit il n'est pas vrai qu'on vous ait ôté le moyen de faire des commandements et des défenses à votre femme. On vous a seulement défendu de l'empêcher de faire les devoirs d'une catholique. C'est de cela seul qu'on vous blâmera, autant qu'on vous louera de lui

---

to 'était bien', 's'augmente' to 's'augmentait', 'fournit' to 'fournissait', 'l'honorent' to 'l'honoraient', 'paraissent' to 'paraissaient', 'il ne faut' to 'il ne fallait'. In addition, the manuscript may read 'sortent' or 'sortaient'. At the end of Mme Peré's letter the lines 'Cette lettre fut sans effet, et cet hérétique laissa mourir sa belle-mère sans la vouloir jamais aller voir' that follow may have been added later.

[39] 'Dernièrement' has been crossed out.
[40] Modified to: 'personne parmi les honnêtes gens, non pas même parmi'.
[41] 'Mlle N.' replaced with 'votre femme'.

Not long ago she sent the following letter to her son-in-law to request him to come and see her:

Dear Sir,

Being who I am to you, and about to go and give an account to God, I had desired that you grant me the grace of putting aside what happened between the two of us, and that of coming with your wife to close my eyes. I appreciate your not having refused me everything, and that of these three requests you have granted me two, but the affection I have for you does not allow me to conceal that the refusal of the third — your visit — upsets me greatly, and, although you deprive me of one of the greatest consolations that I wished to have in dying, it was nonetheless not for my interest alone that I desired it, since your honour and your salvation are at stake. For you will find nobody decent, not even amongst those of your religion, who does not think that the way you have treated me is contrary to your honour and to the Gospel that you profess to read more often than we do. Nevertheless, do not think that I am resentful in the state I am in. I try to console myself through embracing my crucifix, with which I am learning to do without everything little by little, and to pray to God for those who say that they forgive me, while at the same time they refuse to see me forever. Mademoiselle X., at least, does much to console me through her presence, and for my part I will never, until my last breath, fail to instil in her the respect and the love that she owes you. I do this with all the more attention in that I learn in your last letter that you have a new distress, which you call her regrettable revolt, for I know that your judgement is too sound for you to use these terms to qualify her conversion to our holy faith. What is more, you will not already have forgotten that you declared, while in good company, that after her conversion you noticed a transformation in her conduct that gave you cause to rejoice, and that if, perhaps, it does not continue, your confreres as well as the Catholics say that you should only blame a man of your own religion. In any case it is not true that the means to give orders and put restrictions on your wife has been taken from you. All you have been forbidden to do is to prevent her from fulfilling her duties as a Catholic. It is for this alone that you would be blamed, as much as you would be praised for forbidding

défendre toute sorte de conversations suspectes: et si le passage de l'Écriture que vous alléguez et que vous expliquez mal dans votre lettre, ordonne à la femme de s'attacher à son mari en quittant son propre père, et sa propre mère (en quoi elle ne reçoit nulle défense de Dieu de les aller voir quand ils se meurent), combien plus devra-t-elle pour ce sujet quitter ceux qui ne lui sont rien. Je vous dis ici le dernier adieu, mon très cher fils, et c'est pour cela que ma lettre est si longue parce que vous ne voulez pas que je vous voie jamais plus; adieu donc pour la dernière fois, et si vous voulez que je meure sans vous voir, et sans vous embrasser du moins vous ne m'empêcherez pas de le faire de cœur, et d'affection. Au reste prenez tous ces avis comme venant d'une belle-mère qui va comparaître devant Dieu; si dans son effroyable jugement j'obtiens mon pardon comme je l'espère de sa miséricorde, je demanderai à Dieu qu'il vous donne une partie des lumières que j'ai maintenant touchant la fausseté de votre religion, Je suis [etc.][42]

Cette lettre fut sans effet, et cet hérétique laissa mourir sa belle-mère sans la vouloir jamais aller voir.[43]

[40^r] Je n'ai pas voulu interrompre le narré de ces conversions, par celui de quelques autres que Dieu a opérées à même temps au Fort Saint-Pierre, car aussitôt qu'à la Fête-Dieu j'y fus de retour du Carbet, j'y reçus la profession de foi d'un jeune Anglais natif créole de Niévès.[44] La cérémonie se fit à Notre-Dame de Foy avec toute la pompe que j'y pus[45] employer; tous nos chantres y firent merveilles, et tous les principaux du quartier ayant à leur tête M. le Gouverneur voulurent honorer de leur présence cette belle fête que je terminai par un discours sur ce sujet, après quoi je trouvai ici de l'emploi pour le converti, de peur qu'il s'allât exposer parmi ses patriotes[46] au péril de l'apostasie.

À même temps que je travaillais pour celui-là, j'étais après le garçon de M. Gase. C'était[47] un jeune homme que son obstination avait fait assez connaître à tout le monde particulièrement au R. P. Farganel[48] qui s'y était employé avec une assiduité digne de son zèle, quoique l'événement n'y ait pas correspondu. Pour moi je puis bien assurer que c'était un des plus obstinés, à la conversion desquels je me suis jamais employé; mais enfin que ne peut la grâce de Dieu? J'en vins à bout après deux mois, et il abjura l'hérésie, avec l'étonnement de

---

[42] 'Je suis' is followed by an addition in the margin which appears to read 'etc.'.
[43] The constricted handwriting of this sentence may imply that it is a later addition. See Letter 1, n. 38.
[44] After insertion: 'de l'île de Niévès'.
[45] Transcribed as 'pûs'.
[46] Modified to 'compatriotes'.
[47] 'le garçon de M. Gase. C'était' crossed out.
[48] Transcribed as 'Fraganel'.

her any sort of suspicious conversation. If the passage from Scripture that you quote, and that you explain badly in your letter, orders the wife to join with her husband and to leave her own mother and father behind (and in which God in no way forbids the wife from going to see them when they are dying) how much more should she not, for this reason, then leave behind those who are nothing to her? Here I say my last goodbye to you, my dear son, and it is because of this that my letter is so long, for you do not want me to see you ever again. Goodbye then, for the last time, and if it is your wish that I die without seeing you and without embracing you, at least you cannot prevent me from doing so with my heart and with sincerity. Moreover, receive these counsels as those of a mother-in-law who is about to appear before God. If in His fearful judgement I obtain my forgiveness, as I hope to with His mercy, I will ask God to give you some of the enlightenment I now have concerning the falsity of your religion.

I am etc.

This letter had no effect, and the heretic let his mother-in-law die without going to see her.

I did not want to interrupt the account of these conversions with that of several others that God effected at the same time in Fort Saint-Pierre, for, once I was back there from Le Carbet at Corpus Christi, I received the profession of faith of a young Englishman, a Creole native of Nevis. The ceremony took place at Notre-Dame de Foy[16] with all the pomp that I could arrange. All our choristers were marvellous, and all the notables of the quarter, headed by the Governor, consented to honour with their presence this fine feast which I closed with a speech on the subject. Afterwards I found employment here for the convert, for fear of him exposing himself to the danger of apostasy amongst his compatriots.

At the same time I was working for him, I was working on [the conversion of] Mr Gase's boy. This was a young man whose obstinacy made him well known to everybody, particularly to Reverend Father Farganel[17] who had applied himself to the task with an assiduity worthy of his zeal, although the outcome did not match it. As for me, I can safely say that he was one of the most unyielding on whose conversion I have ever worked, but, in the end, what can the grace of God not do? I managed it after two months, and he abjured heresy to the

---

[16] The manuscript reads 'Notre-Dame de Foy'. However, no record of a church of this name on Martinique has been located, although the Jesuits had a devotion to Notre-Dame de Foy (modern-day Belgium). The Dominicans maintained the church of Notre-Dame du Bon-Port at Saint-Pierre. Chatillon has 'Notre-Dame du Port', p. 47.

[17] Jean-Jacques Farganel ('Fraganel' in the manuscript), Jesuit.

bien des gens. Quelque temps après on commença de me donner plusieurs fois quelque alarme sur quelques bruits qui portaient que ce converti[49] [40ᵛ] avait ensuite renoncé à la foi catholique dans quelque maison. Je reconnus tout autant de fois que ce n'était qu'une pure calomnie; et en ayant enfin découvert l'auteur j'allai chez lui pour l'en convaincre; c'était le nommé Bernon[50] marchand, et qui le porte assez haut, et fait profession de la Religion P. R. heureusement je le trouvai avec M. Turpain dont la présence, le mérite, et l'autorité m'animèrent assez pour représenter à ce calviniste sa témérité, dont je le convainquis avec tant de confusion pour lui, que depuis il ne s'est nullement embarqué en telles affaires, et que je n'ai plus ouï conter ces fables.

De ce mal qui était particulier je voulus passer à celui qui était public. Pour cet effet après quelques perquisitions je découvris une espèce de prêche à la rue de la galère, une synagogue au mouillage, et des débauches pendant l'office chez les gargotiers; de ceux-ci j'en surpris trois dans la visite que j'en fis, qui furent bientôt après condamnés à l'amende. Pour les hérétiques par le moyen du père Du Jonglar[51] j'en fis donner avis à M. le Général suivant la commission qu'il m'en avait donnée, ensuite de quoi le major du fort reçut un ordre d'aller chez le[s] calviniste[s] qui tenai[en]t l'assemblée de ces confrères pour se plaindre de sa désobéissance aux ordres du roi, et pour le menacer de la punition qu'il avait méritée, s'il ne désistait pas, ce qu'il a fait entièrement.[52] Les juifs que [41ʳ] la cour favorise,[53] ont été traités avec plus d'indulgence, on leur a seulement donné un garde pour les empêcher de crier trop dans leurs assemblées. Ainsi voilà trois sortes d'ennemis que j'ai sur les bras: gargotiers, juifs, et calvinistes. Ceux-ci paraissent les plus déchaînés contre moi ayant à la tête le Sieur Bourgeois[54] qui semblait s'ériger en ministre.

Depuis j'avais commencé, et avancé quelques autres affaires de cette nature,[55] mais j'ai reçu ordre de tout laisser pour aller prendre la place du P. La Pierre par un ordre de V.R.[56] le P. de Kerenor[57] n'ayant pas été jugé avoir assez de santé pour y aller à son tour; cet aimable père a fait depuis peu une mission de

---

[49] The manuscript may have been altered from 'ces convertis' to 'ce converti'; however, the auxiliary 'avait' that follows implies that only the second convert was rumoured to have renounced Catholicism.
[50] 'Bernon' replaced with 'B.'.
[51] 'par le moyen du père Du Jonglar' has been crossed out.
[52] The manuscript appears to have originally read 'chez les calvinistes qui tenaient l'assemblée de ces confrères', which has been modified to 'chez le calviniste qui tenaient [sic] l'assemblée de ses confrères'. The grammatical inconsistency, complicated by the mention of an individual threatened with punishment, makes it unclear if one or instead several people were the target.
[53] 'que la cour favorise' has been crossed out.
[54] 'Bourgeois' replaced with 'B.'.
[55] 'et de cette importance' inserted after 'cette nature'.
[56] 'La Pierre par un ordre de V.R.' replaced with 'notre bon ami'.
[57] 'Kerenor' replaced with 'K.'.

astonishment of many people. Some time afterwards alarming rumours began to reach me, and did so on many occasions, according to which this convert had thereafter renounced the Catholic faith in some house or other. I realized that it was all pure calumny, and, having finally discovered the source, I went to his house to accuse him of it. It was Bernon the merchant, who is quite haughty, and professes the so-called Reformed Religion. Fortunately I found him with Mr Turpain, whose presence, merit, and authority inspired me to upbraid the Calvinist for his temerity. My rebuke caused him such embarrassment that he has not been up to anything similar since, and I have heard no more of these tales.

I wished to move on from this wrongdoing, which was an individual's, to tackle one that was public. For this, I discovered after some investigation that there was a sort of Protestant temple on *rue de la galère*, a synagogue at the anchorage, and debauchery taking place in the taverns during the office. I surprised three of the tavern keepers with an inspection, and they received a fine soon afterwards. As for the heretics, through Father Du Jonglar, I notified the General, according to the order he had given me. Following this, the major of the fort received an order to go to the house of the Calvinist[s] who held the assembly of these confreres to upbraid [him] on his disobedience of the king's orders, and to threaten him with the punishment he merited, if he did not desist; he did so completely. The Jews, who are favoured by the court, have been treated with more indulgence, and they have only been assigned a guard to prevent them from making too much noise in their assemblies. So I have three sorts of enemy to look out for: tavern keepers, Jews, and Calvinists, and the last seem to oppose me with most violence, having as their head Mr Bourgeois, who seemed to have set himself up as a minister.

Since then I had started, and had made progress with, a number of other matters of this sort, but I received an order from your Reverence to leave everything to go and take the place of Father La Pierre, as Father de Kerenor was not thought to be in sufficiently good health to go there himself. This amiable Father had, a short time ago, gone on a very active mission of several

quelques semaines à la partie septentrionale de l'île avec beaucoup de force, et il se disposait à en faire une autre dans la méridionale, lorsque le départ du P. La Pierre[58] l'en a empêché.

M. R. P. Je suis[59]

Votre très humble,
et très obéissant serviteur

Mongin[60]

---

[58] 'La Pierre' replaced with 'L.'.
[59] 'M. R. P.' crossed out.
[60] 'Mongin' crossed out.

weeks to the northern part of the island, and he was preparing to go on another one to the southern part, when the departure of Father La Pierre prevented him from doing so.

My Reverend Father,

I am

Your most humble and most obedient servant,

Mongin

LETTER 2[1]

Paris,
BM, Ant MS 9, fols 23^r–39^v.

[**23^r**] Copie de la lettre du R. P. Jean Mongin, écrite au R. P. Antoine Pagez provincial de la Compagnie de Jésus en la province de Toulouse, de l'île de la Martinique le 10e mai 1679[2]

Mon R. P.
Pax Christi[3]

La réponse dont V. R. voulut bien m'honorer l'année passée, ne me fut rendue qu'à Pâques, et apparemment elle ne recevra pas plutôt cette réplique qu'elle m'a demandée. Le porteur n'en sera pas la seule cause. J'y aurai eu ma bonne part, pour avoir si longtemps tardé à l'écrire. Mais Dieu merci, j'ai la meilleure excuse que je pourrais souhaiter, qui est le précieux et continuel accablement des travaux de ma chère mission. Les occupations me donnent si peu de loisir d'écrire que je ne saurais le faire un [**23^v**] peu au long, sans être obligé de faire de très longues, et très fréquentes interruptions. Mais aussi je prie V. R. de joindre ses prières aux miennes pour m'obtenir de Dieu qu'il me garde d'un plus grand loisir.

   Voilà déjà M. R. P. une idée en général des sentiments que j'ai de ma mission. Mais je ne croirais pas avoir satisfait à son désir et à l'ordre qu'elle m'en a donné dans sa lettre, si je ne lui expliquais en détail mes emplois, ce que je lui promets de faire avec toute la sincérité possible, sans parler de ce que font

---

[1]   This letter has been compared with the alternative version in Carcassonne, MdC, MS 73, fols 51^r–68^r. In the present transcription, the number of textual variations of six words or less, as a rule of thumb, indicated in the footnotes has been limited; syntactical reformulations have not been indicated.

[2]   MdC, MS 73, fol. 51^r: 'quatrième lettre au R. P. provincial des jésuites de la province de Toulouse contenant la relation de la mission de la Martinique'. This letter is dated '29 décembre 1678'.

[3]   MdC, MS 73, fol. 52^r: 'Mon Révérend Père' has been crossed out in MS 73, and further references in the same manuscript to the title of the recipient have been removed or replaced.

Paris,
BM, Ant MS 9, fols 23^r–39^v.

Copy of the letter written by Reverend Father Jean Mongin to Reverend Father Antoine Pagez, provincial of the Society of Jesus for the province of Toulouse, from the island of Martinique, 10 May 1679.

Reverend Father,
Pax Christi,

The reply with which your Reverence was kind enough to honour me last year, was only delivered to me at Easter, and it appears that you will not receive the reply that you requested of me any faster. It is not just the messenger's doing. I am at fault too, having for so long delayed writing it. But thanks be to God, I have the best excuse I could wish for, which is the precious and continuous burden of the labours of my dear mission. My tasks allow me so little free time to write that I could not imagine doing so for any length without having to make very long and very frequent interruptions. But I also ask your Reverence to join your prayers to my own, to obtain from God that he will keep me from a much greater leisure.

This should, Reverend Father, give you a general idea of my sentiments with regard to my mission. Yet I would not think my reply satisfactory, according to the order that you gave me in your letter, if I did not explain my tasks to you in detail, which I promise to do in all sincerity, without discussing what is

---

[1]   Only the most significant variants in MdC, MS 73, fols 51^r–68^r (dated 29 December 1678) have been indicated/translated here.

tous nos autres pères qui remplissent si dignement tous les devoirs de leurs charges.[4] V. R. sait quelle différence ont mise, la nation, la religion et la couleur entre les personnes, qui sont le sujet des travaux apostoliques dans ce pays: car il y a des Français, des Portugais, des Castillans, des Anglais, des Irlandais, des Écossais, des Flamands, des Hollandais, des Allemands; des Africains de quasi toute la côte occidentale d'Afrique; des Américains, tant des îles que de la terre ferme soit septentrionale soit méridionale. Enfin toutes les quatre parties du monde contribuent à peupler nos îles, quoiqu'inégalement; car l'Afrique y a la meilleure part, et l'Asie la moindre. De là vient qu'il y a ici des athées, des idolâtres, des juifs, des luthériens, des huguenots, et des catholiques, aussi bien que des blancs, des noirs, des bruns, qui sont les créoles, nés en ce pays de parents européens; des tannés, fils d'un blanc, et d'une noire; des rouges qui sont les Caraïbes, ou sauvages originaires de ce pays, etc. Mais la religion catholique, et la nation française sont les dominantes, et la couleur noire est la plus considérable pour le seul nombre; car c'est la couleur des [24^r] esclaves. On peut facilement juger si cette admirable diversité de gens ne remplit pas l'idée la plus vaste qu'un missionnaire puisse avoir de son emploi; et si ceux qui ont pris plaisir de peindre saint Xavier, le crucifix à la main, au milieu d'un tas de visages barbares et diversifiés n'auront pas beau jeu s'ils pouvaient lui donner un auditoire composé de tant de religions, de tant de nations, et de tant de couleurs, que nous en voyons ici dans nos églises. En vérité M. R. P., ces choses m'ont paru toujours fort touchantes et entretiennent toujours dans mon esprit une estime incroyable pour ma mission, laquelle porte en cela le vrai caractère d'une mission étrangère, qui est la qualité qui nous charme si fort dans ces emplois.

Car enfin ce sont les différentes matières, sur lesquelles travaillent ici les missionnaires, pour leur donner une même forme, *donec formetur in eis Christus*, ce qui se fait, avec une facilité, et un succès admirable, quasi à l'égard de tous, excepté des juifs, et des Caraïbes. Ceux-ci portent de grandes marques d'une nation réprouvée dans leur brutalité, et dans leur obstination, qui s'est augmentée depuis que leur perfidie a obligé les Français de les chasser de nos îles, à la réserve d'un fort petit nombre. Néanmoins on ne peut pas encore désespérer de leur conversion puisqu'à dire le vrai, le défaut d'ouvriers, qui, par un principe de justice, sont obligés de s'arrêter parmi les autres nations, qui sont dans ces îles,[5] a empêché de soutenir cette entreprise avec la vigueur, et la constance nécessaire pour en voir le succès. Outre que pour faire croître une Église dans un tel pays, il faut autant l'arroser du sang des missionnaires, que de leur sueur; et que d'ailleurs il n'y a eu encore que deux de nos pères

---

[4]   MdC, MS 73, fol. 52^r: 'si je ne les lui expliquais en détail, avec la nature, et les particularités de cet emploi, ce que je promets de faire avec toute la sincérité possible'.
[5]   MdC, MS 73, fol. 53^r: 'cette île'.

done by all our other Fathers, who carry out all the duties of their care in such a worthy manner. Your Reverence knows how nation, religion, and colour have distinguished the people who are the object of apostolic works in this land, for there are French, Portuguese, Castilians, English, Irish, Scottish, Flemish, Hollanders, Germans; there are Africans from almost the whole western coast of Africa, and Americans from the islands and the mainland, north and south. Indeed the four parts of the world contribute to the peopling of our islands, although they do in unequal measure, for Africa gives the largest share and Asia the least. This means that here there are atheists, idolaters, Jews, Lutherans, Huguenots, and Catholics, as there are whites, blacks, and brown-skinned people, or the Creoles born in this land to European parents. There are people with coloured skin, who are the sons of white men and black women, there are red-skinned people, that is, Caribs, who are the savages who are native to this land, etc. But the Catholic religion and the French people are dominant, and the colour black is the most significant in terms of number, for it is the colour of the slaves. One may easily judge whether or not this admirable diversity of people corresponds to the widest idea a missionary can have of his occupation, and if those who enjoy painting Saint Xavier,[2] crucifix in hand, in the middle of a crowd of barbarous and varied faces, would not have a field day if they could give him an audience composed of so many religions, peoples, and colours, that we see here in our churches. In truth, Reverend Father, these things have always seemed to me to be very touching, and nourish in my spirit a constant and remarkable esteem for my mission, which in this has the true mark of a foreign mission, the trait that delights us so much in these occupations.

For these are the different sorts of matter on which the missionaries work to give them the same form, *Donec formetur in eis Christus*,[3] which is done with admirable facility and success with regard to nearly all, with the exception of the Jews and the Caribs. The latter show telling signs of being a damned people, with their brutality, and their obstinacy which has increased since their perfidy obliged the French to chase them from our islands, except for a very small number. Nevertheless all hope of their conversion is not lost, for it is the lack of workers — who, from a principle of justice, are obliged to stay amongst the other peoples in the islands — that has prevented this enterprise from being supported with the vigour and constancy that is needed for its success. Aside from this, for a Church to expand in such a land, it must be watered as much with the blood of missionaries as with their sweat, and moreover, only two of

---

[2]   Saint Francis Xavier.
[3]   *'Donec formetur in eis Christus'*: 'Until Christ be formed in them'. Reference to 'Donec formetur Christus in vobis', Galatians 4. 19 ('Until Christ be formed in you', 1582, p. 505).

massacrés par ces barbares. Enfin que ne doit-on pas espérer, depuis qu'on a vu les florissantes Églises de nos pères espagnols, dans le Paraguay province de notre Amérique [24ᵛ] méridionale.[6] Aussi nos missionnaires, n'ont pas moins de désir, que d'espérance, de pouvoir aller chercher ces pauvres sauvages dans la terre ferme, et dans leurs îles. Et il y a longtemps que nous y serions tous, s'il nous était possible d'abandonner nos postes, sans successeurs, où il y a déjà de l'occupation pour vingt fois plus de missionnaires que nous ne sommes.

Cependant nous avons abondamment de quoi nous en consoler, par la grandeur, et l'utilité des travaux pour les autres nations. Les nègres, tant ceux qu'on porte, tous les ans, en très grand nombre, que ceux qui naissent ici tous les jours, sont une moisson assurée,[7] à grand peine en trouvera-t-on un, entre mille, qui ne demande le baptême, aussitôt qu'il a quelque connaissance de nos mystères. Il est vrai qu'ensuite, il y a quelque peine à l'égard de plusieurs, pour les faire vivre en bons chrétiens,[8] parce que le mauvais traitement de quelques-uns de leurs maîtres les oblige à être fugitifs dans les bois, ou a dérober pour vivre, et que la difficulté qu'ont force habitants d'acheter des hommes, ou des femmes pour faire le mariage de leurs nègres, quand il leur en manque jointe à[9] la grande communication qui est entre les nègres, qui sont d'ordinaire demi-nus, et particulièrement pendant la nuit, dans les travaux des sucreries, sont une occasion de grands désordres. Mais la vigilance des missionnaires, diminue notablement tous ces maux, par les voies que la prudence, et le zèle leur suggèrent, accourant partout, où est le péril et représentent efficacement, tantôt aux maîtres, tantôt aux esclaves, le devoir de leur conscience, et le danger de leur salut. Avec ces moyens et une infinité d'autres qu'il serait trop long de particulariser on fait de ces nègres une Église très florissante, et on apprend qu'on ne perd pas toujours sa peine en lavant un Ethiopien.

[25ʳ] En vérité M. R. P. je suis sensiblement touché toutes les fois que je fais réflexion à des actions généreuses qui se pratiquent parmi ces gens-là, et à une sensibilité admirable, qu'ils ont pour les choses de Dieu, quoique j'avoue qu'il est d'eux comme de nous, et que tous les baptisés ne sont pas saints.[10] Ces pauvres gens font ici des actions qui sont comparables à celles que l'on voit dans la vie des saints. Car, ne prétendant pas, de cette lettre en faire une relation, je me contenterai de dire a V. R. que nous avons vu, ici des femmes, faire des actions héroïques en souffrant les outrages, les coups et le feu même qu'on leur appliquait, pour les obliger à s'abandonner à leurs maîtres, et à leurs

---

[6] MdC, MS 73, fol. 53ʳ: 'depuis qu'on a vu les florissantes Églises des Iroquois'.
[7] MdC, MS 73, fol. 53ʳ: 'sont une moisson assurée car pour les adultes'.
[8] MdC, MS 73, fol. 53ᵛ: 'bons catholiques'.
[9] MdC, MS 73, fol. 53ᵛ: 'et que la difficulté qu'ont force habitants d'acheter des maris, ou des femmes pour leurs esclaves jointe à'.
[10] BM, Ant MS 9, fol. 25ʳ: the text that follows, from 'Ces pauvres gens font ici des actions' to 'pour résister à toutes ces attaques', does not feature in MdC, MS 73.

our Fathers have been murdered by these barbarians. Indeed, what can one not hope for, given the flourishing Churches of our Spanish Fathers, in Paraguay, that province of our South America? Our missionaries have no less desire than they have hope that they will be able to search out these poor savages on the mainland and in their islands. We would all be there already, and for a long time now, if it had been possible for us to abandon our posts, with no one to succeed us, and there is already enough work here for twenty times more missionaries than we are.

However, we have more than enough to console ourselves here, with the extent and the usefulness of [our] labours for the other peoples. The black slaves, both those who are brought here every year in great number, and those who are born here each day, are a sure harvest. With great difficulty will you find one in a thousand who does not request baptism as soon as he has knowledge of our mysteries. It is true that afterwards there is some difficulty in making many of them live as good Christians, for bad treatment by some of their masters obliges them to flee to the woods, or to steal to survive, and the difficulty many planters have in buying men or women to marry their slaves when they lack them — along with the great promiscuity between the slaves who are normally half naked and particularly so at night in the sugar plants — are the cause of great corruption. But the missionaries' vigilance greatly mitigates all these evils, in the ways that prudence and zeal suggest to them. They rush everywhere there is danger, and they effectively instruct masters as well as slaves about the duty of their conscience and the danger for their salvation. With these means, and an infinite number of others that it would take too long to describe here in detail, we make a flourishing Church of these slaves, showing that one's labour is not always wasted in washing an Ethiopian.[4]

In truth, Reverend Father, I am deeply moved each time I think about the generous actions of these people, and their admirable sensibility with regard to divine matters, although I admit that it is with them as it is with us, and all those who are baptized are not holy.[5] The deeds of these poor people here are comparable to those you read about in the lives of the saints. As my intention is not to make this letter into a relation, I will limit myself to telling your Reverence that we have seen women here act in a heroic way in suffering offence, physical violence, and even punishment by fire, to force them to submit to their masters and overseers.[6] This is all the more admirable in that everybody

---

[4] A reference to Aesop's fable on the same subject; Aesop, *Fables*, bilingual French–Greek edn, ed. by Émile Chambry (Paris: Société d'édition Les Belles Lettres, 1927), Fable 11, 'Le Nègre', p. 8.

[5] BM, Ant MS 9, fol. 25ʳ; the text that follows, from 'The deeds of these poor people' to 'to resist all these onslaughts', does not feature in MdC, MS 73.

[6] On the *commandeur* as 'overseer' in earlier colonization, see Robert Chaudenson, *Des îles, des hommes, des langues: essai sur la créolisation linguistique et culturelle* (Paris:

commandeurs, ce qui est d'autant plus admirable, que tout le monde sait que ces pauvres gens en dépendent absolument pour toutes choses, et que leur bonne ou mauvaise fortune est entre les mains de leur maîtres, qui hors la mort, et la mutilation, peuvent faire à leurs esclaves tout le mauvais traitement qu'ils voudront, sans que personne y trouve à redire ce qui joint à l'avantage qu'ils tirent, de leurs maîtres pour leur vivre, leur vêtement et soulagement du travail, et pour tout autre chose, quand ils consentent à leurs désirs, avec la pente naturelle qu'ont tous les Africains au vice de la chair, est capable de faire concevoir à tout le monde, qu'il faut une très grande grâce de Dieu, et une vertu héroïque, pour résister à toutes ces attaques. Le moins occupé de nos missionnaires a pour le moins mille nègres pour sa part, et quelques-uns deux ou trois mille.[11] Jugez de là, quelle consolation c'est de les voir[12] assemblés les jours de fête, dans l'église, pour la dévotion, et de se souvenir à même temps que Dieu s'est voulu servir de nous, pour se faire connaître à ces gens-là, qui sans ce bonheur, étaient perdus, sans ressource. Je vous [25ᵛ] avoue que leurs assemblées, avec les chansons dévotes, qu'ils y chantent, entonnées par des voix très agréables me paraissent aussi nouvelles, et aussi touchantes que le premier jour, et qu'il m'est bien difficile de retenir les larmes, dans ces occasions. J'ai connu ici fort particulièrement un gentilhomme d'un très bel esprit, que sa mauvaise conduite avait obligé, depuis quatre ans, de quitter la cour, où il était fort avancé, qui prenait ici un grand plaisir d'assister à ces assemblées, pour ouïr chanter un dialogue d'une âme damnée, qui décrit ses tourments, à une personne qui l'en interroge. Et il m'assurait que tous les prédicateurs, les plus pathétiques, qu'il avait ouïs longtemps dans Paris, ne l'avaient pas plus touché que faisait cette chanson spirituelle qui était entonnée par une négresse, et poursuivie par tous les autres esclaves dans l'église. Dieu pardonne à un auteur, qui a donné au public, une idée fausse de ces pauvres nègres, touchant leur disposition pour le christianisme. Il est religieux de profession, et il a fait une histoire assez longue de ce pays, à même temps qu'un ministre huguenot a travaillé sur le même sujet, mais il y a de certains endroits propres à faire juger, que l'ouvrage du religieux, est de la façon d'un ministre; et celui du ministre de celle d'un religieux: tant ce religieux et ce religionnaire font mal leur personnage.[13] Il ne se passe point d'années que chaque missionnaire ne fasse, aux fêtes solennelles, bon nombre de baptêmes, de ces pauvres gens, tant des nouveaux venus d'Afrique que des originaires du pays.[14]

---

[11] MdC, MS 73, fol. 53ᵛ: for this sentence read 'Chacun de nos missionnaires a pour le moins mille nègres pour sa part'.
[12] MdC, MS 73, fol. 53ᵛ: 'Jugez de là quelle consolation c'est de les voir et ouïr.'
[13] MdC, MS 73, fol. 54ʳ: from 'Il est religieux de profession' to 'font mal leur personnage' is crossed out.
[14] BM, Ant MS 9, fol. 25ᵛ: this sentence, from 'Il ne se passe point d'années' to 'originaires du pays', does not figure in MdC, MS 73.

knows that these poor people absolutely depend on them for everything, and that their good or bad fortune is in the hands of their masters who can, death or mutilation excepted, treat their slaves as cruelly as they want, without anyone having anything to say about it. Add to this the benefits they receive from their masters with regard to their food, clothing, relief from labour, and everything else when they consent to their desires, and the natural inclination of all Africans towards the vice of the flesh, and anyone can well see that both a great grace from God and heroic virtue are needed to resist all these onslaughts. The least busy of our missionaries looks after at least a thousand slaves, and some have two or three thousand. You may imagine, then, what a consolation it is to see them assembled on feast days in the church for devotion, and to recall at the same time that God wished to use us to make Himself known to these people who, without this good fortune, would have been irretrievably lost. I avow to you that their assemblies, with the devotional chants that they sing with such delightful voices, seem to me as new and as touching as the first day [I heard them] and that I find it very difficult to hold back my tears on such occasions. I was very well acquainted with a gentleman here, of excellent understanding, who four years previously had been obliged to leave the court where he was very well advanced, on account of his misconduct. He took great pleasure in attending these assemblies here, listening to the sung dialogue of a damned soul describing its torments to a person questioning it about them. And he assured me that he had not been more moved by the most affecting preachers that he had long heard in Paris, than by this spiritual song, sung by a female slave, and continued by all the other slaves in the church. May God forgive a certain author who has given the public a false idea of these poor slaves, with regard to their disposition towards Christianity! He is an ecclesiastic by profession, and he wrote a history of this land which is long enough, at the same time as a Huguenot minister was working on the same subject. However, there are some parts which would make one think that the priest's work is in the style of a minister, and that of the minister in the style of a priest, so badly do both cleric and Protestant act their parts.[7] Not a year goes by without each missionary baptizing a good number of these poor people during the solemnities, both those newly arrived from Africa and those born in the land.

L'Harmattan, 1992), revised with Salikoko S. Mufwene, trans. by Sheri Pargman et al. as *Creolization of Language and Culture* (London: Routledge, 2001), p. 112.

[7] Reference to Jean-Baptiste Du Tertre's *Histoire générale des Antilles* and Charles de Rochefort's *Histoire naturelle et morale des Îles Antilles* (see Introduction to the present book). From 'He is an ecclesiastic by profession' to 'act their parts' is crossed out on MdC, MS 73, fol. 54^r.

Pour les huguenots de[15] différents lieux de l'Europe [26^r] on travaille efficacement à leur conversion, et à réprimer l'envie qu'ils ont de l'exercice public de leur religion. On leur fait garder rigoureusement les ordonnances.[16] Il y a deux ans et demi que je découvris une assemblée secrète, qu'ils faisaient pour leurs prières, et en ayant donné avis à Monsieur le Général, il leur fit une répréhension, et une menace, qui fut la disposition à une grosse amende, à laquelle ils ont été condamnés depuis pour la récidive, par une sentence du juge, qui a été confirmée par le Conseil Souverain, auquel ils s'étaient rendus appelants. Il y en a un entre eux qui m'incommodait notablement dans mon quartier par ses scandales, tant en matière de religion, que pour les mœurs. Mais il est devenu sage, depuis que je l'ai fait mettre une fois en prison, et deux fois à l'amende. Il est évident que, sans ce soin des missionnaires, nos îles seraient bientôt pires que Genève. Car c'est ce qui empêche une infinité de familles huguenotes, particulièrement de La Rochelle, de venir s'établir ici. D'ailleurs on convertit quelques-uns de ces gens-là, assez souvent, et depuis environ un an, il y en a eu environ cent qui ont fait profession de notre sainte foi, dans cette seule île, dont la plupart étaient des prisonniers de guerre, qu'on avait menés de nos dernières conquêtes dans ces pays. Mais comme une marque de la véritable religion, consiste dans ce soin de l'étendre toujours davantage, les hérétiques ont ici une marque bien particulière, et bien sensible de la fausseté de leur secte, en ce que, dans les îles, où les Hollandais et les Anglais, sont les maîtres, ils empêchent constamment qu'on instruise, qu'on baptise, et qu'on marie leurs esclaves, les laissant vivre, et mourir dans leur infidélité et dans toute sorte de concubinage, sous prétexte que les chrétiens ne doivent pas être esclaves; comme [26^v] si c'était un plus grand mal, pour ces pauvres nègres, d'être esclaves des hommes pour un temps, que d'être esclaves du démon, pour une éternité.[17] Voilà cependant une chose qu'on peut opposer aux protestants, avec autant de raison, que le feu Pierre [sic] Pardies,[18] dans son traité de miracles, et le sieur Arnaud dans ses *Préjugés*, leur reprochent la manière avec laquelle les Hollandais trafiquent dans le Japon, en y renonçant, pour le moins extérieurement, au christianisme, pour n'en être pas recherchés, à même temps qu'une infinité de fosses, et de croix encore sanglantes, leur font connaître de quelle manière bien différente, en ont usé les catholiques, en de pareilles occasions pour étendre leur sainte foi dans ce pays.[19]

---

[15] MdC, MS 73, fol. 54^r: the sentence beginning 'Pour les huguenots' is preceded by the insertion 'a capite'.

[16] MdC, MS 73, fol. 54^r: 'l'ordonnance'.

[17] MdC, MS 73, fol. 55^r: instead of 'que d'être esclaves du démon, pour une éternité' read 'que des démons pour une éternité' (apparently an insertion).

[18] MdC, MS 73, fol. 55^r: 'Père Pardies'. See n. 9 in the English translation of this letter.

[19] MdC, MS 73, fol. 55^r: from 'Voilà cependant une chose qu'on peut opposer aux protestants' to 'pour étendre leur sainte foi dans ce pays' has been distinguished from the rest of the text by a border.

With regard to the Huguenots from the different parts of Europe, we work effectively towards their conversion, and in opposing their desire to publicly exercise their religion. They are made to follow the ordinances rigorously. Two and a half years ago, I discovered a secret assembly that they had for their prayers, and, after I had informed the General, he reprimanded them and threatened them with a large fine. They have since been sentenced to pay it because they reoffended, by sentence of a judge, and confirmed by the Sovereign Council to which they appealed.[8] One of them was of considerable bother to me in my quarter, because of the trouble he stirred up in matters of both religion and morality, but he is well behaved now, since I had him put into prison once, and fined twice. It is clear that our islands would soon be worse than Geneva without the attention that missionaries pay to this matter. For it is this that prevents an infinite number of Huguenot families, particularly from La Rochelle, from coming and settling here. Some of these people have been converted, and this happens often enough. Since about a year ago, about a hundred of them have professed our holy faith, on this island alone, most of them prisoners of war brought here from our last conquests in these lands. But given that a sign of the true religion consists in ensuring that it is continually spread, the heretics here have a very clear and perceptible sign of the falseness of their sect, for, in the islands where the Hollanders and the English are masters, they continually prevent the instruction, baptism, and marriage of their slaves. They let them live and die in their infidelity and all manner of cohabitation, under the pretext that Christians should not be slaves — as if it were a greater evil for these poor slaves to be the slaves of men for a time, than to be the slaves of the devil for eternity. This is nonetheless a criticism that can be made of the Protestants with as much justice as the late Pierre [sic] Pardies, in his treatise on miracles, and Master Arnaud in his *Préjugés* reproach them for the way the Hollanders trade in Japan by renouncing Christianity — outwardly, at least — to avoid being troubled for it, while an infinite number of graves, and still-bloody crosses, show them how differently the Catholics behaved in similar occasions so as to extend their holy faith in that land.[9]

---

[8]   The Sovereign Council of Martinique.
[9]   Mongin is referring to Ignace-Gaston Pardies (1636–1673), translator of extracts of Daniello Bartoli (1608–1685), *Dell'historia della compagnia di Gesù: l'Asia descritta*, 1 (Genoa: Benedetto Guasco, 1656) into French, published as *Les Miracles de S. François-Xavier, apostre des Indes* (Paris: Michel Le Petit, 1673). On the Dutch, see Pardies, *Les Miracles*, preface, non-paginated. Antoine Arnaud [Arnauld] (1612–1694); Arnauld's collaborator Pierre Nicole (1625–1695) is the author of *Préjugez légitimes contre les calvinistes* (Paris: Veuve de C. Savreux, 1671).

Pour les catholiques je puis assurer que je n'ai vu nulle part tant de probité. J'avoue bien, que, selon le bruit commun cela n'a pas toujours été ainsi, parce que, quand les îles commencèrent d'être habituées, on tâchait de les peupler, comme on pouvait, et comme on fait les premiers établissements, à cause de quoi c'était un refuge de personnes de l'un, et de l'autre sexe, qui, en quittant l'Europe, ni quittaient pas leurs désordres. Mais depuis environ 50 ans, que cela était, nos îles ont heureusement changé de face, par le grand nombre d'honnêtes gens, qui s'y sont venus habituer, et surtout par la bénédiction que Dieu a bien voulu donner aux travaux des missionnaires, qui mettent en usage tous les moyens, que le zèle, et la prudence leur dictent, pour maintenir tout le monde dans le devoir des chrétiens, car ils sont éternellement en campagne pour leurs fonctions, et les excursions continuelles, causent un bien qui n'est pas croyable. Ils ne [27ʳ] sont pas moins occupés dans leurs églises, car ils y prêchent, tous les dimanches, et toutes les fêtes;[20] il n'y en a point de solennelle, qui ne soit accompagnée de ses 40 heures avec un concours admirable de personnes qui viennent de quatre ou cinq lieues. Et ces dernières fêtes de Noël, j'ai vu dans mon église, plusieurs familles entières, et nombreuses, qui étaient venues de quinze à seize lieues. Certes c'est une merveille bien consolante, de voir comme Dieu supplée dans ces gens-là le défaut des sacrements, ou plutôt comme l'effet des sacrements est en eux de longue durée, car ne pouvant que rarement, à cause de leur éloignement, faire leurs dévotions,[21] ils conservent, durant ce temps-là, une innocence qui donne également aux missionnaires, de l'étonnement, et de la consolation.

Mais de toutes les nations, et de toutes les religions, que nous avons ici, les juifs sont ceux qui profitent le moins de nos travaux, je n'ai encore vu la conversion d'aucun. Le peu d'espérance, qu'on y voit, jointe aux continuelles occupations des missionnaires, dont le fruit est ailleurs plus assuré, ne contribue pas peu à ce malheur; quoique la plus [p...able][22] raison, pour laquelle ces gens sont partout inconvertibles, est leur crime et leur déicide, qui étant le plus grand de tous les sacrilèges, a mérité la plus grande de toutes les peines, dans l'obstination universelle et particulière de cette nation.

Voilà M. R. P. les différentes couleurs, nations et religions qui sont la matière sur laquelle travaillent ici les missionnaires mais avec[23] quelle facilité, quelle application et quelle douceur [27ᵛ] ils s'y emploient; ce sont des choses, qu'eux-mêmes ne sauraient bien expliquer.

Cette facilité se prend en partie de la langue qui n'est autre ici que la française,

---

[20] MdC, MS 73, fol. 55ᵛ: 'car ils y prêchent, et de leur mieux toutes les fêtes'.
[21] MdC, MS 73, fol. 55ᵛ: 'car ne pouvant revenir que rarement dans l'année pour faire leurs dévotions'.
[22] BM, Ant MS 9, fol. 27ʳ: this word has been modified (possibly to begin with the letter 'v') but is illegible. MdC, MS 73, fol. 55v: 'véritable'.
[23] BM, Ant MS 9, fol. 27ʳ: 'avec' is an addition.

With regard to the Catholics, I can assure [you] that nowhere have I seen such probity. I readily admit that, according to what is commonly said, it has not always been such because, when the islands were first settled, they were inhabited in the way of initial settlements, which need to be populated. Because of this, they were a refuge for people of one and the other sex who, in leaving Europe, did not leave their immorality behind them. But in the fifty-odd years since then, our islands have completely changed for the better thanks to the great number of decent people who have come to settle here, and especially because of the blessing that it pleased God to give to the work of the missionaries, who employ all the means that zeal and prudence prescribe to keep everybody in their Christian duty, for with their duties they are always in the field, and these constant expeditions bring unbelievable good. They are no less busy in their churches, for they preach there every Sunday and on every feast day. There is no solemnity that it is not accompanied by its *Forty Hours* with an admirable number of people who come from four or five leagues around.[10] During the last feast of Christmas I saw in my church whole families, and large families with that, who had come fifteen or sixteen leagues. It is certainly a marvel that brings great consolation to see how God compensates the lack of sacraments in these people, or rather, how in them the effect of the sacraments is of long duration. For even though their remoteness means that they can only rarely offer their devotions, during this time they conserve an innocence which both astonishes and consoles the missionaries.

But of all of peoples and all the religions that we have here it is the Jews who profit least from our labours; I have not yet seen one convert. The little hope there is thought to be of this, along with the missionaries' continuous tasks — which are, moreover, more assured of bearing fruit — contributes in no small way to this unhappy state of affairs, although the most [......] reason that these people are everywhere impossible to convert is their crime and their deicide. As this is the greatest of all sacrileges, it has merited the greatest of all punishments, in the generalized and individual obstinacy of this people.

These, Reverend Father, are the different colours, peoples, and religions which are the matter on which the missionaries work here, but with such ease, such application and such gentleness; these are things that even they could not fully explain.

This ease is in part due to the language, which is French alone here. For, as

---

[10] A *solemnity* is a Catholic celebration of the highest rank. The *Forty Hours* was a collective penitential devotion, of forty hours' duration; Bernard Dompnier, 'Un aspect de la dévotion eucharistique dans la France du XVIIe siècle: les prières des Quarante heures', *Revue d'histoire de l'Église de France*, 178 (1981), 5–31.

car comme elle est ici celle des maîtres, il n'est presque personne, parmi tant de différentes nations, qui, en peu de temps, n'en ait appris suffisamment pour nous entendre, et pour se faire entendre; sans que le jargon particulier des commençants y forme aucun obstacle considérable. Je suis bien assuré, du moins, que les personnes de notre pays pourraient apprendre de force nègres à parler français. Notre mission possède donc en cela un avantage, qui ne peut être assez estimé que par ceux, qui savent, qu'elle est la seule de nos missions étrangères, à qui cela appartient, et que le défaut de cette commodité, donne dans toutes les autres une difficulté très considérable, à cause du temps qu'il y faut employer, avant que de pouvoir faire la moindre chose pour le salut des peuples, qu'on va chercher si loin. Aussi il me souvient d'avoir vu il y a bien des années dans le volume des passions du père Caussin qui met la peine dégoutante que les pauvres missionnaires souffrent à apprendre ces langues, parmi les plus rares exemples de la patience.[24] Heureux celui qui peut arriver à sa fin, sans des moyens qui la retardent si fort,[25] car nous travaillons en cette mission, au salut des fidèles, et des infidèles, sans apprendre de langue, et à moins que nous n'allions demeurer parmi les Indiens des îles qu'ils habitent et dans la terre ferme, ce que nous ne pouvons pas faire, faute de [28^r] missionnaires, la langue française suffit pour tous nos autres emplois près des autres nations.

Une autre source de cette facilité, est le respect que toutes ces sortes de gens, ont pour les missionnaires. Pour les nègres, la qualité humiliante d'esclave, les rend respectueux à l'égard de tout le monde, mais particulièrement de nous, il arrive assez souvent, que nous rencontrant en chemin, et ne pouvant nous saluer de parole, pour ne l'avoir pas encore assez libre, ils le font par leur geste, se mettant à genoux, baisant la terre, et faisant le signe de la croix. Il ne faut pas dire de quelle manière ces pauvres gens reçoivent les avis, et les répréhensions des missionnaires, puisqu'il n'est pas possible de voir rien de plus humble, et de plus humilié, quoique, quelques-uns de leurs maîtres, dans les plaintes, qu'ils nous font de leurs nègres, les accusent quelquefois d'être orgueilleux; ce que je n'ai jamais pu concevoir. Nous sommes respectés à proportion, des juifs, et des hérétiques, qui, pour leur religion se voyant chargés de la haine du peuple, ne manquent pas d'adoucir leur disgrâce, par les témoignages extérieurs de leur modestie; et il y en a beaucoup parmi eux, qui nous aiment, autant qu'ils nous craignent. Aussi il n'y a point de catholique, qui soit plus exact qu'eux, pour nous avertir d'administrer le baptême, ou les derniers sacrements à leurs esclaves, quand il en est temps, y étant obligés d'ailleurs par les lois du pays, aussi bien que de leur laisser chômer les fêtes, venir faire leurs dévotions,[26] un

---

[24] BM, Ant MS 9, fol. 27^v: this sentence, from 'Aussi il me souvient d'avoir vu' to 'parmi les plus rares exemples de la patience', does not feature in MdC, MS 73.
[25] BM, Ant MS 9, fols 27^v–28^r: the text that follows, from 'car nous travaillons en cette mission' to 'près des autres nations', does not feature in MdC, MS 73.
[26] MdC, MS 73, fol. 56^v: 'venir faire leurs Pâques'.

here it is the language of the masters, there is almost nobody, amongst so many different peoples, who in a short time has not learned enough to understand us and to be understood, and without the curious parlance of beginners being a serious obstacle to this. I am quite assured, at least, that people from our country could learn how to speak French from many black slaves. Thus, this gives our mission an advantage that can only be adequately understood by those who know that it is the only one of our foreign missions to have it, and that the lack of this convenience causes a great difficulty in all the rest, because of the time that must be spent in this before doing the slightest thing for the salvation of the peoples whom we seek out so far away. I remember reading many years ago, in Father Caussin's volume on the *passions*,[11] the tiresome effort that poor missionaries have to make in learning these languages placed among the most exceptional examples of patience. Happy is he who can achieve his ends without means that would hold him back so much. For in this mission we work towards the salvation of the faithful and the infidels without learning another language, and short of going to live amongst the Indians who live on certain islands and on the continent — which we cannot do, given the lack of missionaries — the French language is sufficient for all our other uses with the other peoples.

Another reason for this ease is the respect that all these sorts of people have for the missionaries. The humiliating state of being a slave makes the black people respectful towards everybody, but particularly towards us. Often enough it happens that when we meet them on our way, they cannot greet us in speech as they do not yet know enough language, and so they do so through gesture, getting on their knees, kissing the earth, and making the sign of the cross. How these poor people receive the missionaries' direction and reprimands — you will never see anyone as humble and as humiliated, even though some of their masters accuse them on occasion of being proud when they complain to us about their slaves; I could never imagine this. We are respected in measure by the Jews and the heretics who, seeing that they are hated by the people because of their religion, ensure they lessen their disgrace through outwardly showing modesty, and there are many among them who appreciate us as much as they fear us. As such, there is no Catholic who is more exact than they are in calling for us to administer baptism or the Last Rites to their slaves, when the time comes. They are, moreover, obliged to do so by the laws of this land, as they are to give [their slaves] feast days off work, to let them offer their devotions on

---

[11] Nicolas Caussin (1583–1651), author of *La Cour sainte; ou, l'institution chrestienne des grands* (Paris: S. Chappelet, 1624).

jour ouvrier, et leur laisser interrompre leur travail, lorsque les missionnaires leur vont faire quelques exhortations[27] [28^v] de piété, dans les champs, où ils travaillent en troupe. De là vient aussi qu'il n'y a, ni n'y peut avoir aucun nègre, qui soit juif, ou hérétique.[28] Ces instructions au milieu des champs où l'on assemble les nègres est d'une très grande utilité pour leur salut, étant très difficile de les instruire suffisamment dans les églises aux catéchismes les jours de fête et de dimanche, où ils ne se peuvent pas tous trouver, et où l'on ne peut pas leur dire les choses si familièrement que lorsqu'ils sont en petit nombre. On les prend même seul à seul, quand on le juge à propos, et comme il y a quelquefois des maîtres qui ont de la peine à souffrir, que l'on détourne leurs esclaves du travail, nous avons obtenu une ordonnance, qui défend aux maîtres, sous de certaines peines de s'opposer à cette pratique.

L'autorité des missionnaires n'est pas moindre à l'égard des maîtres catholiques, qui ont une extrême déférence pour eux. C'est pour cela que chaque père dans son quartier, est l'arbitre de leurs différends ordinaires, aussi dans leurs démêlés, ils ont recours à lui. Il est le premier dépositaire de leurs plaintes, et celui qui lui a parlé le premier, s'imagine avoir emporté gain de cause. S'il y a quelque avis à leur donner, on les mande avec un billet, quand on ne peut pas aller chez eux, et ils reçoivent les avis avec respect. S'ils le perdent, c'est ici la dernière impudence de laquelle ils reviennent facilement. Ainsi il y a quelques mois qu'un homme de mon quartier, et officier, m'avait désobéi avec contumace, en une affaire importante du temporel de mon église;[29] peu de jours après, à l'issue de ma messe [29^r] je le vis se prosterner devant moi, et me serrant les genoux me demander pardon, en pleurant, et promettant d'obéir, comme il fit sur-le-champ. En voici une autre preuve; dernièrement je fus averti, à neuf heures du soir, que quelques débauchés, que j'avais fait citer depuis peu, devant le juge de la police, soupaient en débauche dans un cabaret pour de là, disaient-ils me venir faire quelque insulte à ma case,[30] qui en est fort proche. Je pars aussitôt pour aller au-devant de ces messieurs et les ayant rencontrés devant

---

[27] BM, Ant MS 9, fol. 28^r appears to read 'quelque [abbreviated to 'quelq.e'] exhortations'. MdC, MS 73, fol. 56^v reads 'quelque exhortation'.

[28] BM, Ant MS 9, fol. 28^v: the text that follows, from 'Ces instructions au milieu des champs' to 'de s'opposer à cette pratique', does not appear in MdC, MS 73.

[29] MdC, MS 73, fol. 57^r: 'Ainsi il y a quelques mois qu'un homme de mon quartier s'emporta [l'emporta?] pour quelque affaire importante [inserted at this point: 'contre moi'] du temporel de mon église.'

[30] MdC, MS 73, fol. 57^r: 'à ma cure', which has been replaced by 'à mon presbytère'.

working days, and to allow them to interrupt their labour when missionaries go to the fields where they work in gangs to exhort them to piety. This is also the reason that there is no slave who is Jewish or a heretic, nor can there be.[12] This instruction in the middle of the fields where the slaves are assembled is of great use for their salvation, as it is very difficult to give them sufficient instruction in catechism in the church on feast days and Sundays, because they cannot all be there then, and one cannot on such occasions talk to them with the same familiarity as when there is a small number of them. You can even talk to them individually, if it seems appropriate, and as there are sometimes masters here who are difficult about allowing their slaves to be distracted from their labours, we have obtained an ordinance which forbids masters from opposing this practice, on pain of punishment.

The missionaries have no less authority over Catholic masters, who show considerable deference to them. It is for this that each priest is in his quarter the arbiter of their day-to-day disagreements, and they appeal to him in their quarrels. He is the first person to whom they relate their grievances, and whoever has spoken to him first thinks he has won his case. If a judgement has to be communicated, they are sent for in writing,[13] if we cannot go to their abode, and they receive this judgement with respect. If the judgement is not in their favour, it is not the type of thing they get over quickly. Several months ago a man from my quarter, an officer, had disobeyed me with insolence[14] in an important affair concerning the temporal interests of my church. A few days later, upon leaving my Mass, I saw him prostrate himself before me, and, while holding onto my knees, apologize while sobbing and promising to obey, as he did immediately. Here is another illustration: at nine o'clock one night recently I was warned that several degenerates whom I had recently summoned before the magistrate were wining and dining in a tavern, and were saying that they were going to come to my residence,[15] which is very near, and cause me some mischief. I left immediately to get ahead of these gents, and, meeting them

---

[12] BM, Ant MS 9, fol. 28ᵛ: the text that follows, from 'This instruction in the middle of the fields' to 'from opposing this practice, on pain of punishment', does not appear in MdC, MS 73.

[13] 'Mander quelqu'un' (the formulation used in the French here): 'to send for someone'; 'mander à quelqu'un': 'to write or send a message to someone'. Antoine Furetière, *Dictionnaire universel*, 3 vols (The Hague: A. and R. Leers, 1690); repr. ed. by Henri Basnage de Beauval and others, 4 vols (The Hague: Pierre Husson and others, 1727); II (1690), entry 'Mander', non-paginated.

[14] While *contumance*, in legal terms, refers to an individual not appearing when summoned to a court case, it means 'to disobey [one's religious superior] with insolence' in religious terms. Augustin Calmet, *Commentaire littéral, historique et moral sur la règle de Saint Benoît*, 2 vols (Paris: Emery, 1734), I, p. 445.

[15] 'Ma case', in BM, Ant MS 9, fol. 29ʳ, would translate as 'my cabin' or even 'my hut', whereas MdC, MS 73, fol. 57ʳ gives the more neutral 'cure' and 'presbytère', or an ecclesiastical residence.

la porte de ce cabaret, je les prie de me souffrir dans leur compagnie pour prendre la fraîcheur de la nuit, à la faveur de la clarté de la lune. Ils me firent une réponse, qui marquait une extrême aigreur; néanmoins je fais semblant de n'y prendre pas garde, et leur demande s'ils n'agréeraient pas que je les entretinsse de quelques histoires arrivées,[31] quelqu'un m'ayant répondu que oui, je leur racontai quelques fins tragiques des débauchés. Ce récit les apprivoise, ils me font porter une chaise, pour continuer, et comme je connus le changement que cet entretien avait produit je les invite à le terminer, par l'examen de conscience. Je le fis tout haut à genoux avec eux au milieu de la place d'armes, où nous étions, et m'étant étendu pathétiquement sur le quatrième point, chacun se retira chez soi assez pensif après m'avoir fait cent amitiés et dit cent choses obligeantes et pleines de respect, et parce que la débauche se devait étendre jusqu'au lendemain, ils furent bien dîner ensemble, mais ce fut avec une modération qui donna de l'étonnement à ceux qui les connaissaient, aussi ils s'entredisaient qu'ils avaient été enchantés la nuit précédente.

[29^{V}] Mais nous n'avons pas toujours besoin de ces industries pour conserver l'autorité, qui est si nécessaire aux missionnaires.[32] Leur fermeté dans les affaires de Dieu, intimide assez leurs ennemis les plus terribles; nous en avons des exemples assez récents, qui nous apprennent à ne craindre que Dieu, dans les fonctions de notre ministère. C'est ainsi que je suis venu à bout d'une cabale, que quelque intérêt particulier, avait formée dans mon quartier, contre le temporel de mon église. Et le chef de parti qui est aussi celui du même quartier, se souvenant que l'année passée j'avais renversé toutes ses machines, et étant interrogé, il y a trois jours du succès que pourrait avoir une assemblée qui se devait tenir le même jour, sur de pareilles affaires, répondit qu'il ne s'y ferait autre chose que ce que le père voudrait. Quelques heures après, l'événement fit voir qu'il avait dit plus vrai qu'il n'aurait souhaité, mais Dieu merci, je ne voulais rien que ce que la piété et la justice demandaient. Voila M. R. P. quelle est l'autorité des missionnaires dans les affaires de Dieu dans ce pays. Les moyens qu'ils emploient pour la maintenir, sont moins humains et plus apostoliques, si je ne me trompe, que ceux qui furent mis en usage par des prêtres séculiers dans le second établissement de Cayenne, où un d'entre eux, s'était fait seigneur de l'île, pour travailler avec plus d'autorité, et d'efficace à la propagation de notre sainte foi. Aussi cette entreprise n'eut aucun succès.

---

[31] MdC, MS 73, fol. 57^{r}: 'et leur demande s'ils n'agréeraient pas que je leur fisse le récit de quelques belles aventures'.
[32] MdC, MS 73, fol. 57^{V}: 'qui est si nécessaire aux missionnaires, pour donner l'efficacité aux travaux qu'ils entreprennent pour le salut des peuples'.

at the tavern door, I asked them to allow me to join them in taking the night air, on this moonlit night. They replied to me in a way that showed they were extremely bitter. Nevertheless, I pretended not to notice, and asked them if they would accept me telling them a few stories.[16] One of them answering yes, I told them a few tales about degenerates who came to an unhappy end. This tale calmed them down and they had a chair brought for me to continue, and as I recognized the change that this conversation had produced in them, I invited them to finish it with the examen of conscience.[17] I performed it out loud on my knees with them in the middle of the parade ground, where we were, and after I had elaborated on the fourth point[18] with pathos, each went off home thoughtfully, after making a hundred expressions of friendship and said a hundred obliging and respectful things to me. As their debauchery was due to go on until the following day, they did dine together, but it was with moderation that astonished those who knew them, with them saying amongst themselves that they had been enchanted the previous night.

Yet we do not always need this sort of manoeuvre to conserve the authority that it is so necessary for missionaries to have. Their firmness in the matters of God also intimidates their most terrible enemies. We have seen instances recently enough, which teach us to fear God alone in the duties of our ministry. It is in this way that I foiled an intrigue against the temporal interests of my church that an individual had formed in my quarter, to further his own interests. The head of the party, who is also the head of the same quarter, remembering that last year I had frustrated all his machinations, was questioned three days ago about the possible outcome of a meeting concerning similar matters that was due to take place the same day. He replied *that nothing would happen there but what Father would like.* Several hours later, it turned out that he had been righter than he would have liked; but, thanks be to God, I wanted nothing but what piety and justice demanded. This, Reverend Father, is the authority of missionaries over the affairs of God in this land. The means they use to maintain it are less human and more apostolic, if I am not mistaken, than those that were employed by secular priests in the second colonization of Cayenne, where one of them had himself made *Lord of the island* so as to work for the propagation of our holy faith with more authority and efficiency; and so this enterprise was not successful.[19]

---

[16] In his *Journal*, Mongin also describes telling devotional tales to combat the 'flirting' ('cajolerie') on board between the sexes during his voyage to Martinique in 1675–76, MdC, MS 73, fols 2ʳ–2ᵛ.

[17] The examen (examination) of conscience invites one to reflect on one's sins, and has a particular importance in Jesuit spirituality.

[18] The fourth point of the *general examen* is to 'request pardon for [one's] sins' ('poscere veniam de delictis'). Ignatius of Loyola, *Exercitia*, p. 62.

[19] Large-scale attempts were made to colonize Cayenne in 1643–44 and in 1652. Antoine

La facilité de nos emplois ne se prend pas seulement [30ʳ] de ce respect qu'ont les[33] peuples pour le caractère de ceux qui font les affaires de Dieu. La docilité, et les autres bonnes dispositions de ces mêmes peuples, y contribuent infiniment. Ces qualités sont proprement le partage des pauvres nègres. Mais, à dire le vrai, elles leur sont bien communes, avec la plupart des Européens, qui habitent ces îles.[34] C'est un effet de la grande solitude dans laquelle chaque famille vit chez soi. Car il y en a bien peu qui soient attroupées, en des bourgs, ou des villes, comme en Europe, leurs maisons sont dispersées à la campagne, comme autant de châteaux, ou de métairies, parce qu'ils ne subsistent que de la récolte qu'ils font de leur sucre, et de leur manioc etc. Ainsi étant loin des uns des autres, ils ne se voient d'ordinaire que les fêtes à la messe, après laquelle, la plupart reprend le chemin de chez eux, pour arriver avant la nuit et c'est cette retraite qui les éloignant des compagnies, qui est le plus dangereux écueil de l'innocence, favorise tellement la leur,[35] que les villes les plus dévotes de la France, ne peuvent avoir rien de semblable. Je laisse à penser, si ce n'est pas une grande disposition, pour la perfection chrétienne.[36] Nous profitons partout de ces avantages, autant que les autres occupations de la dernière nécessité, nous le permettent; et le fruit en est véritablement admirable. Pour moi je remarque tous les jours que Dieu semble exiger de moi en cela bien peu de coopération, car pour peu que je m'y applique je vois des progrès qui me donnent de l'étonnement; je vois des jeunes filles et des jeunes femmes venir de deux ou trois lieues à pied et à jeun pour fréquenter les sacrements et s'en retourner tout de même, nonobstant les chaleurs du pays. Je vois de si grandes ferveurs pour la mortification, que sans [30ᵛ] le soin d'un directeur pour la modérer, elle aurait ruiné déjà bien des santés. J'en connais, même parmi celles qui ne savent ni lire ni écrire, qui ont une très grande communication avec Dieu, une desquelles m'a assuré qu'elle ne saurait regarder un crucifix avec application, sans tomber en défaillance: une autre m'a fait voir des papiers où elle marque ses pensées et je n'ai rien vu qui approche davantage des ardeurs,[37] qui paraissent dans les livres de sainte Thérèse, à cela l'on pourrait ajouter les libéralités continuelles qui se font pour l'Église, ou pour les pauvres. Pour cet effet, je n'ai qu'à avertir publiquement des besoins extraordinaires des gens, on y remédie aussitôt. L'année passée le feu se prit à une maison d'une fort honnête famille, où tout fut brûlé; la chose était trop publique, pour avoir besoin d'en avertir le monde. Aussi sans que je m'en mélasse, dans le moment on lui trouve une autre maison, on la meuble, et

---

[33]   BM, Ant MS 9, fol. 30ʳ: possibly 'ces'.
[34]   MdC, MS 73, fol 58ʳ: 'cette île'.
[35]   Chatillon writes 'L'éveil de l'innocence favorise tellement la leur' (p. 58).
[36]   MdC, MS 73, fol. 58ʳ: 'pour la perfection chrétienne et pour la spiritualité la plus sublime'.
[37]   MdC, MS 73, fol. 58ᵛ: 'une autre m'a fait voir des papiers où elle marque les pensées qui font plus d'impression sur son esprit dans la méditation, et je n'ai jamais rien vu qui approche davantage des ardeurs'.

The ease of our tasks is not only due to the respect [these] peoples have for those who do the work of God. The docility and the other good inclinations of these same peoples also contribute greatly. These qualities are characteristic of the poor slaves, but, in actual fact, most of the Europeans who inhabit these islands have the same traits. It is a consequence of the great solitude in which each family lives on their settlement. For there are very few who are clustered together in villages or towns as in Europe. Their houses are dispersed in the countryside like castles or smallholdings, because they only live off their harvests of sugar, manioc etc., and so, being far from one another, they usually only see each other on feast days at Mass. After this, most make their way back home, to arrive before nightfall. It is this remoteness that, keeping them far from human society, which is the most serious danger to innocence, so favours their own that the most pious cities in France would have nothing like it. I leave it to you to judge if it is not a great disposition for Christian perfection. Everywhere we draw profit from these advantages, as much as our other occupations of extreme urgency allow us to, and the fruit is truly admirable. For my part, I notice every day that God seems to demand little effort from me, as with even a little application on my part I see progress that astonishes me. I see young girls and young women come from two or three leagues away on foot and fasting, to frequent the sacraments, and then returning the same way, notwithstanding the heat of this land. I see such a great zeal for mortification that, without a director's care to moderate it, it would have ruined the health of many people. I know many of them, even amongst those girls who do not know how to read or write, who have great communication with God. One girl assured me that she could not look upon a crucifix with concentration without fainting, and another showed me her papers where she writes down her thoughts, and I have never seen anything which comes closer to the ardour that can be seen in the books of Saint Teresa.[20] To this can be added the continual liberalities that are made to the Church, or to the poor. For this purpose I only have to make it publicly known that people are in exceptional need, and it is immediately remedied. Last year, there was a fire in the house of a very decent family, and everything went up in flames. The matter was too well known for me to have to alert everybody. So, without me intervening, another house was quickly found for them, and it was furnished and supplied with provisions for

Biet, a secular priest and member of the disastrous second expedition, relates that the Abbé de l'île de Marivault was 'chosen to be *premier Directeur dans le pays*', but drowned before the expedition left Paris in May 1652. Biet, *Voyage de la France équinoxiale en l'isle de Cayenne* (Paris: François Clouzier, 1664), pp. 4, 11–12.

[20] Saint Teresa of Ávila (1515–1582), Spanish saint of the Catholic Reformation known for her mystical writings; her works include the autobiographical *Libro de la vida*.

on la fournit de vivres pour six mois, et ce qui était de plus considérable dans cette charité, c'est qu'elle imitait celle de saint Nicolas, car ceux qui la faisaient, m'envoyaient dans ma case pendant la nuit, les barriques de vin, de farine, et de viande; afin que la nuit suivante je les fisse passer chez ces pauvres gens, sans leur nommer du tout les auteurs de ces aumônes, qui me l'avaient ainsi recommandé, *pour leur épargner*, disaient-ils, *la confusion qu'ils pourraient avoir en notre compagnie, s'ils savaient qu'ils nous ont une obligation de cette nature.* Aussi peu de temps après, le chef de cette famille, qui avait reçu ces aumônes considérables dans une occasion, où je me trouvai, se laissa aller à un furieux [31ʳ] emportement contre un de ces bienfaiteurs, sans que celui-ci lui ait jamais dit la moindre parole, pour lui faire entendre les obligations qu'il lui avait, quoique même du depuis il en ait reçu des déplaisirs bien plus considérables.[38]

Pour ce qui est des malades, pauvres ou riches, ils n'ont rien ici de plus commun que de se faire porter au lieu qu'ils croiront leur être plus utile pour l'air, pour le voisinage des chirurgiens, ou pour autre chose, et là ils demeurent et sont entretenus, tant qu'ils veulent aux dépens de leur hôte. Ainsi il y a tel qui n'est jamais sans quelqu'un de ces pensionnaires, quoiqu'il faille partager avec eux le peu de chose qu'ils ont souvent pour vivre. Pour des hôtelleries, il y a peu de temps qu'il a commencé d'y en avoir ici, quoique les voyages y soient extrêmement fréquents, tant par mer, que par terre; parce qu'on a accoutumé de s'arrêter au lieu où l'on arrive aux heures des repas, et du sommeil, et l'on y est d'ordinaire bienvenu, quelque inconnu que l'on soit. Nous avons eu ici quantité de prisonniers de guerre, que Monsieur le Comte d'Estrées avait faits sur les Hollandais, et tous ont eu grand sujet de se louer de la charité de nos insulaires. Il y avait parmi ces prisonniers, une famille fort honnête, et assez nombreuse, qui vint chercher un asile dans mon quartier, et parce qu'il y avait deux filles nubiles extrêmement bien faites, je m'employai pour les mettre en lieu d'assurance, dans des maisons d'honneur. Ce fut à cette occasion qu'il y eut une émulation admirable, entre les plus gens de bien, qui faisaient des offres considérables pour loger, et pour nourrir ces gens, jusque-là, qu'il y en eut qui leur offrirent une des plus belles maisons de l'île fournie des meubles, et des vivres afin qu'ils y fissent seuls leur ménage.

[31ᵛ] Et il fallut enfin partager cette famille pour contenter la dévotion de tout le monde. De là l'on peut juger si les pauvres souffrent en ce pays, pour moi je n'en connais aucun, qui mendie son pain, tant à cause de la facilité qu'ils ont à gagner leur vie, que de celle qu'on a à les secourir. C'est avec la même promptitude qu'on fait du bien à l'église, quand on les y invite, car il ne me souvient pas d'avoir jamais rien demandé pour la mienne; (et je demande assez souvent) sans l'obtenir tout aussitôt. Aussi va-t-elle être bientôt dans

---

[38] MdC, MS 73, fol. 59ʳ: 'des déplaisirs bien plus considérables que ceux des paroles'.

six months. What was most noteworthy about this charity was that it resembled that of Saint Nicholas, for those who performed it sent barrels of wine, flour, and meat during the night to me at my lodgings, so that the following night I would send them to these poor people, and without telling them who had given them these alms. The almsgivers had requested that I do so, so as, they said, 'to spare them embarrassment in our company, if they knew they had an obligation of this nature to us'. Indeed, a short time afterwards on an occasion when I was present, the head of this family who had received such considerable alms got into a furious rage with one of these benefactors. The benefactor never said the slightest thing to make him aware of the obligations he had towards him, even though he has since received much worse affronts from him.

As for the sick, whether rich or poor, the most common thing here is for them to be brought to the place they think will most benefit them, whether because of the air, the proximity to surgeons, or something else, and there they stay and are provided for as long as they like, at their host's expense. Indeed, there are hosts who are never without such lodgers, even though they have to share with them the little they have to live on. There have only been hostelries here for a short time, even though voyages by sea and land are extremely frequent here, because it is customary to stop wherever one finds oneself at meal times and at bedtime, and normally one is welcome, even if one is unknown. We have had a good number of prisoners of war here who were captured amongst the Hollanders by the Count d'Estrées, and they all had good reason to praise the charity of our islanders.[21] Amongst these prisoners there was a very decent, and large enough, family who came to seek refuge in my quarter, and, as there were two girls, of marriageable age and very well made, I set about having them put in a safe place in honourable houses. There was admirable rivalry then amongst the most virtuous folk, who generously offered to lodge and to provide for these people, until one of them offered them one of the best houses on the island, furnished, and with provisions so that they could live independently.

In the end, this family had to be split up to satisfy everybody's devotion. From this, one may judge if the poor suffer in this land, and for my part I know of none of them who have to beg for their bread, as much because of the ease in making a living, as the readiness there is to help them out. [The islanders] show a similar readiness to be generous to the church, when they are invited to do so, for I cannot remember ever having asked for anything for my own (and I ask often enough) without obtaining it straightaway. Indeed, it will

[21] Jean d'Estrées (1624–1707), vice-admiral of France, retook Cayenne from the Dutch in 1676, and would take Tobago in 1677.

sa perfection quoiqu'elle soit déjà la plus belle de toutes celles qui sont dans l'île.[39] Voilà M. R. P. quelles sont les bonnes qualités, et les dispositions de nos insulaires, pour faciliter les affaires de Dieu. C'est sur cela qu'on peut faire fond pour les élever, avec sa grâce à une sublime spiritualité, pourvu qu'on eût des missionnaires, qui en eussent le loisir; car je vous avoue que je ne donne pas la centième partie de mon temps à cette sorte d'occupation,[40] étant bien souvent obligé, à l'exemple du divin pasteur, de laisser ces brebis qui sont dans le bercail, pour en aller rappeler une seule de son égarement.

Mais quoique le respect, et la docilité[41] des peuples d'ici causent une grande facilité dans nos emplois, notre application n'en est pas moindre. Je crois que je ne le pourrais mieux justifier, qu'en vous marquant la distribution de notre temps pour les jours de fête et les jours ouvriers. Les fêtes[42] nous ne quittons pas notre église que dans la dernière nécessité de porter les sacrements aux moribonds; ainsi dès la pointe du jour, chacun de ceux qui sont seuls dans leur quartier, s'en va au confessionnal; je ne saurais aller si matin [32ʳ] au mien, que je ne le trouve assiégé de nègres, venus de bien loin, ils m'occupent seuls pendant une couple d'heures, qui est le temps de l'arrivée des blancs, dont ensuite j'entends les confessions pendant un même espace. Après ces quatre heures, je suis obligé d'aller chanter la grand-messe avec toutes ses cérémonies, ce que nous faisons avec plus[43] de pompe et d'exactitude qu'il est possible. Après l'Évangile je quitte la chasuble, pour monter en chaire, et faire le sermon: ensuite duquel, après avoir achevé la grand-messe, je remonte en chaire pour faire le catéchisme aux nègres qui remplissent l'église à l'issue des blancs. Cette occupation me tient jusqu'environ le temps qu'on va commencer à sonner vêpres: alors je me retire pour aller prendre quelque réfection qui est toujours beaucoup moindre que le besoin, et plus grande que l'appétit. Je reviens ensuite à l'église chanter les vêpres, ce que nous faisons à proportion de la solennité de la messe, et les vêpres sont suivies du catéchisme que nous faisons aux petits enfants blancs, ce sont les occupations fixes de chaque jour de fête. Et si elles ne suffisent pas pour faire des jours pleins, quelques demi-heures qui pourraient rester devant ou après vêpres, sont remplies par plusieurs autres occupations bien différentes, que les gens nous viennent donner, pour profiter de l'occasion du jour de fête, qui les oblige de se mettre en chemin, pour venir à l'église. Car c'est alors que nous sommes accablés ou pour les enterrements, ou pour les baptêmes ou pour les mariages, et toujours pour écouter des avis, des plaintes et des affaires de toute sorte, pour maintenir partout le bon ordre. Enfin ce n'est d'ordinaire qu'au commencement de la nuit, que je me retire chez moi, avec un

---

[39] MdC, MS 73, fol. 59ᵛ: 'dans nos îles'.
[40] MdC, MS 73, fol. 59ᵛ: 'cette sorte d'occupation de la direction'.
[41] MdC, MS 73, fol. 59ᵛ: 'Mais quoique la langue, le respect, et la docilité'.
[42] MdC, MS 73, fol. 59ᵛ: 'la distribution de notre temps, pour les jours de fête'.
[43] MdC, MS 73, fol. 60ʳ: 'avec le plus'.

soon be perfected, although it is already the loveliest of all those on the island. These, Reverend Father, are the qualities and the humour of our islanders to facilitate the work of God. One can count on this to raise them, with His grace, to a sublime spirituality, once there are missionaries who have the time to do so. For I acknowledge that I do not spend one hundredth of my time on this occupation, being very often obliged — like the divine Shepherd — to leave the sheep in the fold, so as to call back one that has been lost.[22]

Yet even though the respect and docility of the peoples here greatly facilitate our work, we are no less attentive to them. I believe that I can no better prove this but by showing you how we divide up our time on feast days and working days. On feast days we only leave our churches for cases of extreme necessity, to administer the sacraments to the dying. So from daybreak onwards, each of those who are alone in their quarter goes to the confessional. However early in the morning I go to my own, I find crowds of blacks there who have come from very far away, and they alone keep me busy for a couple of hours, at which time the whites arrive, and I then hear their confessions for the same duration. After these four hours I have then to sing High Mass with all its ceremonies, which we do with as much pomp and exactness as is possible. After the Gospel, I remove my chasuble to go into the pulpit and give the sermon, and after this, having finished High Mass, I go back into the pulpit to teach catechism to the blacks who fill the church when the whites have left. This task occupies me until about the time that Vespers begins to be rung; I then retire for some refreshment, which is always much less than I need, and more than I have appetite for. I then return to the church to sing Vespers, which we do according to the solemnity of the Mass, and Vespers are followed by our catechism for the little white children. These are the set duties of each feast day. And if they are not sufficient to fill the entire day, the few half hours that might remain before or after Vespers are taken up with many other quite different tasks, that the people come to us with, as they take advantage of the feast day which has obliged them to make their way to the church. It is then that we are inundated with burials, baptisms, or marriages, always hearing opinions, complaints, and matters of all sorts, so as to maintain good order everywhere. In fact, I do not usually return to my residence until night begins to fall, so greatly exhausted that I am incapable of

---

[22] A reference to the parable of the lost sheep; Matthew 18. 12–14; Luke 15. 4–7.

grand épuisement qui me rend incapable de tout autre chose que de me jeter sur mon lit. Il faut néanmoins se relever bientôt pour dire l'office du jour, et si ensuite m'étant couché, on vient m'appeler pour un malade [32ᵛ] qui presse et qui est éloigné, cela ne contribue pas beaucoup à me délasser.

Voilà nos fêtes, les jours ouvriers ne sont pas à mon avis, si rudes, et si fatigants, quoiqu'ils ne soient pas moins remplis, car je dis ma messe le plus matin, que je puis, tant pour satisfaire la dévotion du monde qui y assiste alors en plus grand nombre, que pour être plus libre pour me mettre en campagne. Néanmoins je suis un peu arrêté, et quasi toujours, après la messe, par quelqu'une de ces occupations que j'ai marquées les jours de fête, quoiqu'elles ne soient point alors en si grand nombre; mais m'en étant débarrassé le plus tôt que je puis, je me mets en chemin pour aller sur mes montagnes, où il y a éternellement à faire quelque chose pour des missionnaires, qui ne jugent pas qu'ils ne doivent faire d'autre travail, que celui dont ils ne peuvent se dispenser, sans péché mortel. Car comme le motif de la charité, non de la justice, nous a amenés ici, c'est aussi la même, qui nous doit faire agir dans ces occasions de la pratiquer sans attendre la dernière obligation.⁴⁴ Ainsi suivant ce principe, nous ne manquons jamais d'occupation, car il y a toujours des malades, ou dangereux, ou non dangereux, des affligés de toutes sortes, des opprimés, et des oppresseurs,⁴⁵ des méchants, qui ont besoin d'amendement, des gens qui ont quelque aptitude, ou quelque volonté pour la spiritualité; des pauvres et des aumôniers; des personnes qui font de grands progrès dans la dévotion, des ignorants qui ne savent rien de la science du salut, des catéchumènes, et des infidèles de toute sorte, et une infinité d'autres choses qui sont capables d'entretenir et d'occuper le zèle d'un missionnaire. C'est aussi pour ces occupations que nous sommes en campagne continuellement, [33ʳ] sans pouvoir trouver une heure fixe pour le repas; car dès que je suis parti la matinée, comme j'ai dit, quoique je n'eusse eu dessein de faire qu'une seule chose, il s'en rencontre tant, néanmoins, dans mon chemin, que j'ai souvent bien de la peine à gagner ma case avant la nuit. Aussi l'heure de mon souper n'est pas toujours fort longtemps devant minuit; pendant la nuit même je suis appelé assez souvent pour des malades. C'est l'emploi ordinaire de notre mission, car pour les fatigues extraordinaires, je ne les mets pas en ligne de compte.

Nonobstant⁴⁶ tout cela, il n'est pas difficile de comprendre la douceur de notre emploi, puisqu'on y peut jouir de toutes les honnêtes satisfactions, dont la vie religieuse est capable, et dont Platus a rempli la troisième partie de son admirable livre. Tous les plaisirs innocents de la campagne, sont ici dans leur perfection; la verdure éternelle de ce pays est un spectacle qui charme et que

---

⁴⁴ MdC, MS 73, fol. 61ʳ: 'les dernières obligations'.
⁴⁵ MdC, MS 73, fol. 61ʳ: 'et des oppresseurs' has been crossed out.
⁴⁶ MdC, MS 73, fol. 61ʳ: 'Nonobstant' preceded by the insertion 'a capite'.

anything else but throwing myself onto my bed. Nonetheless, it is soon time to get back up again to say the daily Office, and, if I am then called from my bed for someone who is urgently ill and lives far away, it does nothing for my repose.

That is what feast days are like. Working days are not, in my opinion, as arduous and tiring, although such days are no less full. For I say my Mass as early in the morning as I can, as much to content the devotion of those who attend in greater number at that time, as to have more liberty to go into the field. Nonetheless, I am nearly always held back after the Mass by one of those duties I mentioned with regard to feast days, although they are not in such great number. So having freed myself from these as early as I can, I am on my way to my mountains, where there is always something to do for missionaries, who do not think that the only work they should do is that from which they cannot abstain, without mortal sin. For as it is charity, and not justice, that brought us here, it is the same motive that should motivate us in these opportunities to practise it, without waiting for the utmost obligation. So, following this principle, we are never without something to do. For there are always those who are ill, whether dangerously so or not, those in all manner of distress, oppressors and the oppressed, the wicked who need repentance, people who have some aptitude or desire for spirituality, the poor and those who give alms, people who make great progress in devotion, the ignorant who know nothing about the way to achieve salvation, catechumens, and all manner of infidels, and an infinite number of other things to keep a missionary's zeal busy. It is also because of these tasks that we are constantly in the field, without being able to eat at a set time. For once I have left in the morning, as I said, even if I had only planned to do one single thing, I nonetheless find so many more along the way that I often have much trouble returning to my cabin before nightfall. Indeed, I do not always have my dinner long before midnight, and during the night I am called out often enough to the sick. These are our usual occupations in our mission, for I have not included our exceptional travails in this.

In spite of all this, it is not hard to imagine the sweetness of our occupation, for here one may delight in all the decent joys that the religious life can procure, and with which Platus filled the third part of his admirable book.[23] All the innocent pleasures of the countryside are in their perfection here; the eternal

---

[23] Platus, or Girolamo Piatti (1545–1591), author of *De bono status religiosi libri III* (Rome: apud Jacobum Tornerium, 1589) of which the third book is entitled *De iucunditate*.

je trouve encore aussi beau que le premier jour que je l'ai vu. Nous ne sommes pas privés de la satisfaction de voir les livres les meilleurs, et les plus récents; nous avons une bibliothèque, qui en est très bien fournie, parce qu'on nous envoie, avec grande diligence, ce qui s'imprime de plus beau, et il est assuré que dans nos provinces, quoique infiniment plus proches de la source de ces belles choses, on ne les voit pas plus tôt, et plus constamment qu'ici. Il faut néanmoins avouer que quoique la lecture ait de grands attraits, pour les gens de notre robe, nous n'avons pas ici le temps d'y vaquer, avec la grande assiduité que demande cette occupation, car il est également nécessaire à nos missionnaires et d'avoir étudié, et de n'étudier pas; ce qui n'empêche point de lire les *Journaux des savants*, qui nous sont tous envoyés trois ou quatre fois l'an, pour le moins, accompagnés de toutes sortes de nouvelles imprimées,[47] où comme nous cherchons celles d'édification, les autres se rencontrent en passant, et quoique pour celles-ci nous ayons plus d'indifférence [33^v] ce n'est pourtant pas un grand déplaisir pour des missionnaires du nouveau monde, de savoir ce qui se passe dans l'ancien.

À la lecture je pourrais ajouter la conversation des honnêtes gens, qui sont ici plus nombreux que la calomnie ne le publie en Europe. Cette satisfaction n'est pas comme la précédente, puisqu'elle est un moyen nécessaire et ordinaire pour travailler au salut du prochain, et d'ailleurs il n'en est aucun qui ne se fasse honneur de converser avec les missionnaires. J'ai vu deux fois ici des flottes du roi et tous les ans, nous y voyons des escadres remplies de gens de mérite et de qualité, qui pendant leur séjour, de plusieurs mois, sont éternellement chez nous. Outre cela il arrive encore, tous les ans, plus de cent vaisseaux marchands, où il y a toujours d'honnêtes gens, qui séjournent environ la moitié de l'année. Mais ceux-là ne font que passer; nous sommes beaucoup plus satisfaits des habitants, d'ordinaire, on trouve de l'honneur parmi eux, à proportion de leur rang. Nous avons entre autres le bonheur de posséder, dans cette île, un juge criminel, et civil, qui a de la science, et de l'esprit, de la probité, du courage, et de la piété,[48] pour le moins, autant qu'il en faudrait pour paraître avec honneur dans un parlement[49] de France.[50]

---

[47] MdC, MS 73, fol. 61^v: 'accompagnés de toute sorte de belles nouvelles imprimées, ou manuscrites'.

[48] MdC, MS 73, fol. 62^r: 'un juge criminel, et civil qui a de la science, de l'esprit, de la mine, du naturel, de la probité, du courage et de la piété'.

[49] MdC, MS 73, fol. 62^r: 'avec honneur à la tête d'un parlement'.

[50] MdC, MS 73, fol. 62^r continues from this point: 'Pour les missionnaires il y en a ici dans cette île 3 séculiers, 2 capucins, 5 jacobins, et 7 jésuites. De tous ceux-là je n'en connais qu'un ou deux qui ne soient fort bons théologiens, et la moitié sont bons prédicateurs; c'est avec ceux-là comme étant associé pour le même dessein, que je passe mes meilleures heures, quand le loisir, et la rencontre me le permettent. L'union entre tous est aussi grande qu'on le puisse souhaiter pour le succès de nos emplois, et parce que les R. P. jacobins sont plus nos voisins, nous entretenons avec eux une familiarité honnête, et une correspondance

green of this land is an enchanting sight, and one that I find as beautiful as the first day I saw it. We are not deprived of the satisfaction of seeing the best and the most recent books. We have a library which is very well furnished with them because we are very promptly sent the best of what is printed, and it is assured that in our provinces, although far nearer to the source of such fine things, they are not seen any earlier or more regularly than here. Nonetheless, it must be acknowledged that, although reading has great appeal for those of our profession, here we do not have the time to do so with the great attention this pursuit requires, for it is equally necessary for our missionaries to have studied, and not to study. We still get to read the *Journal des savants*;[24] all the issues are sent to us at least three or four times a year, along with all sorts of printed news in which, while looking for what is edifying, we come across other subjects. Although we are more indifferent about the latter, it is nonetheless not all that disagreeable for missionaries to the New World to know what is happening in the Old.

To reading I might add conversation with decent people, of whom there are more here than rumour in Europe would have it. This source of satisfaction is not like the one I have just mentioned, since it is a necessary and habitual means to work towards the salvation of one's fellow man, and moreover there is nobody who is not honoured to converse with missionaries. I have twice seen the king's fleet here, and every year we see naval squadrons carrying many worthy and noble people who, during their stay which lasts for several months, are always amongst us. As well as this, more than a hundred merchant vessels arrive here every year, which always bring decent people who stay for about half the year. However, these people are only passing through; we are much more satisfied with the settlers, usually they are honourable, according to their rank. Amongst these, we have the good fortune to have on this island a magistrate who presides over criminal and civil matters, and who is knowledgeable, astute, upright, courageous, and pious, at least as much as it would take to sit with honour in a *parlement*[25] in France.[26]

---

[24] The *Journal des savants*, published from 1665 onwards, contained articles on the latest scientific discoveries as well as book reviews.

[25] The *parlements*: the regional courts in France.

[26] MdC, MS 73, fol. 62ʳ continues at this point: 'With regard to the missionaries, there are on this island three seculars, two Capuchins, five Jacobins, and seven Jesuits. Of all these I only know of one or two who are not solid theologians, and half of them are good preachers. Associated with them for the same aim, it is with these that I pass my best hours, when I have some time, and we happen to be about. We are as unified as one might wish for the success of our work, and, because the Jacobins are our closest neighbours, we maintain a good mutual relationship, with us inviting them to our most popular sermons, to dine with us, and showing them our sincere friendship in everything, and they reciprocate in everything, which is of great edification for the people.' This extract does not feature in BM, Ant MS 9, or in Chatillon.

Mais il n'est pas difficile de s'imaginer que dans toutes les amitiés nos pères se réservent quelque chose de particulier, les uns pour les autres. Nous nous visitons quelquefois, mais avec quelle joie, il faudrait l'avoir expérimentée pour le dire. Nous n'oublions rien alors des devoirs que l'hospitalité prescrit, et comme c'est la charité qui dresse le festin, il est toujours très agréable.[51] Outre cela nous nous assemblons tous à certains jours, au Fort Saint-Pierre, qui est le principal bourg de l'île, et la résidence de nos supérieurs. C'est là, que l'âme et le corps se refont à merveille, quoique d'ordinaire nous [34r] n'y séjournions qu'une nuit,[52] qui sont [sic] assez souvent interrompus par des exprès, qui nous rappellent auprès des malades de nos quartiers. Voilà une partie des douceurs de notre mission; ses intérieurs sont bien plus sensibles, et d'un ordre bien plus relevé. Elles naissent du fruit des travaux des missionnaires que Dieu donne toujours à ceux, qui s'abandonnent à lui.[53] Pour moi je ne puis jamais le louer assez quand je considère, qu'il s'est bien voulu servir de moi pour coopérer, au bien inestimable de cette mission. Il m'est difficile, de retenir les larmes, lorsque voyant la dévotion de mes nègres, assemblés au nombre du mille dans mon église, je dis en moi-même, *voilà des gens qui connaissent Dieu, et qui ne l'eussent jamais connu, sans ceux que sa miséricorde leur a envoyés; Quomodo credent, nisi mittantur?* Quelle consolation de se voir réduit à cette heureuse nécessité que de ne chercher que Dieu seul, et de dire, ce que V. R. me marque dans sa lettre, *Dieu et moi*? C'est le motif et la pensée, qui m'ayant fait demander pendant quatorze ans une mission étrangère, avec de très grandes satisfactions intérieures, me fait maintenant goûter la possession de ce bonheur, avec autant de constance et de joies. Enfin mon R. P. je suis extrêmement consolé, quand je me ressouviens de ce solitaire de Cassien, qui calmait tous ses chagrins pour la seule vue des murailles de sa cellule, et par la prononciation de ces paroles *propter Christum parietes cellae istius custodio.*[54] Car je vois que le même motif m'a mis dans un état, tout opposé à celui de la solitude, et que par suite je puis dire, avec le même sentiment, en regardant ce nouveau monde, et le chemin que j'ai fait, que j'y suis enfin, par le bon plaisir, et pour le bon plaisir de notre Seigneur. Car j'ai prétendu embrasser un état où je puisse diminuer [34v] un

---

réciproque en les invitant à faire nos sermons les mieux suivis, à prendre le repas chez nous, et en toutes les autres démonstrations d'une sincère amitié, en quoi ils ne nous cèdent nullement; et tout cela avec une grande édification du peuple.' This extract does not feature in BM, Ant MS 9, or in Chatillon.

[51] MdC, MS 73, fol. 62v: 'et comme c'est la charité qui dresse le festin, elle n'y souffre la frugalité, qu'autant qu'il est nécessaire'.

[52] MdC, MS 73, fol. 62v: 'quoique d'ordinaire nous n'y séjournions qu'un jour, et qu'une nuit'.

[53] MdC, MS 73, fol. 62v: 'elles naissent du fruit des travaux des missionnaires, qui est infaillible à la faveur de la bénédiction qui y donne Dieu'.

[54] MdC, MS 73, fol. 63r: 'qui calmait tous les chagrins, par les seules paroles, propter Christum parietes cellae istius custodio'.

But it is not difficult to imagine that, amongst all the friendships those of our order have, there is something unique about those the members have with one another. We visit one another on occasion, but with a joy that you would have had to have experienced to describe. We neglect none of the duties that hospitality prescribes, and, as it is charity that prepares the feast, it is always an agreeable one. As well as this, we also gather on certain days at Fort Saint-Pierre, which is the main town on the island and the site of our superiors' residence. There, body and soul are wonderfully restored, although we usually only stay there for one night, which is interrupted often enough by messengers who call us back to the sick of our quarters. These are some of the joys of our mission; its inner joys are far more marked, and far more sublime in degree. They are born from the fruit of missionaries' labour, which God always gives to those who abandon themselves to Him. For my part, I can never praise Him enough when I consider that He has indeed chosen to make use of me to work towards the priceless good of this mission. I find it difficult to hold back my tears when, seeing the devotion of my slaves,[27] a thousand of them gathered in my church, I say to myself *these are people who know God, and who never would have known Him, without those whom His mercy sent them: Quomodo credent, nisi mittantur?*[28] It is such a consolation to see oneself reduced to that happy necessity of only seeking God alone, and of saying, as your Reverence writes in your letter, *God and I.* It is the motive and the thought that, having led me to request a foreign mission for fourteen years, with very great inner satisfactions, now leads [*sic*] me to savour the possession of this happiness with as much constancy and joys. Indeed, Reverend Father, I am very much consoled when I think of that solitary, in Cassian, who calmed all his turmoil, from seeing only the walls of his cell, and by pronouncing these words: *propter Christum parietes cellae istius custodio.*[29] For I see that the same motive has brought me to a position which is the complete opposite of solitude, and that in consequence I can say with the same sentiment, in looking on this new world and the journey I have made, that I am ultimately here because it pleases God, and so as to please God. For I desired to embrace a state where I could lessen the terrible

---

[27] By 'his slaves', Mongin can be understood to mean 'those of his flock'.

[28] 'Quomodo credent, nisi mittantur?'('How can they believe, if they are not sent?') paraphrases 'Quomodo credent ei, quem non audierunt? [...] Quomodo vero praedicabunt nisi mittantur?', Romans 10. 14–15 ('How shall they believe him whom they have not heard? [...] But how shall they preach unless they be sent?', 1582, p. 408).

[29] 'I am the custodian of the walls of this cell because of Christ.' Mongin is referring to John Cassian (*c.* 360–*c.* 435), author of *De institutis coenobiorum* and *Collationes patrum XXIV*. The quotation is attributed to Saint Macarius, in Laurentius Surius (1522–1578), *Historiae sanctorum omnium nationum*, 13 vols (Turin: Eq. Petri Marietti, 1875–80), I (1875), 77.

peu l'effroyable incertitude de mon salut éternel, et venir mourir dans un lieu, et dans un emploi, qui étant de soi le plus pénible de tous ceux de la Compagnie, m'a paru aussi le plus propre à me faire espérer que Dieu me fera miséricorde à la fin de ma vie.

Je voudrais ici finir cette lettre, qui n'est déjà que trop longue, pour les occupations de la personne à qui elle est adressée, et de celle qui l'écrit; mais le dessein pour lequel j'ai pris la plume m'oblige à continuer encore pour répondre à ce qu'on oppose, contre les grands avantages de notre mission. D'abord il se présente à moi deux objections des plus considérables, mais comme elles sont contraires ensemble, il est d'autant plus difficile d'y répondre, qu'il y a danger que la solution de l'une ne fortifie l'autre. Néanmoins j'espère que la vérité nous délivrera de ce péril.

Il y en a donc, qui pour détourner les gens de venir en cette mission, leur disent, les uns qu'il y a trop de souffrance, et les autres qu'il y a trop de délices, et qui conséquemment, blâment ceux qui y sont déjà, ou de témérité, ou de délicatesse. Pour les souffrances, quand bien il serait vrai, comme ils l'entendent que nos maisons[55] d'ici ne seraient que des infirmeries qui remplissent celles de la France, je ne les avais jamais ouï compter que parmi les attraits, et les louanges d'une mission,[56] et la nôtre est bien malheureuse puisqu'on prétend en diminuer l'estime, par les mêmes choses, qu'on admire dans les autres. Cependant ce mot de cet Ancien [35^r] *N Serpens, sitis, ardor, Arenae Dulcia virtuti* ne convient pas si bien au pays, pour lequel il a été dit, qu'à celui de notre Martinique, comme savent ceux qui en connaissent les qualités, d'ailleurs on ne dira pas que les souffrances des autres missions, y fassent des martyrs d'autre manière que ceux d'ici. Enfin quoique autrefois cette île ait été une terre qui dévorait ses habitants,[57] elle a bien changé de nature, à l'égard de tout le monde, à la faveur de l'augmentation du commerce, qui porte ici de l'Europe, avec abondance, toutes les commodités de la vie, et pour nous en particulier. N. R. P. Supérieur général[58] y a mis un si bon ordre, que depuis longtemps, par la grâce de Dieu, nous n'avons eu aucun malade. Je le bénis de ce que je ne l'ai pas encore été du tout. Ceux qui trouvent trop de délices dans notre mission se fondent sur ce que nous y sommes honnêtement bien nourris, habillés, logés, et montés. Ils pourraient encore ajouter ce que j'ai dit ci-dessus sur le chapitre de la douceur de notre emploi: mais de tout cela, on ne peut rien conclure, si ce n'est que nos supérieurs qui ont enfin mis les choses sur ce pied, ont agi par un zèle, selon la science, après avoir appris, par une expérience de tant d'années, que la ferveur toute seule, est un mauvais guide, qui n'a pas nui seulement à

---

[55] MdC, MS 73, fol. 63^v: 'comme ils l'entendent que nos missions'.
[56] MdC, MS 73, fol. 63^v: 'je n'avais jamais ouï compter les souffrances que parmi les attraits, et les louanges d'une mission'.
[57] MdC, MS 73, fol. 63^v: 'habitations' has been changed to 'habitants'.
[58] MdC, MS 73, fol. 63^v : 'N. R. P. Supérieur général des îles'.

uncertainty of my eternal salvation a little, and come to die in a place, and in an occupation, that, being the harshest of those of our Society, also appeared to me to be the best suited to give me hope that God will have mercy on me at the end of my life.

I would like at this point to end this letter, which is already far too long, given how occupied are the person to whom it is addressed and the person writing it. However, the purpose for which I took up the quill obliges me to continue further so as to reply to what is said against the great advantages of our mission. First, there seem to me to be two very considerable objections, but, as they are opposed to one another, it is all the more difficult to reply to them in that there is a danger that the response to one may strengthen the other. Nevertheless, I hope that truth will deliver us from this danger.

There are those who, wishing to discourage people from embarking on this mission, say to them either that there is too much suffering, according to some, or too much comfort, according to others. In consequence, those who are here already are accused either of temerity or of softness. Regarding the suffering, even were it to be true that, as they insinuate, our houses here are nothing more than infirmaries that fill those of France, I had never heard such suffering counted anywhere else but amongst the attractions and merits of a mission. Our own is most unfortunate since they try to undermine its value with the same reasons that are admired in others. However, the expression used by the Ancient: *N. Serpens, sitis, ardor, Arenae Dulcia virtuti* less suits the land it referred to than it does our Martinique, as those who are familiar with it well know.[30] Moreover, it cannot be said that the sufferings of other missions make their martyrs otherwise than those here. In fact, although this island was in former times a land that devoured its inhabitants, it is much changed in character with regard to everybody, thanks to the increase in commerce which brings here from Europe, and in abundance, all the comforts, and particularly for us. Our Reverend Father Superior General has so well ordered this that for a long time, and by the grace of God, we have had no one ill. I praise Him that I have not yet been sick at all. Those who find that this mission is too comfortable draw such a conclusion from us being decently fed, clothed, and lodged, and with good horses. They might also add what I wrote above about the sweetness of our occupations, but all that can be concluded from this is that our superiors, who have finally got the mission on its feet, have acted through zeal tempered by wisdom, having learned by the experience of so many years, that fervour alone is a bad guide that harmed not just the health of many of our

---

[30] 'Serpens, sitis, ardor harenae dulcia virtuti' ('Serpents, thirst, burning sand — all are welcomed by the brave'), M. Annaeus Lucanus, *De bello civili*, trans. by J. D. Duff (Cambridge, MA: Harvard University Press; London: Heinemann, 1988), Book IX, ll. 402–03.

la santé de plusieurs de nos premiers missionnaires,[59] mais encore au salut de quantité d'âmes, qui n'ont pu être secourues pendant que les missionnaires se mouraient,[60] ou s'en allaient chercher la santé en France. Voilà, avec quel succès, on nous objecte les souffrances et les délices, car enfin ces deux objections[61] sont deux couronnes [35^v] pour notre mission, quoique l'une soit d'épines, et l'autre de roses.

Mais dans nos îles, dit-on, il n'y a rien à faire pour des gens de notre profession; de sorte qu'en France le moins occupé, et le moins utile de nos pères, l'est beaucoup plus qu'on ne l'est ici. Sans toucher à cette comparaison, je puis répondre, que c'est celle de toutes les objections, qui nous fait plus de pitié, sur ce qu'elle allègue le défaut d'occupation. Ce que j'ai [dit] ci-dessus,[62] justifie assez l'assiduité du travail de nos missionnaires. Avant que j'eusse le bonheur d'être de leur nombre, je n'avais jamais pu me persuader du contraire, de ce que je vois, quelques efforts qu'on ait faits pour cela; et il me souvient que lorsque je passais par le Languedoc, avec le P. Bonnal, quelqu'un désespérant de nous faire reculer, nous dit, comme pour nous consoler, que de vrai les jours de fête, nous ne serions pas dans l'inaction, mais qu'aussi il était constamment vrai, que le reste de la semaine, nous pourrions préparer nos sermons sans nulle interruption. Le souvenir de cette parole, nous divertit quelquefois dans notre entrevue avec le même père qui connaît, aussi bien que moi, comme tous les autres, par expérience, combien cela est éloigné de la vérité. J'avoue bien que nos auditoires, et pour le nombre, et pour la qualité, étant préférables à presque tous ceux de nos églises de la province de Toulouse, mériteraient bien un sermon préparé, pendant toute une semaine. Mais il est impossible de trouver ce temps-là, et d'ailleurs l'éloquence apostolique d'un missionnaire, jointe avec ses occupations continuelles, lui imposent une heureuse nécessité, de se contenter du solide[63] dans ses prédications; ce qui est une épargne de temps aussi grande que tout le monde sait, et laquelle est ici [36^r] absolument nécessaire, au moins pour moi, continuant de prêcher depuis trois ans dans la même église, tous les jours de fête, sans y avoir manqué, et il y en a qui l'ont fait plus longtemps dans une même église pareillement. Aussi j'en sais un qui ne trouve pas d'autres temps, pour penser à ses sermons, que pendant que le chœur chante à la grand-messe, à laquelle il doit prêcher. On pourra connaître par là, si nous sommes occupés, et avec combien peu de fondement, on avance le contraire, à moins qu'on ne l'entende de ceux qui ne trouvent rien à faire, que de dire leur messe, et aller confesser les malades, qui sont à la dernière extrémité, quand ils en sont requis; ce qui ne remplit nullement l'idée d'un missionnaire zélé.

---

[59] MdC, MS 73, fol. 64^r: 'plusieurs de nos missionnaires'.
[60] MdC, MS 73, fol. 64^r: 'pendant que les confesseurs se mouraient'.
[61] MdC, MS 73, fol. 64^r: 'car enfin ces objections'.
[62] MdC, MS 73, fol. 64^r: 'j'ai dit ci-dessus'.
[63] MdC, MS 73, fol. 64^v: 'lui imposent une heureuse nécessité de laisser tout à fait le brillant, pour le solide'.

first missionaries, but also the salvation of many souls that could not be saved while the missionaries were dying, or were going back to France to try and regain their health. So these are the ways our sufferings and our comforts are objected to, for these two objections are, in the end, two crowns for our mission, although one crown is of thorns and the other of roses.

But in our islands, they say, people of our profession have nothing to do; so that those of our clerics in France who have the least tasks to do, and are least useful, still do much more than we do here. Without addressing this comparison, I can reply that of all the objections it is the one that we consider most pitiful, in that it alleges that we lack occupation. What I said above sufficiently justifies the diligence of our missionaries in their work. Before I had the good fortune to be amongst their number, I never believed the opposite of what I [now] see, whatever efforts were made to make me do so. I remember when I was passing through Languedoc with Father Bonnal, when somebody who was losing hope of getting us to turn back said to us, as if to console us, that in truth on feast days we would have something to do, but for the rest of the week we could prepare our sermons without any interruption.[31] The memory of these words amuses us sometimes when in conversation with this same priest who knows through experience, as well as I and all the others do, how far removed from reality these words are. I readily admit that as our audiences, in terms of number and rank, are superior to nearly all those of our churches in the province of Toulouse, they well deserve a sermon which had been prepared for a week. However it is impossible to find such time, and what is more, the apostolic eloquence of a missionary, along with his continuous activities, impose on him the happy necessity of contenting himself in his sermons with what is solid. Everyone knows how considerable a saving in time this is, and it is absolutely necessary here, at least for me; I have been preaching continuously for three years now in the same church on every feast day, without having missed any of them. And there are those who have done the same, in their own church, and for longer. Indeed, I know one [missionary] who has no other time to think about his sermons except while the choir is singing at High Mass, at which he has to preach. One may judge from this if we are busy, and the little basis there is for advancing the opposite of this, unless it is meant about those who find nothing to do but to say their Mass and confess the sick who are near death, when they are called for, and this is not at all the image one has of a zealous missionary.

---

[31] On Bonnal (spelled *Bonal*), who accompanied Mongin on his 1675–76 Atlantic crossing, see Camille de Rochemontrix, *Le Père Antoine Lavalette à la Martinique d'après beaucoup de documents inédits* (Paris: Alphonse Picard et fils, 1907), p. 26, n. 1.

Il me souvient encore d'une autre chose qu'on me disait autrefois contre cette mission; savoir que nous y faisions toutes les fonctions curiales. Je ne sais pas si ceux qui font cette objection, et ceux qui s'y laissent surprendre, prétendent que dans la mission éclatante de la Chine, les missionnaires de Pékin, envoient quérir quelque bon prêtre à Macao pour faire les enterrements, et les baptêmes du menu peuple, ou autres choses semblables, pendant qu'ils se réservent pour les sermons, et pour les baptêmes des mandarins. Cette pensée serait tout à fait ridicule, et nul ne doute que ces missionnaires ne fassent toutes les fonctions curiales que tous les apôtres, et tous les hommes apostoliques ont toujours faites dans les missions étrangères. Après tout que trouve-t-on de rebutant dans cet exercice après qu'on a admiré, avec raison, une si grande diversité d'étranges personnages qu'on fait,[64] et que font tant de missionnaires dans les pays étrangers, de maître d'école, [36ᵛ] de chirurgien, de valet, de mendiant, d'esclave et de forçat, pour gagner tout le monde à Jésus-Christ, en se faisant tout à tout le monde.[65] Et si dans toute la chrétienté, mais particulièrement dans la France, on voit force gens considérables pour leur vertu, ou pour leur science, ou pour leur naissance, qui se font honneur, et un mérite des fonctions curiales, quoique ce ne soit pas tout à fait sans désintéressement, puisqu'ils en recueillent les fruits, et en perçoivent les émoluments temporels, avec assez d'exactitude pourquoi est-ce que des religieux, n'auront pas le même sentiment pour des emplois, où ils ne cherchent[66] que la bénédiction de la rosée du ciel, et nullement celle de la graisse de la terre, après avoir quitté, pour embrasser ces travaux, les espérances le repos, et toutes les satisfactions de leur pays? En effet quoique le profit du dedans des églises médiocres, outre les pensions que le roi donne se monte ici assez souvent jusqu'à 10 000 livres de sucre l'année,[67] nous n'y touchons pourtant pas, que pour les partager entre les pauvres, qui sont en fort petit nombre, et avec l'église que nous desservons, conformément à notre règle.

Enfin comme le chœur fait une de ces fonctions, on ne saurait croire de quelle douceur elle est accompagnée, nommément quand on se souvient qu'on chante solennellement les louanges de Dieu, dans un nouveau monde, qui avait demeuré près de six mille ans sans le connaître. Aussi nous n'oublions rien pour rendre le service divin le plus auguste et le plus dévot qu'il se peut et nous suppléons au défaut du nombre d'ecclésiastiques par des petits [37ʳ] enfants, bien appris, et bien dressés, qui en habit de chœur, font à l'autel tout ce que les rubriques permettent aux acolytes non sacrés: comme c'est depuis peu, que les

---

[64] MdC, MS 73, fol. 65ʳ: 'qu'ont fait'.
[65] MdC, MS 73, fol. 65ʳ: 'pour gagner tout le monde'.
[66] MdC, MS 73, fol. 65ᵛ: 'pourquoi est-ce que des religieux n'auront pas le même sentiment pour des curés qui ne cherchent'.
[67] MdC, MS 73, fol. 65ᵛ: 'En effet quoique le verrou des églises médiocres, se monte ici assez souvent jusqu'à 10 000 [figure after modification] livres de sucre dans l'année'.

I still remember something else that was said to me in the past against this mission, which was that we performed all of the curial duties. I do not know if those who make this objection, and those who are taken in by it, claim that in the illustrious mission to China the Peking missionaries send to Macao for some worthy priest to perform the burials and the baptisms of the common folk, or similar things, while they keep themselves for the sermons, and for the baptisms of the mandarins. Such an idea would be ridiculous, and nobody is in doubt that these missionaries perform all the curial duties that all the apostles, and all apostolic men, have always carried out in the foreign missions. After all, what is thought so off-putting in such practices after one has justly admired such a great diversity of strange roles that we play,[32] and that are played by so many missionaries in foreign lands: schoolmaster, surgeon, valet, beggar, slave, and convict, so as to bring everybody to Jesus Christ by being everything to everybody.[33] And if, in all of Christendom but particularly in France, we see many people who are remarkable for their virtue, their learning, or their birth, who see curial duties as a source of honour and merit — although they are not entirely disinterested, because they gather the fruits and collect the temporal profits — why would clerics not feel the same way about occupations for which they are only looking for the blessing of the dew of the heavens, and not that of the fertility of the earth, having left behind the hope of repose and all the joys of their country to take on these labours?[34] Indeed, although the profit of a smallish church here, aside from the stipends from the king, can often enough be as high as 10,000 pounds of sugar in a year, we do not use it except to share it amongst the poor, who are in very small number, and with the church that we serve, in conformity with our rule.[35]

Indeed, one of these duties being the choir, you would not believe how agreeable it is, notably when one reflects that one is solemnly singing the praises of God in a new world, which had subsisted for nearly six thousand years without knowing Him. So we spare nothing to make the divine service as sublime and as devout as can be, and we make up for the lack of ecclesiastics with little children who have been well taught and well prepared, and who, in choirboys' garb, perform all the tasks at the altar that are permitted to unordained acolytes. As things have only recently begun to be set up so, the devotion this

[32] BM, Ant MS 9, fol. 36^r has 'qu'on fait' ('that are played', or 'that we play'), whereas MdC, MS 73, fol. 65^r gives 'qu'ont fait' ('that were played').
[33] This paraphrases 'omnibus omnia factus sum', 1 Corinthians 9. 22 ('To all men I became all things', 1582, p. 443).
[34] This paraphrases Isaac's 'Det tibi Deus de rore caeli et de pinguedine terrae et abundantiam frumenti et vini', Genesis 27. 28 ('God give thee of the dew of Heaven, and of the fatness of the earth abundance of corn and wine', 1635, p. 82).
[35] See *Constitutions and Norms*, Part IV, Chapter 2, pp. 226–54.

choses ont commencé d'être sur ce pied, il n'est pas croyable quel sentiment
de dévotion cela cause dans les assistants.[68] Nous savons tous combien le
chœur était au goût de notre saint patriarche, en même temps qu'il le jugeait
incompatible avec nos emplois en Europe, malgré son inclination même.[69]
Mais depuis Dieu a tellement disposé les choses, que les enfants goûtent ici
une douceur qu'il a refusée à leur père, puisqu'elle est presque inséparable de
l'emploi des missionnaires, qui a toujours été non seulement le principal, mais
aussi le premier de ceux que saint Ignace a eus en vue.

Il me vient encore à la pensée qu'il y en a qui sont rebutés de cette mission,
voyant le nombre de ceux qui en sortent pour s'en retourner en France.
J'avoue que ce sentiment est plus raisonnable, puisqu'il part d'une volonté
de se consacrer à Dieu de telle manière, qu'on ne puisse plus revenir de l'exil
volontaire de la mission. Mais aussi en quelle de nos quatre missions de France
trouvera-t-on ce qu'on veut exiger de cette cinquième?[70] Est-ce qu'on ne revient
point de la Perse, de la Grèce, de la Syrie ni du Canada?[71] Ce n'est pas que nos
missionnaires qui sont de retour en France, aient quitté nos îles sans de bonnes
raisons, puisque tout le monde sait que ce n'a été qu'à cause des maladies, qui
ont été autrefois aussi fréquentes, qu'elles sont maintenant rares, par la grâce de
Dieu; aussi comme ils ne se retiraient que pour reprendre haleine, et des forces,
qu'ils avaient perdues par l'excès de leur travail, causé [37ᵛ] par la multitude
des occupations de la mission, qui a toujours manqué, et qui manque encore à
présent du nombre nécessaire de missionnaires, la plupart y sont revenus pour
achever l'holocauste comme fit le P. Brion jusqu'à quatre fois. J'avoue pour moi
que quand je me trouverais dans la même nécessité d'employer un tel remède,
je n'en ferais pas grande difficulté quoique dans ce malheur, je n'aurais pas de
plus grande et de plus sensible consolation, que l'espérance de venir mourir
dans mon poste; mais celle de n'avoir jamais besoin d'en sortir, m'est bien plus
douce sans comparaison.[72]

---

[68] MdC, MS 73, fol. 65ᵛ continues with 'et beaucoup plus dans l'officiant, qui est l'âme de
toutes ces cérémonies, et qui anime les chantres qui y font de leur mieux'.
[69] MdC, MS 73, fols 65ᵛ–66ʳ: 'et malgré son inclination même, et celle de quelques
puissances ecclésiastiques'.
[70] MdC, MS 73, fol. 66ʳ: 'cette quatrième', replaced with 'celle-ci'.
[71] From this point in MdC, MS 73, fols 66ʳ–66ᵛ, the original text has been covered over by
a replacement text, in another hand.
[72] BM, Ant MS 9, fols 37ʳ–37ᵛ: instead of the text from 'Ce n'est pas que nos missionnaires'
to 'm'est bien plus douce sans comparaison', MdC, MS 73, fols 66ʳ–66ᵛ now reads as follows:
'que si on revient plus souvent de cette mission, c'est qu'il en vient aussi plus dans celle-ci
que dans toutes les autres ensemble, le chemin en est plus battu, le voyage se fait à moins de
frais par le moyen des vaisseaux du roi, et enfin la liberté des missionnaires est plus grande,
comme nous l'ont appris le fondateur et le restaurateur de cette mission; le premier par son
exemple, et le second par sa déclaration et tous deux de la province de France. Le fondateur
était le P. Bouton dont Sotuel fait un grand éloge dans la bibliothèque de la Compagnie, et
qui de professeur de théologie étant devenu le premier des ouvriers de cette mission, dont

inspires amongst the attendees is unbelievable. We all know how much our holy Patriarch appreciated choirs, even as he thought them incompatible with our tasks in Europe, and despite his own inclination.[36] However, God has since so disposed things that here the children enjoy a delight that was refused to the father, since it is near-essential to the missionaries' charge, a charge which has always been not simply the most important, but also the first of those for which Saint Ignatius strove.

Another thought has occurred to me, which is that some have been put off from this mission, when they have seen the number of those returning to France from it. I allow that this is more reasonable thinking, as it is based on the wish to devote oneself to God to such a degree that one can never return from the voluntary exile that a mission is. But in which of our four French missions will one find what is demanded of the fifth? Does one not come back from Persia, Greece, Syria, or Canada? It is not that our missionaries who have returned to France left our islands without good reason, for everybody knows that it was only because of the diseases that were, in the past, as frequent as they are now rare through the grace of God. And, as they only withdrew to catch their breath and regain the strength they had lost in their excessive labours, the result of the multitude of duties in the mission — which has always been lacking in sufficient number of missionaries as it does today — most went back to offer themselves up, as Father Brion did, up to four times.[37] I avow that on my part, were I to find myself in need of using such a remedy, I would have little difficulty in doing so, although in this misfortune I would have no greater and more keenly felt consolation than the hope of coming here to die in my station, but that of never needing to leave it is far sweeter to me, and incomparably so.[38]

---

[36] 'Because the occupations which are undertaken for the aid of souls are of great importance, proper to our Institute, and very frequent; and because, on the other hand, our residence in one place or another is so uncertain, they will not regularly hold choir for the canonical hours or sing Masses and offices'. *Constitutions and Norms*, Part IV, Chapter 3, [586] 4, p. 258.

[37] Gérard Brion, who would be Superior General of the Jesuit mission in the Caribbean and coastal South America. See Jean Grillet, Letter of 1668 to Pierre de Saint-Gilles, in *Mission de Cayenne et de la Guyane française* (Paris: Julien, Lanier, Cosnard, 1857), pp. 183–210 (p. 184).

[38] Instead of the text from 'It is not that our missionaries' to 'is far sweeter to me, and incomparably so' in BM, Ant MS 9, fols 37ʳ–37ᵛ the following now appears in MdC, MS 73, fols 66ʳ–66ᵛ: 'if [missionaries] return more often from this mission, it is because many more come to this one than to all the others together. The path has already been trodden, the voyage is cheaper on the king's vessels, and missionaries have greater freedom, as the founder and the restorer of this mission have taught us, the first by his example and the second by his declaration, and both were of the province of France. The founder was Father Bouton, who was greatly praised by Sotuel in his *Bibliotheca scriptorum Societatis Iesu* and who after being a professor of theology, and becoming the first worker on this mission, of which he wrote the first printed account, returned to France. The restorer is Father Le Mercier; one of his excellent regulations so as to rejuvenate this mission with a great number

Voilà M. R. P. ce que j'avais à répondre à la lettre de V. R. touchant les sentiments que Dieu me donne pour ma mission; ils sont pleins d'estime et de tendresse, à cause de la grande diversité de personnes pour lesquelles on travaille, de la facilité à y réussir, et de l'assiduité de ces travaux. Cette occupation est universelle, efficace et assidue, étant quasi pour toutes les nations de la terre, étant ordinairement suivie de son effet, et enfin étant presque toujours sans nulle interruption. C'est ce que j'ai expliqué dans la suite de cette lettre, qui paraîtra sans doute trop longue et sans aucun ordre, ce que j'espère que V. R. me pardonnera bien quand elle saura que j'ai été si souvent interrompu, depuis un mois que je l'ai commencée et qu'à grand'peine ai-je pu remplir une page sans quitter la plume.[73] Mais du moins cette lettre quelque mal suivie [38^r] qu'elle soit, la confirmera sans doute dans le sentiment qu'elle m'a fait la grâce de me témoigner, qu'elle était résolue de ne point refuser le congé, à ceux de sa province qui auraient le courage de venir prendre part à nos travaux.[74] Aussi

il composa la première relation imprimée, s'en retourna en France. Le restaurateur est le P. Le Mercier, dont un des beaux règlements pour faire refleurir cette mission par le grand nombre de missionnaires est la déclaration qu'il fit qu'on n'en refuserait le retour à aucun; il me la signifia lui-même le lendemain de mon arrivée, il m'ajouta qu'il l'avait envoyée en France avec une circulaire pour toutes nos communautés, afin que tous reconnaissent comme un attrait de cette mission, qu'on y sert Dieu avec cet esprit d'amour que saint Ignace a si fort [66^v] recommandé, et qu'on n'a pas moins de liberté de repasser en Europe que d'une ville à l'autre, ce qui corrige l'idée de ceux qui veulent bien regarder les missionnaires comme des esclaves. Les deux autres héros de notre mission ont été le P. Pelleprat, et le P. Brion; et l'un et l'autre l'ont quittée plusieurs fois, pour de bonnes raisons. Cette lettre étant écrite pour détruire les obstacles qui nous privent de force bons ouvriers, je ne devais pas omettre de parler de cet engagement imaginaire que quelques-uns craignent dans cette mission.' MdC, MS 73 continues in the original hand from 'Voilà M. R. P.'.

[73] BM, Ant MS 9, fol. 37^v: instead of this sentence, from 'C'est ce que j'ai expliqué' to 'sans quitter la plume', MdC, MS 73, fol. 66^v reads: 'C'est ce que j'ai expliqué dans la suite de cette lettre, qui paraîtra sans doute trop longue, et dont on excusera peut-être la prolixité, quand on saura que ce n'est qu'une effusion de cœur, et nullement une production d'esprit, le style en est une marque assez évidente; et quand j'eusse prétendu faire autrement il m'eût été impossible d'écrire rien de suivi ayant été obligé d'interrompre si souvent depuis plus d'un mois que j'ai commencé, qu'à grand'peine ai-je pu jamais remplir une page sans quitter la plume.'

[74] BM, Ant MS 9, fols 37^v–38^r: instead of the sentence from 'Mais du moins cette lettre' to 'venir prendre part à nos travaux', MdC, MS 73, fols 66^v–67^r reads 'Je crains que la longueur de cette lettre n'en détruise quelques [pr......?] puisqu'elle semble marquer un grand loisir qui n'est guère le partage des missionnaires fort [67^r] occupés, mais loin de détruire ce que j'ai dit de l'assiduité de notre travail, je puis dire que cela même le prouve davantage, car si j'eusse eu plus de loisir, les choses eussent été mieux pensées, mieux digérées, et mieux serrées, en retranchant, et les superfluités, et les redites qui sont un effet ordinaire de la précipitation; ainsi je pourrais dire comme un bel esprit de notre temps: pardonnez la longueur de ma lettre, elle aurait été plus courte, si j'eusse eu plus de temps pour l'écrire. j'avoue néanmoins que j'ai quelque peu de scrupule, d'avoir dérobé à ma mission force moments précieux que j'ai employés à mettre mes pensées sur ce papier; mais à même temps je m'en console par l'espérance que j'aurais été pour le moins aussi utile, à cette même mission par cette lettre,

This, Reverend Father, is my reply to your Reverence concerning the sentiments God has given me for my mission; they are full of esteem and tenderness, because of the great diversity of people for whom we work, the ease of our success, and our diligence in these labours. This task is universal, effective, and continuous, for it is for the benefit of nearly every nation on the earth, usually leads to a result, and, finally, is nearly always without interruption. This is what I have explained in the rest of this letter, which will doubtlessly seem too long and without order, which I hope that your Reverence will excuse me when learning that I have been so often interrupted, in the month since I began it, and that it is only with great difficulty that I have managed to fill a page without having to put down my quill. But at least this letter, however disorganized it may be, will confirm your Reverence in the sentiment you had the grace to communicate to me: that you are resolved not to refuse leave to those of your province who have the courage to come and participate in our labours.[39] Indeed, we have great need of them, because of the losses that the

of missionaries, is his declaration that nobody would be forbidden from returning [to France]. He made it known to me the day after I arrived here, and added that he had sent it to France with a circular for all our communities, so that all of them recognize as one of the attractions of this mission, that we serve God here with the spirit of love that Saint Ignatius recommended, and that one has no less freedom to return to Europe than one has to go from one town to another. This corrects the idea of those who consider missionaries as slaves. The two other heroes of our mission are Fathers Pelleprat and Brion, and each one left it many times and with good reason. This letter having been written to remove the obstacles that deprive us of many good workers, I had to ensure that I discussed this imagined engagement that some fear in this mission.' Jacques Bouton (1592–1658) left a *Relation de l'establissement des François depuis l'an 1635 en l'isle de la Martinique*. Nathaniel Sotuello, co-author of *Bibliotheca scriptorum Societatis Iesu* by Petrus de Ribadeneira and others (Rome: J. A. de Lazzaris Varesii, 1676); the article on Bouton ('Iacobus Boutonus') is on pp. 359–60.

[39] In place of the sentence in BM, Ant MS 9, fols 37^v–38^r from: 'But at least this letter' to 'come and participate in our labours', MdC, MS 73, fols 66^v–67^r reads: 'I fear that the length of this letter will [...] as it seems to indicate a great leisure which should not normally be the lot of missionaries who are very busy, but far from disproving what I have said about how busy we are, I can say that this actually proves it more. For, if we had more free time, [I would have] been able to think things through more and edit it more carefully, in cutting out the excess and repetitions which ordinarily result from haste. So I may say, like a wit of our time, *excuse the length of my letter; it would have been shorter if I had had more time to write it.* I acknowledge nonetheless that I have some scruples about taking from my mission much precious time that I used to put my thoughts to paper. Yet at the same time I console myself with the hope that I will have been as useful for this mission with this letter as I would have been through the work I neglected so as to write it, since your Reverence has already told me you are resolved not to refuse leave to any of those who request it, to come and participate in our labours; this letter will perhaps inspire amongst some the desire to do so.' From 'your Reverence has already told me' to 'participate in our labours; this' has been crossed out. The 'wit' is Blaise Pascal (1623–1662), *Les Provinciales* (Cologne: Pierre de la Vallée, 1657), Letter 16, p. 12.

en avons-nous grand besoin, à cause des pertes que la mission a faites depuis deux ans, car Cayenne, et toute la terre ferme de l'Amérique,[75] a été longtemps abandonnée[76] après la mort du père Frémond, arrivée par un excès de son zèle, plutôt que par l'intempérie de l'air et comme quatre des nôtres allaient lui succéder, ils se perdirent en mer avec le vaisseau.[77] Ensuite comme V. R. sait un père de la province de Lyon s'étant rendu à La Rochelle pour s'embarquer pour le même voyage, il y est mort en attendant l'occasion, et le P. Mayenoue, son compagnon qui y était en même temps, a été enfin obligé par une maladie qui lui survint au point de son départ de s'en retourner dans sa province,[78] au grand regret de toute notre mission, qui lui tendait les bras, comme à celui qui devait nous consoler de tant de pertes que l'on jugera être encore plus grandes, si l'on y ajoute celles de deux de nos pères, qui se perdirent il y a trois ans dans nos mers avec le vaisseau, après des aventures, qui étant jointes à celles des pères Méland, Boislevert, Pelleprat, Frémond et autres, pourront faire un jour, dans la belle histoire de cette mission, des endroits capables de contenter tous les hommes apostoliques, et même les curieux.[79]

Après quoi M. R. P. il ne me reste plus rien qu'à implorer le secours des prières de V. R. et pour notre mission et pour moi qui en ai plus de besoin,

que par les travaux que j'ai omis pour l'écrire, puisque V. R. me témoigna déjà qu'elle est résolue de ne refuser nullement le congé à ceux qui le lui demanderont, pour venir prendre part à nos travaux; cet écrit pourra peut-être en faire naître l'envie à quelques-uns.' From 'V. R. me témoigna déjà' to 'prendre part à nos travaux; cet' has been crossed out.

[75] BM, Ant MS 9 has 'la Merique' here, and on fol. 38[v].

[76] MdC, MS 73, fol. 67[r]: 'Aussi en avons-nous grand besoin, car quoique le Frère de Saint-Gilles [name crossed out and replaced with 'N'] nous ait répondu depuis peu, qu'il vient plus de missionnaires ici que dans toutes les autres missions ensemble qui sont de l'assistance de France, néanmoins nous sommes extrêmement accablés, par les pertes qu'a faites la mission depuis deux ans; car Cayenne a été longtemps abandonnée'.

[77] MdC, MS 73, fol. 67[v]: 'ils se perdirent en mer avec le vaisseau; un cinquième qui y alla ensuite pour suppléer à leur défaut, y est tombé malade, étant obligé seul de travailler à cette belle mission.'

[78] MdC, MS 73, fol. 67[v]: 'et le P. Mayenoue, qui y était à même temps, ayant été sur le point de faire le voyage de l'Amérique, aussi bien que celui de l'autre monde a été enfin obligé de s'en retourner dans la province'.

[79] MdC, MS 73, fol. 67[v]: 'pourront un jour dans la belle histoire de cette mission faire des endroits les plus capables de contenter les curieux, et les hommes apostoliques'. MdC, MS 73, fol. 67[v] continues with the following paragraph: 'Ce sont ces pertes, et la bonne volonté que V. R. me témoigne de contribuer à leur réparation, qui m'ont obligé de faire mes efforts pour en lever les obstacles, en dissipant par cette lettre les préoccupations injustes de quelques-uns contre notre mission; c'est aussi pour cette même raison que j'y étais exhorté depuis plus d'un an par le R. P. Le Mercier, notre Supérieur général, ayant connu que j'étais tout pénétré de l'estime, et de l'affection pour nos emplois; il a fallu tous ces motifs pour me faire écrire si au long sur une matière qui n'est inconnue à personne, quoique la connaissance de quelques-uns soit fondée sur des rapports peu conformes à la vérité, et faits par des personnes qui en sont convaincus eux-mêmes intérieurement par leur propre expérience.' From 'qui n'est inconnue à personne' onwards has been crossed out.

mission has suffered in the last two years, for Cayenne, and all the mainland of America, has been long abandoned,[40] after the death of Father Frémond,[41] which was due to his excessive zeal, rather than the poor air, and then as four of our own were on their way to succeed him, they were lost at sea with their vessel. Then, as your Reverence is aware, a priest from the province of Lyon who had gone to La Rochelle to embark on the same route died there while waiting to embark. His companion who was there at the same time, Father Mayenoue, was obliged to return to his province in the end because of a sickness that came upon him as he was about to leave. This was a source of great regret to our entire mission, who held our arms out to him, as to someone who would be a source of consolation after so many losses. These [losses] will be thought all the more significant, if those of two of our Fathers who were lost with their vessel in our seas three years ago are added to them. Their adventures, alongside those of Fathers Méland,[42] Boislevert,[43] Pelleprat, Frémond, and others, may one day be a part of the fine history of this mission that will content all apostolic men, and even the curious.[44]

After this, Reverend Father, there is nothing left for me to do but to implore the assistance of your Reverence's prayers for our mission and for myself; I

---

[40] MdC, MS 73, fol. 67^r: 'Indeed, we have great need of them, for although Brother de Saint-Gilles [name crossed out and replaced with 'X'] has recently replied that more missionaries come here than in all the other missions put together that are of the assistancy of France, we are nonetheless extremely weakened by the losses the mission has suffered in the last two years for Cayenne has been long abandoned.'

[41] Louis Frémond (16..–1677?). See *Mission de Cayenne et de la Guyane française*, p. 265.

[42] Denis Méland (Mesland) (....–16..). An experienced missionary who arrived in Cayenne in 1651 to administer to the Amerindian population. See Pelleprat, Part 2: *De la terre ferme*, p. 3.

[43] Antoine Boislevert (1618–1669). See José del Rey Fajardo, 'Antoine Boislevert (1618–1669): Fundador de los llanos de Casanere', *Boletín de la Academia Nacional de la Historia*, 77.308 (1994), 81–104.

[44] MdC, MS 73, fol. 67^v: 'may one day, in the fine history of this mission, be the parts that will most content the curious, and apostolic men'. This continues with the following paragraph: 'It is these losses, and the will to contribute to their repair that your Reverence communicates to me, that have obliged me to try to remove the obstacles to it, by dissipating with this letter the unjust preoccupation our mission causes some people. It is also for this same reason that Reverend Father Le Mercier, our Superior General, encouraged me to do so over a year ago, as he knew I am filled with esteem and affection for our tasks. All these reasons were required to make me write for so long about a subject that is unknown to nobody, even if some people's knowledge is based on reports which contain little truth, and that were made by people who are prejudiced and reliant on their own experience.' From 'that is unknown to nobody' onwards has been crossed out.

quelque saint et quelque avantageux que soit mon emploi. Je sais que ce n'est pas beaucoup d'avoir été en Jérusalem, mais d'avoir bien vécu en Jérusalem; ce qui est [38ᵛ] d'autant plus vrai, pour notre Amérique, que les dangers y sont plus grands de s'y oublier de son salut, en travaillant à celui des autres. Dans nos cases nous sommes souvent sans compagnon, et dans nos petits voyages, nous le sommes toujours.[80] Notre Seigneur y supplée par sa sainte crainte,[81] et par sa présence réelle dans le Saint-Sacrement auprès duquel nous sommes logés, et que nous avons souvent pendu au col, et caché sur le cœur pour l'aller assez loin porter aux malades: et enfin la confiance en la miséricorde de Dieu qui nous voit exposés au péril par le seul désir de lui plaire, nous console dans notre crainte, qui ne laisse pas d'être assez grande, pour vous prier[82] instamment, d'obtenir, par vos saints sacrifices, que Dieu ait pitié de moi car la vie de mes compagnons me fait bien de la confusion. Et si dans cette lettre, je n'ai rapporté que ce qui se passe dans le quartier dont les supérieurs m'ont chargé, ce n'a été que pour rendre les choses plus croyables voyant que celui qui les rapporte en est le témoin oculaire.[83] Je ne parle pas non plus à Votre R. de la mission de Cayenne et de la terre ferme de l'Amérique, où je n'ai pas été, et où il n'y a aucun autre prêtre, ni missionnaire, que de notre Compagnie. Tout ce que j'en puis dire est que cette mission est très désolée, ayant été ruinée deux fois, par les Anglais, et par les Hollandais et grandement affligée par la perte du vaisseau qui y portait quatre des nôtres avec tout ce qui était nécessaire pour son rétablissement. C'est néanmoins le poste du monde le plus avantageux pour la conversion d'une infinité de nations indiennes qui habitent ce vaste et grand pays, qui sont très dociles, d'un naturel très doux, dont les langues sont fort aisées à apprendre et à prononcer, et qui vivent toutes [39ʳ] en une parfaite intelligence avec les Français, quoiqu'ordinairement elles aient guerre ensemble, dans lesquelles les Français ne prennent aucun parti. Cette seule mission capable d'occuper un nombre très grand de missionnaires n'en a cependant qu'un seul qui est de la province de Guyenne, et un autre de celle de France que nous venons tout présentement d'apprendre y être arrivé avec un de nos frères. *Sed quid Inter tantos.* Aussi dans la crainte qu'a N. R. P. Supérieur général que les deux pères ne s'abandonnassent par trop au travail, il leur a ordonné de s'appliquer uniquement aux Français, et aux nègres sans penser du tout aux Indiens, jusqu'à tant[84] qu'ils aient reçu du secours.

---

[80] MdC, MS 73, fol. 68ʳ: 'dans nos cases nous sommes quelques-uns sans compagnon, et dans nos voyages nous le sommes tous.'
[81] MdC, MS 73, fol. 68ʳ: 'par sa sainte miséricorde'.
[82] MdC, MS 73, fol. 68ʳ: 'par le seul désir de lui plaire retranche tout ce que notre crainte pourrait avoir de chagrin; elle ne laisse pas d'être assez grande en moi pour vous prier'.
[83] MdC, MS 73, fol. 68ʳ: 'Et si dans cet écrit j'ai plutôt marqué ce qui se passe dans mon quartier, que dans le leur, ce n'a été que dans l'intention de rendre les choses plus croyables à l'égard de ceux qui verront que celui qui les rapporte en est le témoin oculaire, quoique je sois assuré d'ailleurs, que je cède en toute façon aux autres missionnaires de qui j'apprends tous les jours, et à vivre, et à travailler. Je suis V. a.' The MdC, MS 73 letter ends here.
[84] BM, Ant MS 9 reads 'jusqu'à temps'.

have more need of it, however holy and advantageous my occupation may be. I know that what matters is not to have been to Jerusalem, but to have lived well in Jerusalem.[45] This is all the more true for our America in that the dangers of forgetting about one's own salvation are greater, while working for that of others. In our cabins we are often without anybody else, and, in the short trips we take, we are always alone. Our Lord compensates for this with His holy fear, and by His real presence in the Holy Sacrament, near which we are housed, and which we often wear around our necks, hidden close to our hearts, when we bring it to the sick who are far enough away. Finally, confidence in the mercy of God, who sees us exposed to danger solely for the desire to please Him, consoles us in our fear, which is nonetheless sufficiently great to entreat you with urgency to obtain, through your holy sacrifices, God's pity on me, for the lives of my companions perturb me greatly. If in this letter I have only reported what is happening in the quarter which my superiors assigned me, this has only been for greater credibility, seeing that the reporter is an eyewitness.[46] I will not speak to your Reverence about the mission of Cayenne and the mainland of America either, as I have not been there, and there are no other priests or missionaries there but those of our Society. All I can say about this is that this mission is very desolate, having been ruined twice by the English, and the Hollanders, and greatly afflicted by the loss of a vessel which was bringing four of ours to it, with everything necessary for its re-establishment. It is nonetheless the most advantageous place in the world for the conversion of an infinite number of Indian peoples who inhabit this great, vast land, and who are very docile, very gentle in nature, whose languages are very easy to learn and to pronounce, and who all live in perfect intelligence with the French, even though amongst themselves they are habitually at war. The French do not take sides in these wars. This mission, which could alone occupy a great number of missionaries, has nonetheless only one member who is from the province of Guyenne, and another from the province of France, whom as we have just learned, has arrived there with one of our brothers.[47] *Sed quid inter tantos.*[48] As our Reverend Father Superior General feared the two priests would take on too much work, he ordered them to devote themselves to the French and the blacks alone, without even thinking about the Indians until such time as they have received assistance.

[45] 'Non Ierosolymis fuisse, sed Ierosolymis bene vixisse laudandum est', Saint Jerome, *Ad Paulinum, de institutione monachi*, in *Opus epistolarum divi Hieronymi Stridonensis* (Paris: apud Carolum Guillard, 1546), fols 35^r–36^r.

[46] MdC, MS 73, fol. 68^r: 'If in this letter I have discussed what is happening in my quarter rather than in theirs, it is only through good faith towards those who will see that the person reporting this is an eyewitness, although I acknowledge moreover that I learn to live and to work each day from the other missionaries. I am'. The MdC, MS 73 letter ends here.

[47] The provinces of Guyenne and of France correspond to the *Provincia Aquitaniae* and *Provincia Franciae*, respectively. The *brother* referred to here would have been an unordained Jesuit.

[48] 'sed haec quid sunt propter tantos?', John 6. 9 ('but what are these among so many?', 1582, p. 233).

Quatre mois après avoir écrit cette lettre je me suis souvenu que je ne l'avais pas encore envoyée. C'est donc le 10e mai 1679 qu'elle part de mes mains, sans savoir quelle sera son aventure durant ce délai, nous avons appris de nos pères de Paris, et de Nantes, que les états de Languedoc ont demandé au pape, la béatification du P. Régis, et supplié le roi de s'y employer près de sa Sainteté. Cette nouvelle nous a donné bien de la joie, et je n'ai pas douté que cette affaire ne fût un effet de l'esprit et du zèle de V. R.: si elle me voulait envoyer quelques images de ce bienheureux, quelques exemplaires de sa vie, et de la terre de son tombeau, ce serait un moyen pour le faire connaître ici, où l'on n'en a d'autres connaissances que celle que j'en ai pu donner dans mon quartier à quelques malades, parmi lesquels, il y a deux ans qu'une femme voulant se mettre dans des remèdes très périlleux, pour guérir d'une maladie habituelle et fort fâcheuse, elle m'appela pour se confesser, et se disposer à la mort. Je lui conseillai de faire [39^V] vœu de se confesser et communier le jour de la mort du P. Régis, elle le fit, se mit dans ces remèdes, guérit parfaitement et vint rendre son vœu. Je prêtai la vie de ce saint homme à une honnête famille de mon quartier, mais comme je redemandai mon livre je trouvai qu'ils avaient eu la dévotion et la patience de l'écrire, tout du long. Le cœur me dit que ce saint va remplir de miracles toute notre Amérique, et comme je sais que V. R. y a très grande dévotion je la prie très humblement de lui demander pour moi cet esprit apostolique dont il était si plein afin que je puisse faire mon salut et travailler utilement à celui de tant d'âmes que Dieu a commises à ma charge. C'est en lui et pour lui que je suis avec toute sorte de respect.

De V. R. Le très humble et très obéissant serviteur Jean Mongin

Four months after having written this letter I remembered that I had not yet sent it. It is as such on 10 May 1679 that it leaves my hands, and who knows what will happen to it, in this time, we have learned from our Fathers in Paris and Nantes that the Estates of Languedoc have asked the pope to beatify Father Régis, and entreated the king to intervene with his Holiness.[49] This news has given us much joy, and I had no doubt that this affair was the result of the intelligence and zeal of your Reverence. If you were so kind as to send me some pictures of this blessed man, some copies of his biography, and some earth from his tomb, that would be a way to make him known here, for here all they know about him is what I have told a few sick people in my quarter. Amongst these there was a woman two years ago who wanted to take some very dangerous remedies, so as to be cured of a very common and troublesome illness. She called for me to confess her and to prepare her for death. I advised her to make a vow to confess and to take Communion on the anniversary of the death of Father Régis. She did so, took her remedies, was completely healed and came to fulfil her pledge. I lent the *Life* of this holy man to a decent family of my quarter, and when I asked for my book back I found that they had had the devotion and the patience to copy it all out. My heart tells me that this saint is going to fill all our America with miracles, and, as I know that your Reverence has a great devotion to him, I humbly request you to ask of him for me the apostolic spirit of which he was so filled so that I may obtain my salvation and work usefully for that of the many souls that God has committed to my care. It is through Him and for Him that I am with all respect,

Your Reverence's very humble and obedient servant, Jean Mongin

---

[49] Régis was beatified in 1716. Daubenton, p. 338.

LETTER 3

Vanves,
AFSI, GBro185, fols 1^{r}–49^{v}.

The beginning of the alternative version of this letter in MdC, MS 73 has been transcribed separately in Letter 4 [Extract].[1]

[1^{r}] Copie de la lettre du père Jean Mongin, missionnaire de l'Amérique, à une personne de condition de Languedoc, écrite de l'île de Saint-Christophe au mois de mai <u>1682</u>.

Monsieur,

La lettre, que je me donnai l'honneur de vous écrire, il y a quelque temps, dans laquelle j'avais touché en peu de mots les travaux de nos pères employés au salut des nègres, n'ayant pas pleinement satisfait votre désir, j'obéis à présent à l'ordre que vous m'avez donné de vous mander les choses plus en détail, ce que je vous prie de trouver bon que je fasse, sans garder aucun ordre, et à mesure qu'elles me viennent dans l'esprit, la multitude d'occupations que j'ai, ne me permettant pas de le faire autrement, je m'acquitte à la vérité de cette obligation un peu tard, mais j'ai cru ne me devoir pas contenter de ce que nos pères qui avaient été pasteurs des nègres, m'avaient appris. J'ai voulu par ma propre expérience en prendre connaissance particulière,[2] avant que de [1^{v}] vous en rien mander, ce que je puis faire à présent, le Révérend Père Supérieur général m'ayant ôté tout autre emploi, et donné le soin des nègres d'un quartier de cette île, je vous ferai donc part de ce que j'ai fait près de ces pauvres gens depuis un an que les supérieurs m'y ont appliqué.

Vous vous souvenez peut-être bien Monsieur, que je vous mandai il y a quelque temps, que nous avons trois sortes de gens à cultiver en ce pays, savoir,

---

[1] Variations between the AFSI, GBro185 and MdC, MS 73 versions will be indicated in the notes here from AFSI, GBro185, fol. 9^{r} onwards; the number of textual variations of six words or less, as a rule of thumb, indicated in the notes has been limited; syntactical reformulations have not been indicated.

[2] AFSI, GBro185, fol. 1^{r}: 'une' has been inserted before 'connaissance particulière'.

TRANSLATION 3

Vanves,
AFSI, GBro185, fols 1^{r}–49^{v}.

Copy of the Letter of Father Jean Mongin, Missionary to the Americas, to a Person of Quality of Languedoc, Written on the Island of Saint Christopher in the Month of May 1682.

Dear Sir,

As you were not fully satisfied by the letter that I had the honour of writing you some time ago, in which I briefly described the labours of our Fathers working for the salvation of the slaves, I am now obeying the order you gave me to send you a more detailed description. I ask you to accept me doing this without following any order, and as things come to my mind, as the multitude of tasks that I have do not allow me to do so otherwise. In truth, I am fulfilling this obligation a little late, but I thought that I should not content myself with what I had learned from our Fathers who had been pastors to the slaves. I wanted to gain first-hand knowledge through my own experience before sending you anything, which I can now do as the Reverend Father Superior General has relieved me of all other tasks, and given me the care of the slaves of a part of this island. I will now tell you about what I have done amongst these poor people in the year since my superiors sent me amongst them.

You will perhaps remember, Sir, that I wrote to you some time ago that we have three sorts of people to instruct in this land. There are the French who are

les Français, qui y sont en grand nombre répandus en diverses îles, et qui y viennent pour y [*sic*] faire fortune; les nègres, qu'on y transporte des côtes d'Afrique, pour les travaux des sucres et des autres ouvrages du pays; et les Indiens originaires de l'Amérique, qui habitent quelques îles, mais qui sont en un nombre presque infini dans la terre ferme de l'Amérique. Ils étaient autrefois les maîtres de toutes les îles, occupées à présent par les Espagnols, par les Anglais, par les Français et par les Hollandais, mais tant par la guerre que ces Indiens ont eue avec les Européens, qui en ont exterminé un grand nombre, que par la facilité qu'ils avaient de se retirer ailleurs, ils ont laissé les Européens en possession de leurs terres, et sont allés pour la plupart en terre ferme.

[2^r] Il en reste cependant encore bon nombre dans deux ou trois îles, où ils sont les maîtres, parmi lesquels mêmes il y a un très grand nombre de nègres, qui y ont été jetés par le naufrage de quelques vaisseaux, qui en étaient chargés, et par leur désertion de la maison de leurs maîtres, ce qu'ils font quelquefois, quand ils en sont maltraités, et qu'ils peuvent se saisir de quelque canot, ou de quelque autre bâtiment, qui facilite leur évasion. Ces nègres fugitifs, que l'on appelle dans les îles *nègres marrons*, étaient autrefois esclaves des Indiens des îles où ils s'étaient sauvés, mais leur nombre s'est tellement multiplié, qu'ils se sont cantonnés tous ensemble, et qu'ils ont obligé les Indiens de les laisser habiter leurs terres. Ils sont quelquefois en paix ensemble, et quelquefois en guerre. Ces nègres marrons, dont une bonne partie a reçu le baptême, conservent encore quelque sorte de souvenir de ce qu'ils ont appris, faisant le signe de la croix, et quelques-uns faisant leurs prières. Si nous avions un peu plus de missionnaires, on en pourrait envoyer quelqu'un demeurer parmi eux, pour ne les laisser pas tout à fait dans l'abandon.

Nous cultivons donc en ce pays des gens de trois parties du monde, des Français, et quelques autres nations [2^v] de l'Europe, qui sont mêlées parmi nous; des nègres qui sont Africains, et les Indiens originaires de l'Amérique. Il n'y a que l'Asie qui ne nous fournisse point d'emploi, et pour parler en termes du pays, nous y avons des blancs, qui sont les Européens, des noirs, qui sont les nègres, et des rouges, qui sont les Indiens. Ce n'est pas qu'ils soient rouges naturellement, mais tant à cause de l'été continuel du pays, et des couleurs, dont ils se frottent le corps, et se peignent le visage, ils paraissent de couleur rougeâtre. Laissant donc les blancs et les rouges, je ne vous parlerai à présent que des noirs, selon que vous avez desiré que je fisse.

La terre de ce pays, et les fruits qu'elle produit, se cultivant comme les jardins à main d'homme, et non par les chevaux et les bœufs, comme font nos laboureurs en France, il est nécessaire d'avoir un grand nombre d'hommes pour cette culture. Nos premiers Français, qui ont passé dans nos îles, ne se servaient pour tous les travaux du pays, que de pauvres gens qu'ils embarquaient sur les ports de mer, et qui s'engageaient à leur service pour trois ans, mais comme ils

scattered around various islands in great number, and who come here to make their fortune; the blacks, who are transported here from the coasts of Africa and made work in sugar production and other labours of this land; and the Indians who are native to the Americas, who live on diverse islands but who are in nearly infinite number on the American mainland.[1] Once they were masters of all the islands now occupied by the Spanish, the English, the French, and the Dutch, but, because of the war between these Indians and the Europeans who exterminated a great number of them, and the ease with which they could withdraw elsewhere, they left the Europeans in possession of their lands, and most of them have gone to the mainland.

Nonetheless, there [are] still a good number of them on two or three islands, where they are the masters, and amongst whom there are a very considerable number of blacks. These blacks are either survivors of the wrecks of vessels carrying slaves, or have deserted from their master's household, which slaves sometimes do when they are mistreated and can get their hands on a canoe or another vessel to enable their escape. These fugitive slaves, who are called *maroon slaves* on the islands, were once slaves of the Indians of the islands where they took refuge, but their number has since multiplied so much that they have settled together and forced the Indians to let them live on their own lands. Sometimes they live in peace, and sometimes they are at war. These *maroon slaves*, a good number of whom were baptized, still have some memory of what they learned, making the sign of the cross, and some of them saying their prayers. If we had a few more missionaries, we could send one to live amongst them, so as not to leave them in complete abandon.

We instruct, then, people from three parts of the world: the French, and some other European peoples who are amongst us; the blacks who are Africans; and the Indians who are native to the Americas. It is only Asia that gives us nothing to do. To speak in the language of this land, we have whites, who are Europeans, blacks, who are African slaves, and the red-skinned, or the Indians. They are not naturally red-skinned, but, because of the continual summertime in this land, and the colours which they rub into their bodies, and with which they paint their faces, they appear a sort of red colour. Leaving the whites and the red-skinned to the side, I will now only talk to you about the blacks, as you desired me to do.

As the earth of this land, and the fruits it produces, are cultivated in the way gardens are, by hand, rather than with horses and oxen as our labourers do in France, a great number of men are needed for this culture. The first Frenchmen who came to our islands only used poor people for all the labour of the land, whom they embarked at the seaports, and who contracted themselves into their service for three years. But, as they saw that they could not find

---

[1]   Mongin is referring to North and South America.

ont vu qu'ils ne pouvaient pas trouver le nombre de Français nécessaire pour leur service, que la dépense des voyages, de la nourriture [3ʳ] et de l'entretien de ces engagés, était fort grande, et qu'au bout des trois ans ils devenaient libres, ils ont voulu imiter les Espagnols et les Portugais, qui, depuis longtemps, se servaient des nègres pour esclaves, dans l'Amérique, de sorte que, encore que dans la France il ne soit pas permis d'avoir des esclaves, qui y mettant le pied à terre acquièrent leur liberté, le droit d'esclavage est établi dans notre Amérique française, soit par déclaration du roi, soit par tolérance et un usage établi, c'est de quoi je ne suis pas bien informé. De sorte qu'à l'imitation des Espagnols et des Portugais, nos vaisseaux français vont à présent tous les ans en bon nombre à la côte occidentale d'Afrique, qui est d'une immense étendue, acheter des nègres, en échange desquels ils donnent des merceries, de la quincaillerie, et autres denrées de peu de valeur. Ils chargent leurs vaisseaux de nègres, tant qu'ils en peuvent porter, tel vaisseau en portera quatre, cinq et six cents, hommes, femmes, filles et garçons. L'on les vend au marché, comme l'on fait les chevaux, selon leur âge, leur force, et la vigueur de leur corps. Ils sont bientôt enlevés, qui en donne le plus, les emporte, en moins de rien un vaisseau qui en est plein, a tout vendu. Un nègre jeune, fort et vigoureux coûtera cent écus, [3ᵛ] celui qui a plus de nègres est le plus riche. Les rois du pays des nègres, dont quelques-uns sont fort puissants, se font la guerre avec des armées de dix, quinze et vingt mille hommes, ils font les uns sur les autres des prisonniers en grand nombre, qu'ils vendent. Les mêmes rois vendent aussi leurs sujets, quand ils leur ont déplu, et même pour très peu de chose, comme par exemple pour avoir ôté une plume des paons de leurs rois, ou touché à une calebasse de celles qui sont attachées aux palmiers, pour en recevoir la liqueur.

La justice qu'ils ont parmi eux condamne à l'esclavage pour peu de chose, ceux qui tombent entre ses mains, un père vendra ses enfants, et quelquefois ses femmes, quand elles lui déplaisent, et même il arrive quelquefois que lorsque les vaisseaux sont en rade pour cette traite, les nègres qui se trouveront sur la côte les plus forts, enlèveront de force ceux qu'ils rencontreront en leur chemin, et les vendront au vaisseau. Nous avons vu dans nos îles des reines du pays qui étaient esclaves, et que les rois qui en étaient mécontents avaient vendues de la sorte, auxquelles cependant les nègres sujets du même prince, qui étaient aussi esclaves, portaient grand respect, faisant quelquefois [4ʳ] leur besogne, portant leurs fardeaux, et leur donnant à manger, de ce qu'ils avaient de meilleur.

Au commencement que les Portugais tirèrent des nègres des côtes d'Afrique, ils usaient de quelque circonscription dans ce trafic, et n'en achetaient point qu'ils ne se fussent informés du droit qu'avait le vendeur sur eux, mais à présent on les achète sans s'informer du droit de ceux qui leur vendent, et on charge dans les vaisseaux tous ceux qui se présentent, et cependant quand ils sont une fois vendus, ils demeurent esclaves toute leur vie et toute leur postérité.

a sufficient number of Frenchmen for their service, and that the expense of these voyages, the food, and the upkeep of these indentured labourers was very great, and that after three years they became free, they did as the Spanish and the Portuguese, who have been using blacks as their slaves in America for a long time. As a result, although in France it is not permitted to have slaves, who gain their freedom once their feet touch French soil, the right of slavery is established in our French America. Whether this is by the king's declaration, or by tolerance and established use, I cannot answer. As such, like the Spanish and the Portuguese, our French vessels now go every year in great number to the west coast of Africa, which is an immense area. There they buy slaves, giving in exchange haberdashery and hardware, and other products of little value. They load their vessels up with as many slaves as they can carry, with one vessel carrying four, five or six hundred men, women, girls, and boys. They are sold in the marketplace like horses, according to their age, their strength, or the vigour of their body. They are soon bought, and whoever gives the most gets them. In no time at all a fully laden vessel will have sold the lot. A slave who is young, vigorous, and strong will cost a hundred *écus*, and whoever has the most slaves is the richest.[2] The kings of the land of the blacks, some of whom are very powerful, make war upon each other with armies of ten, fifteen, or twenty thousand men. They take great numbers of prisoners from each other, and they sell them. The same kings sell their subjects when they are displeased with them, and even for minor things, for example for taking a feather from their kings' peacocks, or touching one of the gourds that are attached to palm trees to collect their sap.[3]

Their form of justice condemns those who fall foul of the law to enslavement for minor infractions. A father will sell his children, and sometimes his wives when he is dissatisfied with them. Amongst the blacks along the coast, sometimes the strongest will take away by force those they cross on their way, and sell them to vessels, when they are lying offshore for this trade. In our islands, we have seen queens of these lands who had been sold into slavery by the kings who were displeased with them. However, the Africans who were subjects of the same monarch, and who were also slaves, would show great respect to these queens, sometimes carrying out their labour, carrying their loads, and giving them the best of what they had to eat.

When the Portuguese first brought black slaves from the African coasts, they showed some circumspection in this trade, and did not buy any without enquiring about the right that the vendor had over them. However, nowadays buyers purchase them without asking questions about the right of those who are selling them, and all those who are up for sale are loaded into the vessels, and once they are sold they remain slaves for their entire lives, as do all their descendants.

---

[2] One *écu* was equivalent to three *livres*; one *livre* to twenty *sous*.
[3] Both claims are made by Molina, with the punishment for taking a peacock's feather attributed to the king of Angola (Molina, *De iustitia et iure*, I, col. 174).

Comme cette côte d'Afrique est d'une très grande étendue, il y a des cantons où les nègres sont bien plus recherchés que d'autres,[3] à cause qu'ils sont plus vigoureux, et de plus grand travail. Ceux d'Angole sont les plus estimés, et ceux du Cap-Vert le sont le moins, à cause de leur paresse, et qu'ils s'estiment entre les nègres comme nos gentilshommes de deçà. Ils sont néanmoins assez propres pour être ouvriers, et non pas pour les travaux de la terre.

Il ne se passe point d'année que les Français, les Espagnols, les Portugais, les Anglais, et les Hollandais n'enlèvent plus de vingt mille nègres, et nonobstant cela le nombre ne diminue pas dans le pays, [4ᵛ] qui est extraordinairement peuplé. Il y a des cantons des royaumes de ces nègres, qui sont aussi peuplés et la terre aussi cultivée que les environs de Paris.

Ces nègres ont les qualités qu'Aristote demande pour être bons esclaves, la force du corps, et la pesanteur de l'esprit, car les nègres sont gens de très grand travail, et de peu d'ouverture d'esprit. Il s'en trouve cependant plusieurs parmi eux qui ne manquent pas d'entendement, et qui sont capables de toute sorte d'arts et de science, si on les y avait élevés.

Les Espagnols ont dans le Pérou et dans leurs autres états de l'Amérique un nombre presque infini de nègres, qu'ils occupent à toute sorte de travaux mais particulièrement à tirer les métaux de la terre, car encore qu'ils se servent aussi des Indiens pour cela, ce n'est que pour un certain temps, le Conseil des Indes ayant ordonné que ces Indiens seraient renvoyés dans leurs maisons après le service de trois mois, au lieu que les nègres servent toute l'année sans aucun relâche, et que leurs enfants et toute leur postérité demeurent esclaves.

Les Portugais en ont aussi un très grand nombre dans le Brésil, pour la culture des sucres et du pétun, et pour la coupe du bois de brésil.

[5ʳ] Les Hollandais et les Anglais en ont pareillement beaucoup dans leurs colonies, particulièrement les Anglais. On fait état, que dans la seule île de la Barbade,[4] il y en a plus de cinquante à soixante mille, qui diverses fois se sont révoltés contre leurs maîtres, mais toujours sans succès.

Outre le trafic que toutes les nations de l'Europe font d'hommes à la côte d'Afrique, ils y font encore commerce de très riches marchandises comme de la poudre d'or, de l'ambre gris, des dents d'éléphant, de la gomme, des cuirs de bœufs ou de vaches, dont le pays est tout plein, et de diverses autres marchandises.

Quoique les vaisseaux qui vont à la traite des nègres les achètent assez peu de chose, ils étaient néanmoins autrefois à meilleur marché, et dans le royaume de Borno l'on donnait vingt esclaves pour un cheval, et autant dans celui d'Angole, pour un chien trois esclaves, dans celui de Congo pour la queue d'un éléphant, et un en Guinée pour un petit couteau.

---

3   AFSI, GBro185, fol. 4ʳ: 'dans' inserted to read 'que dans d'autres'.
4   AFSI, GBro185, fol. 5ʳ reads 'la Barbaude'.

As this coast of Africa is great in area, there are cantons where slaves are sought far more than in others, because they are more vigorous and laborious. Those of Angola are most esteemed, and those of Cape Verde least so because of their sloth, and because they think of themselves amongst Africans as our gentlemen think of themselves amongst us. They are nonetheless suitable enough for more skilled labour, and not for working the land.

Not a year goes by without the French, the Spanish, the Portuguese, the English, and the Dutch taking away more than twenty thousand African slaves, and in spite of this the number in the land, which is extraordinarily populous, does not lessen. There are cantons in the kingdoms of these blacks which are as heavily populated, and the land as cultivated, as the hinterland of Paris.

These blacks have the traits that are needed in good slaves according to Aristotle: bodily strength and slowness of thought, because they are people who can work very hard, and have little mental capacity.[4] There are nonetheless many among them who are not lacking in understanding, and who would be capable of all manner of arts and science, if they had been brought up studying them.

The Spanish, in Peru and in their other possessions in the Americas, have a near-infinite number of black slaves whom they put to all sorts of labours, but particularly to extracting metals from the earth, for, although they also use Indians for this, it is only for a set time. The Council of the Indies ordered that these Indians should be sent back to their homes after a period of service of three months, but the blacks serve all year long with no let-up, and their children and all their descendants are slaves.[5]

The Portuguese also have a great number of slaves in Brazil for the cultivation of sugar and tobacco, and for logging Brazil-wood. The Dutch and the English also have a great number in their colonies, particularly the English. It is reported that on the island of Barbados alone, there are more than fifty to sixty thousand, who have at various times rebelled against their masters, but always without success.

Apart from the trade in men that all the nations of Europe engage in on the African coast, they also deal in very costly merchandise like gold dust, ambergris, elephant tusks, gum,[6] the hides of oxen or cows, of which the land is full, and diverse other merchandise.

Although the vessels that trade in slaves buy them for very little, they used to be cheaper nonetheless, and in the kingdom of Borno they would give twenty slaves for a horse, and the same number in the kingdom of Angola, three slaves for a hound, [the same number] in the Congo for an elephant tail, and one in Guinea for a little knife.[7]

---

[4] Aristotle, p. 23.
[5] The Council of the Indies (Consejo de Indias), founded in 1524, administered the Spanish colonial possessions in the Americas.
[6] *Gum*: potentially gum Arabic (*Acacia Senegal*).
[7] *Borno*, or Bornu. The claim that, in this kingdom, 'ils donnent 15 voire 20 [esclaves] pour

Le traitement que l'on fait aux nègres est très misérable, car ils n'ont point d'autre vêtement qu'un caleçon et les femmes une jupe de grosse toile. Leur nourriture est de quatre livres de cassave par semaine, qui est un pain fait de racines, qui est moins bon que celui de blé, et une livre et demie de viande salée aussi par semaine. Leur case pour leur logement et [5ᵛ] pour toute leur famille, est d'environ vingt-quatre pieds de long sur douze de large, en laquelle ils pratiquent divers petits appartements. J'en vis l'autre jour une, qui dans ce petit espace avait huit petits réduits qui n'avaient aucune vue l'un sur l'autre. Il y en a parmi eux de fort industrieux qui par leur adresse, et par la culture de quelques terres qu'on leur donne, vivent fort commodément et souvent se traitent mieux que plusieurs de nos Français. On les fait continuellement travailler, et quelquefois, au temps que les travaux sont pressés, la plus grande partie de la nuit, et nonobstant ce grand travail, et le mauvais traitement, ils ne laissent pas d'être très joyeux, de se railler les uns des autres, et ils danseraient nuit et jour, qui les croirait. Ils tiennent toujours du feu dans leurs cases pendant la nuit, ce que font pareillement les Indiens, car la nuit est froide, et les uns et les autres se portent bien.

Vous me demanderez peut-être: d'où vient cette différence de couleur des peuples de la plus grande partie de l'Afrique, qui sont noirs, et des autres parties du monde, dont les habitants sont blancs, et même d'une partie de l'Afrique, où ils sont pareillement blancs. Je ne crois pas que personne vous en puisse rendre aucune raison la moins du monde vraisemblable, car de dire ce que croit le vulgaire, que cette noirceur vienne de la chaleur de la zone torride, [6ʳ] qu'habitent les nègres, qui les brûle, et qui leur donne cette couleur, est une erreur toute pure, car outre que la chaleur n'est pas telle que nous la croyons, à cause des vents continuels, qu'il fait dans la zone torride, qui tempèrent extrêmement la chaleur, aussi bien que la froideur et la longueur des nuits, et les grandes rosées qui rafraîchissent notablement l'air, et qui rendent la terre plus fertile, il est certain que, communément sous la zone torride il ne fait point plus chaud qu'en France en été, et bien moins qu'en Italie et en Espagne. Si cette chaleur était si grande, comment serait-il possible que la zone torride fût si pleine de peuples, qu'elle est, car en beaucoup d'endroits elle est notablement plus habitée que l'Europe. Mais pour faire voir invinciblement que ce n'est point la zone torride, qui donne cette couleur aux peuples qui l'habitent, c'est que la plus grande partie de l'Asie et de l'Amérique, étant aussi bien que l'Afrique sous la zone torride, ces peuples y sont cependant blancs, du moins basanés, comme sont en Europe les gens, qui en été travaillent à la campagne. Ce n'est pas seulement en la couleur que les nègres sont différents de toutes les autres nations. Ils le sont encore dans les traits du visage, dans la couleur des yeux, et la figure du nez, dans les cheveux qui sont toujours frisés et retroussés, dans la peau qui est douce et lisse comme du satin, et en la couleur des dents, qui est

The blacks are very poorly treated, as they have no other clothing but a pair of breeches, and the women wear a coarse fabric skirt. They have, per week, four pounds of cassava, which is a type of bread made of roots, and which is not as good as that made from wheat, and a pound and a half of salted meat.[8] The cabins that house them and their families are about twenty-four feet long and twelve wide, and they divide them up into various little rooms. I saw one the other day in which such a little space had been divided up into eight little cubicles, not one of which looked upon another. Some slaves are very industrious, and, through know-how and cultivating a little land they are given, they live very well and often better than many of our own Frenchmen. They are put to work continuously and sometimes, when the work is urgent, for the greater part of the night, and, despite this harsh labour and bad treatment, they are still very joyful, never tire of making fun of one another, and could dance night and day. Who would believe it?[9] They always have a fire going in their cabins at night, as do the Indians, because the night is cold, and one and the other are in fine fettle.

What, you may ask me, causes the difference in colour between the peoples of the greater part of Africa, who are black, and those inhabitants of the other parts of the world who are white (and even those of part of Africa, where they are also white)? I do not think that anyone can give you an explanation that is in any way satisfactory, as to say, as it is commonly believed, that this blackness is due to the heat of the Torrid Zone inhabited by the blacks, and which burns them and gives them this colour, is completely erroneous. For, apart from the fact that the heat there is not as we imagine, because of the continual winds that greatly temper it, there is in addition the coldness and the length of the nights, and the great dews that greatly cool the air, and that make the land more fertile. It is certain that, in the Torrid Zone, it is ordinarily no hotter than summer in France, and a lot less so than in Italy and Spain. If the heat were so extreme, how would it be possible for the Torrid Zone to be as full of people as it is, for in many places it is considerably more populous than Europe? Yet what incontestably demonstrates that it is not at all the Torrid Zone that gives this colour to the people who live in it is that the greater part of Asia and America is in the Torrid Zone, as much as Africa is, and their peoples are nonetheless white, or at most olive-skinned, as with people in Europe who work in the countryside in summer. It is not only in their colour that black Africans are different from all other peoples. They are also distinct in their facial features, in the colour of their eyes and the shape of their nose, in their hair which is always frizzy and which sticks out, in their skin which is soft and smooth like satin, and in the colour of their teeth which are as white as can be. This difference

un cheval' is made in d'Avity (p. 372), and that in Congo 'une seule ['queue d'éléphant'] se troque contre trois esclaves' (p. 446). Of Angola, d'Avity writes 'il y a des chiens de la grandeur des dogues d'Angleterre, pour lesquels on a donné vingt-deux esclaves' (p. 455).
[8] Under the *Code Noir*, masters were obliged to give 'two pounds of salted beef' ('deux livres de bœuf salé') to their slaves each week. *Code Noir*, Article 22 (1718), p. 6.
[9] The French reads 'qui les croirait'; the sense implies 'who would believe it?'.

de la dernière blancheur. Cette différence vient sans doute [6ᵛ] de race, et non point par aucune température de l'air, ni par aucun principe étranger, car des noirs engendreront immanquablement toujours des noirs, en quelque pays du monde qu'ils se trouvent, comme pareillement des blancs engendreront toujours des blancs, quand ils seraient au milieu du pays des nègres. L'on assure même que dans la Guinée il y a quelques cantons de blancs, dans l'île de Madagascar, qui n'est séparée de la côte orientale d'Afrique, que d'un petit bras de mer, les originaires de l'île sont blancs, quoique ceux de la côte voisine soient tout noirs.

Un blanc et une noire engendreront un enfant, qui sera d'une couleur, ni si noire que celle d'un nègre, ni aussi blanche que celle d'un blanc, mais entre les deux. On appelle des gens de la sorte des mulâtres, dont l'Amérique possédée par les Européens est toute pleine. Si ce mulâtre a communication avec une blanche, les enfants en seront encore plus blancs, et si c'est avec une noire, les enfants seront encore plus noirs, et ainsi toujours de la sorte, jusqu'à tant qu'une des couleurs l'ait entièrement emporté sur l'autre.

On aura peine à croire une merveille que nous voyons tous les jours, qu'un enfant des nègres n'est pas noir en sa naissance, à la réserve d'un endroit du corps, et en trois semaines, ou un mois il devient tout à fait noir. Dieu seul peut savoir la véritable raison de cette différence des hommes qui viennent tous d'Adam et de Noé.

[7ʳ] Toute la côte tant orientale qu'occidentale d'Afrique à la réserve des côtes de Barbarie et des terres voisines, est toute peuplée de noirs, aussi bien sans doute que le dedans du pays. Il ne se tire néanmoins de nègres pour notre Amérique, que de la côte occidentale, l'orientale que l'on appelle la Cafrerie ou le pays des Cafres, à l'extrémité duquel est l'Éthiopie, est trop éloignée pour aller chercher des esclaves si loin.

Quand les vaisseaux nous ont mis à terre ces pauvres gens, ce qui arrive plusieurs fois l'année, et qu'ils ont été distribués dans les cases des habitants, le père missionnaire du quartier, où sont ces nègres nouveaux venus, s'informe de quel pays d'Afrique ils sont, et si par exemple il trouve que celui qu'il voudra instruire, est d'Ardes ou de Juda, royaumes de Guinée, il dira à quelque nègre de son pays, qui est déjà chrétien, qu'il apprenne au nouveau venu les principes du christianisme, et lui promettra récompense pour cela. Cet ancien nègre s'en acquitte le mieux qu'il peut, jusqu'à tant que ce nègre nouveau venu ait appris le français, ce qu'il fait en très peu de temps du moins de la manière que les nègres l'apprennent ordinairement, ce qu'ils font en assez peu de temps, dépendant pour toutes choses de leurs maîtres et de leurs commandeurs qui leur parlent toujours français, et pour de très bonnes raisons leur étant défendu de parler leur langue [7ᵛ] naturelle, ils auraient même de la peine à s'entendre autrement, y ayant quelquefois dans une case des nègres de dix ou douze langues. Leur pays est d'une si grande étendue, qu'il y a parmi eux un très grand nombre

is no doubt due to race, and by no means due to the temperature of the air or any external factor, because blacks will invariably beget blacks in whichever country in the world they are, as whites will similarly beget whites, were they to be in the middle of the land of the blacks. It is even assured that in Guinea there are several cantons of whites. On the island of Madagascar, which is only separated from the east coast of Africa by a narrow channel, the native peoples are white, although those of the neighbouring coast are all black.

A white man and a black woman will beget a child who will be of a colour that is neither as black as an African, nor as white as a white man, but between the two. People like this are called *mulâtres*, and [those parts of] the Americas possessed by the Europeans are full of them. If this *mulâtre* has congress with a white woman, the children will be still whiter than him, and if it is with a black woman then they will be blacker, and it will be like this always until one of the colours has entirely suppressed the other.

It will be difficult to believe a marvel that we see every day, which is that a child of black parents is not black at birth, except for one part of the body, and in three weeks or a month he becomes completely black. Only God alone may know the real reason for this difference between men who are all descended from Adam and Noah.

The entire coast of Africa, east as well as west, is inhabited by black people, with the exception of the Barbary Coast and the neighbouring lands. No doubt it is the same with the interior. Nonetheless, it is only from the west coast that blacks are taken for our Americas. The east coast, which is called the land of Cafraria,[10] and which has Ethiopia at its furthest limits, is too distant to go looking for slaves that far.

When the vessels have put these poor people ashore for us, which occurs many times during the year, and when they have been shared out in the planters' cabins, the missionary father of the locality where these slaves have recently arrived finds out what part of Africa they are from. If, for example, he finds out that the slave he has to instruct is from Ardra or Ouidah,[11] which are kingdoms in Guinea, he will tell some other slave from the same land who has already been Christianized to teach the new arrival the principles of Christianity, and promise him some reward for this. The elder slave will do the best he can, until the new arrival has learned French, which he will do in very little time, at least in the way the slaves ordinarily learn it. They usually learn it in little enough time, dependent as they are for everything on their masters and their overseers, who always speak French to them. There are very good reasons for it being forbidden for them to speak their native language. They would even have some trouble understanding one another otherwise, as there are sometimes ten or twelve native languages spoken by slaves living in the

[10] The term 'land of Cafraria' is used in Caesar Frederick, *The Voyage and Travell*, trans. by Thomas Hickocke, in *The Principal Navigations, Voyages, Traffiques and Discoveries of the English Nation*, ed. by Richard Hakluyt, 12 vols (Glasgow: James MacLehose, 1903–05), V (1904), 365–449 (p. 444).

[11] Ardra and Ouidah (Whydah) were states in modern-day Benin. The variations in Mongin's spelling of *Ardra* have been standardized in the translation of this letter.

de langues, de sorte que ce serait une chose infinie à un missionnaire de les apprendre. Nous avons cet avantage en notre mission en convertissant les nègres, qui n'est en aucune autre, en ce que nous travaillons au salut des infidèles, sans apprendre de langues. Il est vrai que ceux de nos pères, qui s'emploient au salut des Indiens originaires de l'Amérique, sont obligés d'apprendre leur langue,[5] mais elle est très aisée et composée de mots faciles à prononcer.

Notre mission des nègres a encore un autre avantage, qui est que le fruit qu'on fait est sûr, constant et assuré, et sans crainte que les nègres après leur instruction et leur baptême retournent à leur infidélité, car ils sont domestiques de nos Français, desquels ils dépendent pour toutes choses, et que même par leur propre intérêt, et par respects humains ils sont obligés de fréquenter l'église et les sacrements comme nous dirons ci-après, au lieu que souvent quand on a converti des infidèles, qui sont maîtres d'eux-mêmes, ils quittent assez souvent la foi et le christianisme, quand ils ne voient plus de missionnaires. Toute l'application doit être à inspirer la vertu aux nègres convertis, et à les entretenir dans les bonnes mœurs après leurs confessions.

[8ʳ] Les nègres ont appris en peu de temps un certain jargon français, que les missionnaires savent, et avec lequel ils les instruisent, qui est par l'infinitif du verbe, sans jamais le conjuguer, en y ajoutant quelques mots qui font connaître le temps et la personne de qui l'on parle, par exemple, s'ils veulent dire, *je veux prier Dieu demain*, ils diront *moi prier Dieu demain, moi manger hier, toi donner manger à moi*, et ainsi en toutes choses. Ce jargon est fort aisé à apprendre aux nègres et aux missionnaires aussi pour les instruire, et ainsi ils le donnent à entendre pour toutes choses.

Il faut ici dire une chose à l'avantage des nations catholiques, telles que sont les Français, les Espagnols, et les Portugais, qu'ils ont grand soin de l'instruction et de la conversion des nègres, au lieu que les Anglais et les Hollandais, qui en font pareillement commerce, n'ont pas seulement la pensée de les faire chrétiens, et de leur dire un mot pour leur rien apprendre, de sorte que les nègres dans les colonies de ces hérétiques, vivent et meurent de la même manière, que font leurs chevaux, sans jamais dire un mot de prières, sans aller à l'église et sans aucune connaissance des choses de l'autre monde. Croirait-on bien que les Anglais, qui ont dans toutes leurs colonies de l'Amérique, plus de cent mille nègres, qu'il n'y en a quasi pas un seul qui soit instruit, et [8ᵛ] qui vive chrétiennement. Les[6] hérétiques, comme disait un saint père, sont bien capables de faire un hérétique d'un catholique, mais on ne verra point qu'ils s'appliquent jamais à faire un chrétien d'un infidèle.

Quoique souvent les nègres des Anglais soient mieux nourris et mieux vêtus que les nôtres, ceux-ci ne voudraient pas cependant, pour quoi que ce soit,

---

5   AFSI, GBro185, fol. 7ᵛ: apparently 'leurs langues'.
6   AFSI, GBro185, fol. 8ᵛ: possibly 'Ces'.

same shack. Their homeland is so vast that there are a very great number of languages spoken amongst them, so that it would be an infinitely difficult task for a missionary to learn them. In our mission for the conversion of slaves, we have an advantage that none other has, which is that we work for the salvation of infidels without learning languages. It is true that those of our Fathers who are occupied with the salvation of the Indians native to the Americas are obliged to learn their language,[12] but it is very easy and composed of words which are easy to pronounce.

Our mission to the slaves has one more advantage, which is that the fruit of it is certain, constant, and assured, and without the fear that the slaves, after their instruction and their baptism, will go back to their infidelity, because they are attached to the households of our Frenchmen, on whom they depend for everything, and even for their own interest and through human respect they are obliged to frequent the church and the sacraments as will be discussed afterwards. This is unlike what often happens with the conversion of infidels who are their own masters; often enough these abandon faith and Christianity when they no longer see missionaries. All our effort has to be directed towards inspiring the virtue of the newly converted, and maintaining their good behaviour after their confessions.

The African slaves learn a sort of French jargon, which the missionaries know and with which they can instruct them. They use the infinitive of the verb, without ever conjugating it, adding a few words to indicate the tense and the person of whom they are speaking. For example, if they want to say, 'I want to pray to God tomorrow', they will say 'Me pray God tomorrow', 'Me eat yesterday', 'You give me eat', and so on in everything. This jargon is very easy to teach both to slaves and to the missionaries to instruct them, and so they use it to make themselves understood in all things.

One thing must be said in the favour of the Catholic peoples, such as the French, the Spanish, and the Portuguese; it is that they take great care in the instruction and conversion of black slaves. However, the English and the Dutch, who also trade in them, do not even think of Christianizing them or teaching them anything at all. The result is that the slaves in the colonies of these heretics live and die in the same manner as their horses do, without ever having said a word of prayer or gone to church, and having no knowledge whatsoever of the things of the other world. Is it believable that the English have more than one hundred thousand slaves in all their American colonies, and that there is hardly one who has been instructed and who lives Christianly? These heretics, as a holy Father said, are quite capable of making a heretic of a Catholic, but you will never see them try to make a Christian of an infidel.

Although the slaves of the English are often better nourished and better clothed than our own are, ours would not wish to change masters for anything,

---

[12] Apparently 'their languages' in the manuscript.

changer de maître, voyant le soin que l'on a de leur salut, et l'honneur qu'ils ont de venir à l'église, ce qui est si vrai, que les missionnaires ne trouvent point de moyen plus efficace dans les répréhensions qu'ils font aux nègres, quand ils sont dans le désordre, que de les menacer en leur jargon, *toi seras traité de même que nègre anglais sans baptême sans église, sans sépulture.*

Il serait à souhaiter qu'il y eût quelques-uns de nos pères au Cap-Vert, au Sénégal ou à Gorée où nos Français ont des établissements, pour pouvoir travailler au salut des nègres dans leur propre pays. On y ferait sans doute bien du fruit, quand ce ne serait qu'en baptisant les enfants qui meurent, ce qui arrive continuellement dans un pays si peuplé, et en baptisant aussi les enfants que l'on embarque, pour porter dans l'Amérique, dont une bonne partie meurt souvent en chemin. Les directeurs de cette compagnie d'Afrique le souhaitent beaucoup, mais nous avons tant de missions à fournir qu'il est impossible de [9^r] tant[7] entreprendre à la fois.

Je m'oubliais de parler de la religion qu'ont les nègres, dans leur pays. Il y a des nations qui ne croient rien du tout, d'autres qui reconnaissent un principe, et d'autres encore qui ont quelque connaissance du mahométisme, et qui sont circoncis, ce sont particulièrement ceux du Cap-Vert, à cause du voisinage des rois d'Afrique mahométans. Il y en a même quelques-uns, qui ont parmi eux des marabouts, qui est le nom que l'on donne aux prêtres mahométans, mais il se peut dire, qu'ils savent tous si peu ce qu'ils croient, que nous n'avons aucune difficulté de leur ôter leur créance, la difficulté uniquement est à introduire la nôtre et particulièrement les bonnes mœurs.[8]

Après avoir expliqué ce qui regarde les nègres en général, le détail dans lequel je vais entrer, en sera plus intelligible. Nous en avons quatre missions dans l'île de la Martinique, une dans celle de la Guadeloupe, deux dans cette île de Saint-Christophe,[9] et une à Cayenne, où comme j'ai dit,[10] nous sommes seuls de prêtres pour les Français, les nègres, et les Indiens. Je ne vous entretiendrai pas de ce que nous faisons parmi les Français, dans tous ces lieux. Il suffit de vous dire, que l'on y vit à présent avec plus de régularité qu'en France, que nous convertissons tous les ans un grand nombre d'huguenots, et rendons [9^v] toutes les assistances nécessaires à environ cent vaisseaux qui y viennent tous les ans en commerce. Il n'y a que les juifs que le commerce, qu'y ont fait autrefois les Hollandais, y a attirés, qui ne sont pas plus dociles qu'en Europe, car on ne peut pas quasi en convertir un seul. Il n'y en a que dans la seule île de la Martinique.

---

[7]   AFSI, GBro185, fol. 9^r: possibly 'tout'.

[8]   For an alternative version of the start of this letter in MdC, MS 73, see Letter 4 and Translation 4 in this book. From this point on, AFSI, GBro185 will be compared with MdC, MS 73 in the notes. The text takes up at MdC, MS 73, fol. 84^r.

[9]   AFSI, GBro185, fol. 9^r–9^v: the text that follows, from 'et une à Cayenne' to 'dans la seule île de la Martinique', does not feature in MdC, MS 73.

[10]   AFSI, GBro185, fol. 9^r: 'comme j'ai dit' has been crossed out.

seeing the care we take of their salvation, and the honour they have of coming to church. This is so true that missionaries have no better way of scolding slaves for their immoral behaviour than to threaten them, by telling them in their jargon, 'you be treated like English slave: no baptism, no church, no grave.'

It would be advisable to have some of our Fathers at Cape Verde, Senegal, or Gorée, where our Frenchmen have settled, to be able to work for the salvation of Africans in their own land. This would be very fruitful without a doubt, even if all that was done was to baptize the children who die, which occurs continually in such a heavily populated land, and the children who are embarked for America, a good number of whom die during the voyage. The directors of the Africa Company[13] are very desirous of this, but we have so many missions to provide for that it is impossible to do everything at the same time.

I was forgetting to talk about the religion of the Africans in their own land. There are peoples who believe in nothing at all, others who recognize a principle, and still others who have some knowledge of Mohammedism, and who are circumcised. These are particularly from Cape Verde, because they neighbour the Mohammedan kings of Africa. There are even some who have *marabouts* amongst them; this is the name that is given to Mohammedan priests, but it may be said that they all know so little about what they believe that we have no difficulty in extirpating it from them. The only difficulty is introducing our own faith, and particularly good manners.[14]

Now that I have discussed the Africans in general terms, this will make what I am going to talk about clearer. We have four missions on the island of Martinique, one on that of Guadeloupe, two on this island of Saint Kitts,[15] and one in Cayenne where we are the only priests for the French, the Africans, and the Indians. I will not tell you about what we do amongst the French in all these places. It is enough to say to you that life is more orderly in them, at present, than in France, and that every year we convert a great number of Huguenots, and provide all the assistance that is needed to about one hundred vessels a year which come here to trade. The only Jews were brought here by the trade the Dutch used to engage in, and are no more docile than in Europe, because hardly a single one can be converted. They are only on the island of Martinique.

---

[13] At the time of Mongin's letter, the Compagnie du Sénégal, formed in July 1681. See Paul Chemin-Duponstès, *Les Compagnies de colonisation en Afrique occidentale sous Colbert* (Paris: Augustin Challamel, 1903), p. 122.

[14] For an alternative version of the start of this letter in MdC, MS 73, see Letter 4 and Translation 4 in this book. From this point on, AFSI, GBro185 will be compared with the principal variants in MdC, MS 73 in the notes. The text takes up at MdC, MS 73, fol. 84^r.

[15] AFSI, GBro185, fol. 9^r–9^v: the text that follows, from 'and one in Cayenne' to 'only on the island of Martinique', does not feature in MdC, MS 73.

Le quartier dont j'ai le soin en l'île de Saint-Christophe, a environ quatre lieues de circuit. C'est une charmante plaine couverte de cannes de sucre en plusieurs endroits, avec un tel profit pour les habitants, que quoique les champs, qui en sont plantés, ne feraient pas plus d'une lieue en carré, on y fait les années ordinaires trois millions de livres de sucre. Cet espace est semé d'un grand nombre de maisons, comme autant de métairies et de hameaux, et fermé d'un côté par la mer, et de l'autre par des montagnes, qui s'élèvent doucement, et qui ne me font nulle peine à monter partout où elles sont habitées. Au milieu de ce beau pays est notre maison qui est très commode pour m'y rendre facilement toutes les nuits, car il est ici nécessaire, du moins pour l'édification, que les missionnaires ne couchent jamais hors de chez eux que quand il faut passer la nuit auprès des malades qui sont à l'extrémité, et enfin la disposition de ce lieu facilite extrêmement le soin que l'on [10ʳ] prend des esclaves lequel consiste à leur administrer les sacrements et à les y disposer.

C'est en quoi s'accordent tous nos missionnaires, aussi bien qu'à être assidus à l'église les matinées des fêtes, pour dire la messe à ces nègres, et pour leur administrer les sacrements, de la pénitence et de la communion, et pour leur faire le catéchisme, mais tout cela n'est que la moindre partie de notre travail, qui nous doit occuper le reste de la semaine, c'est ce que chacun fait, comme il juge plus à propos devant Dieu, selon les temps, les lieux et les personnes. La méthode que j'y garde est je crois ce que vous me demandez si instamment, Monsieur, lorsque vous dites que vous me priez de vous mander les manières,[11] que je tiens pour la conversion de ces gens, et de vous faire savoir les routes que le Saint-Esprit m'y fait tenir. C'est sur ce chapitre que je dois maintenant vous satisfaire, après vous avoir dit un mot des travaux[12] d'une personne à qui j'ai succédé dans cet emploi, et dont la mission si j'en avais pu savoir le détail, serait ici un plus digne sujet de votre lecture, que tout ce que vous m'obligez à vous écrire de mes manières.

Ce missionnaire est un homme en qui Dieu a voulu faire paraître un exemple du zèle et de la fidélité qu'un apôtre doit à son emploi, laquelle n'éclate jamais tant que dans les difficultés qui se présentent [10ᵛ] dans l'exécution,[13] car je n'ai jamais vu un homme qui travaillât avec tant d'application. Il ne paraissait guère dans nos entretiens, à grand'peine dans nos repas, et l'on ne savait quel temps il prenait pour le sommeil. On le voyait continuellement auprès de ces pauvres esclaves, tantôt d'un côté tantôt de l'autre. Il était assez souvent les heures entières[14] à en exhorter et instruire quelqu'un en particulier au milieu d'un champ exposé aux ardeurs du soleil de notre zone. Il ne se contentait pas de les attirer au bien par plusieurs beaux présents de dévotion, comme des images,

---

[11] MdC, MS 73, fol. 84ᵛ: 'lorsque vous dites que <u>vous me suppliez de vous donner les maximes</u>'.
[12] MdC, MS 73, fol. 85ʳ: 'travaux prodigieux'.
[13] MdC, MS 73, fol. 85ʳ: 'laquelle n'éclate jamais tant que dans le défaut du succès, que nous devons tous abandonner à la Providence'.
[14] MdC, MS 73, fol. 85ʳ: 'Il était assez souvent, dit-on, les 3 et les 4 heures de suite'.

The neighbourhood I look after on the island of Saint Kitts is about four leagues in circumference. It is a charming plain covered, in many places, with sugar cane, which brings in such profits for the planters that, even though there is no more than a square league of cane fields, in a typical year three million pounds of sugar are made. This space is dotted with a great number of houses, farms, and hamlets, enclosed on one side by the sea, and on the other by gently sloping mountains that I can walk up with no difficulty, wherever they are inhabited. In the middle of this fine land is our house, which is convenient for me to return to every night. For here, for reasons of edification, missionaries should never spend the night away from their own residence, except when they must spend the night caring for the sick who are on their deathbeds. The location of this place is of considerable help indeed for our care of the slaves, which consists in preparing them for the sacraments, and administering the same.

Our missionaries are together in this, as they are in assuring Mass in church for these slaves on the mornings of feasts, and in administering the sacraments of penance and communion, and in teaching them their catechism, but all this is only the least part of the labours that occupy our time the rest of the week. Each does as he judges appropriate before God, according to the time, the places, and the people. The method that I use is, I think, what you ask me about with so much insistence, Sir, when you implore me to inform you of the methods I use to convert these people, and the paths that the Holy Spirit has me follow in this. I must now satisfy you on this point, after saying a little about the labours of a person whom I succeeded in this task, whose mission, if I had been able to know the detail of it, would be a much more worthy subject to read about than all that you oblige me to write to you of my methods.

This missionary is a man whom God wanted to serve as an example of the zeal and fidelity that an apostle must have in his task, which is never clearer than in the difficulties that present themselves. For I have never seen a man work so diligently. He was hardly ever there while we were in conversation, rarely present at mealtimes, and we did not know at what time he got any sleep. He was always to be seen somewhere or other with these poor slaves. Often enough he would spend hours preaching to and instructing just one of them in the middle of a field, exposed to the strong sun of these parts. He was not happy bringing them to goodness with many fine devotional gifts, such as images, medals, and rosaries, that are ordinarily our prizes here, but he added

des médailles et des chapelets, qui sont ici nos prix ordinaires, il y ajoutait toute
sorte de quincaillerie et même des habits de toile, dont son industrie lui faisait
trouver moyen d'avoir provision.[15]

Le défaut de ces talents, et de ces subsides était capable de me faire perdre[16]
la volonté de travailler après un ouvrier de cette force, si je ne me fusse senti
très disposé à me passer de la consolation du succès et à n'en chercher d'autre
que celle qu'on goûte en faisant ce qu'on peut pour le service de Dieu, qui n'a
nul besoin ni de notre industrie ni de notre travail,[17] pour retirer les âmes de
l'erreur et du péché.

Ce fut dans cette pensée que je commençai cette mission [11ʳ] avec beaucoup
de joie au mois d'août de l'année 1680. Mon premier recours fut à la prière, en
recommandant à celles des gens de piété le travail que j'allais entreprendre. Je
commençai dès lors ce que j'ai continué depuis, de dire à cette intention deux
messes la semaine, l'une pour le salut de ces pauvres nègres, l'autre[18] pour ceux
que j'enterrais, afin que par leurs prières ils secondassent en paradis la peine que
je prenais pour leurs compatriotes.

Ensuite je me résolus de travailler avec ordre sachant bien que dans l'embarras
et la multitude des choses, il ne faut pas tant compter sur la peine, que sur la
méthode. Je m'en formai une dès lors que je n'ai point quittée depuis, et je
partageai tous les mois du reste de l'année et de la suivante, de telle manière, que
ce qui restait de cette année, ne fut employé quasi qu'à bien connaître le mal à
quoi il fallait apporter remède, et à m'appliquer à ce qui pressait davantage, qui
était le baptême des adultes arrivés.[19] Le premier semestre de l'année suivante
fut employé à disposer aux sacrements ceux qui en pouvaient être capables,
et l'autre semestre pour remédier en particulier aux vices, qui avaient exclu
plusieurs nègres des sacrements.

Cette tâche demandait un homme tout entier qui fût toujours en campagne,
où ces pauvres esclaves sont [11ᵛ] disposés par troupes, les uns aux fourneaux

---

[15] MdC, MS 73, fol. 85ᵛ continues from this point with the following paragraph: 'Mais Dieu
qui voulait éprouver sa fidélité a permis que le succès ne correspondît pas entièrement au
travail de ce fervent missionnaire, car après avoir tant sué durant 7 ou 8 ans il jugea que
les débauches de ces esclaves étaient si grandes et si universelles qu'il ne pouvait pas leur
faire faire la Pâques, ni les marier, ni baptiser les adultes que rarement. Il m'assura de ces
misères en me laissant cet emploi, et il en était si persuadé [que] quelque temps après son
départ ayant reçu une de mes lettres, où pour le consoler, je lui écrivis que je commençais de
connaître que les désordres n'étaient pas tout à fait si grands, qu'il m'avait dit, il répondit un
peu fâché de ce que je ne l'en voulais pas croire entièrement, que quand je m'y appliquerais
je connaîtrais qu'il avait dit vrai.'

[16] MdC, MS 73, fol. 85ᵛ: 'Et certes le mal était assez grand pour me faire perdre'.

[17] MdC, MS 73, fol. 85ᵛ: 'qui n'a nul besoin ni de notre travail' ('ni' crossed out).

[18] MdC, MS 73, fol. 86ʳ: 'l'une pour le salut de ces pauvres nègres conformément à ma tâche
particulière de chaque mois, et l'autre'.

[19] MdC, MS 73, fol. 86ʳ: 'qui était le baptême de quelques adultes arrivés depuis plusieurs
anneés'.

to these all sorts of metal objects, and even clothes, which he obtained through his industry.[16]

Lacking these talents and these resources, I might have lost the will to work following such a formidable labourer, if I had not felt very much disposed to do without the consolation of success, instead seeking no other but that which can be had by doing what one can for the service of God, who has no need of our industry or of our labour to take souls out of error and sin.

It was with these thoughts that I started this mission with much joy in the month of August of the year 1680. My initial recourse was to prayer, asking pious people to pray for the labour I was about to begin. From that point onwards, I began what I have continued to do since: to say two Masses a week for this intention, the first for the salvation of these poor slaves, and the second for those I buried, so that, in Paradise, they assist through their prayers the trouble I took for their compatriots.

Then I resolved to work with order, knowing well that, faced with so many challenges and with a multitude of things to do, one should rely more on method than on one's toil. At this stage, I devised a method that I have kept since, and I divided up the remaining months of the year, and the following, in such a way that what was left of [the first] year was almost completely devoted to getting to know the affliction for which a remedy was needed, and to working at what was more urgent, which was the baptism of the adults who had arrived. The first six months of the following year were employed in preparing those who might be capable of the sacraments, and the following six in remedying, individually, the vices that had caused many slaves to be excluded from the sacraments.

This task required a man who would be constantly out in the countryside where these poor slaves are divided up into teams, some at the furnaces of the

---

[16] MdC, MS 73, fol. 85^{v} continues from this point with the following paragraph: 'But God, who wanted to test his fidelity, made the success of this fervent missionary not equal his labour, for, having toiled so much for seven or eight years, he judged that the debauchery of these slaves was so extensive and widespread that he could not allow them to take the sacraments at Easter, nor marry them, nor baptize the adults except in rare cases. In leaving this post to me he assured me of these hardships, of which he was so persuaded that some time after his departure, having received one of my letters — in which, to console him, I had written that I was beginning to understand that the [slaves'] excesses were not as serious as he had said — he answered, somewhat annoyed that I did not want to completely believe him, that when I applied myself to the task I would realize he was right.'

des sucreries, les autres aux moulins, les autres à leurs repas, et en plus grand nombre dans les champs, où nous avons partout la permission de leur faire quitter leurs travaux pour leur parler de leur salut. Il y a néanmoins deux sortes d'occupations, l'une fixe, l'autre casuelle, qui causent de temps en temps des interruptions dans mes courses, qui à cela près sont assez réglées et continuelles. La fixe est pour la veille et la matinée de toutes les fêtes, sans exception pour penser et prêcher un sermon pour le moins à un auditoire célèbre, et composé de gens de considération,[20] qui mériterait un prédicateur qui eût plus de talent, de science et de loisir, que je n'en ai, tout cela sans préjudice du catéchisme, et des confessions des nègres, qui occupent constamment le reste de ces matinées de tous les missionnaires, comme j'ai tantôt dit, car pour l'après-dîner[21] comme les esclaves sont rarement chez eux les jours de fête, je l'emploie à voir ceux qui sont à la prison, que je ne puis pas manquer d'y trouver, et les nègres de notre maison, parce que sont [sic] ceux, qui aiment le moins à sortir.

L'occupation casuelle est la visite des malades, à qui il faut être exact à donner de jour et de nuit les sacrements,[22] dont ils ont besoin. J'entends les nègres malades, car pour les blancs, je ne vois, pour mieux [12ʳ] secourir les nègres, que ceux[23] qui m'appellent nommément ou qu'au défaut des autres missionnaires, qui sont chargés de ce soin. À ces deux occupations près, le reste du temps est entièrement pour mes courses ordinaires, ayant remarqué combien il est nécessaire qu'un missionnaire soit assidu pour ne pas perdre aucune occasion de faire de grands biens.[24]

Pour prévenir donc toute sorte de distractions, et pour ne m'occuper que de ma mission, j'ai coutume de dire la messe, le plus tôt que je puis pour partir incontinent après. Je porte avec moi de quoi prendre quelque réfection, au lieu où je me trouve à midi à l'ombre de quelque arbre. Si je ne pars pas si matin, je prends quelque chose à la maison, ce qui me suffit jusqu'à la nuit,[25] qui est le temps que je me retire en compagnie d'un nègre des plus spirituels, qui n'a d'autre occupation que de me suivre partout.

[20] MdC, MS 73, fol. 86ᵛ: 'La fixe est pour la veille et pour la matinée de toutes les fêtes sans exception, pour faire un sermon pour le moins à un auditoire'.
[21] MdC, MS 73, fol. 86ᵛ: 'l'après-midi'.
[22] MdC, MS 73, fol. 87ʳ: 'la consolation et les sacrements'.
[23] MdC, MS 73, fol. 87ʳ: 'car pour les blancs, je n'en vois, pour plus d'une raison, que ceux'.
[24] MdC, MS 73, fol. 87ʳ continues from this point: 'comme on a vu qu'il est arrivé ici à un ecclésiastique qui eût fait encore de plus grands progrès qu'il n'a faits dans la mission par les rares talents naturels et surnaturels dont Dieu l'a comblé, s'il n'avait jugé plus à propos de donner une bonne partie de son temps à la direction d'une dévote d'éclat; laquelle de vrai n'a pas moins de solidité quoiqu'il lui ait toujours fallu presque tout un directeur, **par un défaut commun au sexe dans les premières et grandes ferveurs**'. Text in bold appears to be a later addition.
[25] MdC, MS 73, fols 87ʳ–87ᵛ: 'Quand c'est bon matin, je porte avec moi de quoi prendre quelque réfection là part que je me trouve à midi, à quelque ombre, si j'en puis trouver. [87ᵛ] Si ce n'est pas si matin, la réfection que je prends avant de partir me soutient jusqu'à la nuit'.

sugar plants, others at the mills, others at their meals, and the greatest number in the fields, where we have permission everywhere to have them leave off their work so we can talk to them about their salvation. There are nonetheless two sorts of tasks, one regular and the other unpredictable, which from time to time interrupt my coming and going, which is otherwise regular and continuous enough. The task that is regular is on the eve and the morning of each feast day, without exception, to reflect about and preach at least one sermon to a distinguished audience made up of esteemed people, who deserve a preacher with more talent, learning, and free time than I have. All this has to be done without impacting on the catechism and the confessions of the slaves, which, for all the missionaries, take up all that is left of the mornings, as I mentioned a moment ago. For, as the slaves are rarely at home on feast days, I use the afternoon to see those who are in the prison, whom I cannot but find there, and the slaves in our house, as it is they who least like going out.[17]

The unpredictable side of my work consists in visiting the sick, to whom one must give the sacraments as soon as possible, whether by night or day. By these I mean the sick blacks because, to better assist these blacks, I only see the whites when they call for me by name or when the other missionaries who look after them are unavailable. These two tasks aside, the rest of my time is devoted to my usual missionary work, having noticed how necessary it is for a missionary to be diligent so as not to miss any opportunity to do great good.[18]

To avoid any sort of distraction and to give myself to my mission alone, my habit is to say Mass as early as I can so as to leave straightaway afterwards. I bring something with me for my refection which I take wherever I am at midday under the shade of a tree. If I do not leave so early, I have something at the house which does me until night-time, which is the moment for me to retire in the company of a particularly keen-witted[19] slave, whose only occupation is to follow me everywhere.

[17] 'après-dîner'; 'dîner' most closely approximates to the modern 'déjeuner' at this time.

[18] MdC, MS 73, fol. 87^r continues from this point: 'as, it was seen, occurred here to an ecclesiastic who would have made greater progress in his mission than he had, given the rare talents, both natural and supernatural, which God bestowed on him, if he had not thought it more appropriate to devote a large amount of his time to the [spiritual] direction of a prestigious woman of ardent devotion. In truth, she is no less solid, although she has always needed a director for herself, **thanks to a fault common to her sex in their initial, great fervour.**' Section in bold appears to be a later addition.

[19] 'Spirituel, se dit aussi d'un esprit éclairé, et qui a de belles lumières et de belle connaissances'. Furetière (1690), III, entry 'Spirituel', non-paginated.

Ce fut de la sorte que je commençai ma mission, par connaître mes pauvres paroissiens, et par en dresser une liste, conforme à celle que le rituel romain prescrit très sagement à tous les curés, et qu'il appelle le catalogue des âmes,[26] ordonnant qu'on y marque ceux qui ont fait leurs Pâques, et reçu quelques autres sacrements. Je ne pouvais mieux faire que de prendre pour mon guide ce divin livre, pour lequel j'ai une attache particulière, à l'imitation de tous les véritables [12ᵛ] missionnaires, qui ne se croient pas exempts de ses lois pour être dans un pays étranger, comme l'a prononcé un concile national tenu à Lima dans la terre ferme de l'Amérique et approuvé du Saint-Siège. J'ajoutai seulement à cette forme de catalogue plusieurs autres articles, que la condition et l'état des nègres me permettaient et m'obligeaient d'y ajouter.[27]

Car j'y marquai le nom et le surnom d'un chacun, aussi bien que celui de leurs femmes, et de leurs enfants, s'ils étaient séparés ou non, en bon ou en mauvais ménage, les veufs, les veuves, les filles et les garçons, frères et sœurs, orphelins et orphelines, les véritables nègres, et les mulâtres nés d'un blanc et d'une noire. Ensuite était marqué leur pays, qui est bien différent, puisqu'il y en a de toutes nos îles françaises, flamandes, anglaises et espagnoles, où ils sont nés, comme aussi de quels royaumes ils ont été tirés, leurs pays occupant presque toute la côte[28] occidentale de l'Afrique, dans l'étendue de plus de quinze cents lieues[29] sans compter les pays méditerranés d'où il en vient beaucoup, ce qui fait dans leur naturel une diversité très grande, dont la connaissance est nécessaire à un missionnaire.

Je marque ensuite leur âge le plus exactement que je puis, car ils ne le sauraient dire eux-mêmes,[30] on y distinguait encore les baptisés, et ceux dont le baptême était incertain, ou qui avait été fait sans [13ʳ] les cérémonies en péril de mort, ceux qui avaient déjà été à confesse et communié, et qui avaient fait leurs Pâques l'année courante, et enfin les degrés[31] de probité, et de capacité pour le catéchisme, c'est-à-dire, ceux qui étaient très capables, médiocrement, moins que médiocrement, et les incapables,[32] dont le nombre n'est pas trop petit, entendant par la capacité médiocre, la science qui est nécessaire de nécessité

---

[26] MdC, MS 73, fol. 87ᵛ: 'et qu'il appelle le <u>catalogue de l'état des âmes</u>'.

[27] AFSI, GBro185, fol. 12ᵛ: 'me permettait et m'obligeait d'y ajouter'.

[28] MdC, MS 73, fol. 88ʳ: 'où ils sont nés et des royaumes qui occupent presque toute la côte'.

[29] AFSI, GBro185, fol. 12ᵛ: 'de côtes' has been inserted here (to read 'quinze cents lieues de côtes').

[30] MdC, MS 73, fol. 88ʳ: 'Ensuite de leur pays on voit l'âge au plus près qu'on le peut marquer car ils ne le sauraient dire eux-mêmes; et pour mémoire, le malheur du temps en étant sans doute la cause' (the word 'mémoire' crossed out and 'ceux qui sont nés ici je n'en trouve [?] presque point de mémoire' inserted).

[31] MdC, MS 73, fol. 88ʳ: 'et enfin 6 degrés'.

[32] MdC, MS 73, fol. 88ʳ: 'ceux qui étaient très capables, bien, médiocrement, et moins que médiocrement, et les ineptes'; in MdC, MS 73, 'et moins que médiocrement' appears to be an addition.

It was in this way that I began my mission, getting to know my poor parishioners and making a list, one which conformed to that which the Roman rite, wisely, prescribes for all parish priests. The rite calls it a catalogue of souls, and prescribes that those who have celebrated Easter and have received some of the other sacraments should be noted within.[20] I could do no better than take as my guide this divine book for which I have a particular attachment, in imitation of all the true missionaries who do not think of themselves as above its laws because they are in a foreign land, as pronounced by a National Council held in Lima on the mainland of America, and approved by the Holy See.[21] I only added to this sort of catalogue many other articles, that the condition and the circumstances of the slaves allowed, and obliged me to add.

For I indicated the name and nickname of each as well as that of their wives and children, if they were separated or not, if they were in a happy or bad marriage, the widowers and widows, girls and boys, brothers and sisters, orphans of either sex, the true blacks, and the *mulâtres* born to a white man and a black woman. After this was marked their homeland, which differs greatly — as there are some born in each of our French, Flemish, English, and Spanish islands — and from which kingdoms they were taken. Their land spans almost the entire west coast of Africa, stretching over more than fifteen hundred leagues, without counting the inner lands from which many come. This means that they are very diverse in the character which a missionary must know.

I then note their age as exactly as I can, because they could not tell me it themselves. Those baptized were distinguished from those whose baptism was uncertain, or who had been baptized without the ceremonies when they had been in danger of death, those who had already made confession and received Communion, and who had received the sacraments at Easter this year, and, lastly, their degree of probity and capacity for catechism, that is those who were very capable, moderately so, less than moderately, and those unsuitable, of whom there is not a small number. By moderate capacity I mean the knowledge that is necessary through necessity of means, and absolutely necessary to be saved, above which was that of necessity of precept which includes prayers.[22]

[20] On the 'catalogue of souls' see Louis Michard and Georges Couton, 'Les Livres d'états des âmes: une source à collecter et à exploiter', *Revue d'histoire de l'Église de France*, 67.179 (1981), 261–75. Michard and Couton write that the practice originated in the injunction of the Council of Trent for the cleric to 'know his flocks' ('oves cognoscere') and was popularized by the implementation by Saint Charles Borromeo (1538–1584) of a *Liber status animarum* in the diocese of Milan. Mongin's description can be compared with the reproductions of French models in Michard and Couton, pp. 262, 264. These findings are also summarized in Chatillon, p. 13.
[21] There were five Councils of Lima between 1551 and 1601, of which the most significant was the third (1582–83), and in which Acosta played a significant role. Its acts, including the creation of a catechism in Amerindian languages, were confirmed by the Holy See. See Enrique Dussel, *A History of the Church in Latin America*, trans. by Alan Neely (Grand Rapids, MI: Eerdmans, 1981), pp. 57–58.
[22] *Nécessité de moyen* ('necessity of means') is considered necessary for salvation, or 'absolutely necessary', as Mongin writes, while *nécessité de précepte* ('necessity of precept')

de moyen, et absolue pour être sauvé, au-dessus de laquelle était celle, qui est de nécessité de précepte et qui comprend les prières, les degrés des mœurs étaient à peu près distingués de la sorte, si ce n'est qu'aux deux plus bas degrés répondaient les méchants et les scélérats, et que j'avais ajouté l'espèce de leurs vices, qui sont l'ivrognerie, l'impudicité, le larcin,[33] l'indévotion, l'impiété, le marronage, c'est-à-dire, l'habitude de fuir, et de s'absenter de chez le maître, et aux concubinaires j'avais marqué le nom de la concubine,[34] en dernier lieu étaient marqués les infirmes, ceux qui faisaient faire la prière aux autres, etc.

Toutes ces listes étaient sous le nom de chaque maître rangés selon l'ordre des compagnies de milice, et celles-ci[35] selon l'ordre topographique du quartier, où elles sont au nombre de cinq. Enfin il n'y avait aucun de ces articles, qui ne fût marqué avec un seul chiffre, exceptés les noms, dont je tirai deux grands avantages, l'un que personne n'y connaissait rien que moi et l'autre [13^V] qu'il était très portatif ne contenant que six feuilles de papier marquées en échiquier sans aucune confusion qui serait autrement inévitable, dans une si grande multitude et diversité. Vous verrez dans la suite la grande utilité que j'ai tirée de ce catalogue.

Ce fut pour cette raison, que je crus bien employer deux mois entiers pour recueillir et ranger ainsi ces mémoires me transportant sur tous les lieux pour cet effet, car pour la capacité je ne m'en rapportais qu'à moi-même, interrogeant tout le monde l'un après l'autre, et pour leurs mœurs je prenais toutes les précautions raisonnables pour n'y être pas trompé, selon les divers rapports des plus sages et parmi eux, et parmi les blancs, faisant de nouveaux changements dans ces mémoires, selon les nouvelles connaissances, qui me venaient de bonne part.[36]

---

[33] AFSI, GBro185, fol. 13^r has the variant 'ladrecin'.

[34] MdC, MS 73, fol. 88^V: 'et aux concubinaires j'avais marqué le nom de la concubine et réciproquement'.

[35] MdC, MS 73, fol. 88^V: 'Toutes ces listes étaient sous le nom de chaque maître, ceux qui étaient rangés selon l'ordre des compagnies et celles-ci'.

[36] MdC, MS 73, fol. 89^r continues from this point: 'Ainsi cette liste étant achevée avec toutes ces diligences, je trouvai que dans mon quartier il y avait alors 200 maisons qui avaient des nègres, desquelles 37 avaient perdu la coutume de faire les prières: que les esclaves en tout étaient 2400. 261 adultes qui n'étaient pas baptisés. 720 étaient mariés, dont 200 étaient en mauvais ménage. 760 en âge de marier, 655 concubinaires, 900 qui savaient les premiers principes de la foi, mais non pas les premières prières. 676 qui ne savaient pas même ces premiers principes, sans compter les ineptes et les petits enfants. 1200 qui disaient avoir commencé d'aller à confesse; 780 avoir communié, 222 qui faisaient profession de ne venir jamais à la messe ni au catéchisme quoique baptisés ou catéchumènes. Enfin il y en avait 26 qui étaient sorciers ou de fait ou de profession ou de réputation. [89^V] Voilà l'état où était mon quartier quand je commençai de travailler; et en même temps voilà assez de quoi me faire perdre toute espérance si j'eusse été si malavisé que de la mettre en mes forces et en mon travail; celui de mon fervent prédécesseur était inimitable [possibly changed from 'inévitable']; mais j'étais résolu d'imiter au moins la fidélité qu'il avait eue pour son ministère, pour ne me laisser pas abattre par les difficultés: heureux encore si le fruit de ma

The degrees of morality were more or less distinguished in this way, except that the two lowest degrees were for the evil and for scoundrels, and that I added the type of their vices, which are drunkenness, fornication, theft, irreligion, impiety, and *marronage*, which means the habit of taking flight and abandoning the master's [plantation]. I noted the name of the concubine for those cohabiting, and in last place the sick, those who led prayer for the others, etc.

All these lists were organized by the name of each master, arranged in order of the militia companies, which were in turn arranged by the topographical order of the locality, where there are five companies. There was not one of these articles that was not marked with one figure, the names excepted, and this had great advantages for me. One was that I was the only person who understood it, and the other that it was very portable, made up of only six leaves of paper in the form of a chessboard without any of the confusion that would be otherwise unavoidable with such a great multitude and diversity. You will see in what follows how useful this catalogue has been to me.

It was this that made me think of spending two full months in gathering and arranging these memoirs, going myself to all these places for this reason. With regard to capacity I relied on myself alone, interrogating everybody one after the other, and with regard to their morality I took all reasonable precautions so as not to be deceived, according to the various reports of the wisest amongst them and amongst the whites. I made changes to these memoirs, according to new information that came to me from reliable sources.[23]

should be known as a 'precept of God, or the Church', Engelbert Sterckx, *Le Catéchisme de Malines* (Malines: Van Velsen, 1851), pp. 17–18.

[23] MdC, MS 73, fol. 89[r] continues from this point: 'This list having been finished with such care, I worked out that in my area there were 200 houses at that point which had slaves, of which it was no longer the custom in 37 to have prayers; that there were 2400 slaves in total, with 261 adults who had not been baptised, with 720 who were married, and 200 unhappily so. There were 760 of marriageable age, 655 cohabiting, 900 who knew the first principles of [our] faith, but not the first prayers. There were 676 who did not even know the first principles, not counting the simple-minded and the little children. There were 1200 who said they had started going to confession, 780 that they had taken Communion, 222 who declared that they never went to Mass or catechism even though they had been baptized or were catechumens. There were also 26 sorcerers, whether in fact, or professed, or reputed as such. [89[v]] This was the state of my area when I started my work, and it would have been enough to make me lose all hope, if I had been so ill-advised as to put any [hope] in my abilities and in my work. I could not hope to equal the work of my fervent predecessor, but I was resolved to have at least as much fidelity as he had had for his ministry, so as not to be put off by the difficulties. I would be happy if my first year bore as much fruit as I have found amongst so much ignorance and wickedness, and that we have been trying to stamp out for so many years now.'

Après avoir donc rangé ces mémoires en octobre, je crus qu'il fallait entrer par la porte du christianisme, et commencer par le premier et le plus nécessaire de tous les sacrements, c'est-à-dire, le baptême, tant parce qu'il y avait longtemps, qu'on n'avait pas baptisé des adultes, que parce qu'il en fallait ainsi disposer quelques-uns aux mariages, que je voulais célébrer après les Rois, pour remédier au plus tôt à tant de débauches.

Une des dispositions essentielles au baptême d'un infidèle est de lui faire changer de religion, ce qui se fait, comme vous dites fort bien dans votre lettre, en lui faisant connaître les imperfections de celle, qu'il tient[37] [14ʳ] et les raisons de la perfection de celle, qu'on lui veut faire prendre, ensuite de quoi vous vous étonnez comment nous pouvons persuader des gens qui n'ont point de raison, comme sont nos nègres.[38] Vous n'êtes pas le seul des gens de qualité, qui ont voulu philosopher sur cette matière. Il y a environ dix ans qu'un intendant de nos îles, qui était un élève du célèbre feu Monsieur de Lesclache sur les principes de la philosophie de son maître, composa ici une méthode pratique et raisonnée pour la conversion des nègres.[39] J'ai trouvé depuis peu ce beau manuscrit, et je l'ai tiré de la poussière pour lui donner une place honorable dans notre bibliothèque.

Mais à dire le vrai tous ces raisonnements sont ici inutiles, et les nègres sont ceux de toutes les nations du monde, à la conversion desquels cadre le mieux cette parole de saint Paul, *non in persuasibilibus humanae sapientiae verbis etc. Il faut donc au moins des miracles*, ajoutez-vous, sur quoi vous me priez de ne vous pas cacher ceux que nous faisons. Je ne vous les cacherai point assurément, en vous disant que sans ce secours la grâce vient à bout de leur infidélité. L'exemple de tous leurs compatriotes, l'estime qu'ils ont des blancs, l'assiduité des missionnaires, l'autorité de leurs maîtres, aident beaucoup sans nulle violence à leur faire demander le baptême, et jamais la foi n'a été plus aveugle, ni moins sujette [14ᵛ] à la tentation que dans ces gens.

Une autre raison encore de cette facilité est qu'ils n'ont pas besoin de changer de religion pour embrasser la nôtre; car ils n'en avaient quasi jamais eu aucune. Ceux qui viennent de la partie plus septentrionale de l'Afrique ont une teinture très légère du mahométisme, à cause du voisinage du Maroc,[40] et de la Barbarie. Ils portent au col des billets écrits en arabe, qui sont des préservatifs, disent-ils,

première année eût eu quelque proportion avec celui que j'ai trouvé parmi tant d'ignorance et de méchanceté qu'on tâche d'exterminer ici depuis tant de temps.'

[37] AFSI, GBro185, fol. 13ᵛ: 'tient' crossed out and replaced with 'a'.

[38] MdC, MS 73, fol. 90ʳ continues: 'voilà ajoutez-vous ce que je cherchais et que je cherche encore.'

[39] MdC, MS 73, fol. 90ʳ: 'la conversion de ces idiots'.

[40] Both AFSI, GBro185, fol. 14ᵛ and MdC, MS 73, fol. 90ᵛ read: 'de Maroc'.

Having put these memoirs in order in October, I thought that I should enter by the gate to Christianity, and start by the first and most necessary of all the sacraments, which is baptism. This was as much because no adults had been baptized for a long time, as because some of them had to be prepared for the marriages that I wanted to celebrate after Epiphany, to remedy so much immorality as soon as possible.

One of the dispositions that is essential to the baptism of an infidel is to make him change religion, which is done — as you put it so well in your own letter — by showing him the imperfections of his own, and the reasons of the perfection of that which we want him to adopt. In consequence, you wonder how we can persuade people who are lacking in reason, as is the case with our slaves, and you are not alone amongst the people of quality who have attempted to philosophize about this matter. About ten years ago an *intendant* of our islands,[24] who had been a pupil of the celebrated late Mr de Lesclache, composed a practical and reasoned method for the conversion of slaves based on the philosophical principles of his master.[25] I found this fine manuscript a short time ago, and I dusted it off and gave it an honourable place in our library.

However, to say things as they are, all this reasoning is useless here. The blacks are those, amongst all the peoples of the world, to whose conversion the words of Saint Paul most apply: *non in persuasibilibus humanae sapientiae verbis etc.*[26] Therefore, you add, there is a need for miracles, and you beseech me not to hide from you those we perform. I will most certainly not be hiding them, in telling you that without such assistance, it is grace that surmounts their infidelity. The example of all their compatriots, their esteem of the whites, the assiduity of the missionaries, and the authority of their masters, are of great help in making them ask for baptism without any force, and never has faith been blinder, or less subject to temptation than with these people.

One further reason for this ease is that they do not need to change religion to embrace our own, because they had hardly ever had one. Those who come from the northernmost part of Africa have a light trace of Mohammedism because of the proximity of Morocco and the Barbary States. Around their necks they wear amulets written in Arabic which, they say, protect them from disease. When I ask them for these amulets upon their arrival they give them to me, and let me

---

[24] According to Moreau de Saint-Méry, Claude Clersellier became *intendant général des îles de l'Amérique pour la Compagnie* in 1642 and was succeeded by *agents généraux* for the companies, until Jean-Baptiste Patoulet became royal *intendant* in 1679; Moreau de Saint-Méry, *Loix et constitutions*, I, p. xxxiii.

[25] Louis de Lesclache [16..–1671], author of *La Philosophie, expliquée en tables*, 5 vols (Paris: [n. pub.], 1651–56).

[26] 'et sermo meus praedicatio mea non in persuasibilibus sapientiae verbis sed in ostensione Spiritus et virtutis', 1 Corinthians 2. 4 ('and my speech and my preaching was not in the persuasible words of human wisdom but in showing of spirit and power', 1582, p. 427).

des maladies, d'abord que je les leur demande à leur arrivée ils me les donnent, et me les laissent brûler sans nulle peine. Je n'en ai eu qu'une fois avec trois qui étaient du Cap Blanc, qui est un lieu plus septentrional que tous les autres d'où l'on nous apporte des nègres. Pour ceux qui sont plus méridionaux, ils m'ont fait connaître qu'ils croient qu'il y a un être, qui a tout fait, et qui envoie, disent-ils, la pluie pour faire mûrir leurs vivres. Ceux d'Angole m'ont dit, qu'ils l'appellent Zambi, ceux qui sont moins éloignés de la fameuse rivière de Sénégal, appellent ce dieu Reboucou.[41] Ils m'ont ajouté, que c'est quelque chose de caché, et qui est fait comme nous. Ceux qui sont d'Ardres ou Arada l'appellent Roudou,[42] et ceux-ci m'ont dit qu'ils enterrent leurs morts dans la maison, font un grand festin sur la fosse, et y en jettent la moitié pour le mort, mais quand je leur ai demandé où allaient les morts [15ʳ] après cette vie, *c'est ce qu'on ne sait pas chez nous* m'ont-ils répondu fort ingénument. D'ordinaire quand ils veulent assurer quelque chose, ils lèvent les yeux et la main en haut d'un air fort tendre et fort respectueux, en disant *Dieu la-haut*.

Je fus bien surpris dernièrement, quand un vieillard m'entretenant de ce qu'on lui avait appris dans son pays touchant ce qu'on peut appeler religion parmi eux, il me fit un récit, qui a assez de rapport avec celui que fait l'Écriture, de la faute que fit Cham à l'égard de son père Noé, durant son ivresse. Il me disait que Robrocou avait trois enfants, deux garçons et une fille, que l'aîné ayant vu son père découvert d'une manière indécente durant son assoupissement, avait appelé les autres pour s'en moquer, que ceux-ci l'avaient couvert avec une espèce de toile de son pays, laquelle il me nommait, et que Robrocou s'étant éveillé avait récompensé le cadet le faisant son successeur, et puni l'aîné en le faisant esclave du premier. Ceux qui croient que la noirceur de ces gens vient de la malédiction que Cham s'attira dans une pareille occasion, pourront dire que les nègres n'ignorent pas tout à fait l'origine de leur couleur.

On peut rapporter en cet endroit ce que je vous écrivis de la sotte impiété de celui, qui pour justifier les railleries qu'il faisait du paradis, dont on lui parlait, disait [15ᵛ] que les poules y avaient été, et que Dieu pour les empêcher d'en sortir, leur disait, qu'elles ne trouveraient nulle autre part de l'eau à boire, et qu'enfin il y en eut une qui s'échappa, et vola sur la terre, où ayant trouvé de l'eau, en la buvant elle leva la tête en haut, comme pour reprocher à Dieu qu'elle en avait trouvé, et qu'à son imitation sa postérité en faisait de même en la buvant.

Voilà donc ce qu'on peut appeler religion parmi les nègres. On n'a pas tant de peine à la leur faire quitter, qu'à leur apprendre les principes de la nôtre pour les disposer au baptême, leur extrême étourdissement en est la cause, car il y en a qui depuis plus de vingt ans n'ont pu mettre encore dans leur tête combien

---

[41] The varying spellings of 'Reboucou' and 'Robrocou' follow both AFSI, GBro185 and MdC, MS 73.

[42] MdC, MS 73, fol. 90ᵛ: 'Boudou'.

burn them without any trouble. The only time I had any difficulty was with three who were from Cap Blanc, which is a place further north than anywhere else from where black slaves are brought. Those from further south told me that they believe in a being who made everything and who, they say, sends rain to ripen their crops. Those from Angola told me that they call him *Zambi*, and those who are not as far away from the famous river Senegal call this god *Reboucou*. They added that it is something hidden, and which is made like us. Those of Ardra call it *Roudou* and they told me that they bury their dead in the house, hold a great feast at the grave, and throw half on it for the deceased. However, when I asked them where the dead go to after this life, they replied with great naivety 'we do not know this where we are from'. Usually, when they want to assure you of something, they raise their eyes and a hand in the air in a very gentle and respectful way, saying 'God above'.

I was recently surprised by an old man, who was telling me what he had been taught in his country about what could be called religion amongst these people. He told me a tale that is comparable with the account, in Scripture, of the offence committed by Ham when his father Noah was drunk. He told me that Robrocou had three children, two boys and a girl, and that the eldest had seen his father uncovered in an indecent manner while in a drowsy state. He had called the others to make fun of his father, but they had covered him up with a sort of fabric from their lands, which the old slave named for me. When Robrocou awoke he rewarded the youngest child by making him his heir, and punished the eldest by making him the slave of the youngest. Those who believe that the blackness of these people is due to the curse Ham brought upon himself on such an occasion, may well say that the blacks are not completely unaware of the origin of their colour.

This may be the place to recount what I wrote to you about the foolish impiety of one who wanted to justify his mockery of Paradise, about which he was being instructed. He said that there had been hens there and that God, who wanted to prevent them from leaving, used to tell them that they would find drinking water nowhere else, and then in the end one of them escaped. [He said] she flew to earth where, having found water, drinking it she lifted her head up high as if to reproach God for this, and that, just like her, her descendants would do the same when drinking water.

This, then, is what might be called religion amongst the slaves. We do not have as much trouble making them leave it behind, as in teaching them the principles of our own so as to ready them for baptism. Their extreme dullness is the cause of this, for there are some of them who, after more than twenty years, have been unable to get into their heads how many gods there are. This is one of the greatest difficulties for our missionaries, and two learned Spanish

il y a de dieux, ce qui est un des plus grands embarras de nos missionnaires. Aussi deux savants théologiens espagnols ont fait des livres entiers sur cette instruction des nègres, contenant ce qu'on leur peut apprendre, et la méthode avec le degré de capacité, qu'on peut exiger d'eux dans la nécessité.

Sur les côtes de l'Afrique, ou dans les îles qui en sont très voisines, il y a des Portugais[43] qui y ont des évêques, qui sont sans doute pleins de zèle, et la plupart religieux selon la coutume de cette nation.[44] Ceux qui y sont présentement selon les mémoires de l'année 1680, s'appellent François de Saint-Diego, évêque des îles du Cap-Vert, cordelier, Laurens de [16^r] Castro à Angra en Guinée, Bernard de Sainte-Marie hieronymitain, à São Tomé, île sous la ligne, Antoine Soli à Luanda île vis-à-vis et tout proche de Congo, à Angole Pierre Sanchez de l'Ordre de Christ.[45]

Mais nonobstant tout cela presque tous les nègres qui viennent de ce[46] pays, sont également ignorants, exceptés quelques-uns, qui viennent de Congo,[47] peut-être parce que ceux-ci sont voisins d'une mission, que les jésuites ont à Luanda, et ils témoignent qu'ils ont été baptisés en disant qu'on leur a fait manger du sel, et j'ai trouvé aussi que c'était la même réponse, qu'ils faisaient dans leur pays à un missionnaire de notre Compagnie, qui y alla en 1581. Autrefois, et peut-être encore aujourd'hui, quelques Espagnols et Portugais baptisaient les troupes des nègres en même temps qu'ils les embarquaient, et sans autre instruction, quoiqu'il soit certain, que le baptême n'était pas valide, si ces pauvres esclaves n'avaient pas l'intention de le recevoir, aussi les prêtres français qui sont à Sénégal, ne baptisent pas maintenant ordinairement ceux qu'on y embarque pour nos îles, parce que ces nègres ne séjournent pas au lieu de la mission suffisamment pour être instruits, à quoi il faut beaucoup de temps, comme je le sais par mon expérience.

Car de trois dispositions qu'ils doivent apporter au baptême, [16^v] celle-là est une des deux qui sont les plus difficiles pour ces gens.[48] Ces dispositions sont

---

[43] MdC, MS 73, fol. 91^v: 'il y a des Espagnols et des Portugais'.

[44] MdC, MS 73, fol. 91^v: 'la coutume de ces deux nations'.

[45] MdC, MS 73, fol. 92^r continues: 'Il n'y a que les deux premiers évêchés qui sont d'Espagne. Outre cela à Sénégal il y a des capucins français.'

[46] MdC, MS 73, fol. 92^r: 'ces'.

[47] AFSI, GBro185, fol. 16^r and MdC, MS 73, fol. 92^r: 'de Congo' (both mentions).

[48] AFSI, GBro185, fol. 16^r–16^v: in this sentence, 'de trois' has been replaced by 'les', 'celle-là est une des deux qui' has been crossed out, and 'les plus' replaced with 'assez', to read 'Car les dispositions qu'ils doivent apporter au baptême sont assez difficiles pour ces gens.'

theologians have written whole books about the instruction of the blacks, including what they can be taught, and the method, with the degree of capacity, that can be required of them in cases of necessity.[27]

On the coasts of Africa or on the islands which are very close by, there are Portuguese who have bishops, who are without doubt very zealous, and most of them members of an order according to the custom of this nation. Those who are there at present, according to the memoirs of the year 1680, are named Francis de Saint Diego, the bishop of the Cape Verde islands, a Franciscan,[28] Lourenço de Castro in Angra in Guinea,[29] Bernardo de Santa Maria, a Hieronymite, in Sao Tomé, an island under the equator,[30] Antonio Soli in Luanda, an island opposite and very near the Congo, and in Angola, Pedro Sanches of the Order of Christ.[31]

But, in spite of all this, nearly all the blacks who come from these lands are equally ignorant except for a few who come from the Congo. This is perhaps because the latter are from near a Jesuit mission at Luanda. They testify to having been baptized by saying that they were made to eat salt, and I have found that this is the same answer that they gave in their own land to a missionary of our company who went there in 1581.[32] Formerly, and perhaps still nowadays, some of the Spanish and Portuguese baptized crowds of slaves at the same time as they embarked them and with no other instruction, even though it is certain that the baptism was invalid if these poor slaves did not have the intention of receiving it. Therefore, the French priests at Senegal do not ordinarily now baptize those who are embarked for our islands, because these slaves do not reside long enough at the site of the mission to be instructed, which requires much time, as I know from my own experience.

For of the three dispositions that they must have for baptism, this is one of the two that are most difficult for these people.[33] These dispositions are intention, faith, and repentance. Without the first the baptism is null, and

---

[27] Presumably Sandoval, *De instauranda Aethiopum salute* (1627); potentially also Acosta, *De procuranda Indorum salute* (1588).

[28] The bishop of Santiago de Cabo Verde from 1676–84 (consecrated 1675) was the Franciscan Antonio de Sao Dionisio, according to André Chapeau and Charles N. Bransom, 'Franciscan Bishops', *Franciscan Studies*, 47 (1987), 287–372 (348).

[29] Angra do Heroísmo, capital of Terceira in the Azores; Lourenço de Castro is listed as a Dominican, bishop of Angra 1671–81 in António Caetano da Sousa, *Historia genealogica da Casa real portugueza*, 13 vols (Lisbon: da Sylva, 1745), XI, p. 664.

[30] Bernardo Zuzarte de Santa Maria, or Zuzarte de Andrade; *Hieronymite*, a member of the Order of Saint Jerome, a hermetical Catholic order.

[31] Pedro Sanches Farinha was consecrated bishop in 1671, succeeded by António do Espíritu Santo, discalced Carmelite (d. 1674), who was succeeded in turn by Manoel da Natividade. Information from José Barbosa Canaes de Figuerido Castello-Branco, *Estudos biographicos ou noticia das pessoas retratadas nos quadros historicos pertencentes a Bibliotheca nacional de Lisboa* (Lisbon: F. A. da Silva, 1854), p. 169. The Portuguese Ordem Militar de Christo was founded in 1318.

[32] This is discussed in Pierre Du Jarric, *Histoire des choses plus mémorables advenues tant ez Indes orientales, que autres païs de la descouverte des Portugais*, 3 vols (Bordeaux: Simon Millanges, 1608–14), II (1610), 68–69.

[33] AFSI, GBro185, fols 16ʳ–16ᵛ, after modification reads: 'For the dispositions they must have for baptism are difficult enough for these people.'

l'intention, la foi, et le repentir. Sans la première le baptême est nul, et sans les deux autres il n'est pas licite, et quand on connaît qu'il en manque une des trois, on ne peut administrer le baptême sans un grand péché, ce qui embarrasse bien souvent les missionnaires.[49]

Pour moi en les disposant durant les mois d'octobre, et de novembre, je ne faisais pas le plus grand fonds sur les catéchismes des jours de fête, que je n'omettais jamais, car la foule était trop grande pour y pouvoir instruire suffisamment chacun en particulier. C'est pourquoi après avoir vu d'un coup d'œil dans mon catalogue, ceux qui étaient à baptiser, j'allais parler à eux dans leur travail pour les instruire, les examiner, et les choisir pour le baptême.

Quant à la volonté du baptême je n'avais pas de peine à la leur faire naître, car aussitôt qu'ils commencent d'avoir la moindre connaissance de notre religion, ils le demandent avec un grand empressement, paraissant tout persuadés, que sans cela ils n'iraient pas *là-haut avec le bon Dieu*, comme ils disent, outre qu'il y en a plusieurs qui assurent qu'avant le baptême, le mabouya, c'est ainsi qu'ils appellent le démon, les bat toutes les nuits, à cause de quoi leurs maîtres les entendent alors jeter de grands cris, et les voient courir à eux tout épouvantés, [17ʳ] et tout en eau, et moulus de coups. Cela fait que les maîtres ne s'empressent pas moins qu'eux pour les baptêmes, et je me sers de cet empressement des uns et des autres pour les porter à contribuer de leur côté ce qu'ils peuvent pour les dispositions nécessaires aux adultes qui demandent le baptême sans quoi je le diffère constamment.

La capacité et la foi qui fait la seconde disposition, n'est pas si facile que la première, à cause de leur étourdissement, quand leur ignorance vient plus de défaut d'esprit que de leur faute, je me contente qu'ils sachent le mystère de la Trinité et de l'Incarnation, en attendant qu'ils apprennent le reste, c'est-à-dire, l'oraison dominicale, la salutation de l'ange, la croyance et les commandements de Dieu.

Mais le repentir de leurs péchés qui est la troisième disposition ne me donne pas moins de peine, et particulièrement à cause de leurs divers concubinages, qu'ils ne paraissent avoir aucune volonté de quitter, quand ils demandent le baptême, sur quoi je m'étonne de l'étonnement[50] que témoignent leurs maîtres, quand je refuse de baptiser leurs esclaves, qui sont actuellement concubinaires. Nonobstant tout cela je tiens ferme jusqu'à ce que par de bonnes informations que je fais à ma façon, je sois persuadé de leur amendement, en quoi pourtant je n'oserais [17ᵛ] assurer, que je ne sois jamais trompé, mais si cela arrive, ce n'est qu'après des précautions, qui mettent ma conscience en repos. Je ne dois

---

[49] MdC, MS 73, fol. 92ʳ–92ᵛ: 'on ne peut administrer le baptême sans un grand péché, ce qui fait suer bien souvent les missionnaires qui ayant à faire à des catéchumènes étourdis, expérimentent qu'un peu de patience et de théologie ne leur sont pas trop superflus dans ces embarras.'

[50] AFSI, GBro185, fol. 17ʳ: 'l'étonnement' replaced by 'la surprise'.

without the other two it is illicit, and, when one recognizes that one of the three is missing, the baptism cannot be administered without committing a great sin, which is very often a source of difficulty for missionaries.[34]

As for me, in disposing them for baptism during the months of October and November, I did not place too much store in the catechism on feast days, which I never omitted, because the crowd was always too large to be able to instruct everyone individually and sufficiently. This is why, having seen who was to be baptized by glancing at my catalogue, I went to speak with them while they were at work, so as to instruct, examine, and select them for baptism.

I had no difficulty in inspiring in them the wish for baptism, because, once they have the least knowledge of our religion, they ask for it with great eagerness, appearing to be completely persuaded that without this they will not go *up on high with the Good Lord*, as they say. What is more, there are many who insist that, before baptism, the Mabouya — this is what they call the demon — beats them every night. For this reason their masters hear them screaming out loud, and see them running towards them scared stiff, sweating and battered and bruised. For this reason, the masters are no less eager than their slaves to have them baptized, and I use the avidity of one and the other to bring them to contribute what they can on their side, towards the dispositions which are necessary for adults who ask for baptism. Without this, I consistently put off the baptism.

The capacity, and faith, which is the second disposition, is not as easy as the first, because of their dull-wittedness. When their ignorance is due to a lack of intelligence rather than their own fault, I content myself with them knowing the mystery of the Trinity and the Incarnation while I wait for them to learn the rest, that is, the Lord's Prayer, the *Ave Maria*, the Apostles' Creed, and God's Commandments.

But the repentance for their sins, which is the third disposition, gives me no less trouble, and particularly because of their various liaisons which they do not seem to have any desire to leave behind when they request baptism. On this point I marvel at the surprise their masters show, when I refuse to baptize their slaves who are presently cohabiting. Notwithstanding all this I remain firm until I have confirmation, which I obtain in my own way, of their having changed their ways, although I would not dare guarantee that I have never been mistaken. Yet, if this happens, it is only after precautions that put my conscience at ease. I must not forget here the amusing way a slave from my neighbourhood tried to circumvent these. He was among the most likeable for his good nature, but not always so for his morals. Everywhere he saw me he would run after

---

[34] MdC, MS 73, fol. 92^r 92^v: 'the baptism cannot be administered without committing a great sin, which is hard work for missionaries who, when faced with catechumens who are completely lost, discover that a little patience and knowledge of theology do not go amiss in such a case.'

pas oublier ici l'agréable défaite d'un nègre des plus aimables de mon quartier pour son bon naturel, mais qui ne l'a pas toujours été pour ses mœurs. Partout où il me voyait il courait après moi, pour me prier de ne pas tant différer son baptême. Un jour je m'arrêtai davantage à lui expliquer la cause de ce délai, et je lui[51] que [sic] c'était parce qu'il n'était pas sage, *et comment moi sage*, répondit-il,[52] *si moi pas chrétien, moi vouloir être chrétien, pour moi devenir sage*, nonobstant quoi il fit enfin ce que je lui dis, et il se rendit digne d'être baptisé avec les autres.

La troupe en fut assez grande par la grâce de Dieu, et la solennité s'en fit à la fin du mois de novembre de l'année <u>1680</u>, auquel temps pour m'assurer de leur persévérance, et de l'amendement de leur vie, j'en mariai une partie le même jour, et immédiatement après les avoir baptisés, à cause que la difficulté qu'il y a de les bien disposer à la confession,[53] rend quasi nécessaire cette jonction immédiate du mariage et du baptême, lequel supplée abondamment au défaut de la confession qu'on fait d'ordinaire avant que de se marier et c'est pour cela que j'ai coutume d'en marier autant que je puis immédiatement après leur baptême.[54]

[18^r] Après ces baptêmes je m'appliquai à marier les autres chrétiens, qui étaient à marier. C'est un remède que leurs grandes débauches ont rendu nécessaire à la plupart, mais autant que les maîtres et les esclaves s'empressent pour le baptême, autant les uns et les autres ont de répugnance à consentir que je fasse ces mariages. Le libertinage de ces nègres est la plus véritable cause de l'obstacle, qu'ils y forment de leur côté, voulant avoir la liberté de prendre et de quitter toutes les femmes qu'il leur plaira, sans être obligés d'entretenir une famille.

L'interêt que les maîtres ont à seconder leur mauvaise volonté, vient de ce qu'ils ne les peuvent plus vendre séparément, dès qu'ils sont mariés, ce qui fait ou qu'ils ne trouvent pas si facilement des acheteurs, ou qu'ils ne peuvent pas se défaire d'un nègre qui leur est inutile, sans se priver d'un autre qui ne l'est pas, outre qu'il y a des Françaises, qui après avoir instruit quelque négresse[55] pour l'employer en qualité de servante dans la maison, ne veulent plus consentir qu'elle se marie, pour ne se pas priver du service qu'elles en retirent, surtout durant la nuit, pour garder les petits enfants de la maison.

Mais la plus grande difficulté vient de la coutume du pays, laquelle malgré les lois anciennes ne permet pas aux esclaves de différents maîtres, de se marier

---

[51] MdC, MS 73, fol. 93^v: 'je lui dis'.
[52] MdC, MS 73, fol. 93^v: '<u>hé comment moi sage</u> (répondit-il)'.
[53] MdC, MS 73, fol. 93^v: 'outre que la difficulté qu'il y a de les rendre capables de plusieurs années, de confesser'.
[54] MdC, MS 73, fol. 93^v continues: 'J'en excepte quelquefois ceux qui appartenant à un [même] maître s'étaient pris avant d'être baptisés réciproquement et pour toujours, ce qui arrive fort rarement parmi eux car alors il n'est pas nécessaire de les remarier.'
[55] MdC, MS 73, fol. 94^r: 'qui après avoir dégrossi l'esprit de quelque négresse'.

me and beg me not to put off his baptism so long. One day I stopped longer to explain the cause of this delay to him, and I [said] to him that it was because he was not good. 'How me be good', he answered, 'if me no Christian? Me want be Christian so to become good!' In spite of this, in the end he did what I told him to, and became worthy of being baptized along with the others.

Thanks to the grace of God, the group was large enough, and the ceremony took place at the end of the month of November of the year 1680. At the same time, to assure myself of their perseverance and of their having changed their lives, I married a number of them the same day and immediately after their baptism. I did so because the difficulty there is in properly disposing them for confession means it is well-nigh necessary to have their marriage follow immediately upon their baptism. Baptism more than makes up for the lack of the confession that is normally made before marriage, and it is for this that my habit is to marry as many of them as I can immediately after their baptism.[35]

After these baptisms, I concentrated on marrying the other Christians who were to be married. It is a remedy that most need because of their great debauchery, but both masters and slaves are as reluctant to let me celebrate these marriages, as they are enthusiastic about slaves being baptized. The licentiousness of these slaves is the real reason for the objections on their side, as they want to be free to have or to leave as many women as they wish, without being obliged to support a family.

The interest that the masters have in supporting their slaves' unwillingness is due to their no longer being able to sell them separately once they are married. This means either that they cannot find buyers as easily, or that they cannot get rid of a slave who is of no use to them without at the same time getting rid of one who is useful. What is more, there are Frenchwomen who, having had a black slave instructed as a domestic servant, do not then want to allow her to marry, because they would deprive themselves of her service, especially during the night, in looking after the little children of the household.

But the greatest difficulty is due to the custom of the land which, despite the ancient laws, does not allow the slaves of different masters to marry. The

---

[35] MdC, MS 73, fol. 93ᵛ continues: 'Sometimes I excuse those who belong to [the same] master and who, before baptism, had been joined for life, which is very rare with them, for in such a case there is no need to wed them again.'

ensemble, ce que les missionnaires tolèrent ici prudemment, [18^v] pour éviter de plus grands maux, qui seraient les séparations fréquentes, les divorces, les adultères des mariés, les procès et les querelles continuelles de leurs maîtres, ce qui met la plupart de ces pauvres esclaves dans l'impossibilité de se marier, tel habitant n'en ayant qu'un seul, tel n'ayant que des garçons, un autre que des filles, et ceux qui ont suffisament des uns et des autres n'en trouvant pas quelquefois deux, qui se veulent réciproquement marier, quoiqu'il arrive à quelques-uns de ceux-là de demeurer ensemble comme concubinaires.

Vous voyez par là que le remède est aussi difficile, que le mal est grand, et voici comme je m'y suis pris, premièrement tous mes catéchismes et exhortations des jours de fête étaient sur ce chapitre, après reconnaissant sur mon catalogue les nègres, qu'on pouvait marier, j'allais leur en parler dans les champs, où ils travaillaient attroupés. À la première proposition, que j'en faisais, ce n'était dans toute la troupe, que risées, qui duraient le reste du jour avec⁵⁶ des railleries très sanglantes, que ces gens, qui sont les plus grands railleurs du monde, faisaient à ceux, que j'avais parlé de marier, n'omettant aucun de leurs défauts, particulièrement de la femme. Cela faisait que la plupart du temps je n'étais pas écouté de ceux à qui je portais cette parole, quoique bien souvent ils ne fussent retenus que par la mauvaise honte de se déclarer au milieu de tant de railleries. [19^r] Je le vis une fois entre autres en une jeune négresse qui voulait assurément se marier avec un nègre de la troupe. Quand je lui en parlai devant les autres, elle le nia nettement et constamment jusqu'à ce que m'ayant vu tirer parole de six autres pour le mariage, comme je me retirais elle courut après moi pour me dire qu'elle en voulait être aussi, mais qu'elle avait eu honte de le dire devant et avant les autres.

Ces railleries ordinaires⁵⁷ ont souvent exercé ma patience, mais pourtant je continuais de travailler en leur représentant la nécessité de changer le concubinage en mariage. Après je tirais à part ceux qu'il fallait marier; je négociai cette affaire avec toute l'application que j'eusse employée pour des gens de qualité. Il fallait savoir les raisons de leur refus, ce qui n'était pas assurément pour la dot, car ils n'ont rien du tout en ce monde. Ils s'objectent réciproquement des attachements qu'ils ont ailleurs, et que le mariage ne leur fera pas quitter. L'homme dit que la femme, que je lui veux donner, est une criarde, elle allègue au contraire qu'il est cruel, et paresseux pour aller amasser et vendre de quoi se nourrir. Les uns et les autres se défendent sur ce qu'ils n'ont point encore de cabane, ni rien pour faire le festin de la noce, qu'ils ne sont pas tous deux d'un même pays ni de même âge, et plusieurs autres prétextes de cette nature, que j'ai bien de la peine à dissiper. Si j'y réussis, et qu'ils [19^v] me donnent leur consentement, il faut avoir celui de leurs parents; ensuite celui

---

⁵⁶ MdC, MS 73, fol. 94ᵛ: 'qui duraient le reste du jour et plus, avec'.
⁵⁷ MdC, MS 73, fol. 94ᵛ: 'Ces railleries ordinaires et ces refus brusques'.

missionaries tolerate this here through prudence, to avoid worse evils such as frequent separations, divorces,[36] the adulteries of the married, and litigation and continuous disputes between masters. All of this makes it impossible for most of these poor slaves to marry. There might be one planter who has just one slave, another who only has boys, another only girls, and those who do have a sufficient number of one or the other sex might sometimes not find two of them who want to marry one another, even if some may well cohabit together.

You can see from this that the remedy is as difficult as the sickness is grave. This is how I tackled it. All my catechisms and my sermons on feast days were, first, on this theme. Then, seeing from my catalogue which slaves there were to marry, I went to talk to them about it in the fields where they were at work in gangs. From the first mention I made of it, the whole lot began laughing, and it lasted the whole day, accompanied by the vicious mockery which these people, who are the greatest jeerers in the world, made of those I had planned to marry. They neglected none of their faults, particularly those of the women, and it meant that most of the time those for whom I intended this message did not listen to me, although very often the only thing that held them back was the shame of revealing themselves amidst so much jeering. I saw it one time amongst others with a young girl who certainly wanted to marry another slave from the gang. When I brought it up with her in front of the others, she denied it straight out, and persistently, until, after having seen me make six others promise to marry, she ran after me as I was on my way, and told me that she too wanted to marry, but had been ashamed to say it before, and in front of, the others.

This habitual jeering has often tested my patience, but I still kept on working by showing them the need to make their cohabitation into a marriage. Afterwards I took to the side those who had to be married, negotiating this business with as much attention as I would have used for people of quality. I needed to know the reasons for their refusal, and it was certainly not because of the dowry, because they have nothing at all in this world. They object to one another that they have other attachments elsewhere which marriage would not make them leave behind. The man will say that the woman I want to give him is a nag, and she will instead claim that he is cruel, and lazy when it comes to gathering and selling what they need to feed themselves. Both of them will argue that they do not yet have a cabin, nor anything with which to have the wedding festivities, that they are not from the same land or of the same age, and many other excuses of this sort, that I have much difficulty dismissing. If I do succeed in obtaining their consent, then I have to get that of their parents,

---

[36] Mongin uses the term *divorce* several times in this letter. *Divorce* could refer to the 'dissolution' of a marriage, or a separation. See Furetière (1690), I, entry 'Divorce', non-paginated.

des maîtres, dont j'ai trouvé quelques-uns si éloignés et si brutaux que j'en ai vu qui menaçaient leurs esclaves, de les assommer de coups, s'ils consentaient à se marier, quoiqu'ils fussent témoins de leurs concubinages, d'autres qu'il m'a fallu forcer par les voies de la justice à ne les pas empêcher, d'autres qui devant moi les voulaient contraindre par menaces à se marier, et en mon absence les en détournaient avec fureur, comme je l'appris une fois de quelques-uns, qui après que leurs maîtres venaient de leur parler ainsi en ma présence me suivirent pour me venir découvrir à l'écart ce mystère d'iniquité.

Mais enfin, quoique de tout temps les lois aient rendu les esclaves indépendants de leurs maîtres pour le mariage, je tâche toujours d'en obtenir le consentement, pour prévenir beaucoup de désordres, à cela ne me sert pas peu l'intérêt qu'ils y ont pour les enfants qui en proviennent, et qui sont bien plus souvent le fruit d'un mariage, que Dieu bénit, que du concubinage, à quoi il donne sa malédiction.

Quand tout est ainsi conclu je fais faire une espèce de fiançailles aux parties qui se promettent réciproquement devant moi de se marier, car on n'a pas besoin de notaire pour écrire les articles, et l'intérêt n'entre jamais dans leurs mariages, comme il fait si souvent [20ʳ] dans ceux du reste des hommes. Après je leur recommande d'être fort sur leurs gardes, leur disant que le démon ne pouvant empêcher leurs mariages va faire les derniers efforts pour y attirer la malédiction de Dieu par quelque nouveau péché.

Après tous ces préparatifs je ne les marie pas d'abord pour m'assurer de leur constance, qui n'étant pas en eux extraordinairement grande, a causé une infinité de mauvais ménages. J'ai vu assez souvent que des maîtres ayant bonne volonté de marier une de leurs négresses, et celle-ci ne trouvant dans la maison aucun nègre à son gré, ils la menaient dans le lieu où l'on venait de mettre les nègres récemment arrivés de leur pays, afin que parmi deux ou trois cents elle en choisît un à sa fantaisie, qu'on lui achetait, mais durant quelques mois qu'on employait à instruire ce nègre pour le baptiser avant que de faire ce mariage, la future épouse s'en dégoûtait et n'en voulait plus du tout. Voici une autre marque de leur légèreté.

Il y en avait deux qui m'avaient demandé de fort bonne grâce de les marier. Tout était conclu et tous les préparatifs achevés, le jour que je leur avais marqué ils partirent pour venir à l'église, où je les attendais pour les marier, mais le chemin fut assez long pour leur donner le temps de prendre querelle. Le garçon se plaignit de ce que la fille n'était pas assez propre pour une telle occasion, la dispute s'echauffa de telle sorte [20ᵛ] qu'ils se battirent, et tous deux s'en retournèrent sur leurs pas.[58] Je les attendis longtemps, mais comme nonobstant cette légèreté, ils ont tous deux le naturel fort bon, ils renouèrent ensemble, et

---

[58] MdC, MS 73, fol. 96ʳ: 'la dispute s'échauffa d'abord et ils se gourmèrent tous deux tout de bon; après il ne faut pas dire s'ils s'en retournèrent sur leurs pas'.

and then that of their masters. I have found some of these to be so unfavourable and so brutal that I have seen them threaten to give their slaves a thrashing if they agreed to marry, even though they were well aware they were cohabiting. There are others against whom I have had to have legal recourse to stop them preventing their slaves' marriage. There are still others who, when in front of me, would threaten their slaves to force them to marry, and when I was gone, would dissuade them from it with fury, as I learned once from some slaves who, after their master had just spoken to them in this way while I was present, followed me so as to reveal this Mystery of Iniquity to me on the quiet.[37]

In any case, although throughout time slaves have always been considered independent of their masters when it comes to marriage, I always try to secure their consent so as to avoid all manner of problems. I am helped not a little by the interest they have in the children who are born, and who are more often the fruit of a marriage blessed by God, than of cohabitation, which He curses.

When, in this way, it is all arranged, I have a sort of engagement ceremony for both parties, who promise before me to marry one another, for there is no need of a notary to write the terms, and money is never a factor in their marriages, as it so often is in those of the rest of mankind. Afterwards, I advise them to be very careful, and I tell them that the demon, unable to prevent their marriage, will make a last attempt to bring the curse of God upon it by some new sin.

Even after all these preparations I do not marry them immediately so as to be sure of their constancy; as this is not a quality they have much of, it has caused an infinite number of bad marriages. I have often seen masters who have been quite prepared to marry off one of their female slaves, and, with her not finding a slave in the household to her taste, they bring her to where the slaves who have recently been brought from their homeland are kept. They do this so that she can choose one to her liking among two or three hundred, and they buy this slave for her. However, in the few months that it takes to instruct him for baptism before this marriage can take place, the future wife becomes tired of him and does not want him at all. Here is another sign of their shallowness.

Two of them had asked me with great respect to marry them. Everything was ready and the preparations had been finished, and on the day I had reserved for them they set off for the church where I was waiting to marry them. However, the road was long enough to give them enough time to start arguing. The boy reproached the girl for not being turned out as such an occasion required, and the argument got so heated that it turned physical and both of them retraced their steps. I was waiting a long time for them. However, as both of them are very good-natured, notwithstanding their flightiness, they got back together,

---

[37] A reference to *mysterium iniquitatis*, II Thessalonians 2. 7 ('the mystery of iniquity', 1582, p. 554).

après une assez longue épreuve de leur constance, je les ai mariés et ils font maintenant bon ménage.

Le temps pour éprouver leur volonté est celui-là même qui est nécessaire pour les trois publications des bans de mariage, à quoi il faut d'ordinaire environ un mois, parce que les fêtes sont ici plus rares qu'en Europe. J'avoue que cette publication est si nouvelle dans les îles à l'égard des esclaves, qu'elle m'a attiré des affaires,[59] surtout quand on voyait que les blancs mêmes s'en faisaient dispenser assez souvent, ce qui fut cause qu'un habitant m'ayant un jour envoyé deux de ses esclaves pour les marier sur l'heure et sans autre formalité, et moi ayant voulu différer jusqu'après les instructions nécessaires, et la publication des bans, il en fut indigné, disant qu'il avait eu assez de crédit depuis peu pour marier deux de ses enfants, sans bans, dans une autre église, et qu'il était surpris de n'avoir pas le même pouvoir pour ses esclaves. À même temps il renvoie ceux-ci dans le même lieu, où ils furent aussitôt mariés, sans instruction et sans confession, quoique tous deux en eussent bien besoin, mais la manière différente, dont ils m'ont vu marier les autres a donné tant de honte à ceux-ci qu'ils me vinrent trouver peu après pour [21ʳ] suppléer aux défauts de leurs mariages, par la confession et par la communion.

Maintenant ces bans se publient avec l'approbation de tout le monde, ayant fait entendre, que j'y étais obligé par le respect que je dois aux ordres de l'Église, et par la nécessité de découvrir les empêchements de mariage, qui sont plus fréquents, qu'on ne se l'imaginait parmi les nègres, principalement à cause de l'affinité, que produisent leurs concubinages, comme je l'ai reconnu assez souvent après les instructions que je leur ai faites sur l'obligation qu'ils ont de m'en avertir, dans les occasions de les marier.

Les trois bans étant publiés, nous choisissons, tant qu'il se peut, un jour de fête, pour faire la cérémonie du mariage, avec un plus grand concours de nègres, car si c'était un jour ouvrier les maîtres ne permettraient pas même aux parents des mariés d'y assister, pour ne pas perdre quelques heures de leur travail, dont ils sont si avares, qu'à l'heure que j'écris ceci, on vient de me dire qu'un habitant a refusé aujourd'hui à quelques-uns de ses nègres, la permission d'aller dire le dernier adieu à leur frère, qu'on embarque pour les galères perpétuelles.

Le jour de fête facilitant ainsi le concours des esclaves, favorise extrêmement le dessein que j'ai en faisant ces cérémonies avec tout l'appareil qu'il m'est possible, et ce dessein n'est autre que celui de l'Église dans [21ᵛ] leur institution,

---

[59] MdC, MS 73, fol. 96ʳ: 'qu'elle m'a attiré la risée de plusieurs'.

and, after testing their constancy for long enough, I married them and they are now getting on well.

The time required to test their will is the same as that necessary for the three proclamations of the marriage banns, which usually requires about a month, because feast days are less frequent here than in Europe. I admit that proclaiming the banns of slaves is so new in the islands that it has caused me a few problems, especially when it was seen that often enough whites themselves got married without them. One day a planter sent me two of his slaves to be married straightaway and without any further ado, but I wanted to put it off until after the required instruction and the proclamation of the banns.

He was outraged as a result, saying that he had had enough credit a short while ago to marry two of his own children without banns in another church, and that he was surprised not to have the same power for his slaves. Meanwhile he sent them both to the same place, where they were married straightaway without instruction or confession, even though these slaves were in good need of both. However, they were so ashamed by the different way they saw the other slaves being married that they came looking for me soon after, to remedy what was lacking from their marriages through confession and Communion.

Nowadays these banns are proclaimed with the approval of everyone, as I have made it understood that I am obliged to do so by the respect I owe to the orders of the Church, and by the need to find out if there are any obstacles to marriage. These are more frequent amongst the slaves than it was thought, mainly because their cohabitations give rise to affinity,[38] as I have myself discovered often enough after instructing them about their obligation to avert me about this, at the time of their marriages.

Once the three banns are proclaimed, we choose a feast day for the marriage ceremony, as much as it is possible, as it allows a greater number of slaves to attend. If it were a working day the masters would not even allow the bride and groom's relatives[39] to attend, so as not to lose a few hours of their labour, of which they are so avaricious. They are so greedy that, at the time of writing, I have just been told that a planter has today refused to allow a few of his slaves to say a last goodbye to their brother, who is being embarked on the galleys to which he has been sentenced for life.[40]

As feast days facilitate the attendance of slaves, they are also favourable to my intention to carry out these ceremonies with as much splendour as I can, and this intention is none other than that of the Church in establishing them. For,

[38] The context would imply 'affinity' as in a blood relationship.

[39] 'parents des mariés' implies relatives beyond parents. Furetière (1690), III, entry 'Parents', non-paginated.

[40] *Les galères*; punishment consisting in being sentenced to row on the royal galleys, for a fixed term or (as in this case) for life, one of the most rigorous punishments in *ancien régime* France.

car enfin on sait assez que les sentiments intérieurs de l'estime et du respect que nous devons aux sacrements et aux choses saintes s'augmentent infiniment dans notre esprit, par ces choses extérieures et sensibles, qui frappent notre vue. Vous vous souvenez peut-être encore de la bénédiction qu'il plut à Dieu de donner aux travaux d'un père,[60] dans un temps où la cour ne favorisait pas tant qu'à présent la conversion des protestants, on me demandait souvent quelle méthode j'avais prise pour y réussir, et je répondis que la plus efficace était la cérémonie, que l'Église prescrit pour la réception des hérétiques, qu'on faisait pour cette raison avec tout l'appareil dont vous fûtes autrefois le témoin, et qui fut quelquefois[61] salutaire aux huguenots à qui la curiosité prenait d'y assister, ou qui l'entendaient dire aux autres.

Ces choses extérieures sont nécessaires pour donner de la dévotion aux nègres.[62] Je l'ai reconnu à l'occasion de quelques anciens mariages de ces pauvres gens.[63] Plusieurs n'avaient aucune estime de ce sacrement, et quelques-uns même ne se croyaient point du tout mariés, et vivaient séparément dans de grandes débauches, sous prétexte qu'on les avait mariés d'une manière différente de celle des blancs, sans bans, sans messe, sans bague, sans bénédiction et sans église, quelques-uns même selon ce qu'on m'a dit plusieurs fois, ayant été mariés dans les champs par un effet d'un grand[64] zèle de quelques ecclésiastiques, qui pour [22r] arrêter au plus tôt le cours de la débauche, mariaient deux concubinaires dans le même temps, et dans le même lieu où ils pouvaient avoir leur consentement, ce qui m'a causé un fort grand embarras, ne trouvant aucun mémoire de ces mariages, et les mariés mêmes le désavouant.

Au contraire j'ai reconnu l'effet de la sage conduite de l'Église par la multitude et le succès des mariages, qui se sont faits conformément à ses ordres, car mes exhortations ne faisaient pas un grand effet sur l'esprit des nègres, jusqu'à ce qu'ils eurent vu marier leurs semblables avec toutes ces cérémonies, car alors je n'avais plus tant de besoin de les aller chercher pour cela. Ils venaient d'eux-mêmes, et en assez grand nombre, pour m'en prier.

C'est pour cette raison que je n'omets rien de ce qui est prescrit par l'Église dans la célébration du mariage, et je permets à ces pauvres gens toutes les réjouissances honnêtes, ainsi dès que le jour de fête que je leur ai marqué, est

---

[60] AFSI, GBro185, fol. 21v: in place of 'd'un père', MdC, MS 73, fol. 97r reads 'de celui qu'on appelait en Roussillon le père des huguenots'.

[61] MdC, MS 73, fol. 97r: 'qu'on faisait pour cette raison avec tout l'appareil dont vous fûtes quelquefois le témoin et qui fut tant de fois'.

[62] AFSI, GBro185, fol. 21v: instead of 'Ces choses extérieures sont nécessaires pour donner de la dévotion aux nègres', MdC, MS 73, fols 97r–97v reads 'Or comme ces choses extérieures sont nécessaires pour donner de la dévotion à une âme tandis qu'elle est dans le corps; plus elle est dans la matière comme est celle des nègres, plus aussi elle a besoin de [97v] ce secours.'

[63] MdC, MS 73, fol. 97v: 'pauvres idiots'.

[64] MdC, MS 73, fol. 97v: 'd'un trop grand'.

ultimately, it is well known that the inner feelings of esteem and respect that we owe to the sacraments and to what is Holy are infinitely magnified in our mind by exterior things that are perceptible by the senses and that strike our sight. Perhaps you still remember the blessing that it pleased God to bestow upon the labours of a priest, at a time when the court was not as favourable towards the conversion of Protestants as it is at present. I was often asked which method I had used to succeed, and I replied that the most effective was the ceremony that the Church prescribes for the reception of heretics, which was carried out for this reason with all the magnificence that you previously witnessed, and which was salutary at times for the Huguenots who attended through curiosity, or who heard it.

These external things are necessary to inspire devotion amongst the slaves.[41] I recognized this from some of the marriages of these poor people which had taken place some time ago. Many attached no value to this sacrament, and some of them did not even think of themselves as married and lived apart from one another and in great immorality, with the excuse that they had been married in a different way to the whites, with no banns or Mass, no ring, no blessing, and no church. Some of them, according to what I have been frequently told, had even been married in the fields thanks to the great zeal of a number of clerics. As the ecclesiastics wanted to put an end to their immorality as soon as possible, they would marry an unmarried couple at the time and place where they could have their agreement. This caused me significant difficulties, as I could find no record of these marriages, with even the couple denying that they had been married.

Instead, I recognized the effects of the wise direction of the Church, through the great number and success of the marriages which took place according to its orders. For my preaching did not have much effect on the slaves' way of thinking, until they had seen their fellows married with all the ceremonies. After this, I did not need to go looking for them quite so much. They came themselves, and in large enough numbers, to request marriage.

It is for this reason that I omit nothing that is prescribed by the Church for the celebration of marriage, and I allow these poor people all decent merrymaking. So, as soon as the feast day I have allotted them has arrived, they arrive at the

---

[41] AFSI, GBro185, fol. 21ᵛ: instead of 'These external things are necessary to inspire devotion amongst the slaves', MdC, MS 73, fol. 97ʳ–97ᵛ reads 'For as these external things are necessary to inspire devotion in a soul while it is within the body, the more it is within matter, as are the souls of the black slaves, the more it needs this help.'

arrivé, ils se rendent de grand matin à l'église ajustés le mieux qu'ils peuvent par le moyen des habits que les maîtres leur prêtent. Ils sont accompagnés d'une bande d'autres nègres bien propres, à leur tête précède un drapeau orné de tous les rubans qu'ils peuvent trouver. Après que les fiancés se sont confessés,[65] je les marie. Je bénis l'anneau, je dis la messe où[66] je donne la bénédiction aux nouveaux mariés qui sont quelquefois [22ᵛ] en si grand nombre, qu'ils occupent tout le banc de la communion, qui a environ trente-cinq pieds de long, après quoi je leur fais sur le sujet une exhortation que je diffère jusqu'après la fin de la messe pour donner la liberté aux blancs de se retirer, car ce qu'il y a de plus considérable dans le quartier se trouve à cette messe pour prévenir la chaleur du soleil. Il n'est pas croyable quelle estime conçoivent les pauvres nègres du sacrement de mariage, et la différence qu'on fait souvent entre ceux, qui ont été mariés de la sorte, et ceux qui ne l'ont pas été, ce qui fait voir qu'il y a quelque bénédiction particulière attachée aux cérémonies de l'Église.

Le mariage est ensuite registré selon toutes les formes, sans omettre celles que le Code Louis a ajoutées. Après les nouveaux mariés se retirent chez eux, dans le même ordre et le même cortège avec lequel ils étaient venus, puis dans une belle prairie ils font leur festin, chantent, jouent de tous les instruments de leur pays, et dansent avec des marques d'une joie extraordinaire, car c'est une chose surprenante de voir l'empressement qu'ils ont pour ces réjouissances, eux qui sont les plus misérables et les plus tourmentés de tous les hommes.

Après midi je vais visiter la noce pour empêcher l'ivrognerie, les querelles et les danses indécentes, que quelques-uns ont apportées de leur pays. J'y séjourne quelque temps, et pendant qu'ils se divertissent innocemment [23ʳ] je me mets à l'écart dans un endroit de la prairie assez près pour pouvoir accourir au besoin, mais assez loin pour pouvoir réciter mon bréviaire et mes prières, que j'offre à Dieu pour ces pauvres gens, d'aussi bon cœur, que Job lui offrait ses prières et ses sacrifices pour ses enfants pendant qu'ils se divertissaient, *offerebat holocausta pro singulis, dicebat enim ne forte peccaverint filii mei, et benedixerint Deo in cordibus suis*; après quoi je fais cesser la danse, et je congédie chacun chez soi, car quand on les laisse faire, ils dansent toute la nuit jusqu'à la pointe du jour, qu'ils vont au travail, comme s'ils avaient bien reposé.

Quelques semaines après je vais voir les nouveaux mariés, pour reconnaître, s'il n'y a pas parmi eux quelque naissance de discorde, qui est ici fort fréquente dans les mariages, mais j'ai eu la consolation de remarquer toujours en ceux-

---

[65] MdC, MS 73, fol. 98ʳ: 'Après que les fiancés ont confessé au lever du soleil'.
[66] AFSI, GBro185, fol. 22ʳ: the manuscript, lacking most accents, reads 'ou', but context implies 'où'. MdC, MS 73, fol. 98ʳ: 'où'.

church early in the morning, turned out as well as they can be with clothes that their masters have lent them. They are accompanied by a very neat group of other slaves with, at their head, a banner embellished with all the ribbons they can find. After the betrothed have confessed, I marry them, I bless the ring, I say Mass and I give the blessing to the newlyweds, who are sometimes in such great number that they occupy the entire Communion bench, which is about thirty-five feet long. After this I give a sermon on the subject, which I delay until after the end of the Mass to allow the whites the freedom to leave, as the most important people in the area attend this Mass to avoid the heat of the sun. The respect that the poor slaves have for the sacrament of marriage is hard to believe, as is the distinction often made between those who have been married in the way I described, and those who have not. This illustrates that there is some particular blessing within the Church's ceremonies.

The marriage is then recorded according to the legal requirements, without neglecting those added by the Code Louis.[42] Afterwards the newlyweds go home, in the same order and the same procession in which they came, and in a pretty meadow they have their festivities, singing, playing the instruments of their land, and dancing with signs of joy which are extraordinary, for it is a surprising thing to see the enthusiasm they — who are the most abject and abused of all men — have for this merrymaking.

In the afternoon, I go to visit the wedding party to prevent drunkenness, arguments, and the indecent dances that some of them have brought from their land. I stay some time, and, while they amuse themselves innocently, I remove myself to a part of the meadow that is close enough for me to rush over if needed, but far enough away to be able to recite my breviary and my prayers. I offer these to God for these poor people with as good heart as Job offered his prayers and his sacrifices for his children while they amused themselves, *offerebat holocausta pro singulis, dicebat enim ne forte peccaverint filii mei et benedixerint Deo in cordibus suis.*[43] After this I put an end to the dancing and I send everyone on their way home, for, if they are left to themselves, they dance the whole night long until daybreak, at which point they go to work as if they had had a good night's rest.

A few weeks later I go to visit the newlyweds, to check that there are no beginnings of discord — which is very frequent in these marriages — between them. But I have been consoled in always observing in them a clear sign of the

---

[42] The Code Louis, or *Ordonnance de Louis XIV donnée à Saint-Germain-en-Laye* (Paris: Chez les associés, 1667), stipulated that a double register be made of marriages, as well as baptisms and burials; one register would remain with the cleric, and the other be sent to the *greffe*, the administrative records office. The marriage deed would be signed by those married, and four witnesses. *Ordonnance*, Title 20, Articles 8, 10.

[43] Job 1. 5: '[Job] offered holocausts for every one. For he said: Lest perhaps my sons have sinned, and have blessed God in their hearts' (1635, p. 947).

là un effet sensible de la bénédiction de Dieu. J'en sais un, qui quelques jours après son mariage ayant été maltraité par son maître, s'enfuit dans les bois. Sa femme, qui est une jeune négresse, ne voulut pas l'abandonner, et demeura auprès de lui près d'un an dans cet exil, où ils étaient logés, couchés, et nourris, comme les animaux. J'en connais deux autres, que j'avais refusé fort longtemps de marier, parce qu'ils étaient extrêmement méchants. La femme était une prostituée, et l'homme quasi toujours, ou fugitif ou à la chaîne, ce qui me faisait craindre un fort mauvais ménage, mais enfin [23ᵛ] croyant que l'amour d'une femme arrêterait la légèreté d'un mari, je me laissai vaincre à leurs prières, car jamais on ne m'a tant fait d'instances.⁶⁷ Depuis le mariage, le mari, nonobstant ses protestations, est retourné à son habitude; cependant c'est une chose qui étonne les gens de voir avec quelle assiduité cette femme lui donne toute sorte de secours, lorsqu'après qu'il a été repris et remis à la chaîne où il est exposé à toutes les injures de l'air le jour et la nuit, elle profite de tous les moments de loisir, que son travail lui laisse pour lui porter à boire et à manger, pour le couvrir de paille; et de tous les haillons qu'elle peut trouver, et le défendre du froid de la nuit, auquel ces pauvres gens sont très sensibles, quoique dans la zone torride.

Mais je ne puis oublier les sentiments d'une bonne négresse récemment venue. Quelque temps après que je l'eus mariée, je la rencontrai en chemin chargée d'un fardeau au-dessus de ses forces, car elle est assez délicate. Elle gémissait sous la charge, lorsqu'elle m'aperçut, mais aussitôt son chagrin disparut, elle jette son fardeau à terre, vient à moi en claquetant des doigts, qui est la marque de la⁶⁸ joie, et m'abordant d'un visage gai, *Ha Père*, dit-elle, *que Louis bon pour moi*, c'était le nom de son mari, *Louis papa pour moi, Louis mama pour moi, Si moi pas tenir Louis, moi mourir de faim*, c'est parmi eux l'effet d'un excellent ménage. La naïveté de cette créature me tira les larmes des yeux, [24ʳ] et comme elle s'aperçut de la consolation que ces paroles m'avaient donnée, elle me les répète quand elle me rencontre.

Le principal effet du mariage des esclaves, est la fin de leurs débauches. C'est sur ce point que j'insiste particulièrement dans les exhortations que je leur fais dans la célébration de leurs mariages. Aussi j'ai appris depuis les combats admirables que de jeunes mariées ont soutenus pour conserver la foi à leurs maris. Quand j'interroge les jeunes mariés, et quelques-uns des anciens sur le sujet de leurs débauches, ils me répondent avec une espèce d'interjection, que je ne saurais ici expliquer, et dont ils se servent d'un ton tout à fait agréable, pour témoigner qu'on leur fait une demande impertinente,⁶⁹ après quoi ils ajoutent, *Toi pas connaître moi, Père. Moi un tel, que toi marier avec une telle, maintenant*

---

⁶⁷ MdC, MS 73, fol. 99ʳ: 'car jamais aucun autre ne m'en importuna si fort'.
⁶⁸ MdC, MS 73, fol. 99ᵛ: 'de leur'.
⁶⁹ MdC, MS 73, fol. 100ʳ: 'une demande inutile'.

blessing of God. I know one of them who was mistreated by his master a few days after his marriage, and who fled into the woods. His wife, who is a young black woman, did not want to abandon him, and stayed with him in this exile for nearly a year, during which they took shelter, slept, and ate like animals. I know two others whom I had refused to marry for a long time because they were extremely wicked. The woman was a prostitute and the man was nearly always either a fugitive or enchained, which made me fear a very bad marriage. However, in the end, thinking that the love of a woman would put an end to the roguishness of a husband, I allowed myself to be won over by their requests, for no one ever entreated me as much. The husband, despite his protestations, has gone back to his old ways since the marriage, but to see the assiduity with which his wife comforts him, in all sorts of ways, is something that astonishes folk. After his recapture, with him once more chained up and exposed to the elements day and night, she uses any free time she may have from her labour to bring him food and drink, to cover him with straw and all the rags she can find, and protect him from the cold of the night, to which these poor people are very sensitive, even in the Torrid Zone.

But I cannot leave out the sentiments of a good-natured slave, who is a recent arrival. Some time after I had married her, I met her along the way, burdened with a load that was far too much for her, for she is frail enough. She was groaning with the weight of it, but, as soon as she saw me, her suffering disappeared. She threw her burden onto the ground, and came to me clicking her fingers, which is a sign of joy for them. Coming to me with a gay expression, she said 'Oh Father, Louis good for me' — it was her husband's name — 'Louis Papa for me, Louis Mama for me, if me no have Louis, me die of hunger.' Amongst them, this is the sign of an excellent match. The naivety of this creature brought tears to my eyes, and, as she noticed that her words were a consolation to me, she repeats them to me whenever she meets me.

The main result of the marriage of slaves is that it puts an end to their promiscuity. I insist particularly on this point in the sermons that I preach when celebrating their marriages, and I have since learned of the admirable struggles put up by young wives so as to be faithful to their husbands. When I question those who are married[44] — the young and sometimes older — on the subject of their debauchery, they answer me with a sort of interjection that I cannot describe here, and which they make with a very agreeable tone, to show that they have been asked a needless question. After this they add, 'You not know me, Father. Me so-and-so, who you marry to so-and-so, now me have wife that the Good Lord give me for save me. Why me chase after other woman that

---

[44] Mongin's use of 'jeunes mariés' may imply that he is only referring to married *men*, as could the '*Moi un tel*' in the slaves' reply.

moi tenir femme que le bon Dieu donner à moi pour moi sauver, pourquoi moi courir après autre femme que le diable donner à moi pour moi damner. C'est avec cette expression qu'ils distinguent le mariage du concubinage.

Le carême m'obligea de mettre fin à la célébration de tous ces mariages, en ce temps-là le festin de la noce n'étant pas permis, sans lequel ces bonnes [24ᵛ] gens ne se croient pas mariés, d'où il leur vient avec le temps des scrupules ridicules sur la validité de leurs mariages. Après avoir donc ainsi marié ceux qui se présentèrent, mon occupation fut de préparer de nouveaux catéchumènes au baptême qu'il fallait faire à Pâques.

C'était à l'occasion de cette fête, car autrefois la primitive Église avait tellement marqué la veille de Pâques et de la Pentecôte pour le baptême solennel des adultes, qu'il était défendu de le faire en un autre temps hors du péril de mort. Saint Léon dans une de ses lettres condamne quelques-uns, qui l'avaient voulu faire à l'Épiphanie, à cause du baptême de notre Seigneur fait à pareil jour, et le Concile II de Chalons, ceux qui le faisaient à toutes les fêtes des martyrs. Toutefois l'Église depuis a levé cette rigoureuse défense, et s'est contentée de déclarer qu'il est convenable de différer jusqu'à ces jours le baptême des adultes, qui le demandent environ ce temps-là, comme on affecte de le faire encore à Rome, et on remet d'ailleurs au jugement de ceux à qui il appartient, la connaissance de la disposition des catéchumènes, sans laquelle on ne peut les baptiser.

Suivant cette règle, quand quelqu'un à qui on a différé [25ʳ] le baptême pour n'être pas assez disposé, se trouve en quelque péril de mort, on y court aussitôt pour en tirer ce qu'on peut, et pour le moins autant qu'il en faut pour le pouvoir baptiser en conscience, dans cette occasion, où assurément on n'est pas obligé d'attendre de lui tous les témoignages qu'on demanderait des autres, qui ne sont pas en cet état. Après cela on l'ondoie différant les cérémonies jusqu'après la guérison, s'il plaît à Dieu [de] l'en favoriser.

Ce n'est pas la seule occasion où je m'empresse davantage à les disposer au baptême. Je le fais encore, quoique beaucoup moins, toutes les fois qu'il faut marier un catéchumène, parce que ce sacrement étant si nécessaire pour arrêter, ou pour prévenir le cours de leurs débauches, et le baptême étant la porte de tous les autres sacrements, il leur sert dans cette rencontre de disposition prochaine et nécessaire.

À ces deux cas près, qui sont assez fréquents, je n'ai garde d'aller si vite pour les autres baptêmes des adultes, parce qu'il faut les instruire, ce qui demande une si grande application que si je voulais employer autant de temps à l'instruction de tous les autres,⁷⁰ il serait impossible que je fisse jamais autre

---

⁷⁰ MdC, MS 73, fols 100ᵛ–101ʳ: 'ce qui demande une si grande application, qui si je voulais être [101ʳ] ainsi après tous ceux qui ne sont pas baptisés jusqu'à ce que je les eusse mis en état de l'être'.

the devil give me for to damn me?' This is the expression they use to distinguish marriage from cohabitation.

Lent obliged me to put an end to the celebration of all these marriages. During this time the wedding feast is not permitted, and without the feast these good folk would not think of themselves as married and would begin, over time, to have ridiculous doubts about the validity of their marriages. So, after having married those who came to me, my occupation was to prepare the new catechumens for the baptism that had to be performed at Easter.

It was upon the occasion of this feast, because in olden times the early Church had designated the eves of Easter and Pentecost for the solemn baptism of adults, so much so that it was forbidden to perform it at another time unless there was a risk of death. Saint Leo, in one of his letters, condemns those who wanted to perform it at Epiphany, because Our Lord was baptized on this day,[45] and the Second Council of Chalon condemns those who performed it on any of the Feasts of the martyrs.[46] Nonetheless the Church has since lifted this rigorous prohibition, and has contented itself with declaring that it is appropriate to defer until these days the baptism of adults who ask for it around this time, as in Rome they assert they do, and it is left to those who have the appropriate authority to judge the catechumens' disposition, without which they cannot be baptized.

According to this rule, when someone whose baptism has been deferred, because they are not sufficiently disposed, is in danger of death, we rush to him straightaway to get what we can out of him, and at least as much as is necessary to be able to conscientiously baptize him. On such an occasion there is, undoubtedly, no obligation to expect from him all the testimonies that would be asked for from others who are not in this state. After this he is anointed, and the ceremonies are put off until after he is healed, if it pleases God to favour him in this way.

This is not the only time that I hurry more than usual to dispose them for baptism. I also do so, although much less frequently, each time a catechumen is to be married. I do so because this sacrament [marriage] is so necessary for stopping, or at least limiting, their debauchery, and, as baptism is the gateway to all the other sacraments, it serves in these circumstances as a necessary and close disposition.

These two cases, which are frequent enough, aside, I am careful not to go as fast for the other baptisms of adults, because they must be instructed. This demands such great application that, if I wanted to devote as much time to

---

[45] Pope Leo I (d. 461), *Epistola XVI ad universos episcopos per Siciliam constitutos*, in *S. Leonis Magni Papae Primi opera omnia*, ed. by P.-T. Cacciari, 2 vols (Rome: Apud Josephum Collini, 1753–55), II, 75–83.

[46] Second Council of Chalon-sur-Saône (813), held at the end of the reign of Charlemagne.

chose que de faire entrer de nouveaux chrétiens dans [25ᵛ] l'Église, sans avoir loisir de voir comme ils y vivent outre que les habitudes que les nouveaux venus, aussi bien que les autres, contractent dans les débauches, sont si invétérées, et ils nous ont fait si souvent de fausses protestations de les quitter, qu'il faut une épreuve assez longue pour s'en pouvoir prudemment assurer.

C'était la cause qu'un certain missionnaire, qui avait la réputation de connaître excellemment les nègres, à cause des perquisitions perpétuelles qu'il en faisait avec beaucoup de zèle, passait les années entières sans baptiser aucun adulte, qu'en cas de mort. Quelques théologiens disent aussi, que la raison pourquoi l'Église primitive différait ces baptêmes jusqu'aux fêtes que nous avons dites, était pour éprouver la disposition des catéchumènes, la foi desquels était en ce temps-là plus suspecte, et moi comme je ne crois pas que parmi toutes les nations, qui ont reçu le baptême il y en ait une à qui on en donnât le désir plus facilement, qu'à nos nègres, je ne crois pas aussi qu'il y en ait aucune, à qui on en fasse prendre les autres dispositions avec plus de difficulté et de lenteur.

Toutes ces choses m'ont fait résoudre à ne choisir que deux temps de l'année pour les baptêmes ordinaires et solennels, et ensuite la vénération, que nous devons avoir pour les coutumes et pour les volontés de l'Église, m'a déterminé, sans balancer, à faire les baptêmes [26ʳ] au temps de Pâques et de la Pentecôte, aussi l'office de la veille et de l'octave de ces deux grandes fêtes, semble être fait autant en faveur des nouveaux baptisés, qu'à la gloire de ces deux mystères, et les prières, que l'Église fait alors pour les nouveaux chrétiens seraient quasi inutiles, ou du moins seraient quasi hors de saison, si on ne faisait dans ce temps-là ces baptêmes dans les pays étrangers, qui est le seul lieu où l'on baptise les adultes, dans un nombre considérable.

J'étais convaincu par toutes ces raisons, lorsque j'employai toutes mes courses pendant le carême, pour disposer les nègres au baptême, et à la fin je choisis ceux que je trouvai suffisamment préparés. À Pâques j'en baptisai assez bon nombre à trois diverses reprises. Les premiers furent baptisés le samedi saint le matin, qui est précisément le jour et l'heure marqués pour cette solennité par l'Église, mais parce qu'à cause du travail de ce jour ouvrier, les maîtres en retinrent quelques-uns de ceux qui étaient avertis de venir, ceux-ci furent baptisés le mardi de Pâques, et comme dans ce nombre de catéchumènes, il y en avait qu'il fallait marier immédiatement après le baptême, ce qu'on ne peut faire à cause de la noce, qu'après Quasimodo, ils furent baptisés d'abord[71] après ce dimanche.

[26ᵛ] Ces baptêmes étant faits, il fallut penser à faire la Pâques. Les nègres ne la font pas ici à la même quinzaine, que les blancs, parce que ceux-ci nous occupent si fort alors, et il faut tant de temps pour ouïr les confessions de tous ceux-là, et de chacun d'eux, à cause de leur peu d'esprit, et de leur grand

---

[71] AFSI, GBro185, fol. 26ʳ: 'd'abord' replaced with 'incontinent'.

instructing all the others, it would be impossible for me to ever do anything but bring new Christians into the Church, without having the chance of seeing how they live. This is to leave to the side that the habits the newcomers — like the others — have adopted in their debauchery are so incorrigible, and they have so often falsely promised to leave them behind, that quite a long trial period is required to be able to assure oneself of it with prudence.

It was for this reason that a certain missionary, who was reputed to have an excellent knowledge of the slaves because of the endless inspections he made of them, with much zeal, passed whole years without baptizing any adults except upon their deathbed. There are also some theologians who say that the reason why the early Church put off these baptisms until the feast days that I have mentioned was to test the disposition of catechumens, because their faith during this time was much more suspect. For my part, as I do not believe that among all the peoples of the earth there is one which more readily acquires the desire for baptism than our slaves, neither do I believe there is one which is made to adopt the other dispositions more slowly and with more difficulty.

All these things made me resolve to choose only two times in the year for the ordinary and solemn baptisms, and then the veneration that we should have for the customs and the wishes of the Church determined me, without hesitation, to perform the baptisms at the time of Easter and Pentecost. What is more, the office of the eve and the Octave of these two great feasts seems to be as much for the newly baptized as for the glory of these two mysteries, and the prayers that the Church makes then for new Christians would be almost useless, or at the least somewhat misplaced, if baptisms in foreign lands were not performed at this time, for it is only there that adults are baptized in a considerable number.

I was convinced by all these reasons, when I devoted all my efforts during Lent to preparing these slaves for baptism. In the end I chose those who were sufficiently prepared, and at Easter I baptized a good number at three different times. The first were baptized on the morning of Holy Saturday, which is precisely the day and time indicated by the Church for this solemnity. However, because this is a working day, the masters kept at their labour a number of those who had been summoned to come, and these were baptized on Easter Tuesday. As, moreover, in this group of catechumens there were some who had to be married immediately after baptism — which, given the wedding, can only be done after Quasimodo Sunday — they were baptized immediately after this Sunday.[47]

Once these baptisms had been performed, it was time to think about Easter Communion. The blacks do not receive it during the same fortnight as the whites, because the latter keep us so busy then, and so much time is needed to hear the confessions of the former, with them so slow-witted, and with such a

---

[47] Quasimodo Sunday, or Low Sunday, the Sunday following Easter Sunday.

nombre, qu'on a jugé à propos dans nos îles, de séparer leurs Pâques de celles des blancs. Quelques missionnaires les font faire aux nègres par anticipation durant le carême, mais je les renvoie après Pâques à cause des baptêmes qu'il faut préparer devant.[72]

C'est à quoi je commençai de m'occuper la semaine d'après Quasimodo, et j'eus besoin d'environ un mois pour en venir à bout. C'était le sujet de mes catéchismes et de mes voyages ordinaires, et je ne me mettais en campagne qu'après midi, et j'allais par ordre avertir diverses bandes de venir le lendemain à l'église faire leurs Pâques. Les maîtres savent les ordonnances et la coutume du pays, et ne manquent pas de faire cesser le travail le lendemain pour cet effet.

Il y en a pourtant un si attaché à son gain, qu'il ne voulut pas envoyer ses esclaves et différa jusqu'aux fêtes de la Pentecôte pour sauver le travail des jours ouvriers. Il les envoya pour lors avec des habits neufs pour se mettre à couvert des reproches qu'on lui fait de ne les nourrir, ni habiller, ceux-ci indignés de l'avarice de leur maître prirent un chemin bien contraire à [27ʳ] celui de l'église, et ont été fugitifs durant longtemps au grand dommage de cet avare, qui ne pouvait pas être mieux puni. C'est ce que je lui représentai, mais inutilement, car ses gens étant enfin revenus, il s'obstina dans son refus, qui lui attira une nouvelle punition de Dieu, car dans un an il a perdu quatorze esclaves qui lui sont morts, par divers accidents, ce qui est ici une perte fort considérable, et fort rare, que j'ai fait valoir pour l'exemple des autres, car il y en a encore un qui lui est semblable. Pour lui il a reconnu sa faute, il m'en a demandé pardon, et m'a promis d'être plus obéissant cette année. Nous verrons ce qu'il fera.

Après donc avoir averti les nègres dans leur travail de venir le lendemain, je m'informe de nouveau de ceux qui continuent dans leurs débauches, et après m'en être assuré autant qu'on peut raisonnablement je leur marque un autre temps pour leurs Pâques, pourvu que dans ce temps-là ils donnent de véritables marques de leur amendement. Pour les autres je leur fais une instruction et une exhortation sur ce sujet, après je m'en vais autre part en avertir une autre bande jusqu'à ce qu'il y en ait assez pour occuper le lendemain deux confesseurs, car un compagnon est également nécessaire et pour mon secours, et pour la liberté des confessions.

---

[72] MdC, MS 73, fol. 102ʳ continues with the addition, apparently in another hand: 'si l'on a quelque respect pour les ordres de l'Église'.

great number of them, that it was judged appropriate on our islands to separate their Easter [Communion] from that of the whites. Some missionaries have that of the slaves in advance during Lent, but I put them off until after Easter because of the baptisms that must be prepared beforehand.

I began to tackle this the week after Quasimodo Sunday, and I needed about a month to do so. It was the subject of my catechisms and my typical voyages, and I would only set out after midday, and would go methodically to alert various groups that they were to come to church the next day for Easter Communion. The masters know the ordinances and the custom of the land, and will halt the labour of the following day without fail for this purpose.[48]

There is, nonetheless, one of them who is so attached to his profit that he did not want to send his slaves and put it off until the feast of Pentecost so as not to lose the labour of working days. He then sent them, and with them wearing new clothes, which was to avoid the criticism made of him that he neither fed nor clothed them. His slaves, who were outraged by their master's avarice, took a path which led in a very different direction from the church, and went on the run for a long time, which was very costly to this miser. He could not have been better punished, as I told him myself, but it was to no avail. For once his slaves had come back, he again refused them, and brought upon himself another divine punishment, for in one year he lost fourteen slaves who died in various misfortunes. This is a very great, and very exceptional, loss here, and I brought the attention of the others to it, for there is another planter here who is like him; for his part he recognized his error and asked for my pardon, promising to be more obedient this year. We will see what he does.

After having averted the slaves who are at work that they are to come the following day, I again enquire about those who continue in their debauchery, and, after having assured myself about them as much as it is reasonably possible to do, I assign them another time for their Communion, once they show true indications of their having changed during that time. I give a lesson and a sermon to the rest of them on this subject, and afterwards I go elsewhere to avert another group of them until there are enough of them to keep two confessors busy the next day, for I need an assistant, as much to help me as to ensure liberty within confessions.

---

[48] The 'Règlement de M. Tracy, lieutenant-général de l'Amérique, touchant les blasphémateurs de la police des Isles', dated 19 June 1664, sanctioned planters who 'forbade their engaged labourers and slaves from attending Mass on Sunday and feast days'; the ordonnance of Mr de Baas, dated 1 August 1669, although directed at 'les religionnaires, les Juifs, les cabaretiers et les femmes de mauvaise vie' ('Protestants, Jews, innkeepers and women of poor morals'), ordered slaveowners to send their slaves 'to Mass each Sunday and feast day, to catechism, to the other exercises of piety, to ensure they commune at Easter ['qu'ils fassent leurs Pâques']'. See Moreau de Saint-Méry, *Loix et constitutions*, I, 177, 180–82; Lucien Peytreaud, *L'Esclavage aux Antilles françaises avant 1789* (Paris: Hachette, 1897), pp. 172–73.

Le lendemain je me rends à l'église de bon matin, j'instruis de nouveau ces gens, je leur fais faire les actes de la [27^v] préparation à la confession, le plus pathétiquement et le plus intelligiblement qu'il m'est possible, après quoi chaque confesseur est occupé jusqu'à midi. Tous s'étant confessés je les fais ranger au balustre pour les communier tous ensemble, j'exige de chacun un méreau ou billet du confesseur pour marque qu'ils se sont confessés, rejettant ceux qui n'en ont pas, sans quoi il y en a beaucoup qui ne feraient pas difficulté de communier,[73] soit par étourdissement, soit par méchanceté.

Après je leur représente, le plus fortement que je puis, le grand malheur de ceux qui communient après avoir trompé le confesseur.[74] Je finis en leur disant à peu près les paroles, que prononçait le diacre aux chrétiens de la primitive Église, dans cette occasion, *Sancta sanctis, si quis non sanctus non accedat.* C'est alors que j'en ai vu plusieurs fois jusqu'à cinq ou six se retirer doucement de la sainte table, avant que de communier, après quoi je fais faire aux autres les actes de devant la communion, je les communie, et leur fais faire les actes d'après la communion, qui consistent dans le bon propos[75] de conserver la pureté d'un corps qui vient de porter celui de Jésus-Christ. Ensuite je marque exactement ceux qui ont fait leurs Pâques, je console ceux qui en ont été exclus, et je profite de leur confusion pour leur faire prendre de bonnes résolutions de s'y mieux disposer dans le temps que je leur marque, comme ils font souvent, enfin je les renvoie tous à une heure après midi, [28^r] et je vois alors tant de joie sur le visage de ceux qui ont communié, qu'elle est capable de tirer les larmes des yeux[76] qui en sont les témoins.

Vers les deux heures je vais prendre quelque réfection, et je regagne la campagne pour aller avertir et préparer une autre troupe pour le lendemain, car dès qu'on a commencé il faut continuer sans interruption. J'ajouterai ici qu'une des choses des plus efficaces que j'ai mises en usage pour les porter à faire leurs Pâques, a été la menace, que je leur ai faite de ne recevoir pas pour parrains ceux qui ont manqué à ce devoir, et de leur refuser la sépulture ecclésiastique, s'ils mouraient sans donner des marques de repentir. L'occasion de cette dernière ne s'est pas présentée si souvent comme de la première, mais l'une et l'autre les embarrassent extrêmement, et ils ont vu des exemples de toutes les deux. Ils ont une grande confusion de se voir rejetés quand ils se présentent pour être parrains, et leur chagrin a passé quelquefois jusqu'à en donner à leurs maîtres. Pour la sépulture ecclésiastique, ils l'ont extrêmement à cœur, et avant que de mourir, ils m'en demandent d'ordinaire des assurances, ajoutant qu'ils mourront contents après cela, aussi je fais tout mon possible pour faire quelque

---

[73] MdC, MS 73, fol. 103^r: 'communier sans avoir confessé'.

[74] MdC, MS 73, fol. 103^r continues: '(ce qui n'est pas trop rare parmi eux)'.

[75] MdC, MS 73, fol. 103^r: 'nous faisons les actes d'après la communion, desquels la plus grande partie consiste dans le bon propos'.

[76] AFSI, GBro185, fol. 28^r: after 'des yeux' is inserted 'de ceux'.

I go to the church early in the morning of the following day and once more instruct these people. I have them perform the preparatory acts before confession, with as much feeling and as intelligibly as I can, after which each confessor is busy until noon. When each of them has confessed, I have them line up at the altar rail so that they all receive Communion together. I require each of them to have a token or a note delivered by the confessor to prove that they have confessed, and I reject those who do not have one. Without this, many of them would have no problem taking Communion, because of either their thoughtlessness or mischief.

After this, I draw their attention to the great wrong that is committed by those who receive Communion after having deceived their confessor, and I do so as forcefully as I can. I finish by saying something approaching the words of the deacon to Christians in the early Church: *Sancta sanctis, si quis non sanctus non accedat.*[49] At this stage, I have often seen up to five or six of them quietly withdraw from the Communion table before receiving. After this I have the others perform the acts before Communion, I administer Communion, and have them perform the post-Communion acts, which have the worthy aim of conserving the purity of a body which has just received that of Jesus Christ. I then note with exactitude those who have made Easter Communion. I console those who have been excluded, and I take advantage of their embarrassment to have them resolve to be better disposed for it within the time that I indicate to them, as they often do. In the end, I send them all off at one o'clock in the afternoon, and I see so much joy on the faces of those who have received Communion that it would bring tears to the eyes of those who witness it.

At about two o'clock I go and have something to eat, and then I am on my way again to avert and to prepare another group for the following day, for once one has started one must continue without interruption. I will note here that one of the most effective ways that I have used to bring them to Easter Communion has been my threat not to accept as godparents those who have neglected this duty, and to refuse them a Christian burial if they die without showing signs of repentance. The latter eventuality is often less frequent than the former, but both bother them immensely, and they have seen both cases occur. They are greatly troubled to see themselves rejected when they appear as godparents, and sometimes their upset has gone so far as to be felt by their masters. They are extremely attached to a Christian burial, and before dying they usually ask me to assure them they will receive it. They add that they will die happily after this. I also do everything I can to lend some dignity to their

---

[49] 'Sancta sanctis, hoc dicit: Si quis non est sanctus, non accedat' ('Holy things for the holy, he says, may he who is not holy not approach'). John Chrysostom (347?–407?), *Epistolae ad Hebraeos*, Chapter 10, Homily 17, in *Opera omnia*, ed. by Bernard de Montfaucon, 13 vols (Paris: apud Gaume Fratres, 1834–39), XII (1838), 245.

honneur à leurs enterrements. L'auteur de l'histoire de nos îles, qui a dit qu'on enterre les nègres chrétiens sans suaire même, verrait maintenant ici, suaire, drap mortuaire, croix, cierges, etc.[77]

Les dévotions de Pâques furent achevées environ quinze [28ᵛ] jours avant la Pentecôte, qui était le temps destiné au reste des baptêmes pour cette fête, j'y disposai les gens de la manière que j'avais fait auparavant. Je les partageai en deux bandes, dont la première était de ceux, qui purent venir le jour ouvrier, et la veille de la Pentecôte, les autres furent pour le mardi, qui fut pareillement le jour du mariage de plusieurs d'entre eux.

Pour donner plus d'estime de cette grâce à ces néophytes, il serait nécessaire de faire ces baptêmes avec grande solennité, nos pères le font ainsi dans les Indes orientales, et dans la terre ferme de notre Amérique. Je souhaiterais bien de les imiter, mais j'y trouve encore des obstacles, qui ne sont pas petits, et je trouve toujours dans ces sortes d'appareils et de cérémonies, de nouvelles difficultés, qui me fournissent de belles occasions de mériter, si j'en sais profiter.[78]

J'avais en ce temps achevé pour cette année les principales fonctions de la mission, qui consistaient à préparer les nègres aux sacrements de baptême, de la confession, de l'Eucharistie et du mariage, qui avaient été reçus de tous ceux qui les avaient pu recevoir, mais avant que de commencer la seconde partie de la mission, que je destinais pour remédier à chaque vice en particulier, j'employai encore un ou deux mois à un travail qui était comme le supplément du précédent. C'était de communier les infirmes, de baptiser les imbéciles, rappeler ceux qui ne s'étaient pas présentés [29ʳ] à faire leurs Pâques, ou qui en avaient été rejetés, et enfin porter les plus sages à la fréquentation des sacrements.

Pour les infirmes, comme le nombre en est petit par la grâce de Dieu, j'achevai de leur porter les sacrements[79] en moins d'une semaine. J'en trouvai un qui a peu de semblables, même parmi les blancs, pour son jugement et pour sa vertu, c'est un autre Job, qui depuis plusieurs années se voit pourrir peu à peu avec une patience admirable, il ne sort d'autre parole de sa bouche, que des bénédictions de Dieu, et de tous ceux qui l'approchent pour lui rendre quelque service. Je voulus lui demander si sa femme avait bien soin de lui, pour réponse, il en fit un éloge, comme s'il eût voulu décrire la charité même. Aussi tous les nègres de cette maison, qui sont en grand nombre, ont un extrême

---

[77] MdC, MS 73, fol. 104ʳ: insertion at this point, possibly in another hand: 'et les autres choses que l'Église emploie à la sépulture des fidèles'.

[78] MdC, MS 73, fol. 104ʳ continues with the insertion, apparently in another hand: 'Car il est vrai ici comme partout ailleurs et je l'ai expérimenté dans toutes les parties de cette nouvelle méthode, qu'on n'y saurait mettre les choses sur un bon pied et y faire son devoir sans être l'objet du chaspin de ceux qui y manquent, *offendit eos qui non imitatur* dit S. Cyprien'. *Chaspin, charpin* or *jhaspin*, 'Fâcherie. Mauvaise humeur.' Joseph-Toussaint Avril, *Dictionnaire provençal-français* (Apt: Edouard Cartier, 1839), pp. 83–84, 249.

[79] MdC, MS 73, fol. 104ᵛ: 'j'eus achevé de leur porter les[?] Pâques'.

burials. The author of the history of our islands who claimed that Christian slaves are buried without even a shroud would now see a shroud, a burial sheet, a cross, candles, and so on here.[50]

Easter devotions were finished about two weeks before Pentecost, which was the time designated for the remaining baptisms, for this feast, I organized these people in the way I had done previously. I divided them into two groups, the first of which was made up of those who could come on the working day, and the eve of Pentecost, and the others were for the Tuesday, which was also the day many of them were to be married.

To instil more respect for this grace in these neophytes, these baptisms should be performed with great solemnity. Our Fathers perform them in this way in the East Indies and on the mainland of our America. I would like to do as they do, but I am still confronted with obstacles which are not negligible, and I always find new difficulties in this sort of pomp and ceremony, which are good opportunities for me to obtain merit, if I know how to profit from them.[51]

At this time I had finished the main functions of the mission for the year. These consisted in preparing the slaves for the sacraments of baptism, confession, the Eucharist, and marriage, which had been received by all those who could receive them. However, before beginning the second part of the mission, which I reserved for the correction of each individual vice, I spent another month or two working on a kind of supplement to the preceding tasks. I had to give Communion to the infirm, baptize the feeble-minded, call back those who had not come for Easter Communion, or those who had been rejected for it, and, finally, lead the best-behaved towards frequenting the sacraments.

As there are few infirm, thanks to the grace of God, I finished bringing them the sacraments in less than a week. There is one of them who has few like him, even amongst the whites, with regard to his judgement and virtue. He is just like Job, and with admirable patience has seen himself gradually wither away for many years now. The only words from his mouth are praise of God, and of all those who offer him some assistance. I asked him if his wife was taking good care of him, and in reply he praised her as if he were describing charity itself. All the slaves of this household, who are in considerable number, have great respect for him. He calls the little ones in front of his cabin, and takes great care

---

[50] See Du Tertre, *Histoire générale des Antilles*, II (1667), 538.

[51] MdC, MS 73, fol. 104ʳ continues with the insertion, apparently in another hand: 'For it is true here as it is everywhere else, and I have experienced it throughout this new method, that one cannot put things in order and do one's duty without being subject to the displeasure of those who neglect this duty. *Offendit eos qui non imitatur*, as Saint Cyprian says.' This paraphrases Cyprian of Carthage (2..–258), '*Malos quisquis non imitatur offendit*' ('whoever does not imitate the bad offends [them]'), *Ad Donatum*, Thascius Caecilius Cyprianus (Cyprian of Carthage), *S. Thasci Caecili Cypriani opera omnia*, ed. by Wilhelm von Hartel, 3 vols (Vienna: apud C. Geroldi filium Bibliopolam Academiae, 1868), I, 3–16 (p. 12).

respect pour lui. Il appelle les petits nègres devant sa cabane, et il a grand soin de leur apprendre à prier Dieu. Il souhaite, que je lui [sic] bien souvent le saint-sacrement,[80] et jamais je ne le vais voir qu'il ne me demande cette grâce avec une dévotion bien tendre.

Parmi les imbéciles je n'en trouvai que quatre qui n'étaient pas baptisés, et ayant reconnu par beaucoup d'indices, qu'ils avaient été tels toute leur vie, je les assemblai tous quatre avec leurs parrains et marraines et je les baptisai comme les enfants.

Mais le nombre de ceux, qui n'avaient pas encore fait leurs [29ᵛ] Pâques, n'était pas si petit. Les uns attendaient que je les appelasse, les autres ne s'en souciaient guère. Je m'occupai à cette recherche durant environ un mois, avec quelque utilité, et avec bien de la consolation pour les heureux changements, que je remarquais en quelques-uns, mais comme je ne faisais que glaner après la moisson que j'avais faite à Pâques, au lieu de gerbe je n'emportais que quelque petite javelle, qui ne laissait pas de me réjouir à mon retour, *venient cum exultatione portantes manipulos suos*, cette satisfaction était assez grande pour modérer le déplaisir, que me causait l'obstination de quelques-uns, que je voyais semblables à l'herbe qui naît sur les toits, qui ne remplira jamais ni la main du moissonneur, ni le sein du glaneur, *sicut foenum tectorum ... de quo non implebit manum suam qui metit, nec sinum suum, qui manipulos colligit*, achevez Seigneur, disais-je, la conversion de nos pauvres esclaves, *converte, domine, captivitatem nostram*.

Cette amertume fut encore adoucie par la recherche que je fis ensuite de ceux qui avaient persévéré depuis Pâques, et de tous ceux, qui avaient quelque disposition pour la fréquentation des sacrements, dans les occasions j'en avais entrevu quelques-uns, que j'espérais pouvoir élever à la dévotion pour servir d'exemple aux autres. Je m'appliquai donc à m'en assurer davantage car il y a grand danger de s'y tromper, comme je reconnus alors que j'avais fait en une jeune négresse [30ʳ] qui par son industrie et son hypocrisie avait si bien gagné sa maîtresse, dont elle était la servante domestique, que cette demoiselle, quoique très spirituelle m'en avait donné une grande idée d'autant plus facilement que son témoignage était accompagné de celui d'un missionnaire grand connaisseur, dit-on, en matière de fourberies des esclaves. Je ne laissais pas toujours d'avoir

---

[80] MdC, MS 73, fol. 105ʳ: 'que je lui porte le saint-sacrement bien souvent'.

in teaching them to pray to God. He wants me to bring the Holy Sacrament to him very often, and I never go to see him without him asking this grace of me, and with a very tender devotion.

I only found four amongst the feeble-minded who were not baptized, and, having recognized by many signs that they had been so their whole lives, I brought the four of them together with their godfathers and godmothers and I baptized them as with children.

However, those who had not yet received Easter Communion were not as few in number. Some of them were waiting for me to call them, and the rest were hardly concerned about it. My search for them took me about a month, and was somewhat useful, and the gratifying changes that I noticed in some of them brought much consolation. Yet as all I was doing was gleaning after the harvest I had made at Easter, instead of sheaves I gathered a few mere stalks, but which nonetheless brought me joy upon my return. *Venient cum exaltatione portantes manipulos suos.*[52] This satisfaction was sufficiently great to mitigate my displeasure, which was caused by the obstinacy of some, who seemed to me to be similar to the grass that grows on rooftops, that will never fill the harvester's hand nor the gleaner's breast, *sicut foenum tectorum… de quo non implebit manum suam qui metit, nec sinum suum, qui manipulos colligit.*[53] Lord, I would say, complete the conversion of our poor slaves, *Converte, Domine, captivitatem nostram.*[54]

This bitterness was further sweetened by the search I then made of those who had persevered since Easter and of all those who had some disposition for frequenting the sacraments. I had, when the occasion arose, questioned some in whom I hoped to inspire devotion, so that they would be models for the others. I set about ensuring myself further of this, for there is a great danger of being mistaken, as I recognized that I had done with a young female slave. She was a domestic servant, who had so won over her mistress through her artfulness and hypocrisy, that the lady, although very astute, had given me a very favourable idea of her. She did so all the more easily in that her testimony was complemented by that of a missionary who was said to be very knowledgeable about the tricks of slaves. Nonetheless, I continued to sense that there was

---

[52] This paraphrases 'Euntes ibant et flebant semen spargendum portantes; venientes autem venient in exsultatione portantes manipulos suos', Psalm 126 (125). 6 ('Going they went and wept, casting their seeds. But coming they shall come with exultation, carrying their sheaves', 1635, p. 236).

[53] This paraphrases 'Fiant sicut fenum tectorum, quod, priusquam evellatur, exaruit: de quo non implevit manum suam, qui metit, et sinum suum, qui manipulos colligit', Psalm 129 (128). 6–7 ('Let them be made as grass in the tops of houses, which is withered before it be plucked up. Whereof the reaper hath not filled his hand, and he that gathereth the sheaves his bosom', 1635, p. 239).

[54] 'Converte, Domine, captivitatem nostram, sicut torrentes in austro', Psalm 126 (125). 4 ('Turn our captivity, o Lord, as a torrent in the South', 1635, p. 236).

je ne sais quoi dans l'esprit qui combattait l'idée qu'on m'en donnait, et je ne pouvais pas bien digérer deux choses qui me choquaient dans cette créature, l'une qu'elle était extraordinairement propre et ajustée, ce qui fait ici un grand préjugé contre les négresses, qui avec tout leur travail peuvent à grand'peine se pourvoir de quelque grosse toile, et l'autre, que quand je lui en donnais quelque avis salutaire, elle me répondait avec une arrogance insupportable. Enfin le péché parut, on découvrit un mauvais commerce qu'elle entretenait, cette découverte la mit en fuite avec son galant, qui est mort misérablement, sans que cette fin tragique eût le pouvoir de rappeler à son devoir cette abandonnée, qui s'est enfin retirée depuis peu dans sa case.

Voici un autre exemple de la fine hypocrisie de ces gens-là. Un jeune nègre qui avait quelque esprit, et qui était de bon naturel, appartenait à une sainte famille, dont quelques-uns étaient de bonnes gens, et faciles à tromper. On l'avait mis dans un poste, qui ne lui agréait pas, pour s'en faire retirer, il allégua [30ᵛ] le besoin qu'il avait, disait-il, d'être auprès d'un certain homme pour apprendre à prier Dieu, et l'on voulut bien l'en croire sur sa parole, quelque incommodité que ce changement causât, peu de temps après on fut obligé de le mettre dans un poste semblable au premier, pour s'en tirer encore, il apporta un motif propre pour l'esprit de ceux dont il dépendait, disant que dans ce lieu il était sollicité par des négresses. On condescendit encore pour la seconde fois, quoique le lieu où il voulut être, fût bien plus dangereux, en effet après beaucoup de semblables adresses, il s'est enfin déclaré pour ce qu'il est, c'est-à-dire, pour un scélérat.

Ces exemples me font tenir sur mes gardes pour discerner les apparences de la solidité, et après avoir employé quelques semaines[81] avec une application particulière à faire ce discernement à l'égard de quelques-uns, j'ai eu tout sujet de bénir Dieu pour le nombre de bonnes âmes, qui conservent une innocence merveilleuse, malgré la corruption qui paraissait universelle. Il me semble que je vois un diamant dans un fumier, quand je considère les trésors que la grâce et la nature ont renfermés dans ces mêmes âmes ensevelies dans des corps hideux.[82] J'ai choisi quelques-uns de ces bons nègres pour la fréquentation des sacrements. Ils sont peu en comparaison de ceux qui font le contraire, parce que le danger qu'il y a d'y être trompé, m'oblige encore à prendre de grandes précautions, de sorte que [31ʳ] tous les mois à grand'peine y a-t-il cent communions, les uns ne communient qu'une fois dans ce temps, les autres tous les dimanches, les autres toutes les fois qu'ils peuvent venir à la messe.

C'est là que ces pauvres gens prennent des forces pour résister à des attaques bien violentes, et pour faire des actions qui me donnent une consolation bien sensible. Il y en a un qui dans le travail prêche ses compagnons avec un zèle et une autorité admirables, surtout quand quelqu'un veut prendre la liberté de dire

---

[81] MdC, MS 73, fol. 106ᵛ: 'quelque semaine'.
[82] MdC, MS 73, fol. 106ᵛ: 'des corps hideux et puants'.

something that did not tally in their impression of her, and there were two things I could not quite accept in this creature, and that shocked me. One was that she was extraordinarily well turned-out, which for the female slaves here is cause for suspicion, given that with all their labour they can barely afford some rough fabric. The other was that, whenever I gave her some salutary counsel, she answered me with intolerable arrogance. In the end the sin came to light. It was discovered that she was having a wicked liaison, and the discovery of this caused her to flee with her lover, who suffered a miserable death. Such an unhappy end was not enough to change the behaviour of this strumpet, who finally returned to her cabin a short time ago.

Here is another example of the sly hypocrisy of these people. A young male slave, who was quite bright and good-natured, belonged to a pious family, some of whom were good folk, and gullible too. He had been assigned to a task that was not to his taste, and, to get out of it, he claimed that he needed to be close to a certain man so as to learn how to pray to God. He was believed on his word, despite the inconvenience this change caused. A little afterwards he had once more to be assigned to a similar post, and, to again get out of it, he gave a reason that was tailored to the wit of those whose dependant he was; he said that he was being solicited by the women there. They acquiesced once more, for the second time, even though the place he wanted to be was far more dangerous. In the end, after many similar tricks, he finally showed himself to be what he is: that is, a rogue.

These precedents have made me wary about distinguishing appearances from firmness, and, after having spent several weeks of considerable effort in doing so with several of them, I had every reason to give thanks to God for the number of good souls who conserve a marvellous innocence, despite the corruption which seemed to be everywhere. It seems to me that I am looking on a diamond in a dunghill when I consider the treasures that grace and nature have hidden in these same souls, deep within their hideous bodies. I chose some of these good slaves for the frequentation of the sacraments. There are few of them in comparison with those who are not,[55] because the danger of being mistaken obliges me to take great precautions, so that every month there are barely one hundred Communions. Some only take Communion once in this time, others every Sunday, and still others every time they can come to Mass.

It is there that these poor people gather their strength for the great resistance they will need, and to do actions that bring me great consolation. There is one of them who preaches to his fellow workers with admirable zeal and authority, especially when one of these takes the liberty of saying something unseemly.

---

[55] Implicitly 'who are not chosen', although Mongin's formulation 'qui font le contraire' signifies 'who behave in the opposite way'.

quelque parole messéante, mais il prêche bien plus efficacement par l'exemple de sa modestie dans l'église, lorsque pour se confesser et pour communier, il attend les deux et les trois heures à genoux, immobile comme une statue au milieu de l'église, environné de sa famille, qu'il mène souvent avec lui à confesse.

Il y en a un autre qui sert de commandeur dans les travaux d'une grande sucrerie, dont il s'acquitte avec tant de probité et d'habilité, que tout le monde tombe d'accord, qu'il n'est point de blanc, dans cet emploi, qui n'est pas d'ordinaire celui des nègres, qui s'en acquitte si bien.

Une jeune négresse, dont le naturel et la vertu sont admirables, me parlait un jour de la peine, que lui donnaient de certaines pensées, dont elle recevait beaucoup de chagrin. *Mais comment faire toi*, lui dis-je, *pour chasser lui pensée*, elle me répondit, *moi faire grand fouet avec bonnes cordes, moi m'en aller* [31ᵛ] *où personne ne voir moi que le bon Dieu et la bonne Vierge, là moi me dépouiller, et moi frapper, et moi frapper toujours, toujours, et partout, jusqu'à ce que mauvaise pensée quitter moi.*

Mais, repliquai-je, *qui celui-là, qui apprendre à toi cela?*

Le bon Dieu Lui apprendre à moi cela, fit-elle.

J'en ai vu pleurer une fort amèrement il y a quatre jours, et lui en demandant la cause, elle m'a répondu, que c'était la Passion de notre Seigneur dont elle se ressouvenait dans ce temps de carême.

J'en connais plusieurs qui se sentant tout à coup saisis de certaines maladies, qui apparemment ne sont que des effets des sortilèges, auxquels aussi on a coutume d'avoir recours pour en guérir, m'ont d'abord consulté pour savoir s'ils le pourraient faire en conscience, mais après que je leur eus répondu, que non, ils ont mieux aimé demeurer longtemps accablés de ces maux, que de demander la guérison à des sorciers, qui la donnaient aux autres.

J'admire l'attachement de quelques-uns pour faire leurs dévotions les jours qu'il y a quelque indulgence, pour cet effet, ils se dérobent de grand matin de la maison de leur maître pour y pouvoir être de retour de bonne heure, quand il en a besoin, mais parce que la faute[83] de confesseurs[84] fait qu'ils ne sont pas toujours en état de retourner chez eux à temps, c'est une source de plaintes. Il a fallu pour y remédier que je leur donnasse quelque médaille bénite pour [32ʳ] gagner les indulgences quelque autre jour, nonobstant quoi ils veulent toujours profiter de tout. Il y a une négresse, qui se distingue par l'ardeur admirable avec laquelle elle donne des avis aux autres, en particulier et en public, mais l'exemple de sa probité est encore une chose plus rare, car elle est jointe avec une gaieté très grande et très modeste.

Je laisse les autres choses que je pourrais dire sur cette matière, qui pendant

---

[83] AFSI, GBro185, fol. 31ᵛ: 'la faute' replaced with 'le manquement'.
[84] MdC, MS 73, fol. 107ᵛ: 'mais parce que la foule de confessions'.

But he preaches even more successfully through the example of his modesty in church when, for confession and Communion, he waits for two or three hours on his knees, as immobile as a statue in the middle of the church, surrounded by his family whom he often brings with him to confession.

There is another who is an overseer in a large sugar plant, where he works with such probity and skill that everyone agrees that there are no whites in this job — which blacks do not usually do — who do it so well.

A young slave women, whose character and virtue are admirable, spoke to me one day about the trouble and bother that certain thoughts gave her. 'What you do', I said to her, 'to chase thought away?'

She replied, 'Me make big whip with good ropes, me go where no one see me but Good God and the Good Virgin, there me undress, and me strike, strike, always, always, and everywhere, until bad thought leave me.'

'But', I replied, 'who he who teach you this?'

'The Good Lord He teach me this', she said.

I saw one of them crying very bitterly four days ago, and when I asked her the cause of this she replied that it was the Passion of our Lord, which she recalled during Lententide.

I know many of them who have felt themselves suddenly struck down with a sort of sickness, which is apparently caused by spells, to which they also have recourse for healing. They have consulted me beforehand to find out if they could do this in good conscience, but, after I replied to them that they could not, they have preferred to remain weighed down by these ills rather than to request the healing that these sorcerers bestow on others.

I admire how attached some of them are to carrying out their devotions on indulgence days.[56] For this purpose, they leave their master's house early in the morning, so that they can be back early, when he needs them. But, as the lack of confessors means that they cannot always return to their household on time, it has resulted in complaints. To remedy this, I had to give them a blessed medal so that they could earn indulgences on another day. Notwithstanding this, they still want to profit from all of them. There is a female slave who stands out for the admirable ardour with which she counsels the others, either privately or in public, but her exemplary probity is even rarer, for it is accompanied by great, and very modest, gaiety.

I will leave to the side what else I could say on this subject which, during

---

[56] Indulgences secured remittance of the punishment of sins which had been pardoned in confession.

quelques semaines, que j'ai employées à cultiver ces bonnes âmes, m'a donné une singulière consolation, qui récompensait très abondamment mes soins.[85] J'eusse bien voulu ne faire jamais autre chose, mais je fus obligé de retrancher la plus grande partie du temps, que je donnais à cette occupation, pour me contenter de beaucoup moins le reste de l'année, c'est-à-dire, de ce que je pouvais faire en passant, comme dans le confessionnal, et dans les autres occasions, où je pouvais dire quelque mot de direction, tâchant ainsi d'entretenir toujours ces bonnes personnes, dans la fréquentation des sacrements,[86] pour m'appliquer à d'autres œuvres absolument nécessaires.

Enfin vers la fin du mois de juillet, je me vis au bout de ce que j'avais entrepris pour la première partie de ma mission, c'est-à-dire de ce que j'avais projeté de faire, pour disposer les nègres à la réception des sacrements, et je commençai de m'appliquer à remédier en particulier aux défauts auxquels ils sont le plus sujets, [32ᵛ] qui devait être mon occupation le reste de l'année. Il est vrai que les sacrements sont les plus efficaces de tous les remèdes, et que j'avais remarqué les grands biens, qu'avaient produits le baptême, la confession, les communions, et les mariages, après les soins que j'avais pris pour en exclure les indignes, mais enfin il restait encore à descendre dans le détail, et attaquer par ordre chacun des désordres, dont il s'en fallait bien que tout le monde fût corrigé, parce que tous n'avaient pas encore reçu les sacrements, dont je viens de parler, et qu'il n'y avait que trop d'apparence que dans un si grand nombre il y en avait, qui les avaient reçus sans disposition ou sans fruit.

J'avais remarqué, dans mon catalogue, que les défauts les plus ordinaires de ces gens, étaient l'omission de la prière, et de la messe, les mauvais ménages, l'impudicité, les sortilèges, l'ivrognerie, la fuite de chez leurs maîtres, qu'on appelle ici le marronage, et l'incapacité pour les principes de la foi. Je me résolus de faire autant de visites dans mon quartier qu'il y avait de ces désordres pour parler à tous, et à chacun des coupables.

Pour y mieux réussir, avant que de commencer ce travail, j'allai visiter tous les commandeurs, ce sont des blancs, pour la plupart assez souvent également misérables pour le corps et pour l'âme. Les habitants les prennent à gages pour commander les travaux de leurs esclaves, envers qui ils exercent quelquefois [33ʳ] des cruautés barbares, dont la plus grande est l'attaque qu'ils livrent à la pudicité des pauvres négresses, abusant du pouvoir qu'ils ont pour les délivrer de la faim, du travail, et du châtiment, qu'elles pourraient mériter d'ailleurs.

Vous devez savoir, Monsieur, que les maîtres de ces esclaves ont droit sur eux, pour en disposer, comme il leur plaira, pour le vivre, le vêtement, le travail, le

---

[85]   MdC, MS 73, fol. 108ʳ: 'Je laisse les autres choses que je pourrais dire sur cette matière avec autant de peine que j'en eus à finir l'application particulière dont j'y travaillais. J'employai quelques semaines à cultiver seulement ces bonnes âmes avec un rapport qui récompensait abondamment mes soins.'

[86]   MdC, MS 73, fol. 108ʳ: the sentence ends at 'dans la fréquentation des sacrements'.

several weeks that I spent cultivating these good souls, gave me a singular consolation which abundantly rewarded my trouble. I would well have liked to do nothing else, but I was obliged to reduce most of the time I had been devoting to this task. I had to content myself with much less time the rest of the year: that is, with what I could do in passing, as in the confessional and on other occasions in which I could give a little direction, trying in this way to maintain these good folk in the frequentation of the sacraments even while I was busy with other tasks that were absolutely necessary.

So, towards the end of the month of July, I saw that I had nearly finished what I had undertaken for the first part of my mission, that is, what I had planned to do so as to dispose the slaves to the reception of the sacraments. I then started to work on remedying, individually, the failings they are most subject to, which was to be my occupation for the rest of the year. It is true that the sacraments are the most effective of all remedies, and that I had noticed the great good that baptism, confession, the Communions, and marriages had produced, after the care I had taken to exclude those who were unworthy. Yet, in the end, I still had to work rigorously, and attack in order each of the sins, of which each slave was far from having been cured. For all of them had not yet received the sacraments which I have just discussed, and it was all too evident that in such a great number there were many who had received them without disposition or fruit.

I had noticed in my catalogue that the most typical faults among these people were the omission of prayer and Mass, unhappy marriages, licentiousness, magic spells, drunkenness, fleeing their masters' households, which is called *marronage* here, and incapacity for the principles of faith. I resolved to make as many visits in my neighbourhood as there were of these failings, to speak to all, and to each of the guilty parties.

To better succeed in my labour, I went to visit each of the overseers before starting. They are whites, often enough, as miserable in body as they are in soul.[57] The planters hire them to direct the labours of their slaves, on whom they sometimes inflict barbarous cruelties. The worst is the way they attack the decency of the poor female slaves, abusing the power they have to deliver them from hunger, labour, and the punishment which they might merit, moreover.

You should know, Sir, that the masters of these slaves have the right to do with them as they wish with regard to their nourishment, clothing, labour,

---

[57] Mongin's formulation in French in AFSI, GBro185, fol. 32ᵛ, with the comma before 'pour la plupart', implies the overseers were white, but might possibly be read as 'they are whites in the majority'. This is likely in MdC, MS 73, fol. 108ᵛ, which appears to read: 'ce sont des blancs pour la plupart, assez souvent également misérables pour le corps et pour l'âme'.

châtiment et pour toutes choses, sans que personne s'en mêle, et y puisse trouver à redire. Il n'y a que la mort et la mutilation, que les lois défendent, les blancs ayant ce pouvoir sur les esclaves, pour leur faire du bien, et pour leur faire du mal. Vous voyez bien qu'il faut que les négresses aient une vertu héroïque pour soutenir les attaques d'un maître ou du commandeur des nègres, quand ils les veulent suborner, nonobstant quoi il y a de ces pauvres créatures, qui soutiennent tous ces assauts pour défendre leur honneur. Nous en avons vu qui ont souffert jusqu'au feu, qu'on leur avait appliqué sans vouloir jamais se rendre, on peut bien dire que ce traitement est *metus cadens in constantem virum*.[87]

Pour arrêter le cours de ce désordre, on a fait il y a longtemps, une ordonnance, qui condamne les pères des enfants qui proviennent de ces débauches, à deux mille livres de sucre d'amende, mais je ne l'ai pu faire garder, qu'à la Martinique, où du provenu on enrichit souvent les hôpitaux et les églises, en même [33^v] temps que la crainte de ce châtiment retient force gens dans le devoir.

Ces raisons me firent juger, qu'il fallait commencer par gagner ces commandeurs, pour faire quelque réforme. J'employai environ une quinzaine de jours, à les aller voir, je leur fis des présents et cent amitiés, pour m'insinuer dans leur esprit, je leur fis entendre le grand bien qu'ils pouvaient procurer aux esclaves, dont ils avaient le soin, et au contraire le grand compte, qu'ils devaient rendre à Dieu, de ceux qui se perdaient par leur faute. Je m'attachai principalement au plus méchant de tous, mais Dieu permit, que malgré beaucoup de promesses, qu'il me fit, ayant méprisé mes avis, dans ce même temps il fut chassé honteusement par son maître. Un autre, qui ne valait pas mieux, n'ayant pas voulu se laisser gagner par la douceur, a été traité de la même sorte par la maîtresse du logis où il demeurait, laquelle fut contrainte de le chasser, par la menace qu'on lui fit de le priver des sacrements, si elle le retenait davantage au grand préjudice du salut des négresses, de tout le voisinage, les autres commandeurs n'ont pas été si obstinés, plusieurs me rendaient des visites les jours de fête,[88] le tout au grand avantage des pauvres esclaves, qui étaient soumis à leur conduite.

Ayant ainsi disposé ces commandeurs, je fis une visite générale de toutes les maisons, où il y avait des nègres, pour remédier à la mauvaise habitude, qu'on avait contractée en plusieurs endroits de n'y faire [34^r] plus la prière le matin ni le soir, contre l'ancienne coutume, ce qui était la cause de l'ignorance de force esclaves. Je trouvai que ce désordre était moins universel, par la grâce de Dieu, que beaucoup d'autres, car je ne le remarquai que dans trente-sept maisons,

---

[87] AFSI, GBro185, fol. 33^r: this paragraph, beginning with 'Vous devez savoir, Monsieur' and ending with '*metus cadens in constantem virum*', does not appear in MdC, MS 73.

[88] MdC, MS 73, fol. 109^r: 'plusieurs me rendaient des visites les jours de fête, et d'autres fréquentaient les sacrements'.

punishment, and all things, without anyone getting involved or being able to say anything about it. The laws only forbid death and mutilation, the whites having the power of doing good or doing evil to the slaves. You can well see that female slaves need to be heroically virtuous to endure the onslaught of a master or an overseer of slaves, when they want to corrupt them. Notwithstanding this, some of these poor creatures resist all this violence to defend their honour. We have seen some who have even suffered fire being applied to them without ever giving in. It can well be said that such treatment is *metus cadens in constantem virum*.[58]

To put an end to this disorder, there was an ordinance a long time ago which condemned the fathers of the children born from such debauchery to a fine of two thousand pounds of sugar, but I have only been able to have it respected in Martinique. The hospitals and churches there are often enriched by such fines, and at the same time the fear of this punishment keeps many people on the right path.

These reasons led me to conclude that, to obtain reform, I had to start by winning over the overseers. I spent about two weeks going to see them. I gave them presents and was extremely affable towards them so as to win them over. I expounded to them the great good they could do for the slaves who were in their care, and conversely the great account that they have to give to God of those who were damned through their fault. I mainly worked on the most wicked of them, but God had it so that, in spite of him making me many promises, he rejected my counsel and at the same time he was sent packing in shame by his master. Another, who was no better, not letting himself be won over by kindness, received a similar treatment from the mistress of the household where he resided. She was obliged to send him on his way because she had been threatened with being deprived of the sacraments if she kept him on, given the great risk he posed to the salvation of the female slaves of the whole neighbourhood. The other overseers were not as relentless, and many of them came to visit me on feast days, all of which was of great benefit to the poor slaves under their direction.

Having thus worked on these overseers, I made a general visit of all the households where there were slaves, to rectify the bad habit that had been adopted in many places of no longer saying prayers in the morning or at night-time. This is a contravention of the former custom, and it has resulted in the ignorance of many a slave. I found that this disarray was less widespread than many others, by the grace of God, for I only found it in thirty-seven houses, and

---

[58]   AFSI, GBro185, fol. 33ʳ: this paragraph, beginning with 'You should know, Sir', does not appear in MdC, MS 73. '*Metus cadens in constantem virum*' ('fear overcoming a constant man'): this reflects debates concerning the degree to which actions taken through fear (*metus*) might be blameworthy. See Tomas Sánchez, *Compendium totius tractatis de sancto matrimonii sacramento* (Seville: Antonio de Toro, 1623), fol. 252ʳ.

aussi eus-je moins de peine à y remédier. Pour cet effet j'établis dans chacune quelqu'un pour faire la prière publiquement. C'est d'ordinaire le commandeur, et où il n'y en a pas, quelque autre, soit blanc, soit noir, à la pointe du jour, avant que d'aller au travail, et le soir quand ils en reviennent, ils s'assemblent devant la maison du maître, là à genoux ils font la prière qui consiste dans l'oraison dominicale, la salutation angélique, la croyance, et les commandements de Dieu, ce qui est terminé par un petit abrégé des principaux points du catéchisme. En quelques endroits on fait cette prière en chantant, et comme ils sont en grand nombre, leur voix avertit leurs voisins de leur devoir. Je marque dans mon catalogue celui qui fait la prière, et j'ai soin de le récompenser de son exactitude, les bonnes gens l'appellent *le curé*, et ce nom est devenu comme héréditaire à quelques familles des nègres.

Mais ce ne sont pas seulement les nègres, ou leurs commandeurs, qui font alors cette prière et cette instruction. Je connais un habitant, qui a une des premières charges de notre île. Il est cassé de vieillesse et de maladies, et néanmoins il se faisait amener tous les soirs dans sa [34ᵛ] chambre, les plus ignorants de ses esclaves, que je lui avais marqués, et sans s'en fier à aucun de ses domestiques, il leur faisait lui-même le catéchisme jusqu'à ce qu'il les eût rendus assez capables. Une demoiselle, qui est des premières de cette île, nonobstant l'embarras d'une très nombreuse famille fait la prière le matin elle-même, à la tête de tous ses nègres, à la pointe du jour. J'en connais une autre fort jeune et fort délicate,[89] qui ayant une vieille négresse, accablée de mal depuis longtemps, se glissait toutes les nuits, dans sa cabane, et se mettant près de ce cadavre animé, elle lui apprenait à prier Dieu, et à se disposer à la mort.

Ce qui m'a le plus étonné et édifié en cette matière, a été la charité et la patience admirable d'une illustre veuve, qui se distingue ici par sa vertu et par sa naissance, étant petite-fille d'un chancelier, et garde des sceaux. Je l'ai vue travailler auprès des[90] nègres des plus stupides et des plus brutaux de ce quartier pour leur apprendre les premiers principes du catéchisme avec la même application qu'aurait la gouvernante d'un jeune prince, sans témoigner la moindre impatience, et le moindre dédain.

Je pourrais apporter plusieurs autres exemples sur ce sujet. Je me contente de remarquer, qu'il y en a, qui ne font pas moins pour le corps que pour l'âme de ces esclaves, dans leurs maladies. Je connais une jeune personne, qui semble posséder toutes les qualités [35ʳ] d'un ange, et qui rend aux nègres malades toute sorte de services les plus bas et les plus rebutants, avec une gaieté, et un esprit admirable. Il ne faut pas omettre ici la piété de plusieurs de ces pauvres gens à l'égard de leurs petits enfants, quand le soir ils se sont retirés dans leur cabane. Ils ne se coucheraient pas qu'après les avoir fait prier Dieu, nonobstant

---

[89] MdC, MS 73, fol. 110ʳ: 'J'en connais une autre fort jeune'.
[90] Both AFSI, GBr0185, fol. 34ᵛ and MdC, MS 73, fol. 110ʳ read: 'après des' (without accent).

I also had less trouble rectifying it. For this purpose, I put somebody in place in each household who would take charge of the prayers before the others. This is usually the overseer, or, when there is none, somebody else, black or white, who does so at daybreak before the slaves go off to work, and at night when they return. They gather before the master's house, and there, on their knees, they say their prayers, which consist of the Lord's Prayer, the *Ave Maria*, the Apostles' Creed, and God's Commandments, ending with a short summary of the principal points of catechism. In some parts they sing these prayers, and, as there are many of them, their voices alert their neighbours to their duty. In my catalogue, I note the one who leads the prayers, and I make sure to reward him for his exactness. The good folk call him *the parish priest*, and this name has become a sort of hereditary title for some enslaved families.

However, it is not just the slaves or their overseers who say such prayers or carry out such instruction. I know a planter who holds one of the most important offices on our island. He is a wreck through old age and sickness, but, in spite of this, he had the most ignorant of his slaves that I had indicated to him brought each night to him in his room. Without trusting any of his servants with the task, he would himself teach them catechism until he had made them capable enough. I know one of the most important women of this island who, notwithstanding the care of a very big family, herself leads morning prayers for all her slaves at daybreak. I know another who is very young and very frail, who had an old slave who had been weighed down with illness for a long time. Every night she would slip into the slave's cabin and, drawing near to this living corpse, she would teach her to pray to God, and to prepare herself for death.

I was most surprised and edified by the charity and admirable patience of an illustrious widow, who stood out here through her virtue and her birth, as the granddaughter of a chancellor, and keeper of seals.[59] I have seen her with the most stupid and brutal slaves of this neighbourhood, laboriously teaching them the main principles of catechism with the same application that the governess of a young prince would have, and without showing the least impatience or disdain.

I could adduce many other examples concerning this subject. I will content myself with observing that there are some who do no less for the bodies than for the souls of these slaves during their sicknesses. I know a young person who seems to have all the qualities of an angel, and who carries out the lowest and vilest duties for sick slaves, and with admirable good humour and gaiety. I must not leave out here the piety of many of these poor people towards their little children, when they have retired to their cabins at night. They would not go to

---

[59] During the *ancien régime*, *chancelier* was a high-ranking office, whose duties included ensuring the functioning of the judicial system; the *garde des sceaux* kept the royal seals.

la prière, qu'ils viennent de faire en public, et l'extrême lassitude dont ils sont alors accablés. Pour les huguenots, qui ont des nègres, sans nul domestique catholique, j'ai obtenu d'eux, qu'ils les envoient chez quelqu'un de leurs voisins, où[91] je leur assigne[92] un catholique pour leur apprendre tous les jours la prière.

C'est ainsi qu'on remet efficacement cet exercice, qui avait été si fort négligé en quelques maisons, particulièrement en une grande sucrerie, où une bande d'esclaves[93] se mutinèrent, et se rendirent fugitifs, lorsqu'après mon règlement l'on voulut commencer de les obliger d'aller à la prière, et une autre case où force grands nègres, qui sont nés dans ce pays ne savaient aucune prière, parce qu'on n'y en faisait point du tout, et quand on voulut commencer à les y obliger, ils répondirent[94] qu'ils étaient trop vieux, pour pouvoir rien apprendre, et ce fut le prétexte avec lequel ils excusaient l'ignorance que je remarquai en eux, quand j'allai quelque temps après examiner leur capacité, mais les uns et les autres se sont rangés depuis à leur devoir.

Après avoir ainsi réglé la prière de chaque jour, il [35ᵛ] fallut penser à la messe des jours de fête. Dans une visite générale, que je fis pour cet effet, j'en trouvai plus de deux cents qui n'y allaient jamais employant ce temps-là à dormir, à courir, ou à dérober. Je les pris par où ils étaient les plus sensibles, les menaçant de les priver de la sépulture ecclésiastique, s'ils venaient à mourir, sans donner des marques de leur repentir, parce que, leur disais-je, il ne fallait pas porter à l'église après leur mort, ceux qui avaient refusé d'y venir durant leur vie. Je remarquai encore qu'ils étaient sensibles à la considération de la juste compassion, qu'ils ont des nègres, qui appartiennent aux Anglais, de sorte qu'aucun des nôtres ne voudrait changer de maître avec eux, quoique fort souvent ceux-là soient mieux nourris et mieux habillés, parce qu'enfin, disent-ils, il n'y a point, ni de messe, ni d'église pour eux, non plus que pour les chevaux. *Si vous ne voulez donc pas venir à la messe*, disais-je, *votre condition n'est pas meilleure, et vous pourriez la changer avec eux.*

Je trouvai que ces pauvres gens goûtaient fort cette raison, et pendant que je la leur représentais dans les champs, ils faisaient des signes des mains, et de la tête, qu'ils estimaient beaucoup l'avantage qu'ils possédaient en ce point sur les autres, et dès que j'avais achevé de parler, ils s'en prenaient à ceux [36ʳ] de leur bande, qui étaient les coupables, les en convainquaient devant moi, et leur faisaient une répréhension assez aigre, mais qui n'avait pas moins de douceur pour moi. Par ce moyen, je vis par la grâce de Dieu un assez grand amendement.

Toutefois je remarquai, qu'il manquait encore bien des gens à la messe, et au catéchisme, qui la suit immédiatement, et que la cause était le marché, que

---

[91] AFSI, GBro185, fol. 35ʳ: the lack of accents in the manuscript means that 'ou' is also a possibility here. MdC, MS 73, fol. 110ᵛ: 'où'.

[92] MdC, MS 73, fol. 110ᵛ: 'assignai'.

[93] MdC, MS 73, fol. 110ᵛ: 'où une bande d'esclaves qui ne valaient rien'.

[94] MdC, MS 73, fol. 111ʳ: 'et quand on voulut commencer ils répondirent'.

bed before having them pray to God, notwithstanding that they have just said prayers in public, and that they are absolutely exhausted. I have obtained of the Huguenots who have slaves, but no Catholic servants, that they send them to one of their neighbours, where[60] I assign them a Catholic to teach them prayers every day.

This is how this practice is effectively being reinstated once more, having been very much neglected in several households. It was particularly so in one great sugar plantation where a gang of slaves mutinied, and became fugitives, when the rule I put in place would have required them to go to prayer. In another house, there were many adult blacks who had been born in this land and who knew no prayers because absolutely no prayers were said in the house. When they began to be obliged to pray, they replied that they were too old to learn anything, and this was the pretext they used to excuse the ignorance I noticed in them, when I went to examine their capacity some time after. However, they have all since fallen into line.

After having settled the daily prayers, I needed to think about the feast-day Masses. In a general visit that I made for this purpose, I found more than two hundred of them who never went to these Masses and who spent this time sleeping, fornicating, or thieving. I went for their weak spot, threatening to refuse them a Christian burial were they to die without giving any sign of repentance, because, I said, those who had refused to come to the church while they were alive should not be brought there after death. I noticed that the just compassion they have of the slaves of the English was a consideration that continued to resonate with them. For none of ours would wish to swap masters with them, even though they are very often better nourished and better dressed because, as [our own] say, there is no Mass or church for them any more than there is for horses. I would say to them, 'If you don't want to come to Mass, your condition is no better than theirs, and you may swap it with them.'

I found that this argument really resonated with these poor people, and, while I was in the fields explaining it to them, they would make signs with their hands and heads to show that they very much appreciated the advantage that they had over the others on this point. Once I had finished talking, they would criticize those amongst themselves who were guilty, and blame them in front of me, while reprimanding them with some bitterness. This was, however, a source of no less sweetness to me. Through these means, and by the grace of God, I saw an improvement which was quite substantial.

All the same, I noticed that there were still quite a few people missing at Mass and at the catechism which immediately follows it, and that the cause

---

[60] AFSI, GBro185, fol. 35^r gives either 'where I assign' or (less probably given context) 'or I assign'. MdC, MS 73, fol. 110^v gives 'where I assigned'. See Letter 3, n. 91 and n. 92.

les nègres tenaient durant ce temps-là pour vendre leurs herbages, et leurs fruits, nonobstant[95] une ordonnance de Monsieur notre Gouverneur qui le défendait, mais elle ne se gardait point du tout, parce qu'il était alors en France, et qu'on lui disputait cette juridiction.[96] Je m'adresse donc au juge de la police, et je lui représente non seulement le motif de la religion, mais encore l'intérêt public, à cause que les hôteliers et les revendeurs profitaient du temps de cette messe, où la plupart du monde assiste pour acheter ce qu'ils voulaient, de ces esclaves, et allaient même quelquefois au-devant pour en frustrer le public, ainsi j'obtins une seconde ordonnance, qui défendait ce marché durant la messe, et durant le catéchisme sous peine de confiscation pour le vendeur, et d'amende pour l'acheteur, le tout applicable à l'hôpital, ce qui ayant été exécuté, j'avais la consolation [sic] mon église[97] parfaitement bien remplie de mes nègres durant le catéchisme, quoiqu'elle soit très longue, et les chapelles [36^v] aussi fort grandes.[98] Je dis qu'elle en était remplie, durant le catéchisme, car très peu d'entre eux y peuvent entrer durant la messe, quoiqu'elle soit appelée la messe des nègres, parce que se disant au lever du soleil, presque tout le monde y vient fondre de plus de trois lieues, pour prévenir la chaleur. Tout ce qu'on peut faire est d'y trouver place pour une centaine de nègres, qui sont mieux dressés à chanter, ce qu'ils font à diverses reprises, les principes du catéchisme et les prières en français, et le tout est terminé par le *Domine Salvum fac* etc. Quelquefois on substitue à ces prières des cantiques conformes aux diverses solennités. Les chantres sont nègres et négresses. Ils sont fort bien dressés et chantent d'ordinaire les lettres de dévotion sur les airs les plus nouveaux, et les plus délicats, non sans exciter de grands sentiments d'admiration et de piété principalement dans l'esprit des Français nouvellement venus. Il y a une vingtaine de petits nègres et de petites négresses, qui ne sont pas moins savants et c'est un singulier plaisir de les entendre chanter.

À la fin de cette messe on est bien édifié de voir communier toutes les fêtes, sans exception, un bon nombre de ces pauvres esclaves, et ensuite l'église ayant été libre[99] des blancs qui la remplissaient, les autres nègres, qui avaient été obligés de demeurer à la porte et aux fenêtres, qui ne sont élevées que de trois pieds de terre, leur succèdent. Alors je monte en chaire,[100] et je leur fais le catéchisme.

---

[95] MdC, MS 73, fol. 111^v: instead of 'nonobstant', read 'à même temps je trouvai'.

[96] MdC, MS 73, fol. 111^v: 'mais elle ne se gardait point du tout soit parce qu'il était alors en France soit parce qu'on lui disputait cette juridiction'.

[97] MdC, MS 73, fol. 112^r: 'j'avais la consolation de voir mon église'.

[98] MdC, MS 73, fol. 112^r: 'quoiqu'elle soit longue de 120 sur une largeur de 30 et que l'espace des chapelles soit quasi aussi grand'.

[99] MdC, MS 73, fol. 112^v: 'et ensuite l'église ayant été vidée'.

[100] AFSI, GBr0185, fol. 36^v: the manuscript reads 'monte en chaize'.

was the market that the slaves held during this time to sell their herbs and fruit. This was in spite of an ordinance of our governor which had forbidden the market, but which was not at all respected, because he was in France at that time, and his jurisdiction was in dispute.[61] I addressed myself to the *juge de la police*,[62] explaining not just my religious motives, but also that of the public interest, because the innkeepers and retailers would take advantage of the time of this Mass, which most of the people attend, to buy what they wanted from the slaves. Sometimes they would even get there beforehand so that there was nothing left for members of the public. So it was that I managed to have a second ordinance passed, which forbade this market during Mass and the time of catechism, under penalty of the vendor having his goods confiscated, and the buyer receiving a fine, all of which would go to the benefit of the hospital. With this carried out, I had the consolation of seeing my church completely full of slaves during catechism, even though [the building] is very long and the chapels are also very big.[63] I say that it was full with slaves during catechism, because very few of them could enter during Mass, even though it is called the 'Slaves' Mass'. This is because, as it is said at sunrise, nearly everyone comes from more than three leagues around to attend Mass before the heat. All that one can do is find space for about a hundred slaves, who are the most accomplished singers. At various points they sing the principles of catechism and the prayers in French, and it closes with the *Domine Salvum fac* etc.[64] Sometimes these prayers are substituted with canticles appropriate for the various solemnities. The choristers are black, male and female, are extremely well trained, and usually sing the letters of devotion on the newest and most graceful airs, and not without inspiring a tremendous sensation of admiration and piety, mainly amongst the newly arrived French. There are about twenty little black children, boys and girls, who are no less learned, and it is a unique source of pleasure to hear them sing.

At the end of this Mass it is very edifying to see a great number of these poor slaves take Communion on all the feast days without exception. Then, when the church has emptied of the whites with whom it was filled, the other blacks, who had been obliged to remain at the door and at the windows, which are only three feet off the ground, succeed them. Then I enter the pulpit and I teach them the catechism.

---

[61]   Claude de Roux, Chevalier de Saint-Laurent, was governor of the French colony on Saint Kitts from 1666. Charles Courbon, Comte de Blénac, had been *gouverneur général des îles* since 1677.
[62]   The *juge de [la] police* (*juge de paix*) had the charge of policing civil order in a locality, and the power to judge minor proceedings.
[63]   MdC, MS 73, fol. 112ʳ: 'even though [the building] is 120 [feet?] long and 30 wide and the space of the chapels is nearly as big'.
[64]   'Domine Salvum fac regem. Et exaudi nos in die, qua invocaverimus te', Psalm 20 (19). 10 ('Lord, save the King, and hear us in the day, that we shall invocate thee', 1635, p. 44).

[37ʳ] Ayant ainsi tâché de remédier à l'indévotion touchant la prière, la messe et le catéchisme, j'entrepris d'en faire autant à l'égard de l'impudicité, qui est le désordre le plus universel. Il m'étonna d'abord, quand je le considérai, et ce fut là particulièrement, que j'eus besoin, pour ne me pas rebuter, de l'assistance et de la confiance que j'avais mises en Dieu pour y réussir, comme aussi de la disposition, où j'étais,¹⁰¹ de me contenter d'y avoir fait mon possible, en remettant le succès à la Providence. Je divisai ce travail en deux parties, premièrement pour les mariés, après pour les autres, car le péché des premiers étant le plus grand, il fut aussi le premier sujet de ma mission.

Ces adultères si fréquents n'étaient que l'effet des mauvais ménages. J'en comptai deux cents, et j'entrepris de les raccommoder, mais j'y trouvai tant d'obstacles, qu'il y paraissait bien que le démon était de la partie par ses maléfices. Une fois j'instruisais une troupe de nègres à la campagne, lorsqu'une femme, pour me répondre de plus près, s'étant approchée par hasard de son mari, avec qui elle était en divorce, celui-ci en fit un cri si horrible, et si soudain, qu'il était capable de faire dresser les cheveux, la vue d'un démon n'en ferait pas faire davantage. Une autre fois exhortant une femme de retourner avec son mari, par la pensée de la mort, qui la pourrait [37ᵛ] surprendre dans son concubinage, elle me répondit d'un ton d'enragée, qu'elle voulait demeurer comme elle était, jusqu'à la mort.

La jalousie est encore assez souvent la cause de ces brouilleries, mais à dire le vrai, rarement est-elle injuste, et plus rarement encore est-elle assez grande, car les mariés ne se mettent guère en peine de la débauche les uns des autres. Je sais qu'une négresse ayant été surprise dans la cabane d'un nègre marié, sa femme prit le soin de la cacher avec grande diligence, pour la garantir du châtiment, qui lui était immanquable.

Les autres causes du divorce sont la paresse du mari pour nourrir, loger, et habiller sa famille, et le mauvais traitement qu'il fait à sa femme, tantôt en la battant rigoureusement, tantôt en lui enlevant son repas.¹⁰² Pour réunir donc tous ces gens, il faut menacer, il faut flatter, il faut parlementer, et porter des paroles de part et d'autre, et enfin faire ainsi la paix après beaucoup de rebuts d'allées et de venues.

Je n'eus pourtant pas cette peine une fois, que je fus appelé pour aller confesser une négresse, qui était en péril de mort, par un effet d'un mauvais ménage elle venait de faire une fausse couche, d'un coup de pied de son mari. Il l'avait donné justement de la manière la plus propre à exécuter ce malheureux dessein, aussi l'en avait-il menacée auparavant, mais [38ʳ] je fus bien étonné

---

¹⁰¹ MdC, MS 73, fol. 112ᵛ: 'que j'eus besoin pour ne pas me rebuter, et de l'espérance que j'avais mise en Dieu pour y réussir, et de la disposition où j'étais'.
¹⁰² MdC, MS 73, fol. 113ʳ: 'tantôt en lui enlevant son repas, car quelques-uns sont extrêmement gourmands'.

Having thus tried to remedy the lack of devotion in prayer, Mass, and catechism, I tried to do as much with regard to licentiousness, which is the most widespread sin. I was greatly surprised by it when I first reflected on it. It was particularly with regard to this that, to avoid discouragement, I needed the help and trust that I had put in God for my success, as well as my disposition to be content with having done what I could and leaving the success of it up to Providence. I divided this task into two parts, with the first for those who were married, and the following one for the others, for, as the sin of the former is greatest, it was also the primary focus of my mission.

These adulteries, which were so frequent, were only due to bad marriages. I counted two hundred of them, and I tried to reconcile them, but I found so many obstacles to this that it very much appeared that the demon was in there somewhere with his spells. One time I was instructing a gang of slaves in the countryside when a woman, wanting to come nearer to me with an answer, accidentally approached her husband, from whom she was separated. He let out such a terrible and unexpected roar that your hair would stand on end; the sight of a demon would not do worse. Another time I was urging a woman to return to her husband, by reminding her that death could surprise her while she was cohabiting. She replied, with the tone of a madwoman, that she wanted to stay as she was until her death.

Often enough jealousy is another cause of these arguments, but, to tell the truth, it is rarely unjustified, and even more rarely is it that serious, for husbands and wives are barely troubled by each other's debauchery. I know of a female slave who had been found in the cabin of a married male slave; his wife took care to hide her with great diligence so that she would not suffer the punishment that she would have inevitably received.

Other causes of separation are the husband's laziness in feeding, lodging, and clothing his family, and his bad treatment of his wife, whether that be in beating her severely, or in taking her meal from her. So, to put all these people back with each other, one must threaten, flatter, and negotiate, and speak on behalf of one or the other, and finally make peace between them after much rejection, and coming and going.

I did not have this problem one time, when I was called to confess a black woman who was in danger of death. Her unhappy marriage had led to her having just had a miscarriage, which was due to a kick her husband had given her. He had done this in precisely the best way to carry out this wretched end, and he had threatened her with it beforehand. But I was very surprised by the

des sentiments de cette pauvre créature. Elle n'attendit pas que je l'exhortasse à pardonner à son mari, elle me pressa avec une douceur, et avec une ardeur incroyable, à m'employer pour le faire délivrer de la chaîne où il était, et du fouet, auquel il était condamné. Il fallut que je lui promisse malgré moi.[103] Je le fis, elle guérit, et c'est maintenant un des meilleurs ménages, cette femme ayant apprivoisé la brutalité de son mari, par son innocence, par sa patience, et par sa douceur.

Mais les débauches de ceux, qui ne sont pas mariés, sont bien plus fréquentes, et plus incurables, aussi toutes choses semblent y contribuer, le tempérament de ces gens, l'éducation qu'ils apportent de leur pays, ou qu'ils reçoivent ici de leurs parents, le mauvais exemple, leurs veilles dans les sucreries, et dans les champs, leur nudité,[104] leur indigence, la difficulté, et quelquefois l'impossibilité de les marier, les poursuites des blancs, la tolérance des maîtres, dont quelques-uns même sont allés à cet excès, que n'ayant que des négresses, ils ont payé des nègres étrangers comme des étalons, pour en avoir les enfants, qui sont toujours au maître de la mère. On accusait un habitant de cette île de ce détestable ménage, aussi il n'achetait jamais des hommes, mais seulement des femmes, après avoir ainsi augmenté le nombre de ses esclaves, il les embarqua avec toute sa famille pour aller [38ᵛ] cultiver une place dans une île voisine, mais une tempête l'emporta si loin hors de sa route, qu'on a appris qu'un an après il[105] avait misérablement péri avec tout son monde, partie sur mer, partie sur terre.

Plus ces débauches sont ordinaires, et moins les filles en ont de honte, on en voit assez souvent quelques-unes chargées de cinq ou six enfants, dont elles ne rougissent pas, et ce n'est pas une chose rebutante, pour un garçon qui les recherche en mariage. Le pis est qu'il y en a, qui ont fait perdre plusieurs fois leur fruit, et quand on leur reproche,[106] avec des paroles un peu fortes, elles en paraissent aussi peu émues, comme si l'on parlait à une statue. Il y a quelque temps que je faisais une répréhension de la sorte à une prostituée en présence d'autres qui savaient sa mauvaise vie, elle mangeait alors une canne de sucre, et continua sans perdre un morceau durant tout le temps que je lui parlai.

Le remède que je tâchai d'apporter à ce désordre m'occupa durant un mois, et l'eût fait durant plus d'un an, si je n'eusse eu tant d'autres choses à faire, qu'il ne fallut pas abandonner, selon le projet, que j'en avais fait dès le commencement de ma mission, je m'en allai donc de maison en maison parler à ceux qui étaient coupables selon mon mémoire, où je trouvais encore marqué le nom du complice de chacun.

---

[103] MdC, MS 73, fol. 113ᵛ: 'à m'employer pour lui, et pour le faire délivrer de la chaîne où il était et des verges à quoi il était condamné. Il fallut que je le lui promisse malgré moi.'

[104] MdC, MS 73, fol. 113ᵛ: 'nudité' has been crossed out and replaced with 'peu d'habits'.

[105] MdC, MS 73, fol. 114ʳ: 'qu'on a appris qu'un an après qu'il' modified to 'qu'on a appris un an après qu'il'.

[106] MdC, MS 73, fol. 114ʳ: 'et quand on le leur reproche'.

sentiments of this poor creature. She did not wait for me to exhort her to pardon her husband, but rather entreated me — with a gentleness and an ardour that was unbelievable — to intervene so as to have him delivered from the chains in which he then was, and from the flogging he had been sentenced to. I had to promise her this in spite of myself. I did so, she recovered, and theirs is now one of the happiest marriages, this woman having tamed her husband's brutality with her innocence, patience, and gentleness.

Yet the debauchery of those who are not married is much more frequent and incurable, and everything seems to contribute to it: the temperament of these people, the education they have received in their land or from their parents, bad examples, their night work in the sugar plants, and in the fields, their lack of clothing, their indigence, the difficulty — and sometimes the impossibility — that there is of marrying them, the harassment by the whites, and the masters' tolerance. Some masters, who have only female slaves, have even gone so far as to pay male slaves from outside to breed children with them, and such children always remain with the mother's master. One planter of this island was accused of this hateful practice in his household, for he never bought men, but only women. After having increased the number of his slaves in this way, he embarked them with all his family to go and set up a plantation on a neighbouring island, but a storm brought him so far off his route, that it was discovered that he had miserably perished a year afterwards with all his suite, some of them on land and some at sea.[65]

The more this debauchery is commonplace, the less shame the girls have of it, and often enough you see girls laden down with five or six children; it does not make them blush, and it would not put off a lad who wanted to marry the girl. The worst is that there are some who have many times caused their fruit to be lost, and, when they are reproached for this with some force, they appear as unconcerned as if you were talking to a statue. Some time ago I was making just such a reprimand to a prostitute, with others present who knew of her wicked life. She was eating sugar cane at the time, and she kept on eating it, all the time I was talking to her.

The remedy I tried to bring to this disorder kept me busy for a month, and would have kept me busy for more than a year, if I had not had so many other things to do that could not be abandoned. Following the plan that I had made since the beginning of my mission, I went from house to house to speak to those who were guilty according to my catalogue, in which I also found the name of each one's accomplice marked there.

[65] The MdC, MS 73, fol. 114ʳ formulation ('qu'on a appris qu'un an après qu'il') implies that it was rather the *discovery* of these deaths that took place a year later.

[**39ʳ**] J'assemblais ceux, qui travaillaient dans un même champ. Je leur parlais avec plus[107] de force, qu'il m'était possible, je m'adressais en particulier à ceux qui étaient notés pour ce vice, car cela est public parmi eux, et je finissais en leur disant, que j'allais leur montrer un nègre, qui était dans l'enfer, pour avoir vécu comme eux. C'était un petit et excellent tableau d'une âme damnée. Je n'ai vu en ma vie rien de plus affreux en ce genre. Je connais plusieurs personnes d'esprit parmi nos blancs, qui y ayant jeté un coup d'œil par hasard, reculaient et détournaient la tête tout épouvantés, comme s'ils eussent vu un démon réel et tout en feu. Quand je commençai de me servir de cette industrie devant les nègres, quoique j'en trouvasse quelques étourdis, qui en riaient, néanmoins dans tous les autres je découvrais une grande consternation, quand je leur avais expliqué ce que c'était, et la cause et la durée de ce tourment. Cela était suivi de grandes protestations, et en public, et en particulier, et ces protestations d'un grand nombre de bons effets, dont Dieu a voulu se servir, pour tempérer la douleur, que me causait l'obstination de plusieurs autres, et certes ces convertis, et ces converties font voir tous les jours, que la grâce abonde, où le péché a si fort abondé.

Il y en a une, qui depuis peu a fait une glorieuse résistance, à un Français, qui durant cinq nuits était entré chez elle par la muraille d'un jardin. La dernière fois, qui était la semaine passée, le monde étant accouru [**39ᵛ**] au bruit, on vit ce méchant homme se battre en retraite, l'épée nue à la main, pour regagner la muraille, en même temps que cette généreuse créature le pressait armée de pierres, qu'elle faisait voler à sa tête. Je fus averti de tout, le matin, la plainte fut faite devant le juge, les témoins ouïs, le criminel cité, et l'on espère qu'il servira bientôt d'exemple pour ses semblables.

Je sais d'autres résistances plus longues et plus difficiles, quoique moins éclatantes. Il y a eu quelquefois de funestes rechutes, mais j'ai vu bientôt après couler des larmes, dont l'amertume extrême a beaucoup tempéré celles que ces malheurs m'avaient causées. Enfin je ne dois pas omettre ici, que plusieurs marchands huguenots servent au démon[108] dans notre île, pour perdre ces négresses, nous y en avons vu deux à demi pourris par les maladies honteuses qu'ils y avaient gagnées. L'un s'est allé mettre dans les remèdes en France, l'autre se fit porter dernièrement pour le même effet dans le quartier des Anglais de notre île, où il a souffert jusqu'à la mort en reniant Dieu. Voilà l'Église réformée.

Cependant la fin de l'année[109] s'avançait et je voulais achever ma tâche, c'est pourquoi après[110] avoir parcouru toutes les maisons, où il y avait de ces

---

[107] MdC, MS 73, fol. 114ᵛ: 'avec le plus'.

[108] MdC, MS 73, fol. 115ʳ: 'que plusieurs marchands huguenots sont la plus grande peste que le démon ait mise'.

[109] AFSI, GBro185, fol. 39ᵛ: 'la fin de' crossed out. MdC, MS 73, fol. 115ᵛ: 'Cependant la fin de l'année'.

[110] MdC, MS 73, fol. 115ᵛ: 'je voulais achever mon prix fait à même temps; ce fut la cause qu'après'.

I assembled those who were working in the same field, and I spoke to them with as much force as I was able. I addressed myself in particular to those who had a reputation for this vice, because it is public knowledge amongst them, and I finished by saying that I was going to show them a slave who had gone to Hell because of having lived like them. It was a small, excellent painting of a damned soul. I have never seen anything of the sort which was so horrible. I know many intelligent people amongst our whites who, having looked upon it by chance, recoiled and turned their head away in shock as if they had seen a real demon who was on fire. Although, when I began to use this device with the slaves, there were a few fools who laughed at it, I nevertheless saw that it was a source of great consternation for all the rest when I had explained what it was and the cause and duration of this torment. This was followed by great declarations, publicly and individually, which were then followed by a great number of good results, which God desired to use, to temper the sadness that the obstinacy of many others caused me. And certainly the converts of both sexes show every day that grace abounds, where there had before been so much sin.

There is one of them who, not long ago, gloriously resisted a Frenchman who, for five nights running, had entered where she lived by getting over a garden wall. The last time, which was last week, everyone came running because of the noise. The wicked man was seen retreating towards the wall, his unsheathed sword in his hand, while this noble creature was after him armed with stones that she was throwing at his head. I was told about it all, in the morning, a report was made to the judge, the witnesses were examined, the criminal was brought in, and it is hoped that he will soon serve as an example for those like him.

I know of other examples of resistance which have been longer and more difficult, although less spectacular. There have sometimes been unfortunate relapses, but I have soon afterwards seen the shedding of tears, whose extreme bitterness has much tempered those tears that these woes had caused me. Finally, I must not omit here that there are many Huguenot merchants on our island who serve the devil by leading these enslaved women astray. We have seen two of them who were half eaten away by the shameful diseases that they had acquired here. One went off to find a remedy in France, the other had himself brought recently to the English part of our island for the same reason, where he suffered to the end rejecting God. That is the Reformed Church for you!

However, the year was drawing on and I wanted to finish my task, which is why, after having been to all the households where there was such disorder, I

désordres,[111] je voulus savoir un peu à fond ce que c'était que ces sorciers, à qui les nègres attribuent tous les jours tant de maux si surprenants. Ce qui me faisait croire, [40ʳ] une partie de ce qu'on m'en disait, c'est qu'il est vrai que plus une nation est grossière, plus le démon a coutume de s'en jouer par ses sortilèges, toutes les relations des pays étrangers en font foi, mais particulièrement celles du pays des nègres, on m'a dit souvent et plusieurs personnes dignes de foi disent l'avoir vu, que ces nègres sorciers devinent des choses qu'ils ne peuvent nullement savoir d'ailleurs, qu'ils tirent de toutes les parties du corps d'un malade des pierres, des coquillages, etc. qu'ils font parler une calebasse, d'où ils font sortir une réponse formée comme la voix d'un homme, qu'ils donnent aux autres des ceintures enchantées pour ne pas sentir les coups, quand on les châtie. Ils appellent encore sorciers de véritables empoisonneurs, à qui [sic] ils donnent[112] des maladies mortelles par de certaines herbes, dont ils[113] connaissent la vertu, c'est ainsi que, quelquefois on voit dessécher peu à peu un malade jusqu'à la mort, d'autres enflent comme les hydropiques, et d'autres sentent de petites tumeurs, qui passent successivement d'un membre à l'autre avec de grandes douleurs.

Ils se donnent ces maux, si imperceptiblement, qu'on n'y peut rien connaître, que par les effets, mais dès que quelqu'un a cette réputation, les autres se jettent de furie sur lui au moindre de ces maux qu'ils ressentent. Dernièrement je fus appelé pour en aller confesser un, qui venait de recevoir un coup de couteau de la main d'une négresse, qui l'accusait d'avoir jeté dans sa marmite [40ᵛ] quelque chose, qu'elle y avait trouvé. J'ai porté plusieurs fois les sacrements à une jeune négresse de quatorze à quinze ans, qui a été consumée par une langueur de celles, que je viens de dire. Il me semblait, qu'il y avait quelque chose de plus qu'humain, dans sa patience, dans sa douceur et dans son jugement. Elle m'a toujours assuré, que son mal lui était venu après en avoir été menacée par un nègre, qui avait fait de vains efforts pour la débaucher.

Ceci est encore plus étonnant: un missionnaire, qui avait plus d'expérience que moi, m'avait averti de ne pas témoigner devant les nègres, l'estime que je faisais de la vertu des uns plutôt que des autres, de peur d'exciter une envie, qui serait suivie de quelque sortilège. Je m'oubliai de cet avis, et l'expérience ne me fit que trop connaître, combien il était salutaire, une fois je voulus citer à quelques-uns l'exemple de deux esclaves, qui étaient fort sages, et peu de temps après ces deux mêmes furent malades de la manière que j'ai dite, dont la fréquentation des sacrements les délivra, n'ayant voulu jamais avoir recours aux sorciers, comme on les en sollicitait tous les jours. Une autre fois il m'échappa de

---

[111] MdC, MS 73, fol. 115ᵛ: 'où il y avait de ces désordres que je viens de dire'.

[112] MdC, MS 73, fol. 115ᵛ: 'Ils appellent encore sorciers de véritables empoisonneurs qui donnent'.

[113] MdC, MS 73, fol. 115ᵛ: from this point (numbered both page 72 and page 249 in the manuscript), three folios are missing. The next folio, fol. 116ʳ (numbered both page 79 and page 256), takes up again with 'rapportaient que de la honte', corresponding to 'remportaient que de la honte' on AFSI, GBro185, fol. 43ʳ.

wanted to know a little in detail about the sorcerers, to whom the blacks every day attribute such astonishing evils. What made me believe a little of what I had been told about them is the fact that, the more simple-minded a people are, the more the demon tends to beguile them with his spells. All the accounts of foreign lands attest to this, but particularly those of the land the blacks come from. I have often been told — and many credible people say that they have seen — that these black sorcerers divine things that there is no way they could know otherwise, that they take stones, shells, etc. from all the parts of a sick person's body, that they make a gourd talk and make a reply which resembles a man's voice, and that they give enchanted belts to the others so that they do not feel the blows when they are punished. They also give the name of 'sorcerers' to true poisoners, who can impart mortal illnesses with certain herbs of which they[66] know the properties. So it is that sometimes you see a sick person shrivel up little by little until they die, others swell up as if they had dropsy, and others feel little tumours that pass successively from one limb to another, causing them great pain.

They afflict one another so imperceptibly that it is only through the results that one knows anything about it, but, once someone has this reputation, the others pounce on him with fury once they feel even slightly unwell. I was recently called to confess one of them, who had just been stabbed with a knife by an enslaved woman, who accused him of having thrown something into her pot that she had found in it. I brought the sacraments many times to a young slave girl of fourteen or fifteen years of age, who was consumed by the sort of languor that I have described. It seemed to me that there was something that was more than human in her patience, gentleness, and judgement. She always assured me that her affliction had fallen upon her after she had been threatened by a slave who had made vain efforts to seduce her.

The following is even more astonishing. A missionary who had more experience than I warned me not to let the slaves see that I esteemed the virtue of some rather than others, for fear of inspiring jealousy that would be followed by some spell. I forgot about this advice, and experience showed me only too well how salutary it was. One time I mentioned, to a few of them, the example of two slaves who were very well behaved, and a little afterwards the same two fell sick in the way I have described. The frequentation of the sacraments delivered them from this, and they never had recourse to the sorcerers, as they were every day invited to do. Another time I let slip that one female slave — whose life is

[66] MdC, MS 73, fol. 115ᵛ: from this point (numbered both page 72 and page 249 in the manuscript) three folios are missing.

proposer pour exemple une négresse, dont la vie est assurément très exemplaire. Elle le sut, et me rencontrant un jour, elle me pria dans un grand sérieux, et un peu fâchée de ne lui faire plus ce tort, *qui est pour m'attirer l'envie des autres*, disait-elle, ajoutant qu'assurément elle n'était pas meilleure.

[41^r] Toutes ces choses m'obligèrent à faire une recherche exacte de ces sorciers, ou prétendus ou véritables. J'en trouvai vingt-six, que j'allai examiner en particulier chez eux, plusieurs me dirent ingénument ce qu'ils faisaient, et me montrèrent leurs drogues, d'autres me nièrent tout, et enfin après beaucoup de discussions, qui sont assez difficiles en cette matière, je reconnus que quelques-uns ne faisaient qu'appliquer de certaines herbes, et remèdes naturels, sans aucune apparence de sortilège, et qu'on ne les appelait sorciers, que parce que les nègres appellent ainsi tous ceux, qui se mêlent de donner des remèdes, quels qu'ils soient, aussi il y en eut un, qui pour se justifier en me répondant fit le geste d'un chirurgien, qui fait une saignée, et me dit, *Français lui guérir comme cela, et nègre lui guérir d'une autre sorte.*

J'en ai trouvé d'autres, qui ont plusieurs fois mérité la mort pour de véritables empoisonnements. Ce sont ceux que je menace fortement, et que je prive des sacrements, jusqu'à ce qu'on voie des marques de leur repentir. Il serait bien nécessaire pour l'exemple, qu'on en punît quelqu'un du dernier supplice, mais les missionnaires à l'imitation de leur maître doivent désirer la conversion, et non la mort du pécheur, outre que ces sortes de crimes sont extrêmement difficiles à prouver juridiquement, et que d'ailleurs la justice prend rarement connaissance de ceux des nègres, parce que leurs maîtres ont soin d'étouffer ces affaires [41^v] pour ne pas perdre leurs esclaves.

J'en vis encore d'autres qui se mêlent de guérir avec de véritables sortilèges. Ils les appellent des *marabouds*. Il y en a ici un, qui en porte le nom, et qui en fait l'office, après beaucoup de protestations, qu'il m'avait faites de le quitter, je lui avais promis de le recevoir aux sacrements, si dans un certain temps il me donnait sujet de le faire, mais pour lors même j'appris qu'un habitant l'ayant voulu employer, il lui vit faire des grimaces et marmotter de certaines paroles sur des remèdes qu'il lui préparait, à cause de quoi il l'avait chassé.

Pour les devins on a recours à eux, quand on a été volé, ou ensorcelé, pour en savoir l'auteur, si celui qui les consulte est marié, le devin agissant en suppôt du démon, lui dit souvent que c'est sa femme qui a fait le mal, ce qui met aussitôt les deux mariés aux couteaux, l'un contre l'autre. Il y a quelque temps, qu'un nègre, qui avait acheté une ceinture d'un sorcier pour ne pas sentir les coups, fut fouetté fort libéralement, et à dessein de mettre à l'épreuve la force de ce charme, en présence des autres, qu'on voulait désabuser. À chaque coup qu'on lui donnait, on lui demandait s'il le sentait, et comme ce misérable se tourmentait d'une étrange manière, il n'excitait que la risée des autres, qui se riaient de sa simplicité et de son charme. On les a tellement châtiés pour ces ceintures, que

assuredly very exemplary — was a model for the others. She learned of this, and, meeting me one day, she requested me with great seriousness and some annoyance not to do her such a wrong again. 'It will attract the jealousy of the others', she said, adding that she was not, assuredly, the better for it.

All these things obliged me to carry out an exact enquiry amongst these sorcerers, whether supposed or true. I found twenty-six of them that I went to examine individually in their homes. Many told me guilelessly about what they did, and showed me their drugs. Others denied everything, and in the end, after many discussions, which on this theme are difficult enough, I recognized that some only applied certain herbs and natural remedies, without any appearance of sorcery. These were only called *sorcerers* because this is what the slaves call all those who are involved in providing remedies, whatever they are; there was one of them who, to justify himself, imitated a surgeon bloodletting and said to me, 'Frenchman he heal like this, black he heal in other way.'

I discovered others who have many times deserved the death penalty for true poisonings. It is these whom I threaten forcefully, and whom I deprive of the sacraments until I see signs of their repentance. To make an example of them, one of them should receive the death sentence, but missionaries, like their master, should desire the conversion and not the death of a sinner. What is more, this sort of crime is extremely difficult to prove legally, and the judicial authorities rarely hear about those of slaves, because their masters make sure to hush them up so as not to lose their slaves.

I have seen still others who are involved in healing with real spells; they call them *marabouds* [*sic*]. There is one of them here who has such a title, and performs the functions. After he had assured me that he would stop, I had promised him that I would receive him at the sacraments if, after some time, he gave me reason to do so. However, I then learned that there was a planter who, when availing of his services, had seen him making faces and mumbling words over the remedies that he was preparing for him, and for this he sent him away.

They have recourse to soothsayers when they have been robbed or bewitched, to find out the perpetrator. If a married man consults them, the soothsayer, acting as the demon's accomplice, will often tell him that it is his wife who has caused the harm, which then has husband and wife at each other's throats. A little while ago a slave, who had bought a belt from a sorcerer so that he would not feel lashes,[67] was very generously flogged. This was to test the strength of this charm in the presence of the others, and so open their eyes. He was asked if he felt each lash as he received it, and, as this wretch was kicking up a terrible fuss, he was the laughing stock of the others, who were laughing at his simplicity and at his charm. They have been punished so much for these belts

---

[67] Possibly 'blows' ('coups'); the context indicates 'lashes'.

dernièrement il y en eut quelqu'un, qui sachant, que j'avais fait [42^r] fouiller dans sa cabane pour y en chercher, et que je les avais fait brûler ensuite devant la même cabane, n'osa pas revenir, et fut fugitif durant longtemps.

Pour tous ceux, dont les remèdes m'ont été seulement suspects, après un long examen, je leur ai défendu d'en donner davantage. J'ai chassé de leurs cases les malades qui s'y étaient retirés pour se faire traiter par ces sortes de gens, et les ai renvoyés aux chirurgiens français, dont il y a bon nombre en ce pays, comme partout ailleurs.

Après avoir ainsi travaillé pour réduire ces sorciers, je me vis enfin au dernier mois de l'année, et par conséquent dans la nécessité de recommencer bientôt la suivante les mêmes soins, et de repasser ainsi sur mes pas, en disposant les gens aux mêmes sacrements, et en m'attachant avec le même ordre à diminuer les vices, et à examiner les causes de leurs rechutes, et de leur obstination. Me voyant ainsi pressé du temps, je fus obligé d'omettre le travail, que j'avais projeté dès le commencement, pour l'amendement des fugitifs, des ivrognes, et des voleurs, outre que ces derniers ne me paraissent pas capables de remèdes cette année, par la faute de plusieurs de leurs maîtres, qui jointe avec la ruine des vivres, causée par deux ouragans consécutifs ont réduit ces pauvres gens à la nécessité de dérober tout ce qu'ils peuvent attraper pour vivre.

En attendant donc une autre occasion de prendre mieux mes mesures une autre année, j'employai le mois de [42^v] décembre à examiner et récompenser le progrès, que chacun avait fait pour le catéchisme et pour les prières, et ensuite à réformer mes mémoires, selon les changements qui avaient été faits dans leur nombre, dans leurs mœurs etc.

Cette mission que je fis alors pour reconnaître la capacité de tout mon troupeau, me fut une des plus agréables. Pour cet effet il fallut bien garnir mon sac de beaux présents de dévotion, et avec cette charge je m'en allais dans les champs, où les esclaves travaillent attroupés quelquefois jusqu'au nombre de cent. Là je me retranchais au pied d'un buisson, dont les branches me servaient de parasol pour étaler ma marchandise; elles étaient toutes garnies d'images, de médailles, de chapelets de toute sorte, et comme cela était enfilé de beau ruban de fil de couleurs les plus vives, il donnait merveilleusement dans la vue de ces pauvres gens. Je crois, Monsieur, qu'en lisant ceci, vous vous représentez la boutique de ces merciers, qui aux bonnes fêtes des villages étalent leur marchandise à la porte des églises.

Au reste jamais les nègres ne quittent leur houe et leur serpe, pour se ranger autour de moi, avec plus de promptitude, que dans cette occasion, après qu'ils y avaient formé un demi-cercle, nous commencions selon la coutume, par le signe de la croix, ensuite tenant mon catalogue à la main, j'interrogeais chacun par ordre, et selon le degré de capacité, que j'avais marqué l'année précédente. Si je trouvais qu'il eut profité, je le [43^r] marquais d'abord, et à proportion de sa science, je lui donnais un prix, que les autres accompagnaient de leurs yeux, avec de petits témoignages d'une jalousie, qui m'agréaient beaucoup.

that there was one of them recently who, upon learning that I had had his cabin searched for them, and that I had had them burned in front of the same cabin, dared not return and went on the run for a long time.

For all those whose remedies seemed merely suspicious to me, after a long review I forbade them to give out any more of them. I drove the sick out of the shacks where they had gone for treatment by this sort of people, and I sent them to the French surgeons, of whom there are many in this land, as there are everywhere else.

After having worked in this way so as to subdue these sorcerers, there I was then in the last month of the year. In consequence, I would soon need to start the same endeavours all over again, ploughing the same furrow, disposing people for the same sacraments, and setting myself to reduce the vices with the same order, and examining the causes of their relapses and of their obstinacy. Seeing that I was pressed for time, I was obliged to omit the work that I had planned from the beginning for the correction of runaways, drunkards, and thieves. In any case, the last of these do not seem to me to be capable of remedy this year because of the fault of many of their masters, which, along with the ruin of victuals caused by two hurricanes one after the other, reduced these poor people to needing to steal everything they can get their hands on to survive.

So, awaiting another chance to better prepare myself another year, I employed the month of December in examining and rewarding the progress that each had made in catechism and in prayers, then in revising my records, according to the changes that had occurred in their number, their manners, etc.

The mission that I then embarked upon to evaluate the capacity of my flock was one of the most agreeable to me. For this I had to fill my bag with fine devotional presents, and with this haul I went into the fields, where the slaves work in gangs, sometimes of up to a hundred. There I tucked myself away at the foot of a bush, on whose branches I spread out my merchandise. The branches were all garnished with images, medals, all manner of rosaries, and, as this was draped with pretty braids of the most vivid colours, it made a marvellous impression on the sight of these poor people. I well believe that in reading this, Sir, you may imagine one of the stalls of those haberdashers, who display their merchandise by the door of churches during village feasts.

Moreover, the slaves never drop their hoes and their billhooks so quickly to gather around me as on this occasion. After they had made a semi-circle, we started according to custom with the sign of the cross. Then, holding my catalogue in my hand, I questioned each one in turn, and according to the degree of capacity that I had noted the preceding year. If I found that he had improved, I noted it, and then according to his knowledge I gave him a prize that the others followed with their eyes, with the signs of a certain jealousy, that very much pleased me.

Pour ceux, qui n'avaient rien avancé, ils n'en remportaient[114] que de la honte, que les autres leur faisaient à l'envie, chacun jetant la faute de son ignorance sur lui seul, et c'est là particulièrement qu'ils faisaient valoir d'une manière, qui ne me déplaisait pas trop, le grand talent qu'ils ont pour être moqueurs. Ce qu'il y avait de plus consolant était l'empressement des parents, pour faire répondre leurs petits enfants à l'âge de cinq à six ans, les maîtres mêmes s'en faisaient un honneur, comme pour les enfants de la maison, enfin je reconnus que pourvu qu'on se prenne à cette instruction avec quelque assiduité et quelque méthode, on justifiera ce qu'on a dit souvent que les esclaves des îles, excepté ceux qui y sont venus de nouveau, ou dans un âge un peu avancé, sont mieux instruits, que ne sont les gens de la campagne en France, ce qui est encore plus vrai à l'égard des nègres créoles, c'est-à-dire, nés dans notre Amérique, dont le nombre est plus grand dans Saint-Christophe, que dans les autres îles, mais leur esprit, qui leur fait apprendre si facilement le bien qu'ils ne font pas, leur fait apprendre avec la même facilité le mal qu'ils ne font que trop, et c'est à cette cause qu'on attribue leurs désordres, qui sont aussi plus communs ici, que dans les autres îles.

[43^v] Enfin j'achevai l'année par la réformation de mon catalogue, qui m'était nécessaire comme l'âme de mon emploi. Pour cet effet je me transportai partout pour marquer tous les nouveaux venus, et tous les autres changements qui avaient été faits en grand nombre. Ce sont les mémoires pour faire une nouvelle liste, qui contienne l'état présent du spirituel de ma mission, et en même temps de ce qu'il y a à faire pour l'année présente, où suivant les traces de la précédente, j'ai fait plusieurs mariages jusqu'au carême où nous sommes,[115] que j'emploie à préparer les catéchumènes au baptême de Pâques, sauf le temps, que j'ai employé à cette lettre, qui ne sera pas inutile, puisqu'elle me procurera le secours de vos prières.

Ayant donc ainsi réformé mon catalogue, j'y trouvai 2522 esclaves, 128 mariés de nouveau, 88 réunis après un ancien divorce ou mauvais ménage, 123 adultes baptisés de nouveau, avec 103 enfants, dont 42 prient en paradis pour les autres, car depuis dix à douze ans, il meurt ici la moitié de ces enfants, d'adultes, il en est mort 80. Il y en a 562 qui ont fait leurs Pâques l'année 1681, 585 qui ont avancé pour la capacité, parmi lesquels j'en vois 343 qui ont quelque avancement dans l'instruction. Il y en a 971 qui savent bien les principes de la foi, et 626 qui outre cela savent [44^r] bien les prières, 335 concubinaires qui ont quitté leur péché, et enfin la prière rétablie dans toutes les maisons, excepté dans une seule. Le nombre des baptisés[116] et des morts, est un peu plus grand qu'il n'est ici marqué, parce qu'il se fait quelques baptêmes et quelques enterrements dans quelque autre église, qui est dans mon quartier.

---

[114] MdC, MS 73, fol. 116^r (numbered both page 79 and page 256 in manuscript) now takes up again from the word 'remportaient', transcribed as 'rapportaient'.

[115] AFSI, GBr0185, fol. 43^v: 'où nous sommes' crossed out. MdC, MS 73, fol. 116^v: où nous sommes'.

[116] MdC, MS 73, fol. 117^r: 'Le nombre des enfants baptisés'.

Those who had not advanced took nothing away[68] but the shame that the others generously heaped on them. They were blamed by each for their own ignorance and it is particularly in this that they exercised their great talent for jeering, in a way that did not displease me too much. What brought most consolation was the eagerness of the parents who had their little children, of five or six years old, answer me. Even the masters thought it an honour, as they would for the children of the household. I recognized, then, that, once this instruction is undertaken with some assiduity and method, what is often said of the slaves of the islands will be justified: that is, that, apart from those who have arrived recently or when not so young, they are better instructed than the country folk in France. It is even truer of the black Creoles, that is, those born in our America, of whom the number is greater on Saint Kitts than on the other islands, but their wit, which enables them to so easily learn the good they do not do, also enables them to learn with the same ease the wickedness that they do so much of. It is claimed that this is the cause of their vice, which is also more common here than on the other islands.

So, I ended the year by reworking my catalogue, which was so necessary to me as it is the very soul of my labours. For this purpose I went all about, noting the new arrivals and all the other changes that had occurred in great number. These are memoirs to make a new list, which contains the current spiritual state of my mission and also what has to be done for the present year. Following the same pattern as the preceding one, I performed many marriages up until Lent, which I am spending in preparing the catechumens for Easter baptism, except for the time I spent on this letter, which will not be wasted as it will procure for me the aid of your prayers.

Having thus reworked my catalogue in this way, I found in it 2522 slaves, 128 newlyweds, 88 reconciled after a separation or an unhappy union, 123 newly baptized adults, with 103 children of whom 42 pray for the others in Paradise, as, for ten to twelve years now, half of the children have died here. Of the adults, 80 are dead; 562 received Easter Communion in the year 1681; 585 have made progress in their capacity, amongst whom I see 343 who have advanced a little in their instruction. There are 971 who know the principles of faith well, and 626 who in addition know their prayers well, 335 who were living in sin and have now left their sin behind, and then prayers are once more being said in all households but one. The number of the baptized and of the dead is a little greater than it is noted here, because there are some baptisms and some burials carried out in another church which is in my area.

---

[68] MdC, MS 73, fol. 116ʳ (numbered both page 79 and page 256 in manuscript) now takes up again.

Voilà, Monsieur l'emploi de cette première année, nous la terminâmes par les actions de grâces, que nous rendîmes solennellement à celui qui est tellement l'auteur de tout bien, qu'il ne partage jamais avec aucune créature la gloire de la conversion d'un pécheur, dont il est toujours l'unique principe. Le jour des Rois vint alors à propos pour cette cérémonie. Comme c'est celui de la vocation et de la conversion des gentils, on l'a choisi[117] pour la fête des nègres, vu même que l'on représente ordinairement dans les tableaux de ce mystère, un des trois rois de la couleur de nos nègres.[118] Le matin de ce jour les nègres de notre maison[119] partirent de chez nous, pour se rendre processionnellement à l'église paroissiale, où le gros des nègres de toute l'île les attendait.

Aussitôt qu'ils y furent arrivés, et placés le mieux qu'ils purent, parmi la foule des Français, qui remplissaient déjà l'église, la grand-messe commença. On fut surpris de voir qu'elle ne fut servie et répondue, que par les seuls nègres, qui avaient occupé tout le chœur et le lutrin. C'était ce qu'on n'avait point vu, [44ᵛ] aussi y avaient-ils été obligés par le refus, que les chantres ordinaires leur avaient fait depuis un an, de chanter dans une pareille occasion, mais comme nonobstant ce refus ces mêmes chantres[120] furent obligés d'implorer le secours de plusieurs nègres, qui ont la voix excellente pour soutenir le chœur toutes les fêtes, en ne pouvant pas se passer d'eux, ils se mirent[121] en état de se passer eux-mêmes de ces chantres, et par ce moyen ces pauvres esclaves ayant appris ce qu'il fallait chanter à la grand-messe, ils le firent comme je viens de dire avec plus d'applaudissement pour la nouveauté, que si l'on eût ouï la plus belle musique du monde.

Après l'Évangile, le sermon se fit sur la conversion des infidèles, et parce que le chevalier[122] de Saint-Laurent notre brave gouverneur[123] avait voulu honorer la cérémonie de sa présence, le prédicateur fit son compliment sur le service utile que ce grand homme avait su tirer des nègres,[124] lorsqu'il sauva notre île des Anglais, par deux victoires prodigieuses ayant à la première armé nos esclaves de flambeaux avec grand succès pour brûler le pays ennemi, et dans l'une et dans l'autre les ayant délivrés du péril imminent de l'apostasie, à quoi ils étaient exposés, s'ils fussent tombés entre les mains des Anglais.

---

[117] AFSI, GBro185, fol. 44ʳ appears to read 'on la choisie', and MdC, MS 73, fol. 117ʳ 'on la choisi'.

[118] AFSI, GBro185, fol. 44ʳ: the text, from 'vu même' to 'de la couleur de nos nègres', does not feature in MdC, MS 73.

[119] MdC, MS 73, fol. 117ʳ: 'Le matin de ce jour les nôtres'.

[120] AFSI, GBro185, fol. 44ᵛ: 'français' has been inserted after 'chantres'; the adjective does not figure in MdC, MS 73.

[121] MdC, MS 73, fol. 117ᵛ: 'ils les mirent'.

[122] AFSI, GBro185, fol. 44ᵛ: 'célèbre' has been inserted before 'chevalier'; the adjective features in MdC, MS 73, fol. 117ᵛ.

[123] MdC, MS 73, fol. 117ᵛ: 'notre très saint et très brave gouverneur'.

[124] MdC, MS 73, fol. 117ᵛ: 'le prédicateur fit son compliment sur le service utile que ce grand homme sut tirer des nègres, et le salut qu'il leur avait procuré.'

This then, Sir, was how this first year was spent. We finished it with Prayers of Thanks, which we gave solemnly to He who is so much the Author of all Good that He will never share, with any creature, the glory of the conversion of a sinner, of which He is always the unique principle. Epiphany was a perfect time for this ceremony. As it is the ceremony of the vocation and conversion of the Gentiles, it was chosen for the *Feast of the Slaves*, with one of the three kings usually depicted in the paintings of this mystery as being the same colour as our slaves. On the morning of this day the slaves of our domicile left in procession for the parish church, where most of the slaves of the island were waiting for them.

As soon as they had arrived and found a place for themselves as best they could amongst the crowd of French who had already filled the church, High Mass began. There was surprise upon seeing that it was only slaves, who had filled the choir and lectern, who served it and gave the responses; this had not been seen before. They had been obliged to do so because the ordinary choristers had been refusing to sing on such an occasion for a year at that point. Yet, despite this refusal, the same [French] choristers were obliged to request the assistance of many slaves, who have excellent voices, to accompany the choir on all the feast days. As such, the choristers not being able to do without the slaves, they enabled the slaves to do without them. Through this means, these poor slaves having learned what had to be sung at High Mass, they did so as I have just said with more praise for the novelty of it than if one had heard the most beautiful music in the world.

After the Gospel, the sermon was about the conversion of infidels, and, because the celebrated Chevalier de Saint-Laurent,[69] our brave governor, had honoured the ceremony with his presence, the preacher complimented this great man on the use he had made of the service of the slaves when he saved our island from the English in two prodigious victories. In the first he armed our slaves with torches to burn the enemy's lands, with great success, and in both he delivered them from the imminent danger of apostasy, to which they would have been exposed were they in the clutches of the English.

---

[69] See n. 61 in this translation. The use of fire by slaves against the English colony the coming night is mentioned in a letter dated 19 April 1666, signed Mousset, *écrivain du Saint-Sébastien*, location: 'Versailles, Archives de la Marine, Colonies, Carton de Saint-Christophe', transcribed in Marie Joseph Eugène Sue, *Histoire de la Marine française*, 5 vols (Paris: Félix Bonnaire, 1835–37), I: *XVIIe siècle-Jean Bart*, 361; see also Du Tertre, *Histoire générale des Antilles*, IV (1671), 24, 27.

La grand-messe et les communions des nègres étant [45^r] achevées, la procession se fit dans le bourg. Six grandes belles bannières marchaient à la tête portées par autant de nègres des plus robustes, la première représentait d'un côté Jésus en croix, le symbole du christianisme, et de l'autre l'adoration des Rois, les autres cinq faisaient voir les divers états de la vie de saint François de Borgia, qui peut être appelé *l'apôtre des nègres* avec la même raison qu'un saint père appelle saint Grégoire le Grand, *apôtre des Anglais*, parce qu'il envoya dans l'Angleterre de célèbres missionnaires, car ce saint[125] en envoya pareillement dans le pays des nègres, en qualité de commissaire des Indes, dont il avait fait la fonction durant le généralat de tous les prédécesseurs, et en qualité de Général de la Compagnie, lorsque pour ce dessein il joignit à son frère envoyé vice-roi en Afrique, des missionnaires pour la conversion de ces peuples,[126] nous avions gardé les étendards de ce saint après sa canonisation.

Ces bannières étaient suivies d'une grande et belle croix d'argent, le porte-croix était encore nègre, aussi bien que les deux assistants,[127] qu'il avait à ses côtés, et qu'on pourrait comparer à deux petits anges, à la couleur près, sur leurs pas marchaient modestement environ mille négresses, et ensuite autant de nègres quatre à quatre, et le chapelet à la main, chantant seuls leur catéchisme en vers, les prières ordinaires, les litanies de Notre-Dame, des noëls et plusieurs autres cantiques, enfin deux [45^v] missionnaires en surplis fermaient la marche.

Ceux qui n'avaient vu cette grande troupe, que dans l'église où il en pouvait entrer bien peu, en avaient conçu une idée bien moindre, que celle, qu'ils avaient eue la voyant ainsi assemblée, et en marche dans une grande et longue rue du bourg, où elle produisait un effet admirable par son nombre, par sa couleur, et par la propreté, où tous ces nègres étaient ce jour-là,[128] on ne pouvait pas voir cette procession, sans des sentiments bien tendres, on la comparait à celle des esclaves, que les RR. PP. de la Merci et de la Trinité rachètent de la servitude des infidèles, et qu'ils conduisent avec cérémonie dans les villes de l'Europe, on y trouvait cette différence que ceux-là par leur liberté triomphent des chaînes des mahométans, et ceux-ci à la faveur de l'esclavage, qui les soumet aux chrétiens, triomphent de celui du démon, et commencent à jouir de la liberté des enfants de Dieu.

---

[125] MdC, MS 73, fol. 118^r: 'car saint François de Borgia'.
[126] MdC, MS 73, fol. 118^r: the paragraph ends with 'pour la conversion de ces peuples'.
[127] MdC, MS 73, fol. 118^r: 'aussi bien que les deux céroféraires'.
[128] MdC, MS 73, fol. 118^v: 'où elle produisait un effet admirable par son nombre et par sa couleur, rehaussée par la blancheur de la toile de leurs habits'.

Once High Mass and the Communions of the slaves were finished, the procession was held in the town. There were six fine, large banners in front, carried by the same number of the most robust slaves. The first represented Jesus on the cross, the symbol of Christianity, on one side, and on the other the Adoration of the Magi. The other five showed the various events in the life of Saint Francis Borgia,[70] who could be called the 'Apostle of the Slaves' for the same reason that a holy father calls Saint Gregory the Great the 'Apostle of the English' because he sent famous missionaries to England.[71] For the former also sent such missionaries to the land of the blacks in his capacity as commissary of the Indies, a function he had carried out during his predecessors' generalate, and in his role as general of the Company. Then, for this purpose, with his brother who had been sent as viceroy in Africa, he sent along missionaries for the conversion of these peoples. We kept the standards of this saint after his canonization.

These banners were followed by a fine, large silver cross. The cross-bearer was also black, as well as the two helpers who were flanking him and who could be compared to two little angels, were it not for their colour. After them were about a thousand female slaves walking modestly, and then the same number of males walking four by four, with rosaries in their hand, each singing their catechism in verse, the ordinary prayers, the litanies of Our Lady,[72] canticles of Christmas, and many others, and the procession was closed by two missionaries wearing surplices.

Those who had only seen this great troop in the church, where very few of them could enter, had imagined there were far fewer, than when they saw them assembled together like this, and in procession in a large and long street in the town. The procession produced an admirable effect because of the number, the colour, and the neatness of all these slaves on that day, and one could not look upon it without sentiments of great tenderness. It was compared to that of the slaves whom the Mercedarian and Trinitarian Fathers redeem from servitude to the infidels, and whom they lead with ceremony in the towns of Europe.[73] The difference that was observed was that the latter triumph over the Mohammedans' chains, and the former, thanks to the slavery that submits them to Christians, triumph over that of the demon, and begin to enjoy the liberty of the children of God.

[70] Saint Francis Borgia, or Francisco de Borja (1510–1572), Duke of Gandia, renounced public life and joined the Society of Jesus in 1548, becoming superior general in 1565. He was canonized in 1671.

[71] Pope Gregory the first (540?–604), pope from 590, sent missions to peoples including the Anglo-Saxons; the most famous such missionary was Saint Augustine of Canterbury (d. 605?). Bede (673–735) writes of Gregory 'quem recte nostrum appellare possumus et debemus apostolum'. Bede, *Venerabilis Bedae Historia ecclesiastica gentis anglorum*, ed. by Joseph Stevenson (London: English Historical Society, 1838), p. 89.

[72] A litany is a supplicatory prayer; the *Litanie de Notre-Dame de Lorette* (*Litany to Our Lady of Loretto*) received papal approval in 1587.

[73] The Mercedarians (founded in the thirteenth century) and Trinitarians (founded in the late twelfth century) were redemptionist orders, which were very active in the seventeenth century, and whose duties included ransoming Christian captives in the Barbary States and returning them to Europe.

J'achèverais enfin ici cette lettre, si le motif qui me l'a fait faire si longue, ne m'obligeait, pour ne rien laisser à dire, à vous parler de la mort des nègres, qui n'a pu trouver de place dans le papier. Je puis dire que jamais aucune nation ne l'a moins appréhendée, puisqu'ils se la procurent eux-mêmes pour des bagatelles; et que quand elle vient d'ailleurs, ils la voient venir avec une tranquillité merveilleuse.

Les nouveaux venus sont plus sujets à se faire mourir eux-mêmes, par la persuasion qu'ils ont, qu'en mourant [46^r] ils retournent dans leur pays. On me vint dire une fois, que dans un quartier voisin du mien un homme et une femme nouvellement arrivés s'étaient pendus à un arbre, et mon quartier ne fut pas exempt de ces malheurs. La même chose y arriva un jour à une négresse, et une autre fois à un nègre aussi nouveaux venus,[129] celui-ci avait à grand'peine expiré dans cet horrible genre de mort, lorsque je passais par hasard auprès d'un arbre, où il venait de se pendre, le lieu était sur le bord de la haute falaise d'une rivière, mais par le moyen des broussailles il était si bien à couvert du chemin, où je passais, qu'il était impossible d'en rien voir, particulièrement quand on n'en a pas la moindre pensée, mais je n'eus pas avancé vingt pas, que j'entendis un grand bruit derrière moi. C'étaient des gens, qui par hasard ayant rencontré cet effroyable spectacle, en témoignaient leur étonnement, et plaignaient la perte, qu'avait faite le maître de ce nègre, mais je plaignis bien plus la perte de son âme. Je retournai vite sur mes pas, et je ne trouvai en lui aucun signe de vie,[130] ce fut une chose étrange, que la charogne étant ensuite tombée dans la rivière, qui n'est pas profonde, on ne l'y put jamais trouver, quelque diligence, qu'on en fît, afin d'empêcher l'infection de l'eau, dont tout le monde boit en ce lieu-là.

Ce funeste accident m'obligea de prendre un étrange thème pour l'exhortation, que je fis aux nègres le [46^v] dimanche d'après, et de leur prouver, qu'il ne fallait pas se pendre. Je leur expliquai, comme celui qui venait de le faire, était allé dans son pays, en un sens, mais non pas comme il l'entendait, et je leur dis, que le pays de ceux, qui se pendent, est l'enfer, sur quoi je leur racontais la mort de Judas, duquel les apôtres disaient en ce temps-là,[131] qu'il était allé en son pays, *ut abiret in locum suum*, mais que ce misérable nègre n'était pas allé dans son pays, comme il l'avait prétendu, puisqu'aucun ne retournait en Afrique par ce moyen-là. Pour prouver cela, je ne fis qu'interroger publiquement les plus sages, qui étaient partis de leur pays, en un âge assez mûr, et leur demander à chacun, s'ils se souvenaient d'y avoir jamais vu retourner aucun de leurs compatriotes, qui étaient morts dans l'Amérique, tous me répondirent, que non, alors je fis valoir cette raison convaincante pour détourner les autres de s'en retourner par le même chemin.

---

[129] MdC, MS 73, fol. 119^r: 'aussi nouveau venu'.
[130] MdC, MS 73, fol. 119^r: 'C'étaient des gens qui par hasard ayant rencontré cet effroyable spectacle en témoignaient leur étonnement et plaignaient la perte de son âme, quand étant retourné vite sur mes pas je ne trouvai en lui aucun signe de vie'.
[131] MdC, MS 73, fol. 119^v: 'duquel les apôtres disaient en ces sens'.

I would finish this letter here if what caused me to make it so long did not oblige me, so as to leave nothing out, to speak to you about the death of the slaves, which can be put nowhere else on this paper. I can say that no people has ever had less fear of it, for they cause their own death themselves for a trifle, and, when there is another cause, they await it with marvellous tranquillity.

The new arrivals are more inclined to kill themselves because of their conviction that upon their death they return to their homeland. I was once told that, in a locality near my own, a newly arrived man and woman had hung themselves from a tree, and my own quarter was not exempted from these woes. The same thing occurred with a female slave, and another time with a male, also new arrivals. He had already expired, after suffering this horrible sort of death, when I passed by chance near the tree where he had just hanged himself. The place was on the edge of a high cliff over a river, but because of the bushes he was so well hidden from the path I had taken that it was impossible to see anything, especially when such a thing is not at all expected. But I had not gone on for twenty paces when I heard a great commotion behind me. It was some people who had by chance come across this terrible sight and who, greatly shocked, were lamenting the master's loss of his slave; but I lamented much more the loss of the slave's soul. I swiftly turned back, and found no sign of life in him. A strange thing was that the cadaver, after having fallen into the river which is shallow, could not be found in spite of all the care that was taken, to avoid corrupting the water which is drunk by everyone around there.

This unfortunate incident obliged me to take a strange theme for my exhortation to the slaves the following Sunday, and to prove to them that hanging oneself is wrong. I explained to them that the slave who had just done so had gone to his homeland, in a sense, but not as he understood it. I said to them that Hell is the homeland of those who hang themselves, and I told them about the death of Judas, of whom the apostles said at this time that he had gone to his homeland, *ut abiret in locum suum*.[74] But this miserable slave had not gone back to his homeland, as he had wished to, because no one returned to Africa by such a means. To prove this, all I did was to question in public the wisest of them, those who had left their homeland when they were quite mature in age. I asked each of them if they remembered having ever seen any of their compatriots who had died in America return home. All of them replied 'no', and I stressed this convincing reason to deter the others from returning along the same route.

[74] Acts 1. 25 ('that he might go to his own place', 1582, p. 290).

Les créoles et les anciens venus ne se donnent pas la mort pour ce sujet, mais ils le font pour d'autres. J'en connais un, qu'on dit être un excellent cuisinier, et qui passerait pour tel en Europe.[132] Son maître lui dit un jour, qu'il l'avait vendu à un hôtelier, lui indigné, que cela eût été fait sans sa participation, prend tout à coup de grands ciseaux, qu'il trouva par hasard, et de furie s'en donne un coup dans le ventre. On y accourt, on m'y appelle, la blessure [47ʳ] n'est pas trouvée mortelle; le blessé revient de sa fureur, je lui représente l'énormité[133] de sa faute, et pour donner exemple aux autres, remarquant qu'il portait au col un petit crucifix, que je lui avais donné autrefois, je le lui ôtai avec cérémonie, comme on ôte le collier de l'ordre à un criminel d'état. Il en fit paraître beaucoup de douleur et de confusion, et peu de jours après se retira chez son nouveau maître. La semaine passée un autre qui n'est pas de mon quartier, se donna un coup de couteau dans le ventre, pour prévenir le châtiment dont son maître l'avait menacé.

Le mal est que quand ces misérables sont morts sous les coups de leurs maîtres, ceux-ci, pour se justifier, disent qu'ils se sont étouffés de rage, et trouvent quelquefois des chirurgiens, qui accommodent leur rapport, à la volonté de ces barbares, comme il est arrivé ici depuis trois mois à une jeune négresse de douze ans, que j'avais baptisée l'année passée. Ce rapport injuste a arrêté toutes mes poursuites, mais un peu de temps auparavant le meurtre d'un autre nègre ne fut pas si impuni, une Française à qui il appartenait étant ivre, l'avait étranglé en plein jour sur un grand chemin, et l'avait enterré. J'en fus d'abord averti, je fis ma dénonciation selon les formes, le procureur du roi, et le greffier se transportent sur le lieu, et font leur procès-verbal, enfin cette femme fut punie d'une peine non pas corporelle, car cela [47ᵛ] arrive rarement ici dans ces occasions, mais d'une peine pécuniaire, qui lui a donné un chagrin aussi grand, qu'il était juste. Il arriverait bien d'autres malheurs plus fréquents à ces pauvres esclaves, si les missionnaires ne prenaient leur parti.

Le mépris, qu'ils font de la mort, paraît encore par l'indifférence, avec laquelle ils l'attendent, soit qu'elle soit naturelle, soit qu'elle soit violente, et ordonnée par la justice. J'en ai assisté quelques-uns[134] au dernier supplice, mais je ne me pouvais jamais assez étonner de leur fermeté. *Peu m'importe*, me disait une fois un d'eux, *par quel chemin j'aille en paradis, pourvu que l'âme y soit, et le corps en terre sainte*, car ils ont fort à cœur cette sépulture, et il fallait toujours que je la leur promisse, pour les consoler.

---

[132] MdC, MS 73, fol. 119ᵛ: 'J'en connais un qu'on dit être un excellent cuisinier et très propre pour donner à manger à des gens de qualité'.
[133] MdC, MS 73 ends here, on fol. 119ᵛ, numbered both page 86 and page 263.
[134] AFSI, GBro185, fol. 47ᵛ: 'quelqu'un' in manuscript.

The Creoles and those who have been here for a long time do not end their own lives for this reason, but they do so for others. I know one, who is said to be an excellent cook, and who would be considered as such in Europe. His master said to him one day that he had sold him to an innkeeper and the slave, indignant that this had been done without consulting him, suddenly took a large pair of scissors which happened to be there, and, in fury, stabbed himself in the stomach. There was a commotion, I was called for, the wound was not found to be mortal, and the patient collected himself. I demonstrated the enormity[75] of his sin to him; to make an example of him to the others, noticing that he was wearing around his neck a little crucifix that I had given him previously, I stripped him of it with ceremony, as a state criminal is stripped of the chain of the Order.[76] He seemed very sad and shameful, and a few days later he went off to join his new master. Last week another one who is not from my quarter stabbed himself in the stomach with a knife, so as to avoid the punishment with which his master had threatened him.

What is evil is that, when these wretches have expired because of their masters' blows, the masters, to justify themselves, say that the slaves had suffocated themselves through rage, and sometimes they find surgeons who will modify their report according to the wishes of these barbarians. This happened here three months ago to a young slave girl of twelve years of age whom I had baptized last year. This unjust report put an end to my proceedings, but a short time afterwards the murder of another slave was not similarly unpunished. The Frenchwoman he belonged to was drunk, and had strangled him in broad daylight upon the highway, and buried him. I was alerted to this straightaway. I made my accusation through the appropriate channels, the king's *procureur*[77] and the chief clerk came to the place and carried out their investigation, and in the end this woman was punished. She did not receive corporal punishment, because that rarely occurs here in such situations, but a fine, which caused her as much upset as it was justified. These poor slaves would suffer much more harm, and more frequently, if the missionaries did not stand up for them.

Their scorn of death can also be seen in the indifference with which they await it, whether it be natural, or violent, and a judicial punishment. I have already consoled some of them during their execution, but I could never get over my astonishment at their resolution. 'It matters little to me', one of them said to me once, 'by which road I go to Paradise, once my soul is there, and my body lies in holy ground', for they are very attached to such a burial place, and I always had to promise them they would have this, so as to console them.

[75] MdC, MS 73 ends here, on fol. 119ᵛ, numbered both page 86 and page 263.
[76] Knights of the Ordre de Saint-Michel, founded in 1469 by Louis XI, and the Ordre du Saint-Esprit, founded by Henri III in 1578, wore a chain of which they could be stripped in the case of a criminal sentence.
[77] The *procureur du roi* represented the monarch's interests in legal cases.

J'ai vu longtemps en prison deux nègres, qui y étaient détenus pour des cas pendables. Je les avais résolus à la mort, sans beaucoup de peine, pendant que sans leur en rien dire, je me faisais leur procureur. Enfin Dieu nous fit la grâce et à eux et à moi de gagner cette affaire, et de leur sauver la vie, aussitôt et durant la tenue du Conseil Souverain, qui venait de les absoudre de la sentence de mort du juge subalterne, je leur portai cette bonne nouvelle le même jour, qu'ils attendaient à être pendus, et je fus bien surpris de l'indifférence avec laquelle ils la reçurent. Aussi il y en avait un, qui quelques jours auparavant [48ʳ] ayant été présenté à la question, avait dit, qu'il aimait mieux mourir, et avouer tout ce qu'on voulait, mais nonobstant cet étrange pas on trouva le moyen d'accommoder tout, et de lui sauver la vie.

Un autre fit paraître une constance plus grande. Il avait été rompu tout vif, et survécut quatre jours sur la roue. Il ne dit jamais pendant tout ce temps-là une seule parole d'impatience. Son confesseur en était charmé, et le procureur du roi, qui selon sa charge, avait été sa partie, ne faisait pas difficulté de s'approcher de lui de temps en temps, pour lui suggérer quelque bonne pensée, que le patient recevait avec action de grâces.

Pour la mort naturelle, on ne peut pas l'attendre avec plus de tranquillité. Ils n'en ont de l'inquiétude que jusqu'à ce qu'on ait appelé le père des nègres pour les préparer à la mort, car avant cela, dès qu'ils sentent le moindre mal, ils ne laissent personne en repos dans la case. Après que je leur ai administré les sacrements, ils sont en paix, et s'ils meurent, c'est avec une grande confiance en Dieu, et avec des marques de prédestination.

Mais leurs proches ne sont pas moins sensibles à la mort des défunts. J'en vois souvent des marques, qui m'attendrissent. Il y a quelques mois, que j'enterrais une négresse de huit à neuf ans, sa bonne mère était debout sur le bord de sa fosse, et quand on commença à jeter la terre dessus, elle se prit à chanter [48ᵛ] d'un air lugubre accompagné de sanglots, et de larmes, ce qu'elle chantait était un adieu qu'elle faisait à sa fille, répétant les paroles, qu'elle lui avait dites en mourant, et racontant les bons services qu'elle lui rendait. Je voulus consoler cette pauvre mère, disant que Dieu lui avait laissé d'autres enfants pour la servir, elle me répondit sans détacher les yeux de dessus la fosse, et toujours en pleurant et avec le même air, *rien que Charlot, rien que Charlot*, c'est le nom du garçon qui lui reste, après quoi elle recommença sa chanson comme dessus. Depuis j'ai reconnu que cette coutume de pleurer ainsi les morts, est particulière aux nègres d'Ardes ou Arada, qui est une partie de la Guinée en Afrique.

Voilà Monsieur, ce que j'avais à vous dire, pour satisfaire au désir, que vous m'aviez témoigné, d'être informé de ma mission des nègres. Je vous prie d'excuser la longueur de cette lettre, et encore plus les incongruités que vous y aurez rencontrées. Je suis aucunement excusable, l'ayant écrite à bâtons

There were two slaves I used to go and see in prison for a long time, and who had been detained for hanging offences. I had reconciled them to death, without much trouble, while without saying anything to them I acted as their advocate. In the end God graced me and them with winning this case, and saving their lives. Immediately, during the sitting of the Sovereign Council which had just absolved them of the death sentence passed by a lower judge, I brought them this good news on the same day they were waiting to be hanged. I was very surprised by the indifference with which they received it. There was also one who, having a few days previously been brought to be tortured, said that he preferred to die and to avow whatever was desired. Notwithstanding this strange step, a way was found to put everything in order and to save his life.

There was another who showed even greater constancy. He had been broken alive, and survived on the wheel for four days. During all this time he did not utter one single word of impatience. His confessor was astonished, and the king's *procureur*, who had played the part his office demands, deigned to come close to him from time to time, with some inspiring reflection, that the sufferer received with gratitude.

With regard to natural death, no one can await it with more tranquillity. They are anxious only until the *Priest of the Slaves* has been called to prepare them for death, for before that, once they feel the slightest bit unwell, they leave nobody in peace in the cabin. After I have given them the sacraments, they are at peace and, if they die, it is with great confidence in God and with signs of [their] predestination.[78]

Yet those who were close to the deceased are no less affected by their death. I often see signs of this that are very touching. Several months ago, I was burying a black girl of eight or nine years of age. Her good mother was standing by the edge of the grave, and, when they started to throw the earth on it, she began to sing in a melancholy tone, broken up by her sobs and tears. She was singing a goodbye to her daughter, repeating the words she had spoken while dying, and recounting the good things that she used to do for her. I wanted to console this poor mother, saying that God had left her with other children to help her. She replied without taking her eyes off the grave, crying all the while and in the same tone, 'Only little Charles, only little Charles'. This is the name of the boy who is left. After this she began her chant all over as above; I have since recognized that this custom of lamenting the dead in this way is particular to the slaves of Ardra, which is a part of Guinea in Africa.

This, Sir, is what I had to say to you to satisfy the desire you expressed to be informed about my mission to the slaves. I pray you to excuse the length of this letter, and still more any mistakes you may have come across. I am to be

---

[78] Here, *predestination* is to be understood in the sense of 'individual salvation'.

rompus,[135] et à diverses reprises, ménageant, le mieux qu'il m'était possible, quelques moments, que mes occupations indispensables près des blancs et des noirs, me permettaient de prendre.

Au reste je vous puis assurer, qu'il n'y a pas un de nos missionnaires, qui ne travaille avec bien plus de zèle et de succès, que moi, dans les divers quartiers qu'ils servent, principalement à la Martinique, où [49ʳ] nous avons soin des quatre grands quartiers, qui font toute la face de l'île, et où tous les vaisseaux abordent, particulièrement ceux qui viennent chargés de nègres, dont la plupart sont vendus en cette île qui en a plus que toutes les autres, et qui est le séjour du Gouverneur Général, de l'intendant et de l'escadre de navires de guerre, que le roi tient toujours en l'Amérique.

J'aurais fort souhaité vous pouvoir envoyer une relation de nos Indiens, comme j'ai fait des nègres, car j'avais demandé à nos supérieurs la mission de la terre ferme, où la porte nous est à présent ouverte; tant par notre établissement à Cayenne, que par la belle disposition de ces Indiens, qui nous invitent d'aller demeurer avec eux, et dont la langue est très aisée à apprendre, la plupart de nos Français la sachant, mais il n'est pas juste, quand on n'est pas un nombre suffisant pour tout faire, d'abandonner les Français et les nègres, qui sont nos domestiques, pour aller chercher de l'emploi plus loin. Nous venons cependant d'apprendre par lettres de Cayenne, qu'un des trois pères, qui y sont, avec un séculier, faute de compagnon jésuite, s'en va dans la grande rivière des Amazones, qui n'est éloignée de Cayenne que de deux ou trois journées, au voisinage de laquelle il y a une infinité de nations d'Indiens, qui n'ont jamais entendu parler de l'Évangile, et qui, à la réserve de celles, qui sont sur les côtes, n'ont jamais vu d'Européen. Les deux autres [49ᵛ] pères demeurent à Cayenne pour l'assistance des Français et des nègres, nos pères ayant seuls le soin de tout le spirituel de la colonie, du zèle desquels dépend ce grand et vaste pays des Indiens.

Je salue avec respect votre illustre famille, et vous suis en particulier

Très humble et très obéissant serviteur en Notre-Seigneur Jean Mongin de la Comp.e de Jésus.

---

[135] AFSI, GBro185, fol. 48ᵛ: 'bâton rompu' in manuscript.

excused, having written it in dribs and drabs, and at various stages, making the best use I can of the few moments my indispensable duties with the whites and the blacks allow me to take.

What is more, I can assure you that none of our missionaries work with more zeal and success than I do, in the various quarters that they serve; [we are] principally in Martinique, where we look after four large districts along the coast of the island,[79] and where all the vessels arrive, particularly those which come laden with slaves. Most of them are sold on this island which has more than all the others, which is where the governor general and the *intendant* reside, and where the fleet of warships that the king maintains in America is stationed.

I would very much have liked to be able to send you an account of our Indians, as I did with the blacks, for I had asked our superiors to send me on the mission to the mainland where the gateway is at present open to us. This is as much because of our establishment at Cayenne, as because of the favourable disposition of these Indians, who invite us to come and live with them, and whose language is very easy to learn, with most of our French knowing it. Yet when one is not in sufficient number to do everything, it is not fair to abandon our French and our black people, who are our domestic servants, to look further afield for our labours. We have just learned in letters sent from Cayenne that one of the three priests who are there — and with a secular, in the absence of a Jesuit confrere — is going to travel along the great river of the Amazons, which is only two or three days away from Cayenne. Along this river there are infinite numbers of Indian peoples, who have never heard of the Gospel and who, aside from those on the coast, have never seen a European. The other two priests are staying in Cayenne to look after the French and the black people; our clergy has sole care of all the spiritual needs of the colony, and this great and vast land of the Indians depends upon their zeal.

I greet your illustrious family with respect and am your own

very humble and very obedient servant in Our Lord, Jean Mongin of the Society of Jesus.

---

[79] Mongin is referring to the north-west coast of Martinique.

Carcassonne, MdC, MS 73, fols 79^r–119^v [title page, fol. 79^r; letter begins fol. 80^r]. Transcription from fols 79^r–84^r.

[79^r] *Septième lettre à un gentilhomme du Languedoc contenant la relation de la mission des nègres, de l'île Saint-Christophe*

[80^r] Monsieur,

Il y a longtemps que vous me demandez une réponse qui descende dans le détail des travaux que les missionnaires entreprennent ici pour le salut des nègres. L'idée générale que vous avez de cet emploi, vous fait dire que vous nous considérez dans notre mission avec plus d'admiration que vous ne pourriez exprimer et que pendant six mois vous avez eu l'esprit si rempli de ce que Dieu opère par nous, en ce pays-ci que vous avez employé tout le temps de votre loisir à les étudier et à les comprendre. Ce sont les termes de la lettre que la charité et la piété vous ont dictée sur le sujet de notre mission; j'espère que vous comprendrez ici avec moins de temps et d'étude ce qui fait votre étonnement et qui vous a porté à me demander avec tant d'instance que je vous apprenne, dites-vous, les routes que le Saint-Esprit me fait tenir pour amener dans ses voies des gens sans religion, et sans raison. Votre qualité et notre amitié (car vous voulez bien que j'ajoute ce mot) exigeaient de moi que je satisfisse plus tôt à un désir si juste et si empressé. J'ai pourtant beaucoup différé; et c'était pour me mieux acquitter de ce devoir, disant en moi-même qu'il fallait [renverser?][2] l'ancien proverbe, et dire <u>assez tôt</u> [80^v] <u>si assez bien</u>. Car enfin je voulais connaître par

---

[1] The manuscript has undergone a number of corrections/interventions; minor reformulations of vocabulary have not been noted in the present transcription.

[2] Chatillon transcribes this word as 'justifier' (p. 73). This interpretation would make sense with what follows, but is not what has been written on the manuscript.

TRANSLATION 4

Carcassonne,
MdC, MS 73, fols 79^r–119^v.
Translation from fols 79^r–84^r.

[Title page]: *Seventh Letter to a Languedocian Gentleman, Containing the Relation of the Mission to the Black Slaves, from Saint Christopher Island*[1]

Sir,

You have, for a long time now, been asking me for a reply describing in detail the labours undertaken by the missionaries here for the salvation of the slaves. The general idea that you have about this task leads you to say that you think of us in our mission with more wonder than you could express, and that for six months your mind has been so occupied with what God is doing through us in this land, that you have spent all your free time in studying and understanding them.[2] These are the terms of the letter, that charity and piety dictated to you, on the subject of our mission. I hope that this letter will help you understand, with less time and study, the subject of your astonishment, that has led you to ask me so insistently to instruct you, as you put it, about the paths that the Holy Spirit has me follow to bring people who are without religion and without reason, on the way towards Him. Your quality and our friendship (because you do indeed want me to use this [latter] word) demanded that I satisfy such a just and insistent request earlier. I have, nonetheless, put this off for a long time; and it was to better fulfil this obligation, saying to myself that one should [turn around?][3] the old proverb, and say *soon enough if well enough*. After all, I wanted to learn through my own experience what I had to tell you concerning

[1] This is the seventh letter in MdC, MS 73; see Introduction of this book for addressees.
[2] 'Them' refers either to the 'labours' of missionaries, or to the slaves themselves.
[3] Despite the apparent use of the verb 'renverser' ('turn around'), what follows is the standard formulation of the proverb.

mon expérience ce que j'avais à vous écrire touchant le christianisme des nègres. Auparavant je n'avais pu m'y occuper avec tant d'application ayant été chargé tantôt du soin des seuls blancs, tantôt des blancs et des noirs ensemble. Mais maintenant je suis tout à ces pauvres esclaves et par conséquent mieux informé de tout ce qui les regarde.

La connaissance que mon expérience m'en a acquise me sera nécessaire pour vous en donner une qui soit telle que vous souhaitez. Aussi quand vous n'auriez pour ce sujet qu'une curiosité qui vous fût commune avec les autres gens de Languedoc, j'aurais assez à dire pour la satisfaire, puisque c'est celle de toutes nos provinces qui sait le moins ce qui se passe dans l'Amérique. Mais vos lettres aussi bien que nos anciennes conversations m'ont assez appris, qu'il ne faut laisser rien à dire dans les réponses qu'on fait à vos demandes; et qu'il faut particulariser toutes choses, comme je fis dans ma première lettre touchant mon voyage, et comme je ferai encore dans celle-ci, ayant reconnu par votre lettre que l'idée que vous vous êtes formée de notre mission est un peu trop générale.

Vous vous souvenez peut-être que je vous ai écrit qu'il y a ici trois sortes de gens, qui sont natifs ou originaires, les uns de l'Amérique, les autres de l'Europe, les autres enfin de [81ʳ] l'Afrique (car pour l'Asie il n'y en a quasi point) parmi lesquels la nation française et la religion romaine sont les dominantes. Ceux du pays sont les sauvages, en très petit nombre, parce que par leur perfidie ils se sont attiré des guerres qui les ont la plupart exterminés, à quelques-uns près, qui sont parmi nous, quasi tous esclaves et chrétiens. Ceux-là sont rouges ou basanés, ceux qui sont natifs ou originaires d'Europe, sont les seuls blancs; ceux d'Afrique parfaitement noirs ou Mores.

Comme les blancs ne sont ici que pour faire du sucre qui est une récolte de tous les mois de l'année, ils ont besoin d'un grand nombre de gens pour y travailler. Les premiers Européens qui habitèrent ce pays y employaient des pauvres qui dans les ports de France s'engageaient à des capitaines qui les passaient ici, à servir durant 3 ans le maître à qui ils les livraient et qui en payait abondamment le passage à ce capitaine, après lequel terme ils commençaient à gagner des gages; avec tant de succès pour quelques-uns, qu'il y a des plus riches habitants qui ne sont venus ici que par cette voie.

Mais le travail, la chaleur et le mauvais traitement de ces pauvres engagés en ayant fait mourir la plupart, on pensa que les Mores d'Afrique seraient plus utiles comme étant accoutumés à une vie misérable et à la chaleur extrême de ce pays, étant d'un même climat, quoique plus orientaux [81ᵛ] que nous de 1200 lieues. Pour cet effet on commença d'en apporter ici des esclaves à quoi ils semblent être nés par excellence possédant par-dessus toutes les autres nations les deux qualités, qu'Aristote demande pour l'esclavage: la force du corps et la faiblesse de l'esprit, aussi sont-ce les gens du monde qui souffrent plus patiemment les misères de cet état.

the Christianity of the black slaves. I could not do it beforehand with so much attention, having been entrusted for a time with looking after the whites alone, then the blacks and the whites together. However, now I am completely occupied with these poor slaves and in consequence better informed about everything that concerns them.

I will need my knowledge, gained from experience, to enable you to gain the depth of knowledge that you wish for. If your curiosity about this subject was simply that of the other people of Languedoc, I would have enough to say to satisfy it, because of all our provinces, it is the one in which least is known about what is happening in America. But your letters, as well as our past conversations, have taught me well that nothing must be left out of the answers to your questions, and that everything must be dealt with in detail. This is what I did in my first letter concerning my voyage, and what I will do in this one, as I recognize from your letter that your idea of our mission is a little imprecise.

You will perhaps remember that I wrote to you that there are three sorts of people here, who were either born here or elsewhere, in either America, Europe, or Africa — for there is hardly anyone from Asia here — and among them the French people and the Roman religion are dominant. Those who are of this land are the savages, who are very few in number, because through their perfidy they brought wars upon themselves which have exterminated most of them, apart from a few who live amongst us and who are nearly all slaves and Christians. They are red- or dark-skinned; those who were born or originate in Europe are the only whites, and the Africans are perfectly black or are Moors.

As the whites are only here to make sugar, which can be harvested all the months of the year, they need a great number of people to work here. The first Europeans who settled the land employed poor people who, in the ports of France, signed themselves up to captains, who brought them here to serve the master to whom they were given for three years. The master would pay a steep price to the captain for this passage. After the servants' time was up they would start to earn a wage, with so much success for some of them, that some of the richest planters here started out in this manner.

However, because the labour, the heat, and the bad treatment of these poor indentured labourers caused the death of most of them, it was thought that African Moors would be more useful, given that they are accustomed to a life of poverty and to extreme heat such as that of this land, as they come from a similar climate, although further east than us by 1200 leagues. For this purpose slaves started to be brought from there to these parts, and they seemed to be born for slavery as they possess, more than any other peoples, the two traits that are necessary for it, according to Aristotle: bodily strength and feeble-mindedness. Amongst all the peoples of the world it is also they who suffer the miseries of this state with most patience.

Les Portugais furent les premiers qui firent ce commerce dans les côtes occidentales de l'Afrique où ils firent les premières découvertes et les premières conquêtes il y a 200 ans. Cet étrange trafic avait d'abord donné de l'exercice aux théologiens: car quoiqu'ils reconnaissent d'un commun accord les titres d'une légitime servitude qui se réduisent à la naissance, à la condamnation, et au droit de la guerre, néanmoins la plupart des auteurs, même dans les universités de Portugal, niaient qu'on pût acheter ces esclaves des mains de leurs compatriotes, parce qu'on devait présumer des peuples si brutaux qu'il n'y avait nulle justice ni dans la guerre où ils se faisaient prisonniers, ni dans le procédé de ceux qui de temps immémorial avaient réduit à l'esclavage de certaines familles avec leur postérité, ni enfin dans la vente que font les pères de leurs enfants dans ce pays.

Pour remédier aux scrupules que ces raisons causaient, les rois de Portugal donnèrent des ordres fort précis, mais qui ne furent peut-être pas toujours trop bien [82^r] observés pour empêcher que les marchands qui allaient sur ces côtes n'achetassent aucun esclave sans être assurés du droit du vendeur. Depuis à l'imitation des Portugais les autres Européens établis dans l'Amérique ont continué ce commerce, mais les Français sont ceux qui le font avec plus d'équité et les catholiques avec plus d'utilité pour ces pauvres nègres, puisque la moindre injustice qui s'y commet est punie très sûrement[3] par ordre de la cour comme je l'ai appris des marchands qui vont faire ce trafic; aussi, le roi ne l'avait-il permis que pour nos îles, et aussitôt qu'un nègre est mené en France il y est libre parce que l'esclavage qui y avait lieu sous la première et seconde race de nos rois, dont les principaux officiers domestiques étaient quelquefois esclaves, y a entièrement cessé par des arrêts du parlement de Paris, de Bordeaux et de Toulouse. D'ailleurs quoiqu'il soit vrai que la religion chrétienne par une prescription ancienne ne permette pas de faire esclave un chrétien prisonnier de guerre, elle veut bien que d'un esclave on en fasse un chrétien, comme dit avec raison un auteur anglais et protestant, dans une plainte qu'il fait contre ses compatriotes qui laissent vivre et mourir ici leurs nègres dans l'infidélité sous prétexte qu'il ne faut pas qu'un chrétien soit esclave; comme si c'était un plus grand mal pour ces misérables d'être esclaves que d'être damnés.

Aussi les nègres des catholiques, sont catholiques [82^v] de même que leurs maîtres et ils doivent leur salut à leur esclavage. Je remarque qu'ils sont notablement attendris quand je leur représente qu'ils n'eussent jamais connu Dieu s'ils n'eussent été tirés de leurs pays pour servir les catholiques: dont ils paraissent plus convaincus quand ils comparent leur bonheur avec le malheur de leurs compatriotes qui appartiennent aux Anglais nos voisins dans cette île, qui ont aussi peu de soin de l'âme de leurs esclaves que de celle de leurs chevaux. C'est pourquoi je ne trouve rien de plus efficace dans les répréhensions que je fais aux nôtres quand leurs débauches les rendent indignes des sacrements, que de leur dire en leur jargon, <u>Toi de même que nègre anglais: sans baptême, sans église, sans sépulture.</u>

---

[3] MdC, MS 73, fol. 82^r reads 'seurement' ('sûrement'); an 'e' has been inserted to give 'severement' ('sévèrement').

The Portuguese were the first to carry out this trade on the western coasts of Africa where they made the first discoveries and the first conquests two hundred years ago. At first, this strange trade exercised the theologians, for, although they all recognize that enslavement due to birth, criminal conviction, or the law of war is legitimate servitude, most authors nevertheless — even in the universities of Portugal — refused that these slaves could be bought from their own compatriots. For it had to be presumed of such brutal peoples that there was no justice in the wars in which they took one another prisoner, nor in the proceedings of those who, since time immemorial, had reduced certain families with their posterity to slavery, nor, finally, in the sale of children in this land by their fathers.

To address the qualms caused by these reasons, the kings of Portugal gave very precise orders — which were perhaps not always very well observed — to prevent merchants who went to these coasts from buying any slaves without being certain of the vendor's right over them. Since then, the other Europeans settled in the Americas have followed the Portuguese and continued this trade, but it is the French who do it with most equity, and the Catholics with most advantage to these poor slaves, since the slightest injustice committed is inevitably punished by order of the court, as I learned from merchants who carry out this trade. What is more, the king only allowed it on our islands, and as soon as a slave is brought to France, there he is free, for the slavery of the time of the first and second dynasties of our kings — whose principal domestic retainers were slaves, on occasion — was entirely ended there by decision of the *parlements* of Paris, Bordeaux, and Toulouse. Moreover, while it is true that the Christian religion, through an ancient precept, does not allow a Christian prisoner of war to be enslaved, it does favour making a Christian of a slave, as has been written with justice by a Protestant English writer, in his condemnation of his compatriots who leave their slaves to live and die in their infidelity here, on the pretext that a Christian must not be a slave: as if it were a worse evil for these wretches to be enslaved than to be damned.[4]

So it is that the slaves of Catholics are Catholic like their masters, and they owe their salvation to their enslavement. I have observed that they are noticeably moved when I explain to them that they would never have known God if they had not been brought out of their lands to serve Catholics. They seem to be even more convinced of this when they compare their good fortune with the misfortune of their compatriots who belong to the English, who are our neighbours on this island, and who take as little care of the souls of their slaves as of those of their horses. It is for this reason that I find, when I reprimand our own slaves when their debauchery has made them unworthy of the sacraments, that nothing works as well as saying to them in their patois 'You same as English slave: no baptism, no church, no grave.'

[4]   Presumably Godwyn's *The Negro's and Indian's Advocate* (1680).

Voilà de quelle manière on apporte ici ces pauvres gens, mais avant de vous expliquer celle dont on travaille à leur salut, il faut vous faire remarquer que de leur fonds ils sont pour le temporel, et pour le spirituel les plus misérables qui soient dans le monde.

Pour le temporel il suffirait de dire qu'ils sont véritablement esclaves avec toute la rigueur que les lois ont établie pour la servitude. Ils sont vendus de même que les animaux pour être employés à toute sorte de travail qu'un maître peut exiger de son serviteur; on a commencé même de les faire servir aux galères depuis qu'un parti qui s'est formé pour ce commerce s'est obligé d'en fournir un certain [83ʳ] nombre pour cet effet. Ce qui augmente leur misère est que par leur travail ils ne gagnent rien, et que les enfants mêmes qu'ils mettent au monde appartiennent au maître de leurs parents. Après quoi vous ne serez pas surpris d'apprendre que la plupart pour tout habillement n'ont rien qu'un caleçon, et les femmes une cotte, le tout de grosse toile. Pour nourriture la semaine une livre et demie de viande salée, quatre livres de cassave qui est une espèce de pain de ce pays, et qui ne vaut pas le pain bis de France. Leur lit est une planche, et leur maison une cabane de feuilles et de roseaux, où ils pratiquent néanmoins tant de séparations, de chambres et de réduits, que dernièrement j'en contai jusqu'à huit, dont l'un n'avait aucune vue sur l'autre, dans un espace de 24 pieds de long, sur 12 de large. Ce que je viens de dire n'est que pour les plus aisés. Le soulagement que tous peuvent avoir pour cette extrême nécessité vient de ce qu'ils gagnent en vendant des herbes ou du bois qu'ils amassent les fêtes ou bien les jours ouvriers durant le temps qu'on leur donne pour prendre leur repas ou leur repos.

Mais la misère de l'esprit est bien plus grande. Il y en a une bonne partie de si étourdis que les Portugais doutèrent jadis s'ils étaient hommes, ce qui n'empêche pas que ceux qui naissent parmi nous n'aient l'esprit plus ouvert. Cela me [83ᵛ] fait souvenir d'un d'entre eux qui me disait un jour assez spirituellement que Dieu les fait esclaves parce qu'ils n'ont pas d'esprit pour chercher à manger, qui est un soin dont le⁴ maître se charge. Aussi il arrive assez souvent aux nègres qui sont libres d'être plus misérables que les autres: et pour cette raison une négresse esclave et des moins étourdies, qui a sa mère et deux sœurs libres, me disait dernièrement qu'elle ne voudrait pas changer de condition avec elles. Enfin le commun de ces gens ne tient pas moins de la bête pour les sens; car comme ils sont quasi insensibles aux coups sous les verges qui les mettent tout en sang, aussi ils sont plongés dans les plaisirs de l'ivrognerie et de l'impudicité d'une manière si épouvantable que force missionnaires allèguent cette raison pour en désespérer et pour en abandonner le soin à ceux de notre Compagnie, dont la plupart n'ont pas vu de plus grand attrait dans cette mission que cette misère même qu'ils sont venus secourir.

---

⁴   MdC, MS 73, fol. 83ᵛ: 'le' modified to 'leur'.

This is how these unfortunates are brought here, but, before I explain to you how we work towards their salvation, you must know that, in temporal and spiritual terms, they are the most utterly wretched people there are in the world.

Concerning the temporal, it is enough to say that they are truly slaves, subject to all the harshness that the laws have established for servitude. They are sold like animals, to be used in all the kinds of labour that a master can exact from his servitor. They have even begun to be made to serve on the galleys, since a faction which developed in favour of this trade undertook to supply a certain number for this purpose.[5] What makes their wretchedness worse is that they earn nothing from their labour, and even the children they bring into the world belong to their own parents' master. Given this, you will not be surprised to learn that most of them have for their only clothing a pair of breeches, and the women a sort of skirt, all of coarse fabric. Their food for the week consists in a pound and a half of salted meat, and four pounds of cassava, which is a sort of bread of this land which is not even as good as *brown bread* in France.[6] For their bed they have a wooden board, and their house is a cabin of leaves and reeds which they, nonetheless, partition into so many rooms and little chambers that I recently counted up to eight of them, not one of which looked upon another, in a space of twenty-four feet long by twelve feet wide. What I have just said only relates to the best-off among them. The relief that all may have from this extreme need comes from what they earn through selling herbs or wood, that they gather on feast days, or even on working days, during the time they are given to take their meals or their rest.

However, their poverty of spirit is far worse. There are a good number of them who are so empty-headed that the Portuguese of old questioned whether they were men, although those born amongst us have greater capacity of intellect. This reminds me of one of them who said to me one day, wittily enough, that God makes them slaves because they do not have the brains to go looking for food, which is their master's duty. And so, it happens often enough that free blacks live in greater misery than the others, and for this reason a black female slave — one of the least scatterbrained — whose mother and two sisters are free, said to me recently that she would not want to swap her condition with them. Indeed, most of these people are not unlike animals with regard to their senses, for, as they are almost impervious to the blows with rods which leave them covered in blood, so they are also consumed by the pleasures of drunkenness and fornication to such a horrendous degree that many missionaries claim this is the reason for their discouragement and for abandoning the care of the slaves to the members of our Society. Most of our missionaries, in turn, see no greater attraction in this mission than this very misery that they came to alleviate.

---

[5] On the existence of *agents* for the supply of slaves to the galleys at Marseille, see Adrien Dessalles, quoting Archives de la Marine, *Volume des ordres du roi, de l'année 1679*, p. 2 (in Dessalles, II, Part 3, pp. 19–20).
[6] *Pain bis*: a grey bread of poor quality with a high bran content.

Car enfin quoique ces misérables soient assez souvent condamnés à l'esclavage dans leur pays avec toute leur famille et leur postérité sans autre crime que pour avoir ôté une plume des paons de leur roi, ou touché à une calebasse sèche, de celles qu'il tient attachées à ses palmiers pour en recueillir la liqueur; quoique autrefois dans le royaume de Borne on donnait 20 esclaves pour un cheval et [84^r] même pour un chien dans celui d'Angole; 3 pour la queue d'un éléphant au Congo;[5] un pour un petit couteau en Guinée, néanmoins cette marchandise vendue à si vil prix et si peu estimée dans le pays de l'idolâtrie, a de beaucoup enchéri à l'égard des hommes apostoliques depuis que Jésus-Christ leur maître et le dernier enchérisseur, a mis ces esclaves à un si haut prix faisant mise de tout le sang qu'il a versé pour les racheter. C'est en considérant[6] de [sic] cette rançon que nous les jugeons assez précieux pour nous obliger à donner pour eux, non pas cent écus comme font nos habitants qui les achètent, mais notre sueur et notre sang que nous employons volontiers pour leur salut, malgré les choses rebutantes qui accompagnent leur misère.

For the continuation of this letter, with variants, refer to Letter 3 (AFSI, GBro185, fol. 9^r onwards) and notes.

---

[5]   MdC, MS 73, fol. 84^r: 'à Congo'.

[6]   MdC, MS 73, fol. 84^r: modified to 'considération'.

For, although these wretches are, often enough, enslaved in their land with their entire family and posterity for no other crime than taking a feather from one of their king's peacocks, or touching one of the gourds which he keeps attached to his palm trees to collect the sap, and although in former times in the kingdom of Borno they would give twenty slaves for a horse, and in the kingdom of Angola the same number for a hound, and three slaves for an elephant's tail in the Congo, and one for a little knife in Guinea,[7] nonetheless this merchandise, which is sold so cheaply and is so little valued in the land of the idolaters, has gained much in price for apostolic men since Jesus Christ, their master and the final bidder, so raised the slaves' price through all the blood He shed to redeem them. It is in consideration of this ransom that we judge them precious enough to oblige us to give not a hundred *écus* for them as our planters do when they buy them, but rather our sweat and blood that we gladly employ in their salvation, despite the off-putting things that come with their misery.

For the continuation of this letter, with principal variants, refer to Translation 3 and notes.

---

[7]   For comparable references from d'Avity, see Translation 3, n. 7 (AFSI, GBr0185, fol. 5ʳ).

LETTER 5[1]

Bourges,
AdC, 2F 788.

[2^r] Au Cap-Français Île et côte de St Domingue, le 19 de janvier 1732.

Mon très cher frère,

Je vous ai promis un détail du caractère, et des travaux des nègres qui sont dans notre colonie de Saint-Domingue. Il y a longtemps que je vous aurais tenu parole, sans une foule d'occupations que j'ai eues successivement depuis plus d'un an et qui ne m'ont pas permis de satisfaire sur ce point votre curiosité et mon inclination. Aujourd'hui que je suis un peu plus libre, je vais entrer en matière avec vous. Ne vous effrayez pas de la longueur de cette lettre. Sur un sujet aussi vaste il est difficile d'être court, et je le serai toutefois si je ne vous dis rien que d'intéressant, c'est à quoi je vise dans cette relation. Si je réussis, je croirai ma peine bien employée.

Vous saurez d'abord en général que presque tous les nègres sont ici esclaves, on les vend et on les achète, sans comparaison [2^v] comme des chevaux ou des bœufs aussi en font-ils toutes les fonctions pour la plupart, et la moitié d'eux, ainsi que les Suisses, n'ont[2] guère de l'homme que la voix et le corps. Ce sont les nègres qui défrichent et labourent les terres, on ne sait ce que c'est que charrue à Saint-Domingue, les terres y sont trop fortes, et la plus grande partie c'est en *mornes*, pour parler le langage du pays, c'est-à-dire en montagnes.

L'esclavage des nègres vous paraîtra peut-être peu conforme aux saintes lois du christianisme mais vous cesserez d'être dans ce sentiment, lorsque vous ferez réflexion au bonheur inestimable qu'ils ont de parvenir à être éclairés des plus pures lumières de la vraie religion; avantage qu'ils n'auraient pas chez eux, tout leur pays étant plongé dans les plus épaisses ténèbres du paganisme.

---

[1] There are omissions in the transcription of this letter in the edition of Dyonet consulted (see BnF 8-G-23098), notably from AdC, 2F 788, fols 5^r–6^r, 10^v, 11^r–12^r, 18^v–19^r, 20^r–22^r, 23^r–25^r, 26^v–28^r. Neither these omissions nor minor errors in Dyonet's transcription have been indicated in this transcription.

[2] AdC, 2F 788, fol. 2^v: 'non'.

Bourges,
AdC, 2F 788.

From Cap-Français, island and coast of Saint-Domingue, 19 January 1732

My dearest brother,

I promised you an account of the character and the labours of the slaves of our colony of Saint-Domingue. I would have kept my word a long time ago, were it not for the many tasks I have had in succession for more than a year and which have not allowed me to satisfy your curiosity and my wish. Now that I have a little more liberty, I will discuss this with you. Do not be alarmed by the length of this letter. It is difficult to be brief about such a vast subject, nonetheless I will be, if I tell you nothing but what is interesting, which is my aim in this account. If I succeed, I will consider my labours worthwhile.

You will know, firstly, that in general nearly all the blacks are slaves here. They are bought and sold, in truth, like horses or oxen; most of them carry out the same duties, and half of them, like the Swiss, have barely anything human about them but the voice and the body. It is black slaves who clear and work the land; there is no place for the plough in Saint-Domingue, for the soil is too heavy, and most of the land consists in *mornes*, to speak as the locals do, that is, in mountains.

The slavery of the blacks will seem to you inconsistent with the holy laws of Christianity, but you will change your mind once you reflect on the priceless good fortune they have in being illuminated by the purest lights of the true religion. This is an advantage they would not have had in their land, all of which is immersed in the thickest darkness of paganism.

Dans toutes les colonies françaises de l'Amérique méridionale le nombre des nègres passe infiniment celui des blancs, c'est ainsi qu'ils appellent eux-mêmes les Européens, à cause de la différence totale de couleur. Il y a pour le moins vingt noirs contre [3ʳ] un blanc, c'est l'effet d'une providence continuelle, et tout à fait miraculeuse que tant d'esclaves toujours demi barbares, accablés des plus épouvantables fardeaux et châtiés avec une sévérité, pour ne pas dire avec une cruauté excessive, ne conçoivent pas seulement la pensée de se révolter, vu la facilité qu'ils en ont, et l'impossibilité absolue qu'il y aurait aux blancs de se défendre d'une conjuration générale.

Il est vrai que pour prévenir tout accident, on a établi des lois extrêmement sévères contre les nègres. Il ne leur est pas permis, sous quelque prétexte que ce puisse être, de lever la main sur un blanc. Toute défense même légitime leur est interdite. Mais malheur à celui qui entreprend de se la faire à soi-même. Il est pendu sans miséricorde; quelque bonne raison qu'il apporte pour sa défense. Cette loi, comme toutes les autres, a ses inconvénients. Les blancs plus brutaux souvent que les nègres, en abusent sans cesse, et font mille outrages aux esclaves qu'ils rencontrent dans les chemins, mais c'est [3ᵛ] un malheur qui doit être compté pour peu de chose, vu la nécessité indispensable de la loi dans un pays, où sans elle il n'y aurait aucune sûreté pour la vie des habitants.

La moitié de nos nègres est originaire de la Guinée qui renferme des pays immenses, la côte principale est Juda, où les Français ont un comptoir. La Guinée est partagée en plusieurs petits états, dont les souverains se font continuellement la guerre. Tout ce qu'ils cherchent dans leurs expéditions militaires c'est de faire des esclaves pour les vendre aux vaisseaux d'Europe, au défaut de prisonniers de guerre, ils vendent leurs propres sujets, et même jusqu'à leurs propres femmes, lorsqu'ils en sont dégoûtés ou mécontents. Ces reines dégradées ne survivent pas longtemps à leur disgrâce. Honteuses de porter des fers après avoir eu la couronne en tête, elles se donnent presque toutes la mort. Un père carme aumônier d'un vaisseau négrier (c'est ainsi qu'on appelle les navires qui font commerce de nègres) me disait l'année dernière, qu'une des femmes du roi de Juda, que son perfide époux leur avait vendue, après avoir reproché au roi sa trahison, et brisé en mille pièces une chaîne d'or qu'il lui [4ʳ] avait laissée par un reste de tendresse, cette malheureuse négresse monta avec un visage plus qu'assuré à bord du vaisseau français, comme pour braver le sort qui l'accablait, mais bientôt toute sa fierté s'éclipsa, elle tomba dans une mélancolie affreuse. Jamais on ne put l'engager à prendre de nourriture. Un jour qu'elle était moins observée que de coutume, elle se précipita dans la mer, préférant la mort à l'esclavage.

Ne vous imaginez pas que ce soit à prix d'or ou d'argent que s'achètent les nègres en Guinée. La monnaie courante du pays ce sont des pouches, autrement de petits coquillages de mer qui ne se trouvent que sur quelques

In all the French colonies of South America the blacks greatly surpass in number the whites, as they themselves call Europeans, because they are of totally different colour. There are at least twenty blacks for each white, and it is thanks to a continual and absolutely miraculous providence that so many still half-savage slaves, weighed down with the most awful burdens and punished with severity — if not cruelty — that is excessive, do not even think of revolt, given how easy it would be, and that it would be absolutely impossible for the whites to defend themselves from an extensive conspiracy.

It is true that extremely severe laws have been put in place against slaves to prevent any trouble. They are not allowed to raise a hand against a white for any reason whatsoever. Their defending themselves, even legitimately, is forbidden. Woe to him who would take matters into his own hands. He would be hung without mercy, however justified the defence he might offer. This law, like all the others, has its drawbacks. The whites, often more brutal than the blacks, abuse them ceaselessly and commit a thousand insults upon the slaves they cross on their way, but it is an evil that must be counted for little, given the unavoidable need in this land for law, without which the lives of the planters would be at great risk.

Half of our slaves are from Guinea, which is made up of immense lands. The principal coast is Ouidah, where the French have a trading post. Guinea is made up of many small states, whose sovereigns are continually at war with one another. All they seek in their military expeditions is to enslave people to sell to the European vessels, and, when they cannot get prisoners of war, they sell their own subjects, and even their own wives when they are tired of them or unhappy with them. These fallen queens do not live for long after their disgrace. From having a crown on their head to wearing irons, the shame leads nearly all to take their own lives. A Carmelite chaplain of a slaver (as they call ships that trade in slaves) told me last year that one of the king of Ouidah's wives, who had been sold to them by her perfidious husband, had reproached the king for his betrayal, and broken into a thousand pieces a golden chain that he had left her from what remained of his affection. This unfortunate slave boarded the French vessel with an assured expression, as if she were facing her overwhelming fate with courage. However, her pride soon withered away and she fell into a terrible melancholy. She could never be made to accept food. One day when she was being watched less carefully than usual she threw herself into the sea, preferring death to slavery.

Do not think that it is with gold or silver that slaves are bought in Guinea. The currency of the country is *pouches*, or little marine shells that are only

rives étrangères. Les vaisseaux d'Europe en font provision, et les donnent à la livre à peu près comme le marc d'argent en France. Les nègres se paient aussi en eaux-de-vie, en armes à feu, en toile etc. Le prix en est différent comme de toutes les autres choses, selon la différence de la marchandise. Autrefois un beau nègre sain et robuste, ne revenait aux commerçants français qu'à 50 livres. Les princes de Guinée, si l'on peut donner ce nom auguste à ces véritables portraits du diable, soit avarice soit raffinement de mœurs, ils ont mis l'enchère [4^v] sur leurs esclaves, de sorte qu'un nègre, pièce d'Inde, comme ils appellent ceux qui sont les mieux faits, vaut aujourd'hui jusqu'à 200 livres en Guinée,[3] on n'achète point de vieillards, ce sont tous enfants ou belle jeunesse de l'un et de l'autre sexe, au dessous de 30 ans.

Ces sauvages, excepté le prince et sa cour, sont nus comme la main dans leur pays, à raison des excessives chaleurs du climat. Les marchands d'Europe, au moins est cela pratique de tous nos Français, à mesure qu'ils achètent des nègres, ils ont soin de leur couvrir ce que des yeux chastes ne sauraient voir sans horreur. Ils leur mettent simplement autour des reins une corde légère à laquelle est attaché un morceau de cuir en forme de gibecière de chasseur, c'est là leur chemise, leur veste, leur culotte, et généralement tout leur équipage. Les femmes comme les hommes, n'ont rien de plus pour se couvrir, on les habille dans nos colonies, et vous verrez par la suite de cette lettre que le luxe et la vanité des parures, qui règnent ici plus que dans aucun endroit du monde ont passé des maîtres à leurs esclaves.

[5^r] Outre le commerce des nègres qui se fait en Guinée on y achète quantité de poudre d'or, cette précieuse pimprenelle[4] se trouve dans les rivières mêlée avec le sable. Les nègres qui n'en font pas beaucoup de cas la trafiquent pour des pouche[s] ou de l'eau de vie. Du reste toute la Guinée, selon ce que j'en ai appris de plusieurs Français qui ont parcouru la côte, est un des plus mauvais pays du monde, il n'y a guère de climat plus brûlé par le soleil. À la réserve de quelques moutons, chèvres et chiens qu'on y trouve, les autres rafraîchissements ce sont des fruits sauvages, qui consistent presque tous dans des racines fades et insipides.

La couleur parfaitement noire des nègres sera longtemps une énigme pour les savants scrutateurs de l'antiquité. On n'a encore pu jusqu'ici en apporter de raison, au moins solide et capable de contenter l'esprit. De dire que la chaleur du pays, en soit la cause, c'est un sentiment sans probabilité puisqu'il est certain qu'il y a dans le monde des climats où les rayons du soleil se font sentir encore plus vivement qu'en Guinée, et les habitants ne sont que basanés, sans avoir cette couche de noir de fumée qui rend les nègres si difformes.

---

[3]   The manuscript might be read as '200 livres. En Guinée'.
[4]   The *pimprenelle* (*pimpinella sanguisorba*) might be used in dyeing, according to Furetière (1727), III, entry 'Pimprenelle', non-paginated.

found on certain foreign shores. European vessels stock up on them, and sell them according to weight much as is done with silver in France. Slaves can be bought with spirits, firearms, cloth, etc. The price varies, as with everything else, according to the merchandise. In the past, French traders could buy a good, healthy robust slave for only 50 *livres*. The princes of Guinea, if such an august name can be given to these very demons, have since raised the price of their slaves, whether through greed or refinement. So it is that a slave, *pièce d'Inde*, as they call the best made of them, is nowadays worth up to 200 *livres*, in Guinea, old men are not bought, but instead children or the flower of youth of both sexes, who are less than thirty years of age.

These savages, except for the prince and his court, are completely naked in their country, because of the excessively hot climate. The merchants of Europe (this at least is the practice of all the French) make sure to cover what chaste eyes would not look upon without horror, as they are buying slaves. They have them wear around their loins a thin cord to which is attached a piece of leather in the shape of a hunter's purse. For them, this is shirt, jacket, and breeches: their whole outfit. The women, like the men, have nothing more to cover themselves. They are clothed in our colonies, and you will see in the rest of this letter that luxury and pride in finery, which reign here more than anywhere else in the world, have been passed on by the masters to their slaves.

As well as the trade in slaves, much gold dust is bought in Guinea. This precious powder is found in the rivers, mixed with sand. The blacks, who care little for it, trade it for *pouches* or for alcoholic spirits. Moreover, the land throughout Guinea, according to what I have learned from many Frenchmen who have travelled along the coast, is among the worst in the world. There is hardly any other climate more burned by the sun. Apart from a few sheep, goats, and dogs, the other fare is wild fruit, nearly all of which consists in insipid and tasteless roots.

For those learned people who pass their time studying antiquity, the completely black colour of Africans will remain an enigma for a long time. Up until now, no one has been able to put forward an explanation, or at least one that is solid and satisfies the mind. To say that the heat of the land is the cause is an unlikely opinion, as it is certain that there are climates in the world where the sun's rays are even more intense than in Guinea, and the inhabitants are only of a swarthy colour, without this smoky black colour that makes Africans so ugly.

[5ᵛ] D'ailleurs les nègres transplantés à Saint-Domingue et à la Martinique, où l'air est beaucoup plus tempéré, lorsqu'ils ont des enfants ils leur donnent tout leur coloris, et ce bel héritage de leurs pères, ils le transmettent à leurs descendants jusqu'à la 10ᵉ et 20ᵉ génération sans en rien perdre. On a interrogé de vieux nègres sur cette différence de couleur qu'ils ont seuls en partage. Ils ont répondu que c'était une ancienne tradition parmi eux qu'ils étaient maudits du ciel, et plusieurs de nos savants prétendent que les nègres sont les véritables enfants de Cham qui fut digne et chargé de toute la malédiction de Noé son père. Je ne vous donne pas ce sentiment pour une démonstration, mais vous vous en contenterez, s'il vous plaît, faute de meilleure raison à vous apporter. Permis à vous de chercher dans les fastes poudreux de l'Antiquité ou dans la source féconde de votre imagination de quoi former un système plus convaincant sur l'encre luisante dont sont barbouillés tous les nègres.

Vous seriez peut-être tenté de croire qu'ils ont horreur d'eux-mêmes, et que lorsqu'ils rencontrent dans une glace fidèle leur hideuse [6ʳ] figure, ils envient alors les lis et les roses des visages européens. Inutilement. Ils préfèrent leur couleur à la nôtre, et nous rendent bien le ridicule que nous leur prêtons. La plus belle négresse parmi eux est celle qui est la plus noire. Ils n'ont que du mépris pour celles qui sont les moins diablesses de visage.

Un autre problème pour les curieux, ce sont les cheveux des nègres. Ils les ont extrêmement noirs, ce n'est pas du crin tels que les cheveux de tous les autres hommes, mais une espèce de laine fine et frisée comme la laine d'un mouton. Qui voit la tête d'un nègre a vu généralement toutes celles de sa nation. La nature les a tous également partagés de ce côté-là, comme pour le teint du visage, mais ce qui mérite une singulière attention, c'est qu'après huit ou dix ans leurs cheveux ne croissent plus, et demeurent dans le même état, à moins que pour cause de maladie ou de blessures ils ne soient obligés de faire les tondailles; pour lors leurs cheveux renaissent, jusqu'à ce que la moutonne soit parfaite. Les vieillards grisonnent, mais ne blanchissent jamais parfaitement. Il en est de même de leur barbe, c'est un petit duvet qui frise par bouquet.

[6ᵛ] Il est temps que nous quittions la Guinée pour suivre ces pauvres Indiens que l'on arrache avec violence du sein de leur pays et des bras de leur famille pour les mener en esclavage. Voilà un vaisseau qui a fait sa traite en Guinée, et qui chargé de chair humaine, vole aux côtes de l'Amérique pour en faire le débit. Il faut bien de la prudence et de l'adresse dans le capitaine pour contenir ces esclaves. Figurez-vous quatre ou cinq cents sauvages, conduits par quarante ou cinquante hommes seulement d'équipage, et tous persuadés qu'on les mène à la boucherie, car ils ont cette idée profondément gravée dans l'esprit qu'on ne

What is more, Africans who have been brought to Saint-Domingue and to Martinique where the air is much more temperate pass on all of their colour to their children, who transmit this pleasant heritage of their fathers to their own descendants, to the tenth and twentieth generations, without any of it being lost. Old slaves have been questioned about this difference in colour that only they have inherited, and they replied that it was an old tradition amongst them that they had been cursed by the Heavens. Many of our own learned men claim that black people are in fact the children of Ham, upon whom the curse of his father, Noah, was laid. I am not asking you to think of this opinion as proof, but you may content yourself with it, if you please, in the absence of a better reason to give you. You may, in the dusty annals of antiquity or in the fertile well of your imagination, look for matter to build a more convincing theory to explain the shiny ink with which all the Africans are daubed.

You might be tempted to think that they find their appearance revolting, and that when they see the reflection of their hideous faces in a faithful mirror, they envy the lily and rose colours of European faces. Not a bit of it. They prefer their colour to ours, and they find us as ridiculous as we find them. They consider the blackest woman to be the most beautiful. They have only scorn for those whose faces appear the least like those of she-devils.

Another riddle for the curious is the hair of Africans. Their hair is extremely black, not like a horse's mane as it is with all other men, but rather a sort of fine, curly wool like a sheep's fleece. Whoever has seen the head of one African has seen those of all of his people. Nature has bestowed the same on all of them in this area, as it is with the colour of their faces, but what merits particular attention is that after eight or ten years their hair no longer grows, but it stays the same, unless it has to be trimmed because of sickness or injury. In such a case their hair grows back until it perfectly resembles a fleece. The old ones go grey, but their hair never goes completely white, and it is the same with their beards, which are downy and curly.

It is time for us to leave Guinea and follow these poor Indians[1] who are violently torn from their country and from the family fold to be led into slavery. Imagine a vessel that has traded in slaves in Guinea, and, laden with human flesh, speeds to the coasts of America to sell them. The captain needs much prudence and skill to contain these slaves. Imagine four or five hundred savages, led by a crew of only forty or fifty, all convinced that they are going to be butchered, because they have the idea etched in their minds that they

---

[1]   The use of the term 'pauvres Indiens' ('poor Indians') to refer to another African population, that of Madagascar, has been identified by Nivoelisoa Galibert, who writes that the term 'has connotations of barbarism' ('[véhicule une] charge de barbarie'); *À l'angle de la Grande Maison: les lazaristes de Madagascar: correspondance avec Vincent de Paul (1648–1661)*, ed. Nivoelisoa Galibert (Paris: Presses de l'Université de Paris-Sorbonne, 2007), p. 113.

les achète que pour les manger. On a toutes les peines du monde à les rassurer si l'on n'a jour et nuit les yeux sur eux, il est à craindre ou qu'ils ne se précipitent dans la mer, ou qu'ils ne se révoltent. L'un arrive assez souvent, et l'autre n'est pas sans exemple.

Il n'y a pas encore deux ans que l'équipage d'un vaisseau français qui revenait de Guinée à Saint-Domingue, allait être égorgé par ses esclaves, si la Providence n'avait pris soin de faire avorter un aussi barbare projet. C'est la coutume que le capitaine des navires négriers choisisse pour [7ʳ] servir à sa table la fleur de la jeunesse, esclave de l'un et de l'autre sexe. Ces valets domestiques conspirèrent secrètement avec les nègres de fond de cale, de tuer le capitaine et les matelots, et de s'emparer du vaisseau pour retourner dans leur pays. Déjà ils s'étaient saisis de tous les couteaux de table, et des haches du navire, et se préparaient à donner sur les blancs, lorsqu'un de ces nègres, moins barbare que les autres vint découvrir au capitaine tout le secret de la conjuration. Sur-le-champ on pendit à la grande vergue les plus coupables. Par ce prompt châtiment les autres furent déconcertés, et ne remuèrent pas davantage. Un service aussi important que celui que venait de rendre le fidèle esclave méritait au moins qu'on lui donnât sa liberté; mais l'avarice du capitaine français ne le permit pas. Son libérateur fut vendu au Cap, comme le plus infâme des conjurés avec cette différence qu'il eut le bonheur de tomber chez nous, où il vit encore avec tous les agréments qu'il peut souhaiter, à la liberté près.

D'autres vaisseaux négriers ont été moins heureux. Les nègres ayant égorgé tous les blancs se sont rendus maîtres des navires, et ne sachant point la manœuvre de la mer, ils ont erré longtemps [7ᵛ] au gré des vents et des flots, jusqu'à ce que faute de vivres, ils ont tous péri de faim et de misère. Des Anglais trouvèrent il y a quelques années sur mer un bâtiment rempli de cadavres infectés, il ne restait plus qu'un nègre, qui traînait à peine un misérable reste de vie, quelques lambeaux de chair humaine faisaient toute sa nourriture, on apprit de lui que son malheur et celui de ses camarades venait d'une conjuration qu'ils avaient tramée contre l'équipage du vaisseau, et qu'après avoir impitoyablement massacré tous les blancs, ils avaient tenté en vain de faire route vers la Guinée.

Vous me direz que pour parer à de semblables désordres il faudrait mettre aux fers tous ces barbares. Mais outre la difficulté et les inconvénients qu'il y aurait à cela, la mélancolie des nègres nouvellement esclaves est toujours plus à craindre que ne l'est leur fureur. Ils mourraient tous de désespoir si on les chargeait de fers. Sans cela on a déjà tant de peines à les égayer. Il faut plus de tambours, plus d'instruments, plus de danses, encore avec tous les ménagements possibles a-t-on le chagrin d'en voir toujours quelques-uns, qui trompant la vigilance de leurs argus, se jettent à la mer, entêtés qu'ils sont [8ʳ] de cette pitoyable idée qu'ils reverront leur patrie, et se rejoindront à leur famille.

Pour les détromper d'une erreur aussi grossière, voici le stratagème dont

have only been bought to be eaten. It is immensely difficult to reassure them. If they are not watched day and night, it is to be feared that they would throw themselves into the sea or revolt. The first occurs often enough, and the second is not unheard of.

It is not yet two years since the crew of a French vessel which was returning from Guinea to Saint-Domingue, would have had their throats cut by their slaves, if Providence had not put a stop to their barbarous plan. The custom is that the captains of slavers choose from amongst the slaves the flower of youth of either sex to serve at table. These domestic servants plotted secretly with the slaves in the hold to kill the captain and the sailors, and to take over the vessel and return to their homeland. They had already seized all the table knives and the ship's axes, and were preparing to attack the whites, when one of these Africans who was less barbarous than the others came and revealed the secret plot to the captain. The guiltiest were immediately hung from the main yard. The rest were shaken by this rapid punishment, and abandoned any thought of rebellion. The loyal slave deserved at least his freedom, for such an important service, but the avarice of the French captain would not allow this. [The captain's] saviour was sold at Cap-Français, just as with the most unworthy of the plotters, the only difference being that he had the good fortune to end up with us, where he now lives with all the advantages he could wish for, except for his freedom.

Other slavers have been less fortunate. The blacks have cut the throats of all the whites and taken over ships, but not knowing how to sail, have drifted for a long time carried by the winds and the tides until, without victuals, they all perished from hunger and hardship. On the seas a few years ago, the English came across a ship full of rotting corpses. There was only one slave left alive, who was at death's door, with only a few strips of human flesh to eat. He revealed that his unhappy fate and that of his comrades was due to a conspiracy they had plotted against the ship's crew, and that after massacring all the whites without pity, they had tried in vain to sail to Guinea.

You will say that to avoid similar insurrections all these barbarians should be put in irons. But apart from the difficulty, and the problems this would cause, it is always the melancholy of newly enslaved Africans that is more to be feared than their fury. They would all die of despair if they were laden down with irons. It is difficult enough to keep their spirits up as it is. For this you need ever more drums, instruments, dances, and all the precautions possible cannot prevent some of them slipping away from their jailers and throwing themselves into the sea, a sorrowful sight. This is because they are convinced of the pitiful idea that they will then see their homeland once more, and be reunited with their families.

Here is the stratagem used to disabuse them of such a gross error. When

on use avec eux, quand il est mort un nègre (il en meurt toujours beaucoup à bord des vaisseaux négriers, soit d'ennui, soit de misère). Le capitaine du navire fait attacher le cadavre au bout de la grande vergue, et le laisse doucement s'approcher de la superficie de la mer. Qu'arrive-t-il de là; c'est que les requins, ces monstres de l'océan, les plus friands de chair humaine, alléchés par la vue ou l'odeur du gibier, s'élancent hors de l'eau, pour gober le cadavre, à mesure qu'ils en approchent, on tire aussitôt la corde. Cela irrite le requin qui fait des sauts plus forts vers sa proie qu'on lui abandonne enfin, et qu'il dévore quelquefois tout entière. Les nègres en présence de qui et pour qui seuls se joue la comédie sont effrayés à la vue de ces effroyables tombeaux de leurs camarades, et n'ont plus tant d'envie de se jeter à l'eau par la crainte de la gueule affamée du requin.

Je ne vous dirai rien des désordres honteux qui se commettent par les blancs dans les vaisseaux négriers. Vous concevez assez que la loi <u>non concupisces</u>[5] reçoit de violentes atteintes de la part des Français, qui ont tous leurs yeux, et à leur entière disposition un [8ᵛ] séminaire de jeunes négresses nues comme la main, excepté la gibecière qui n'a que quelques pouces de circonférence. Ajoutez que ces belles ne savent guère ce que c'est que d'être cruelles à leurs galants. La différence de couleur est une des plus faibles barrières à la continence de nos Français, leur fureur sur l'article passe tout ce que je pourrais[6] dire. Je vous en donnerai bientôt des preuves convaincantes, et vous conclurez que si les plus délicats en fait de volupté se prodiguent si libéralement aux négresses, il faut que les matelots poussent bien loin le désordre et le crime.

Avant que de vous tracer de si affreux portraits entrons au Cap-Français avec les nègres que nous avons tirés de Guinée. Le vaisseau négrier n'est pas plutôt mouillé en rade qu'aussitôt le médecin du roi et le chirurgien major de l'Amirauté vont en faire la visite, pour voir si les nègres n'ont point de maladies contagieuses. Ensuite on paie les droits; deux nègres passent au commandant général de la colonie, un pour le gouverneur de la ville, et un pour l'intendant. Comme ils les prennent à leur choix ils ont toujours ce qu'il y a de plus beau dans la cargaison.

Après qu'on a bien lavé et frotté les nègres, comme [9ʳ] des chevaux qu'on va exposer au marché, on ouvre la vente par une décharge du canon de bord. Les habitants en chaloupe se rendent de toutes parts au vaisseau pour acheter ce qu'ils ont besoin de nègres. Le prix est plus ou moins considérable, selon le plus ou le moins de vaisseaux négriers qui abordent au Cap. Communément les beaux nègres se vendent cent pistoles, les négresses valent toujours moins,

---

5   AdC, 2F 788: '<u>non concupices</u>'.
6   AdC, 2F 788: modified to read 'je vous en pourrais'.

a slave dies (many of them often do die on board slave ships, from either melancholy or privation), the ship's captain has the corpse tied to the main yardarm, and it is slowly lowered towards the surface of the sea. What happens is that sharks, these ocean monsters who most appreciate human flesh, are enticed by the sight or the smell of the quarry and hurl themselves out of the water so as to gulp down the corpse. When they get near to it, the rope is pulled up straightaway. This irritates the shark, which launches itself with more and more energy towards its prey, which is eventually left to it, and which the shark sometimes entirely devours. The slaves in whose presence, and for whom alone, this spectacle takes place are terrified at the sight of the horrible sepulchres of their fellow slaves, and are not quite as eager to throw themselves into the water, through fear of the shark's ravenous mouth.

I will say nothing to you about the shameful indecencies committed by the whites in slave vessels. You can well imagine that the law *non concupisces*[2] is violently infringed by the French, who all have their eyes, and a cluster of young black girls completely at their disposal, completely naked except for the loincloth which is only a few inches wide. Along with this, these lovelies are not in the habit of rejecting a suitor's advances. The difference in colour is one of the weakest reasons for our Frenchmen to control themselves. Their fury in this area goes beyond anything I could say to you. I will soon give you convincing proof of this, and you will conclude that, if the most modest, in terms of debauchery, give themselves over so freely to slave women, then the sailors must take dissolution and crime very far indeed.

Before I sketch out such awful portraits for you, picture the arrival at Cap-Français with the African slaves we have taken from Guinea. The slave ship has no sooner anchored than the king's doctor and the surgeon major of the Admiralty visit it to verify that the slaves have no contagious diseases.[3] Then the duties are paid. The commander general of the colony receives two slaves, the governor of the town has one, and the *intendant* has one. As they have their choice, they always get what is best in the cargo.

After the slaves have been well washed and scrubbed, like horses to be displayed in the market, the sale is opened with a shot from the ship's cannon. The planters come to the ship by boat from all over to buy the slaves they need. The price is higher or lower, according to how few or how many slave vessels have arrived at the Cape [Cap-Français]. Good male slaves are usually sold for

[2]   A reference to the ninth commandment: 'Non concupisces domum proximi tui: non desiderabis uxorem eius, non servum, non bovem, non asinum nec omnia, quae illius sunt', Exodus 20. 17 ('Thou shalt not covet thy neighbour's house: neither shalt thou desire his wife, nor servant, nor handmaid, nor ox, nor ass, nor anything that is his', 1635, p. 197).
[3]   On the *médecin du roi*, which had existed at Saint-Domingue since 1701, see Karol K. Weaver, *Medical Revolutionaries: The Enslaved Healers of Eighteenth-Century Saint-Domingue* (Urbana; Chicago: University of Illinois Press, 2006), pp. 30–33.

le prix des enfants se règle sur leur âge et leurs forces. Remarquez s'il vous plaît que je ne parle ici que des nègres nouvellement débarqués de Guinée, car pour les créoles, c'est-à-dire ceux qui naissent dans nos colonies, on les vend toujours davantage, comme étant déjà faits à l'air, au langage, et au travail du pays. S'ils savent un métier cela rehausse encore leur prix, par exemple un nègre qui sera charpentier, ou maréchal, ou boulanger, ou bon serrurier, il n'a point de prix. Il en est qu'on estime jusqu'à 10 000 livres. Ceux-ci gagnent à leur maître au moins 6 livres par jour. J'en dis autant des négresses qui sont bonnes couturières ou bonnes lingères. Jugez par là des pertes considérables que fait un pauvre habitant qui n'ayant qu'un ou deux nègres bons ouvriers, les voit mourir, et emporter avec eux au tombeau toute la richesse de leur maître.

Pour vous donner une idée claire et distincte [9^v] des travaux de nos nègres, il faut les réduire à deux classes, les uns sont occupés aux emplois domestiques de la maison du maître, les autres travaillent à la culture des terres, ou à préparer le sucre, l'indigo, et le tabac. Il faut pour cela comme vous voyez, grand nombre d'esclaves, aussi nos habitants surtout ceux qui entretiennent des sucreries en ont-ils une quantité prodigieuse. Tel habitant en a jusqu'à six et sept cents, le moins qu'on puisse en avoir pour faire marcher un moulin à sucre, c'est une centaine. Cela demande beaucoup de logement et d'ordre dans une sucrerie, ni l'un ni l'autre n'y manque.

Vous seriez charmé de voir nos habitations, c'est ainsi que nous appelons les maisons de campagne de la colonie. Une habitation ressemble à un bourg de France. Vous y comptez jusqu'à cent cases, avec leurs rues, toutes tirées au cordeau. Les cases sont de la même hauteur, de la même figure, et à égale distance les unes des autres. Cela forme un aspect qui fait plaisir à l'œil. La maison du maître est toujours séparée des cases à nègres, et située au-dessus du vent à cause de l'insupportable fumet des nègres qui sentent le musc de bouquin plus ou moins les uns que les autres, mais tous répandent des parfums auxquels il est extrêmement difficile de [10^r] s'accoutumer.

Ce sont les nègres les mieux faits, et les plus belles négresses qu'on emploie aux offices domestiques. Il en est de la maison d'un habitant de Saint-Domingue comme des hôtels des grands seigneurs à Paris, on y voit maîtres d'hôtel, cuisiniers, marmitons, cochers, palefreniers, valets et femmes de chambre, laquais portant livrée, mais différente, comme bien croyez de celle que portaient la plupart de leurs maîtres en France. Une autre partie des domestiques a le soin de la basse cour, et du jardin potager. Ces sortes de nègres s'acquittent parfaitement bien de leur emploi. J'ai été surpris de voir des nègres faire l'ordonnance d'un grand repas, et servir plusieurs tables avec autant de goût et de délicatesse que le pourraient faire les plus habiles traiteurs de Paris.

Mais où paraît davantage l'adresse des nègres valets, c'est à monter un cheval et à le manier, ils sont tous excellents cavaliers et si bien plantés sur leurs

one hundred *pistoles*,[4] with females always worth less, with the price of children determined by their age and their strength. Please note that I am only talking here about slaves newly landed from Guinea because Creoles, that is, those born in our colonies, are always sold for more, as they are already used to the air, the language, and the work in this land. If they know a trade this brings up their price still more, for example, a slave carpenter, ironsmith, baker, or a good locksmith is priceless; some are worth up to 10,000 *livres*. These can earn at least six *livres* a day for their master. The same can be said about female slaves who are good seamstresses or good linen maids. From this you can imagine the great losses suffered by a poor planter who has only one or two slaves who are good workers, and then sees them die, bringing all their master's wealth with them to the grave.

To give you a clear and distinct idea of the work done by our slaves, they must be divided into two classes. Some are put to work in domestic tasks in the master's house, the others in cultivating the land or in preparing sugar, indigo, and tobacco. You can see that a great number of slaves are needed for this, and our planters, especially all those who keep sugar plants, have a prodigious number of them. There are planters who have up to six or seven hundred, and the least number with which one can run a sugar mill is one hundred. A lot of space and order are required in a sugar plantation, and neither one nor the other is lacking.

You would be charmed to see our *habitations* [plantations], as we call the country houses of the colony. An *habitation* is like a village in France. There are up to one hundred cabins with streets, all in a straight line. These cabins are of the same height and appearance, and of the same distance from each other. It is a pleasant sight. The master's house is always apart from the slaves' shacks and located above the wind because of the intolerable odour of the slaves, who all smell of goat to some degree, but all have a scent that it is extremely difficult to get used to.

It is the best-made male slaves, and the prettiest females, who are put to work in domestic tasks. The house of a planter in Saint-Domingue is like a great lord's *hôtel* in Paris. There you can see majordomos, cooks, scullions, coachmen, grooms, valets and chambermaids, lackeys wearing livery which, you can well believe, is different from that which most of their masters used to wear in France. Another set of domestics look after the farmyard and the vegetable garden. These sorts of slaves do a perfectly good job; I was surprised to see slaves lay out a great feast, and serve many tables with as much taste and refinement as the best caterers in Paris could do.

However, the skill of black valets can be seen even more in mounting and riding horses. They are all excellent horsemen, and so well mounted on their

---

[4] A *pistole* was the equivalent of 10 *livres*.

chevaux, qu'ils paraissent ne faire qu'un corps avec leur monture. Cet heureux talent ils le gâtent par le peu de ménagement qu'ils ont pour les chevaux. S'ils ne sont pas sous les yeux de leur maître, ils vont toujours le grand galop, [10ᵛ] quelque longue traite qu'ils aient à faire. Vous ne verrez jamais un nègre seul dans les chemins qui se contente d'aller le pas de son cheval, il court à bride abattue jusqu'à ce qu'il voie la maison de son maître, alors il tire les rênes pour faire prendre haleine à son cheval, et entre à petits pas comme pour donner à entendre qu'il a toujours été le même train. Il n'y a pas un mois qu'un habitant faisant voyage trouva le nègre d'un de ses amis qui doublait la poste sans aucune nécessité. Il l'arrêta lui disant qu'il voulait le charger d'un mot de lettre pour son maître. Sur-le-champ il entra dans une case voisine, et manda à son ami l'équipée de son esclave. Le nègre qui ne se défiait de rien fut le porteur de sa propre sentence, et ne tarda pas à en recevoir le châtiment ce qui le surprit si étrangement qu'il regarda son maître comme un sorcier, ne pouvant pas concevoir qu'il eût eu connaissance de sa faute, sans l'avoir vue.

Une des principales raisons pourquoi les nègres crèvent leurs chevaux à la course, surtout la nuit, c'est leur penchant presque insupportable [11ʳ] à la volupté. Ils ont des maîtresses dans les habitations circonvoisines, et profitent des messages que leur donnent à faire leurs maîtres pour aller voir leurs belles. Comme on sait à peu près le temps qu'il leur faut pour une commission, en allant d'un pas modéré, nos Mercures galants prennent le vol et trouvent le moyen de servir leur maître et leur maîtresse. Souvent ils n'attendent pas qu'on leur commande de marcher, durant la nuit ils montent un cheval à poil, et vont courir la gueuse. Ils ont soin de se rendre avant jour à leur case, afin qu'on ne s'aperçoive pas de leur manège.

Quoique tous les nègres soient naturellement voleurs on peut dire que les valets domestiques le sont infiniment davantage, on ne saurait trop veiller sur eux. Ils s'accommodent de tout ce qui leur tombe sous la main. Le plus habile joueur de gobelets à la foire de Saint-Germain n'est pas plus adroit qu'un nègre à escamoter une bouteille de vin de dessus un buffet, et quand le fripon de valet la tient il l'avale tout d'un train sans verre.

Voici un de ces tours de gibecière qui fut découvert il y a quelques semaines dans une riche habitation. [11ᵛ] Un nègre valet de la chambre passait pour un modèle de fidélité, il avait toutes les clefs de la dépense, et jamais n'avait bu un verre de vin, au dire de son maître. Cependant le maître était la dupe de cette prétendue sagesse. Par hasard un blanc qui était devenu fou rodait une nuit autour de la case du nègre, et s'aperçut au travers de palissades que l'homme de bien buvait fort dévotement de grandes rasades d'un vin d'une couleur

horses that they seem to be of the same body. They spoil this useful talent by their lack of care for horses. If they are not in their master's sight, they always ride at a fast gallop, however long the journey they have to make. You'll never see a slave on the roads on his own who is happy to go at his horse's pace. He rides as fast as he can until he sees his master's house, then he pulls the reins to allow his horse to catch breath, and he arrives at a slow pace to have you believe that this was his pace all along. Not one month ago there was a planter who, while on a journey, came across one of his friend's slaves riding twice as fast as he should, and for no good reason. He stopped him, telling him that he wanted to give him a note for his master. Straightaway, he went into a nearby cabin, and wrote a letter to his friend in which he described his slave's escapades. The slave, who suspected nothing, delivered his own sentence, and it was not long before he received the punishment for it. He was so astounded that he looked on his master as if he were a sorcerer, being unable to fathom that he could have learned of his offence without having seen it.

One of the main reasons that slaves exhaust their horses by racing them, especially at night, is their near-intolerable inclination for the pleasures of the flesh. They have mistresses in the surrounding plantations, and take advantage of the messages that their masters give them to do to go and see their *belles*. As masters have a rough idea of the time their slaves need to do an errand, going at a moderate pace, their amorous messengers take off at speed and find a way to lend service to both master and mistress. Often, they don't wait for an order to be on their way; they get on a horse at night, bareback, and are off after the tramp. They make sure to be back in their cabin before daybreak so that nobody sees what they have been up to.

Although all the slaves are thieves by nature, domestic valets are by far the worst. You cannot watch them too closely. They take everything they come across, and the most skilful swindler at the Fair of Saint-Germain would be no more able than a slave when it comes to swiping a bottle of wine from the top of a sideboard, and then, when the wretched valet has it, he drinks it all in one go without a glass.[5]

Here is one of these ruses, that was discovered a few weeks ago in a rich plantation. There was a black slave, a valet, who seemed to be a paragon of fidelity. He had all the keys to the pantry, and had never even drunk a glass of wine, according to his master. However, the master had been taken in by this appearance of good behaviour. By chance, a white who had gone mad was roaming one night near the slave's shack, and he saw through a gap in the wood that the good man was drinking, with great reverence, a generous quantity of

[5] The *foire de Saint-Germain* was a large covered market which enjoyed a dubious reputation in Paris near the Abbey of Saint-Germain-des-Prés. It was destroyed by fire in 1762.

charmante. Le fou lui demanda bien humblement à boire, et fut rebuté avec
mépris. Cela le piqua si fort que le lendemain il donna avis au maître de tout ce
qu'il avait vu, le maître visita la case du nègre, et n'y trouva qu'un grand coffre,
ou étaient seulement ses hardes. La curiosité le porta à remuer le coffre, et
jamais il ne fut plus surpris que de trouver en terre un canari plein de vin. C'est
un grand pot de terre glaise qui tient une demi-barrique. Le coffre en bouchait
l'ouverture, et quand le nègre avait soif, il allait puiser à la source, n'ayant besoin
pour cela que de retirer son coffre. Il serait inutile de vous dire que tout ce vin
était le fruit des vols de [12^r] l'hypocrite, et qu'il ne tarda pas à être étrillé en
chien courtaud.

Avec cette inclination qu'ont les nègres à voler, ce sont les plus effrontés
menteurs de la terre. Ils nient opiniâtrement tous les vols dont ils sont
coupables. Les prenez-vous sur le fait, et saisis encore de leur larcin, ils font mille
protestations de leur innocence, ou bien ils disent froidement en leur langage;
c'est diable même qui metté ça dans poche à moi. Il est vrai que le libertinage
occasionne assez souvent leurs vols, ils ont leurs maîtresses à entretenir, et le
moyen de le faire qu'aux dépens du maître de l'habitation? Mais le maître lui-
même est la cause la plus ordinaire des larcins de ses esclaves, ayant la dureté
de leur refuser jusqu'aux choses les plus nécessaires à l'entretien de la vie. Ils ne
leur donnent pas même de quoi couvrir leur nudité. Le vol est-il si criminel en
ce cas? À la place des nègres nous en ferions tout autant, et plus qu'eux peut-être.

Je viens aux manufactures de sucre et d'indigo. Il faut dans une sucrerie des
maréchaux, qu'on nomme ici *machoquets*, des charpentiers, des tonneliers,
des bûcherons, des maçons, des [12^v] charretiers qu'on ne connaît à Saint-
Domingue que sous le nom de *cabrouetiers*, du mot de cabrouet qui se prend
pour toute sorte de chariots et charrettes. Ce sont les nègres qui exercent ces
métiers avec assez de succès.[7] Tout le reste de l'atelier est occupé à l'agriculture,
dès la petite pointe du jour la cloche sonne pour la prière qu'ils font en commun,
et après laquelle ils vont travailler à la place, c'est-à-dire au champ du maître. Ils
y demeurent jusqu'à midi, sans qu'il leur soit permis d'être oisifs un moment,
si ce n'est qu'une nécessité pressante les oblige de se relâcher.

Pour les tenir toujours alertes et appliqués à leur travail ils ont derrière eux
un nègre commandeur armé d'un grand fouet, et qui n'a d'autre occupation que
de réveiller de la ferme façon ceux que tient la paresse. Les filles et les femmes
ne sont pas plus épargnées que les hommes. Elles travaillent de concert avec
eux, et chantent presque toujours en travaillant. Toutes leurs chansons [13^r]

---

[7]   Dyonet, p. 119: 'science'.

wine of a delightful colour. The madman asked him for a drink, with great humility, but he was sent on his way with scorn. This irritated him so much that the next day he informed the master of everything that he had seen. The master went and searched the slave's cabin, and all he found was a great trunk which held only his odds and ends. Curiosity moved him to budge the trunk, and he had never been more surprised than when he found a *canari* full of wine; this is a great clay pot which holds a half *barrique*.[6] The trunk was covering the opening, and when the slave was thirsty he would go and draw from his well, for all he had to do was to move his trunk out of the way. There is no need to tell you that all this wine was the fruit of the hypocrite's robberies, and that it was not long before he was thrashed like a miserable dog.[7]

Along with the slaves' inclination towards theft, they are the most brazen liars on earth. They stubbornly deny all the thefts they are guilty of, even if you catch them in the act, and even caught red-handed they protest their innocence a thousand times, or coolly say in their language: 'the very devil put this in me bag.' It is true that their promiscuity is often enough the cause of their thefts. They have their mistresses to keep, and how else can they do so but at the expense of the master of the plantation? But the masters themselves are the most frequent cause of the slaves' thievery. They are so harsh that they will refuse them the things that are most necessary for their upkeep, not even giving them something to cover their nakedness with. Is theft criminal in such a case? If we were in the blacks' place we would do the same, and worse perhaps.

It is time to talk about the sugar and indigo manufactories. A sugar mill must have blacksmiths, who are called *machoquets* here, and carpenters, coopers, loggers, masons, and carters who are only referred to in Saint-Domingue as *cabrouetiers*, from the word *cabrouet* which is the word for all sorts of chariots and carts. It is the blacks who practise these occupations, and with some success. The rest of the workforce is given to agriculture, from the crack of dawn, when the bell tolls for communal prayer, after which they go to work in the *place*, which is the master's field. They stay there until noon, and are not allowed a moment of idleness, unless some urgent necessity obliges them to slacken their pace.

To keep them constantly alert and applied to their work they have a black foreman behind them who is armed with a great whip, and who has no other occupation but to firmly wake up any of them who are a little lazy. The girls and the women are no more spared than the men. They work at the same rhythm as the men, and they nearly always sing while they are working.[8] All their songs

---

[6] A *barrique* was a measure of liquid volume which varied regionally. That of Saint-Domingue is listed as 227.11 litres in Doursther, p. 49.

[7] A 'chien courtaud' was, literally, a dog which had had its tail cut off. Furetière (1727), I, entry 'Courtaud', non-paginated.

[8] AdC, 2F 788, fols 12^v–13^r: Breban's formulation here ('Elles travaillent de concert avec eux,

ont un refrain, c'est ordinairement une des plus jeunes négresses qui chante les couplets. Le chœur répond avec une justesse admirable. Ils battent la mesure avec leurs houes, qu'ils élèvent et laissent tomber à terre en cadence. Le chant est tellement du goût des nègres que du matin au soir ils fredonnent des airs barbares qui vous écorchent les oreilles, mais eux les trouvent gracieux, et comme dit le proverbe, il ne faut point disputer des goûts. Ce que vous auriez peut-être de la peine à croire, ils ont des poètes qui se mêlent de faire des chansons sur le tiers et le quart. Les blancs comme les nègres, et plus encore que les nègres font le sujet de leurs satires, surtout nos Françaises qui n'ont pas leur honneur en recommandation et qui cessent d'être hydropiques après neuf mois. Il faut voir comme les nègres les habillent, s'il n'y a pas de rime dans leurs chansons, il y a du sens au moins, et l'on ne saurait disconvenir qu'ils attrapent assez bien le ridicule des gens.

À midi les nègres reviennent de la place à leurs cases où ils n'ont que deux heures de répit. Encore faut-il qu'ils aient la peine d'apprêter leur dîner; obligés souvent d'aller le [13ᵛ] fouiller en terre à plus de demi-lieue du gîte. À deux heures sonnant ils retournent à la place, et n'en sortent qu'à l'entrée de la nuit. Ils font la prière tous ensemble comme le matin, et de là vont à la veillée, c'est-à-dire à de menus travaux qu'ils continuent jusqu'à dix heures. Les habitants qui sont moins avides de gain, et qui par charité ménagent leurs esclaves, leur épargnent la peine de la veillée; avant que les nègres aient pu souper, il est presque toujours minuit, ainsi n'ont-ils que quatre à cinq heures de sommeil, encore ces malheureux s'en dérobent-ils souvent une partie pour aller au rendez-vous que leur donnent les infâmes[8] objets de leur lubricité.

Les sucreries qui roulent partout nuit et jour sans s'arrêter que les jours de fête, demandent des travaux particuliers. Il y a des nègres qui ne font d'autre métier que de fouetter les chevaux au moulin, d'autres fournissent les paquets de cannes. Ceux-ci font chauffer les fourneaux, ceux-là ont soin des chaudières, sans parler de plusieurs négresses dont les unes donnent à manger au moulin, et les autres emportent les bagaces qui sont les pailles des cannes. Les négresses doivent [14ʳ] prendre bien garde de s'endormir la nuit, en faisant passer les cannes au moulin. Il n'y va de rien moins pour elles que de subir la plus épouvantable mort qu'on puisse imaginer.

Pour bien comprendre ce point de ma relation, je dois vous donner une notion des cannes à sucre, et du moulin qui les écrase pour en tirer l'eau douce dont elles sont pleines. Les cannes à sucre ressemblent assez à ces gros roseaux dont on se sert dans les églises de France pour allumer les cierges, à cette différence près que nos cannes sont quatre fois plus grosses que nos roseaux ecclésiastiques, mais elles ne sont pas si hautes. Les plus longues, leur tête coupée pour avoir du plan, ne passent pas huit pieds. Pour le moulin, c'est

---

[8]   Dyonet, p. 120: 'profanes'.

have a chorus, and normally one of the youngest girl slaves sings the verses. The choir answers her with admirable harmony. They beat time with their hoes, which they raise and let fall in step. The slaves have such a taste for singing that from morning to night they hum these barbarous tunes that grate on your ears, but that they find graceful; and as the saying goes, *there is no accounting for taste*. What you may perhaps have some trouble believing is that they have poets who are in the business of composing songs about absolutely everybody. The whites, as with — and even more than — the blacks are the subject of their satires, especially those of our Frenchwomen whose honour is in doubt and who, after nine months, are relieved of the dropsy. You should see how the blacks describe them. If their songs are without rhyme, they are not without sense, and it has to be said that they are pretty good at capturing the ridiculous side of people.

At noon the slaves come back from the *place* to their shacks, where they have only two hours of rest. They still have to go about preparing their meal, and are often obliged to dig the earth for it more than half a league from the hut. At exactly two o'clock they return to the *place* and they do not leave it until dusk. They all pray together as in the morning, and then they go *to the vigil*, that is, to little jobs that go on until ten o'clock. The planters who are less greedy, and who are somewhat charitable towards their slaves, spare them the nuisance of the vigil. Before the slaves can have their supper, it is nearly always midnight, and so they only have four or five hours of sleep, and on top of that these wretches often use some of this time on a tryst with the abject objects of their desire.

The sugar factories, which are at work night and day and only stop on feast days, require specialized labour. There are slaves who have no other task but to whip the horses at the mill, others bring the bundles of cane, some heat the furnaces, some look after the cauldrons, without speaking of many female slaves, some of whom feed the cane into the mill, and others take away the *bagaces*, or the residue of the cane. The women slaves have to take care not to fall asleep at night while they are feeding the cane into the mill. For, if they do, they risk nothing less than the most horrific death that can be imagined.

To clearly understand this part of my account, I must give you an idea of the sugar canes, and of the mill that crushes them to extract the sweet water with which they are filled. Sugar canes look similar enough to those large reeds that are used in churches in France to light the candles, with the difference that our canes are four times thicker than the ecclesiastical reeds but they are not as long. The longest, with the top cut off to give a flat surface, is no more than eight feet long. The mill is a machine, and its essential components are three

et chantent presque toujours en travaillant') implies that women and girls sang; what follows implies that both sexes did so.

une machine dont les pièces essentielles consistent en trois cylindres de fer appelés *tambours*, parce qu'ils ont toute la forme des caisses d'armée. À l'aide de deux grands leviers, tirés chacun par deux chevaux, ces tambours placés perpendiculairement, roulent sur leur pivot, le premier et le troisième dans le même sens, celui du milieu dans un sens [14$^\text{v}$] contraire; ils sont si proches les uns les autres qu'il n'y a que quelques lignes de distance entre eux. C'est entre le 1$^\text{er}$ et le 2$^\text{e}$ tambour qu'il faut insinuer les cannes pour les moudre, quand les tambours ont mordu, la canne avance toujours jusqu'à ce qu'elle ait passé de l'autre côté, où se trouve une autre négresse qui fait repasser la canne entre le 2$^\text{e}$ et le 3$^\text{e}$ tambour. Je ne sais si je me fais entendre, mais je ne saurais vous expliquer plus clairement la chose. Si je savais l'art de manier un pinceau, je vous tracerais le dessin de nos moulins, mais j'ai pour tout savoir ma plume, encore a-t-elle besoin que vous lui fassiez grâce. Venez à Saint-Domingue vous éclaircir[9] des choses par vous-même. Vos yeux vous en apprendront plus en un moment, que tous les plus habiles pinceaux du monde.

Je suppose, vrai ou faux, n'importe, que vous êtes au fait de nos tambours roulants. Une négresse peu attentive aux cannes qu'elle fait passer, court risque d'engager sa main avec [15$^\text{r}$] la canne. La main une fois engagée, il faut de toute nécessité, si le moulin n'arrête court, et la chose n'est pas facile, lorsque les chevaux sont animés à marcher avec vitesse, il faut dis-je que tout le corps de la négresse passe et se brise plat comme la canne. Il n'est guère de plus affreux supplice que celui-là, et quelques négresses à demi endormies en ont fait l'horrible preuve. C'est pour prévenir un pareil malheur qu'il y a dans chaque moulin une hache toute prête pour abattre vite le bras de la négresse qui aurait par mégarde laissé engager ses doigts entre les tambours. Il n'y a pas d'autre moyen de sauver le reste du corps. Les négresses qui veillent sur les chaudières courent un autre danger non moins affreux; c'est de tomber la tête la première dans ces flots de sucre bouillants, et d'aller en un moment dans l'autre monde toutes confites comme des citrons.

Dans les indigoteries quoique les travaux soient différents, l'ordre du jour y est le même. Les nègres n'y ont pas plus de repos. Vous pourriez me [15$^\text{v}$] faire ici une question, savoir si le maître d'une habitation peut seul suffire pour conduire tant de travaux différents? Je vous répondrai que la chose n'est pas possible, quand elle le serait nos habitants qui ont toutes les manières des grands seigneurs, regarderaient comme au-dessous d'eux le détail infini des soins que demande une habitation. Semblables à ces princes qui font la guerre par leurs généraux, se contentant de régler tout du fond de leur cabinet,[10] nos riches Français de Saint-Domingue ont tous un blanc à leurs gages avec le titre d'*économe*, c'est sur lui qu'il se repose du soin de faire marcher la sucrerie. Tous

---

[9]　Dyonet, p. 121: 'éclairer'.
[10]　Dyonet, p. 122: 'cabine'.

iron cylinders called *drums*, because they have the same shape as the drums in the army. Thanks to two great levers, each pulled by two horses, these drums, which are positioned perpendicularly, rotate about the fulcrum. The first and the third rotate in the same direction, and that in the centre in the opposite direction. They are so close to one another that there are only several fractions of an inch between them. It is between the first and the second drum that the canes must be passed to crush them. When taken in by the drums, the cane goes forward until it has passed to the other side, where there is another female slave who passes the cane through the second and third drum. I don't know if you can understand me, but I cannot explain it more clearly. If I knew how to wield a paintbrush, I would draw a picture of our mills, but my quill is the extent of my talents, and it already demands your indulgence. Come to Saint-Domingue to enlighten yourself about these things yourself. Your eyes will teach you more in a moment than the most able paintbrushes in the world.

I suppose — rightly or wrongly, what of it — that you know about our rotating drums. A female slave who is paying little attention to the canes that must be fed into them risks having her hand caught along with the cane. Once her hand is trapped, what will certainly happen — if the mill does not stop short, which is not easy when the horses have been made to trot at speed — is that the slave's body will, I say, be pulled through and broken flat like the cane. There must hardly be a worse torture than this, and a number of women slaves who were half-asleep have shown this in a horrible manner. It is to prevent such a misfortune that in each mill there is an axe kept ready to cut off the arm of a slave who has, through her inattention, let her fingers be caught between the drums. There is no other way to save the rest of the body. The women slaves who watch over the cauldrons risk another danger that is no less awful; it is to fall head first into a sea of boiling sugar, and to go in an instant to the other world candied like a lemon.

Although the work is different in the indigo works, the agenda is the same. The slaves have no more respite here. You might ask me here if the master of a plantation can manage to direct so many different tasks on his own. I would answer that it is not possible, and, even if it were, our planters, who all behave like they are great lords, would think the endless attention that has to be given to a plantation to be beneath them. Just like these monarchs who go to war through their generals, and are happy to lead everything from their *cabinet*,[9] our rich Frenchmen of Saint-Domingue all employ a white man who has the title of *overseer* [*économe*], on whom they rely for the care of running the

---

[9]   A *cabinet*: a small room which might be reserved for the direction of reserved business, or private study.

les soirs le maître donne pour le lendemain ses ordres à l'économe, celui-ci les porte au nègre commandeur, et veille si on les observe. Il doit avoir l'œil sur tout, parce qu'il répond de tout. Ses appointements ne sont jamais au-dessous de 1000 livres. C'est la pierre philosophale qu'un bon économe dans une habitation.

Revenons à nos nègres. Vous croiriez peut-être qu'il en doit coûter des sommes immenses [16^r] à l'habitant, pour nourrir journalièrement des centaines d'esclaves; mais vous allez être détrompé. L'habitant de Saint-Domingue se charge d'habiller ses esclaves, ce qui consiste précisément en deux chemises par an, qu'il donne à chacun. Pour leur nourriture c'est leur affaire. Ils se pourvoient comme ils veulent, ou plutôt comme ils peuvent, sans que leur maître s'en embarrasse autrement, si ce n'est qu'ils viennent à tomber malades, auquel cas il en prend quelque soin particulier.

Comment et de quoi donc vivent les nègres? Voici tout le mystère. Dans toutes les habitations on assigne à chaque nègre un morceau de terre à faire valoir à son profit. Le nègre en possession de son jardin y plante des vivres pour lui, et pour sa famille. Il a tous les fruits qu'il veut, la terre ne refusant rien à la main qui la cultive. Avec ce secours les ateliers de nègres ne seraient pas à plaindre, si tous les maîtres leur donnaient au moins un demi-jour[11] dans la semaine pour travailler à leur jardin, mais combien en est-il de ces maîtres que l'esprit d'avarice et d'irréligion possède tellement, que tout le travail de la semaine, ils l'exigent sans pitié pour eux seuls, sans même excepter le saint jour du Seigneur qu'ils font [16^v] travailler leurs nègres à la sucrerie, et leur donnent à peine quelques heures dans tout le cours du mois pour sarcler leur jardin. D'autres moins avares et un peu moins impies laissent à leurs esclaves tous les jours de fête pour planter ou ramasser leurs vivres. Le désordre qui s'ensuit encore, c'est que les nègres qui sont éloignés de l'église quelquefois de trois lieues, et qui n'ont pour s'y rendre que les chevaux des Capucins, sont dans l'impuissance absolue d'entendre la messe et l'instruction du dimanche. Ils mourraient de faim toute la semaine s'ils ne profitaient pas du seul jour qu'ils ont pour ramasser de quoi vivre. Les missionnaires ont beau crier à l'injustice et à l'impiété de ces maîtres tyranniques. L'envie sacrilège d'avoir <u>auri sacra fames</u> l'emporte sur toutes les remontrances chrétiennes.

Il est vrai qu'on permet aux nègres d'élever de la volaille et d'avoir un petit parc à cochons pour eux. Mais le peu de gain qu'ils en retirent à peine leur suffit à s'acheter les vêtements qu'on leur refuse et les petits ustensiles du ménage.

---

[11] Dyonet, p. 122: 'deux jours'.

sugar factory. Every evening the master gives his orders for the next day to the overseer, who passes them on to the black foreman, and who ensures that they are observed. He has to keep an eye on everything, because he is answerable for everything. His wages are never below 1000 *livres*. A good overseer is the philosopher's stone of a plantation.

Let us return to our slaves. You may think that it costs a planter a fortune to feed hundreds of slaves every day, but let me set you right. The planter on Saint-Domingue takes care of clothing his slaves, which consists, to be exact, in the two shirts a year he gives to each of them. Their food is for them to take care of themselves. They provide for themselves as they wish, or rather as they can, without their master getting otherwise involved, unless they fall sick in which case he takes some care of the individual.

How and on what do the slaves live? This is the mystery. In each of the plantations, each slave is given a plot of land to work for himself. The slave plants crops in his own garden for himself and his family. He has all the fruit of it that he might want, because the earth refuses nothing to the hand that cultivates it. With this assistance, the slave workforce would not be deserving of pity, if all the masters gave them at least a half day in the week to work in their gardens. But how many are the masters so possessed by avarice and irreligion that they pitilessly exact the whole week's labour for themselves alone, without even excepting the Holy day of Our Lord, when they make their slaves work in the sugar plant, and barely give them a few hours in the whole month to weed their garden. Others who are less avaricious and a little less impious allow their slaves all the feast days to plant and harvest their food. The evil that this causes is that, because the slaves are sometimes three leagues distant from the church, with nothing to get them there but shanks's pony,[10] it is completely impossible for them to hear Sunday instruction and Mass.[11] They would be starving all week if they did not take advantage of the one day they have to gather something to eat. The missionaries may well decry the injustice and impiety of these tyrannical masters; the sacrilegious desire to possess, *auri sacra fames*, prevails over the objections of the Christian.[12]

It is true that the slaves are allowed to raise poultry and to have a little piggery for themselves. However, the little profit they make from it is barely sufficient to allow them to buy the clothes that are refused them, and little household utensils.

[10] On foot. 'Les chevaux des Capucins' translates literally as 'the Capuchins' horses'.
[11] *Instruction* might also refer to a sermon; in this case it can be expected to refer to religious instruction.
[12] 'quid non mortalia pectora cogis, auri sacra fames' ('To what crime do you not drive the hearts of men, accursed hunger for gold?'). Virgil, *Aeneid*, III, 56–57, in *Eclogues, Georgics, Aeneid: Books 1–6*, bilingual Latin–English edn, trans. by H. Rushton Fairclough, rev. by G. P. Goold (Cambridge, MA: Harvard University Press, 1999), pp. 376–77.

Les habitants qui ont la crainte de Dieu devant les yeux, et qui veulent remplir toute obligation envers leurs esclaves [17ʳ] leur accordent un demi-jour¹² entre les deux dimanches pour cultiver leur jardin, et par ce moyen ils les mettent en état d'avoir le nécessaire et même le commode. Sans vouloir nous donner ici pour exemple, nous avons à notre habitation des ménages de nègres aussi à leur aise, par leur industrie aidée de notre indulgence que les riches paysans de France.

Les mets les plus chers des nègres sont la <u>cassave</u>, les <u>ignames</u>, les <u>patates</u> et les <u>ignames</u> [*sic*]. La cassave est une espèce de galette fort plate cuite sur une platine de fer, et faite de la raclure d'une grosse racine appelée <u>manioc</u>.¹³ C'est là le pain des nègres. Ils le préfèrent au pain de froment, et tous nos blancs créoles le mangent avec délices, quoiqu'il n'ait pas plus de saveur qu'une galette de pur son de froment, ce qu'il y a de plus particulier dans cette racine, c'est que l'eau qui en sort est un poison des plus subtils. On l'exprime dans une chausse entre deux poutres, et quand le marc est sec, on le cuit au feu, de la manière que j'ai dite.

Les patates et les ignames sont d'autres racines grosses comme la cuisse, et d'un assez bon goût, selon moi. On les mange bouillies ou cuites sous la cendre, le goût de la patate est absolument le même que celui de la [17ᵛ] châtaigne bouillie. Il y a dans le pays quantité d'autres fruits excellents, et tous fort sains, les melons y sont délicieux et ne causent jamais d'incommodité comme en France. Pour les arbres fruitiers d'Europe ils avortent tous à Saint-Domingue. Il n'y croît que des figues qui sont exquises. Croiriez-vous que les pommes qu'on nous apporte de Normandie se vendent jusqu'à 4 livres la douzaine, et 5 à 6 livres une poire de bon chrétien d'hiver mais en récompense nous avons les quatre saisons de l'année, tous les légumes¹⁴ de France, on mange en tout temps de petits pois, de la laitue pommée, des asperges, et toute sorte de petites et grosses fèves.

Après avoir donné à manger aux nègres, faisons-les parler. Leur langage est tout à fait bizarre, et je ne crois pas qu'aucun de ces Messieurs puisse jamais avoir l'honneur d'être admis à l'Académie française. Ce n'est qu'après bien du temps et des peines que j'ai pu enfin trouver la clef du dictionnaire nègre. Ils parlent la langue française et la nègre tout à la fois, c'est-à-dire qu'ils s'expriment en notre langue de la même façon qu'ils s'exprimeraient en langue de Guinée. Ils n'ont point tant de mots ni de circonlocutions que nous, conjuguer [18ʳ] les verbes c'est ce qu'ils ignorent parfaitement. Ils se servent toujours de l'infinitif ou du prétérit passé, qu'ils font précéder du pronom. Par exemple au lieu de dire, <u>je vais là</u>, <u>je ferai cela</u>, ils disent, <u>moi aller là</u>, <u>moi faire ça</u>. Ils ont surtout un

¹² Dyonet, p. 123: 'deux jours'.
¹³ AdC, 2F 788, fol. 17ʳ: 'magnoc'.
¹⁴ AdC, 2F 788, fol. 17ᵛ: 'toutes les légumes'.

Those planters who fear God, and who want to fulfil all their obligations towards their slaves, grant them a half day between Sundays to cultivate their garden, and with this they give them the means to have what is necessary and even comfortable. Without wanting to set ourselves up as an example, we have households of slaves here on our plantation who, thanks to their industry along with our indulgence, are as well off as rich French peasant folk.

The finest foods for the slaves are cassava, yams, and potatoes. Cassava is a sort of very flat pancake, which is cooked on an iron plate, and made from the shavings of a large root called *manioc*. It is the slaves' bread. They prefer it to wheat bread, and all our white Creoles eat it with delectation, although it has no more flavour than a pancake made from pure wheat bran. What is most singular about this root is that the water that comes from it is a most subtle poison. It is extracted by squeezing it in a filter cloth between two wooden blocks, and, when the residue is dry, it is cooked on the fire, in the way I have described.

Potatoes and yams are other sorts of roots that are as big as the thigh, and have a pleasant enough taste, in my view. They are eaten boiled or roasted in hot ashes, and potatoes taste exactly the same as boiled chestnuts. In this land there are many excellent fruits, and they are all very wholesome. The melons are delicious and never cause you any indisposition as they do in France. European fruit trees never reach maturity on Saint-Domingue. Only figs grow, and they are exquisite. Can you believe that the apples brought to us from Normandy are sold for as much as four *livres* the dozen, and a *Bon-chrétien* pear for five or six *livres*? In compensation we have all the vegetables of France for the four seasons of the year; we eat peas, lettuce, asparagus, and all sorts of beans of all sizes, all year round.

Now that we have fed the slaves, let us have them talk. Their language is completely bizarre, and I don't think that any of these gentlemen could ever have the honour of being admitted to the Académie française. It is only after much time and trouble that I have been able, in the end, to decipher the slaves' vocabulary. They speak the French and the black language at the same time, that is, they express themselves in our language in the same way they would express themselves in the language of Guinea. They do not have as many words or circumlocutions as we do. Conjugate verbs? They have absolutely no idea of how to do this, and they always use the infinitive or the preterite, which they precede with a pronoun. For example, instead of saying, 'I am going there', 'I will do that', they say 'Me go there', 'Me do that'. They have, above all, a

talent merveilleux pour estropier les mots, et les défigurer de manière à ne pas les reconnaître. Ils appellent le procureur du roi, <u>Perroquet du roi</u>, la chicorée sauvage <u>caca cheval</u>, Monsieur Trocmorton Anglais, Monsieur <u>Croque mouton</u>, ainsi du reste, ce n'est pas un nègre seul, tous donnent dans ce travers.

Il faut pourtant convenir qu'ils s'expriment quelquefois d'une manière fort pathétique, et qui fait des images d'après nature. Pour faire connaître qu'ils sont fort en colère, ils emploient cette phrase <u>Cœur à moi brûler trop</u>. De même lorsqu'ils veulent dire qu'il y a bien du temps qu'ils n'ont vu quelqu'un; <u>y a longtemps, temps, temps que moi n'a pas mirer yeux à moi dans yeux à toi</u>. Un de nos nègres vit pour la première fois un bon père capucin qui allait à Mississippi (en qualité de missionnaire, car vous pourriez peut-être vous y tromper). Savez-vous comment le nègre définissait [**18**^V] l'homme séraphique à un de ses camarades? <u>Moi voir iune</u>[15] <u>bête faite comme monde</u>[16] (pour dire faite comme un homme) <u>qui gangner</u>[17] <u>barbe à cabri, sac à manioc, licol à bourrique pour serrer ventre à li</u>. Cela s'appelle peindre naturellement les choses.

Voici une autre peinture aussi naïve quoiqu'un peu moins honnête. La scène est encore au Cap dans la maison des pères jésuites. Un nègre de 16 ans dormait dans notre galerie à plate-terre, et la bouche béante, mon petit nègre valet qui est malin comme un espiègle se déculotta, et fit baiser son derrière au dormeur qui s'éveilla ayant encore les yeux, le nez et la bouche sur les deux hémisphères de l'autre, à l'instant *cœur à li brûler*, et il donna les étrivières à mon petit coquin de valet. J'accourus au bruit, et je demandai quelle était la cause de la querelle, le baiseur de médaille me conta l'affaire en ces termes, <u>Moi sienta là, et dromir</u> [*sic*], <u>et bien petit nègre-là mettre cul dans main à li, et péta dans bouche à moi</u>.

Je ne finirais point si je vous rapportais tous les dictons facétieux des nègres. Je me contenterai de vous en citer encore un qui a son mérite. Monsieur [**19**^r] notre gouverneur étant venu pour nous rendre visite ne trouva aucun de nos pères à la maison. Un des nègres qui garde la salle nous ayant dit le soir que <u>grand monde venir haler pères</u>, nous lui demandâmes qui c'était, il ne sut nous répondre autre chose, sinon que c'était <u>grand monde là qui gangner soldat dans cul à li</u>. C'est que le gouverneur ne marche jamais sans avoir un garde à sa suite, et c'était le soldat *dans cul à li*.

Le caractère des nègres est comme leur langage. C'est un mélange monstrueux de bonnes et de mauvaises qualités. Il serait difficile de dire s'ils ont plus de

---

[15] In the *patois* of Berry, where Breban was born, *iun* and *iune* are the indefinite singular articles. Hugues Lapaire, *Le Patois berrichon*, 2nd edn (Paris: J. Gamber, 1925), p. 85.

[16] In the Creole of Saint-Domingue, *monde* equated to 'person', 'man' ('l'homme'), or 'people' ('Les gens'), according to S. J. Ducoeurjoly, *Manuel des habitans de Saint-Domingue*, 2 vols (Paris: Lenoir, 1802), II, 313, 346, 377.

[17] *Gagner*. Dyonet transcribes this verb as 'ganguer' (p. 124 and passim). However, the verb *gagné* had the sense of *avoir* or 'ce qu'on possède' in the Creole of Saint-Domingue. See for example Ducoeurjoly, II, 294.

marvellous talent for mangling words, and for deforming them so much that you cannot recognize them. They call the king's *procureur*, *The King's parakeet*, wild chicory, *Why-the-Gee-gee*, an Englishman named Mr Throckmorton, *Mr Took-mutton*, and so on. It is not just one of them; they all have the same fault.

One must admit that sometimes they express themselves with great pathos, and with images that are drawn from life. To express that they are very angry they use this phrase 'Me heart too much on fire.' Also, when they want to say that it has been a while since they have seen someone, 'Too much time, time, time that I no stare me eyes in your own eyes.' One of our slaves saw a good Capuchin Father for the first time, who was on his way to Mississippi (as a missionary, just in case you misunderstood). Guess how the slave described this seraphic man[13] to one of his fellows? 'Me see aaan animal look like *monde* (which means, who looked like a man) him with a little goat's beard, with manioc bag and donkey's halter because things are tight.' Now that's what you call painting a portrait from life!

Here is another portrait that is just as simple, although a little less decent. The scene takes place once more at Cap-Français in the Jesuits' house. A slave of sixteen years of age was sleeping in our gallery on the floor with his mouth wide open. My black valet, who is a mischievous little demon, took off his breeches and made the sleepyhead kiss his backside. He woke up with his eyes, nose, and mouth on the other one's behind. Straight away, *His heart too much on fire*, he started whipping my little rascal of a valet, I rushed over because of the noise, and I asked what was the reason for this quarrel. The one who had just kissed the *medal* told me what happened in these terms, 'I sitting down there and I sleeping, and little black fellow there take his behind in him hand, and he fart in me mouth.'

I would never end if I were to tell you all of the slaves' facetious sayings. I will limit myself to quoting one more which has its merits. Our honourable governor, having come to visit us, found that none of us priests was at the house. One of the slaves who guards the hall told us that evening that 'Big man he come look for Fathers.' We asked him who it was, but all he could say to us in reply was that it was 'Big fine man there with a soldier following his arse around.' For the governor never goes anywhere without having a guard with him, and this was the soldier *following his arse around*.

The character of the slaves is like their language. It is a monstrous mix of good and bad qualities. It would be difficult to say if they have more virtues

---

[13] *Seraphic*: term traditionally applied to Saint Francis of Assisi (c. 1181–1226), and to members of the Franciscan order he founded.

vertus que de vices. Ils ont pour la plupart la mémoire extrêmement dure, l'esprit épais, et incapable de sérieuses réflexions. On a toutes les peines imaginables à leur apprendre les principaux mystères de notre sainte religion. Il faut des années entières pour les disposer à recevoir le baptême. Rarement leur permet-on de communier parce qu'ils sont rarement disposés à la Communion. Notre méthode est de les interroger à la Sainte Table sur l'action sainte qu'ils veulent faire. Nous leur demandons s'ils se sont confessés, et à qui, si bon Père leur a permis de communier? Ce que c'est que [19ᵛ] l'Eucharistie? S'ils croient fermement les vérités de ce sacrement adorable? Et lorsqu'ils répondent bien à tout, nous les admettons à la participation de nos plus saints mystères. S'ils ne savent pas répondre, on leur refuse la Communion, sans que cela cause le moindre scandale, parce que les blancs connaissent la conduite et le génie grossier du nègre.

En général ils ont un respect infini pour tout ce qui regarde la religion. Dans les églises ils sont modestes et recueillis comme des anges. Le scandale que leur donne sans cesse l'immodestie des blancs dans le lieu saint, ne fait sur eux aucune impression. Bien différents des autres idolâtres, ils renoncent sans peine aux superstitions païennes, et nous fatiguent de leurs importunités pour nous engager à les baptiser. Leurs parrains et marraines leur tiennent lieu de Papa et de Maman, c'est le nom qu'ils leur donnent. Ils les honorent comme tels, et réciproquement ils en sont chéris avec la dernière tendresse, qu'un nègre ou une négresse fasse une faute considérable, le parrain ou la marraine les châtie aussi sévèrement que ferait le père le plus rigide, et le coupable quelque âge qu'il ait, reçoit les coups, sans oser seulement murmurer. Bel exemple pour les blancs qui sont [20ʳ] si peu fidèles aux engagements qu'ils ont contractés en tenant des enfants sur les fonts de baptême.

Une autre excellente qualité des nègres c'est que quoiqu'ils soient tous fort enclins au mensonge, jamais ils ne déguisent leurs pensées au tribunal de la confession. S'ils vous[18] disent qu'ils renoncent au péché et à certain commerce honteux auxquels ils ne sont que trop sujets, vous pouvez les en croire sur leur parole. Ils vous tiendront promesse à coup sûr, et ne tomberont pas, au lieu que s'ils sont encore attachés à leurs passions, ils vous l'avoueront ingénument: <u>Tiens bon Père, moi aimer encore femme-là trop: moi pas savé encore quitter li.</u> Quand ils vous ont une fois lâché ce mot, il ne faut plus songer à les exhorter à la pénitence. Vous les menaceriez de la mort, du jugement, et de tous les diables d'enfer, que ce serait peine perdue.

<u>Toi donc pas voulé que moi bailler absolution à toi</u>, leur disons-nous?

<u>Ah ah, répliquent-ils froidement, Si toi pas voulé, toi pas bailler absolution à moi, qu'est-ce à moi faire ça?</u>

Que de sacrilèges s'épargneraient nos Français, s'ils avaient la même sincérité dans leurs confessions?

---

[18] Dyonet, p. 125: 'nous'.

than vices. Most of them have an extremely bad memory, are thick-witted and incapable of serious reflection. We have all the trouble imaginable to teach them the principal mysteries of our holy religion. Entire years are needed to dispose them to receive baptism. They are rarely allowed to receive Communion because they are rarely disposed to Communion. Our method is to interrogate them at the altar rail about the holy act they wish to do. We ask them if they have confessed, and to whom? If the good Padre has allowed them to take Communion? What is the Eucharist? Do they firmly believe the truths of this adorable sacrament? If they reply correctly to everything, we admit them to participate in our most holy mysteries. If they do not know what to answer, we refuse them Communion, without this causing the least scandal, because the whites know the blacks' behaviour and their thick-wittedness.

In general, they have infinite respect for anything concerning religion. In the churches they are as modest and composed as angels. The constant, scandalous immodesty of the whites in this holy place has no effect on them. Quite unlike the other idolaters, they renounce pagan superstitions without difficulty, and tire us out by constantly requesting that we will agree to baptize them. Their godfathers and godmothers take the place of Papa and Mama, which is the name they give them. They honour them in this way, and they are cherished in return with the greatest tenderness. If a slave, male or female, commits a serious misdeed, the godfather or godmother punish them as severely as would the most inflexible of fathers, and the guilty party, however old he is, accepts the blows without daring to as much as murmur. What an example they are to the whites, who so little respect the commitments they entered into while holding children at the baptismal font!

Another excellent quality of the black slaves is that, while they are all given to lying, they never hide their thoughts at the tribunal of confession. If they tell you that they are renouncing sin and a shameful liaison, to which they have such a great tendency, you can take their word for it. They will certainly keep their promise and will not falter, whereas, if they are still given over to their passions, they will avow it to you frankly: 'Here, good Father, me still love that woman there too much, me still not know how me leave her.' Once they have said this to you, there is no point urging them any more to penitence. You could threaten them with death, with the Last Judgement, and with all the devils in Hell and you would be wasting your time.

'So you no want me grant you absolution?' we say to them.

'Ah, ah', they coolly reply. 'If you no want, you no grant me absolution; can I do it meself?'

How much less sacrilege would our French commit, if they were as sincere in their confessions?

Avec toutes ces bonnes et mauvaises dispositions des nègres, vous ne sauriez croire quelle peine a un confesseur à leur tirer de la bouche l'aveu de leurs fautes. Ce sont tous [20ᵛ] des saints, lorsqu'ils se présentent au prêtre. Ils n'ont jamais rien fait. Ce n'est qu'à force d'interrogations qu'on découvre leurs péchés. Voici un modèle de leurs confessions:

Demande: Qu'est-ce à toi faire depuis que toi venir dans petite boutique-là?
Réponse: Moi n'a pas faire à rien, bon Père
D Toi pas offenser bon Dieu
R Moi n'a pas jamais [connais?] offenser bon Dieu
D Toi pas jures?
R Si fait, bon Père, moi jurer assez.

Et là-dessus ils vous enfilent une longue kyrielle de jurements, dont se feraient honneur les plus brutaux charretiers de France.

D Toi n'a pas savé voler?
R Moi voler pour bouche à moi, voler [c]assave, voler ignames, voler patates.

Nous leur faisons [sic] pas grand scrupule sur ces sortes de vols, parce que c'est la nécessité qui les y contraint presque toujours.

D Toi n'a pas voler à rien autre chose?
R Oui bon Père, moi voler pain, moi voler vin, moi voler viande

Pour ces sortes de choses nous les grondons horriblement, parce qu'ils s'exposent à des châtiments terribles de la part de leurs maîtres, et que le vin d'ailleurs les rend fort mauvais.

[21ʳ]
D Toi n'a pas tout dire encore.
R Qu'est-ce à toi voulé que moi dire à toi?
D Mais toi dire que toi volé viande? viande-là bêtes à maître à toi? Nenni?
R Si, bon Père, moi voler iune bœuf dans savane à maître à moi, moi voler deux moutons à li, moi voler cochons, moi voler poules etc.

Vous étiez-vous attendu à celui-là? Rien n'est pourtant plus ordinaire aux nègres que d'escamoter les bestiaux de leurs maîtres. Ils les conduisent furtivement dans le bois, et en régalent leurs amis durant la nuit. Il ne leur faut ni broches, ni chaudières pour apprêter leur festin. Ils font boucaner les chairs au feu, le reste ils l'abandonnent aux chiens, ou le salent pour leur case.

D Toi courir?
R Non, bon Père, moi courir jamais. Le mot de courir signifie avoir quantité de maîtresses

For all the slaves' good and bad inclinations, you would not believe how much trouble a confessor has in getting them to admit to their sins. They are all saints when they appear before the priest. They have never ever done anything wrong. It is only through interrogation that one discovers their sins. Here is a model of their confessions:

Question: *What you do since you come to that old place there?*
Reply: *Me no do nothing, good Father.*
Q: *You no offend Good Lord?*
R: *Me not never offend Good Lord.*
Q: *You no swear?*
R: *Indeed, good Father, me plenty swear.*

And then they regale you with a long litany of oaths, that the most brutish carters in France would be proud of.

Q: *You no steal?*
R: *Me steal for me own mouth, steal cassava, steal yams, steal potatoes.*

We do not dwell too much on these sorts of thefts, because it is nearly always necessity which obliges them to commit them.

Q: *You no steal anything else?*
R: *Yes, good Padre, me steal bread, me steal wine, me steal meat.*

For these sorts of things we scold them terribly, because they risk terrible punishment from their masters, and, moreover, because wine makes them very bad-tempered.

Q: *You still no say everything.*
R: *What you want me that I tell you?*
Q: *But you say that you steal meat? This meat your master's animals? Isn't it?*
R: *It is, good Padre, me steal aaaaan ox in the meadow and it was me master's, me steal two 'a his sheep, me steal pigs, me steal hens* (etc.).

Were you expecting that, then? Yet there is nothing more typical of slaves than making off with their masters' livestock. They lead the beasts away furtively into the forest, and they regale their friends throughout the night. They need neither spit nor cauldron for their feast. They smoke the meat over the fire,[14] and leave what is left for the dogs, or they cure it for their shack.

Q: *You go a-chasing?*
R: *No, good Padre, me never go a-chasing.* The word 'chasing' means to have a number of mistresses.

[14] *Boucaner*: the technique consists in smoking according to the description of Oexmelin (Exquemelin) (1699), I, 116–17. For Furetière, who (unlike Oexmelin) had never been to the Americas, it might also consist in grilling or roasting. Furetière (1727), I, entry 'Boucan', non-paginated.

D　Toi marié?

R　Moi pas marié devant Père Boutin. C'est un de nos plus anciens missionnaires, curé des nègres et des matelots

D　Mais toi gangné femme?

R　Moi gangner femme deux assez, et moi cabaner [21ᵛ] tout plein avec yeux.

Parmi les nègres ce n'est pas grand péché d'avoir une ou deux femmes pour maîtresses, et de *cabaner*, pour dire, coucher avec elles. Ce sont là des peccadilles pour eux. Jugez du reste de leurs confessions par le petit tableau en raccourci que je viens de vous présenter.

Il y a souvent à mourir de rire en confessant ces sottes pécores. Une jeune négresse de 17 ans s'accusa d'avoir un amant. Le confesseur lui demanda combien de fois ils avaient cabané ensemble.

Attends bon Père, dit la négresse, ve là Pierrot homme à moi qui bouger là dans église; moi aller demander à li combien de fois.

Elle alla en effet, interroger son adonis qui sortit tout honteux de l'église, sans oser lui répondre un mot. La négresse de retour au confessionnal dit ingénument au père que Pierrot n'avait pas voulu répondre, et qu'elle reviendrait après avoir tiré raison de lui.

Une autre négresse commença brusquement sa confession par dire, Moi gangner six hommes. Voilà ce qui s'appelle dire bien des choses en quatre mots. Cela me fait songer à la confession de ce moine espagnol qui s'étant déjà habillé pour dire [22ʳ] la messe, pria un de nos pères de le réconcilier, *Pater reverendissime, verbulum reconciliationis...* Ego vixi tres annos inter Moniales tanquam taurus inter vaccas. Peto absolutionem. Meâ culpa, meâ culpa etc.

Je défie l'homme le plus grave de tenir son sérieux, en confessant certains nègres. Mais quelles tristes réflexions à faire après cela sur l'incontinence de ces demi-bêtes. Il n'y aurait que demi-mal, si les blancs ne leur donnaient pas l'exemple de la plus horrible brutalité. Mais nos Français sont les premiers à abuser de l'esclavage des négresses. La facilité qu'ils ont d'en venir à bout, les rend voluptueux au suprême degré. Il n'y a point ou presque point d'habitation qui soit exempte de la contagion. Les négresses n'oseraient presque se rendre difficiles. Ce serait s'exposer à être à tout moment maltraitées. Elles trouvent mieux leur compte à se rendre. Plusieurs mêmes se disputent entre elles l'honneur de partager le cœur et le lit de Monsieur. C'est de cet abominable mélange de sang différent que viennent tant d'enfants mulâtres dont la colonie est pleine. De là les dissensions[19] domestiques entre le maître et la maîtresse du logis. Combien de Françaises sont obligées d'essuyer les hauteurs et les mépris insultants d'une insolente esclave qui se prévaut arrogamment de la préférence que lui donne son infâme maître. De là les intrigues galantes, les rendez-vous,

---

[19]　AdC, 2F 788, fol. 22ʳ: possibly 'discussions'; Dyonet, p. 126: 'dissensions'.

Q: *You married?*
R: *Me no married in front of Father Boutin.* This is one of our oldest missionaries, the priest for the slaves and sailors.
Q: *But you have woman?*
R: *Me have enough two woman, and me shack up a lot.*

Among the slaves it is not a big sin to have one or two mistresses and to *shack up*, which means to lie with them. These are little sins, for them. Moreover, you may judge their confessions by the little sketch I have just made for you.

Confessing these little ninnies would have you die laughing often enough. A young girl slave of seventeen years of age confessed she had a lover. The confessor asked her how many times they had *shacked up* together.

'Wait, good Father', said the slave, 'I see Pete, my own man, he's there in church, me go an' ask him how many times.'

And indeed, off she went to question her Adonis, who left the church in shame, without daring to say one word to her. The girl, upon returning to the confessional, said naively to the priest that Pete hadn't wanted to answer, and that she would come back when she could get him to tell her.

Another female slave started her confession by saying straight out 'Me got six men'. That is what you call saying a lot with a few words. It reminds me of the confession made by that Spanish monk who, having already put on his vestments for Mass, asked one of our priests to reconcile him, 'Pater reverendissime, verbulum reconciliationis... Ego vixi tres annos inter Moniales tanquam taurus inter vaccas. Peto absolutionem. Mea culpa, mea culpa etc.'[15]

I defy the gravest of men to remain serious while confessing some of these slaves. But what sad reflections are to be made after this about the incontinence of these half-animals. There would only be small harm if the whites did not give them the example of the most horrible brutality, but our French are the first to abuse of the slavery of black women. It is so easy for them to overcome them that it makes [the men] lustful to a supreme degree. There are few plantations, or none, that are free from this contagion. The female slaves would hardly dare be difficult about it. It would mean leaving themselves constantly open to mistreatment. They get more out of it by giving in. Many even quarrel amongst themselves for the honour of sharing the heart and the bed of *Sir*. It is from this abominable mix of different blood that come the *mulâtre* children, of which the colony is full. This leads to the master and the mistress of the household having domestic problems. How many Frenchwomen are obliged to endure the insulting scorn and disdain of an insolent slave, who arrogantly vaunts the preference that her debased master shows her? It is this that leads to the affairs, the assignations, and the adulteries — so very common — of these women who

[15] 'Most reverend Father, a little word of reconciliation. I lived for three years amongst nuns as a bull amongst cows. I ask for absolution. *Through my fault, through my fault,* etc.'

les adultères si communs [22ᵛ] de ces femmes indignement méprisées. De là la rage et le désespoir des pauvres maris nègres qui comme dit la chanson, n'ont de leur moitié que la moitié. Ils se portent quelquefois aux plus violentes extrémités, et après avoir égorgé leurs femmes, ils vont se pendre au premier arbre. Il n'y a pas six mois que nous eûmes encore un exemple de cette sanglante catastrophe.

Il est rare de voir des négresses qui (comme la chaste Suzanne) choisissent plutôt la mort, que de consentir à être déshonorées. Il s'en trouve cependant de ce caractère, et j'en connais plus d'une qui ont mieux aimé souffrir les plus rudes traitements de la part de leurs maîtres, que de servir leur infâme convoitise.

L'ivrognerie est un autre vice commun parmi les nègres. Ils aiment avec passion une espèce d'eau-de-vie faite avec le sirop de sucre, et qui a beaucoup plus de feu que nos eaux-de-vie de France, on l'appelle tafia ou guildive. Lorsque les nègres en ont pris plus qu'il ne convient, ils sont comme des bêtes brutes, qui n'ont que la fureur en partage. Ce n'est pas qu'ils ne soient adonnés au vin. L'histoire que je vous ai rapportée du canari en terre vous en est une bonne preuve. Mais il n'est pas aussi facile aux nègres d'avoir du vin comme du tafia, qui n'est fait que pour eux.

Le tabac à fumer fait aussi leurs délices. Tous [23ʳ] les nègres hommes et femmes ont tout le jour la pipe à la bouche. Cela ne les empêche pas de vaquer au travail. Jamais ils ne prennent de tabac par le nez. Ils se rient de nous quand ils nous voient la tabatière à la main, nous farcir les narines d'une chose qui n'est faite, disent-ils, que pour bouche à chrétien. L'art de fumer s'est tellement communiqué des nègres aux blancs, qu'il n'est presque point d'habitants créoles, et même d'habitantes, grosses dames, qui ne fument leurs 15 à 20 pipes par jour. Le petit coup d'eau-de-vie ou de tafia ne manque pas après la pipe. Cela leur fait des bouches odoriférantes qui les annoncent d'aussi loin que le fumet des nègres. Le beau spectacle de voir dans nos plaines une dame parée comme une déesse, tirée dans une chaise à quatre chevaux, et fumant sa pipe avec autant de complaisance, que si elle sentait un bouquet de roses, ou buvait un verre de limonade. C'est là une des merveilles du nouveau monde. Chaque pays, chaque mode.

Vous ne serez plus surpris que nos créoles prennent si facilement les manières et les mœurs des nègres, lorsque vous saurez qu'il n'y a à Saint-Domingue de [23ᵛ] nourrices et de gouvernantes d'enfants que les négresses. Il est certain que les enfants sucent avec le lait les inclinations de leurs nourrices. Ces premières inclinations se fortifient ensuite par la force persuasive de l'exemple, de sorte, qu'à la couleur près, il n'y a presque pas de différence entre un enfant blanc et un négrillon. Les plus riches de nos habitants envoient de bonne heure leurs enfants en France, pour tâcher de rectifier leur première éducation; mais quelque chose qu'on fasse, il reste toujours quelque chose de la première empreinte.

have been unjustly scorned. It is this that leads to the rage and despair of these black husbands who, as the song says, *Only have one half of their other half.* They sometimes go to the most violent extremes, and, after having cut their wife's throat, they go and hang themselves from the first tree they find. It is not yet six months since we had yet another instance of such a horrific event.

It is rare to see female slaves choosing (like the chaste Susanna) death rather than consenting to be dishonoured.[16] Still, there are some like this, and I know more than one who has preferred to suffer the harshest treatment at the hands of their masters than to serve their base desire.

Drunkenness is another common vice amongst the blacks. They have a passion for a sort of brandy made with sugar syrup, and which is much more fiery than our French brandies. It is called *tafia* or *guildive*. When the slaves have had more than they should, they are like brute beasts who are driven by fury. It is not that they are not given to wine. The story I related about the *canari* in the ground is a good proof of that. But it is not as easy for the slaves to get wine as tafia, which is made for them alone.

Smoking tobacco is also among their delights. All the black men and women have a pipe in their mouth all day long. It doesn't stop them going about their work. They never take tobacco through the nose. They laugh at us when they see us with a snuffbox in our hand, stuffing our nostrils with something meant, they say, for 'a Christian's mouth' alone. The art of smoking has passed so much from the blacks to the whites that there are hardly any male Creole planters, and even females, important ladies, who do not smoke their fifteen or twenty pipes a day. A little nip of brandy or tafia will not be lacking after the pipe. This gives them fragrant mouths that announce their presence from as far away as the slaves' scent does. It is a pleasant sight in our plains to see a lady dressed up like a goddess, pulled in a carriage drawn by four horses, smoking her pipe with as much delectation as if she were sniffing a bunch of roses, or drinking a glass of lemonade. This is one of the wonders of the New World. Every country has its customs!

It would not surprise you that our Creoles so easily adopt the ways and manners of the blacks, once you know that on Saint-Domingue the only wet-nurses and governesses of children are black. It is certain that the children suckle their wet-nurses' inclinations along with their milk. These first inclinations are then fortified by the persuasive force of example so that, colour apart, there is hardly any difference between a white and a black child. The richest of our planters send their children off young to France, to try to correct their early upbringing, but, whatever is done, something always remains of the first imprint.

---

[16] Susanna was falsely accused of adultery and exonerated by Daniel: Daniel 13.

Quand les négresses sont nourrices, même[20] de leurs propres enfants, elles vivent séparées de leurs maris, jusqu'à ce que l'enfant soit entièrement sevré. Elles sont toutes idolâtres de leur progéniture, légitime ou non, elles craindraient pour le fruit de leur fécondité, si elles ne vivaient pas dans la plus exacte continence. Cette sage conduite des négresses mères occasionne quantité de désordres de la part de leurs maris, qui n'ont pas toujours assez de vertu pour se contenir eux-mêmes deux années entières, ils cherchent à se dédommager ailleurs, et le trouvent toujours assez, souvent trop pour leur malheur, car il n'y a guère de pays au monde où la tisane de Bavière [24ʳ] et le mercure de Suède soient plus en usage qu'à Saint-Domingue.

Il y a parmi les nègres, comme parmi les blancs des charlatans, des diseurs de bonne aventure, peu de véritables sorciers; mais des empoisonneurs beaucoup. Ce sont nos habitants eux-mêmes qui n'ont point de honte, ni de scrupule de consulter les nègres sur mille choses cachées qu'ils veulent savoir. Tout l'éclaircissement qu'ils en tirent presque toujours, c'est qu'ils sont la dupe de leur sotte et impie crédulité, et qu'ils ont perdu leur peine et leur argent à vouloir éclaircir des mystères, dont la connaissance n'appartient qu'à Dieu seul.

Les nègres empoisonneurs réussissent mieux dans leur exécrable métier. Ils connaissent quantité d'herbes venimeuses, par le moyen desquelles ils se défont en peu de temps de tout ce qu'ils ont d'ennemis. On est quelquefois surpris de voir périr presque en même temps des 20 et 30 nègres dans une habitation. On en cherche la cause, et l'on trouve que c'est un malheureux nègre qui les a tous empoisonnés. Un de nos plus riches habitants en perdit l'année dernière plus de soixante morts de poison. Le coupable fut découvert, et mourut dans les fers comme [24ᵛ] possédé du Démon, on brûla son corps et sa case en présence du reste de l'atelier, et les cendres furent jetées au vent. Le dessein de ce scélérat, si Dieu ne l'avait pas prévenu, était de faire périr tous les nègres de son maître qui en a près de quatre cents. Il est assez ordinaire que l'empoisonneur aille se pendre, s'il s'aperçoit qu'on le soupçonne.

Jugez de la malice diabolique d'un nègre mauvais par le trait suivant. Un de nos habitants voyant périr de langueur plusieurs de ses esclaves, soupçonna qu'il y avait du poison, et jeta ses soupçons sur un vieux nègre de son atelier. C'était effectivement ce monstre d'enfer qui, pour je ne sais quelle raison, donnait un poison lent à ses camarades, mais le maître n'en avait aucune certitude. Il crut cependant devoir agir, comme s'il avait eu toute l'évidence du fait. Il menaça le nègre de le faire brûler vif, s'il ne rendait la santé à deux de ses meilleurs esclaves qui dépérissaient à vue d'œil. Le nègre le promit, et dit à son maître qu'il fallait pour cet effet que les malades allassent avec lui dans le bois où étaient les herbes convenables, et qu'il fallait les leur appliquer sur le lieu même. Le maître consentit à tout. Les deux nègres entrèrent bien avant dans la

---

[20] AdC, 2F 788, fol. 23ᵛ: 'mêmes'.

When the black women are nursing, even their own children, they live apart from their husbands, until the child is completely weaned. They are all devoted to their offspring, legitimate or not, and they would be afraid for the fruit of their fertility if they did not live in the strictest continence. This wise conduct of black mothers gives rise to much moral disorder on the part of their husbands, who are not always virtuous enough to control themselves for two whole years. They look elsewhere for their compensation, and they always find enough of it, and sometimes too much, unfortunately for them. For there is hardly anywhere in the world where Bavarian infusions and Swedish mercury are used more than in Saint-Domingue.[17]

Amongst the blacks, as amongst the whites, there are charlatans, fortune tellers, few true sorcerers, but many poisoners. Our planters themselves have no shame or scruples about consulting the slaves about a thousand hidden things they want to know. Nearly always, the only enlightenment they receive is that they have been taken in by their own foolish and impious credulity, and that they have wasted their effort and their money trying to understand the kinds of secrets that God alone knows.

The black poisoners are more successful in their execrable trade. They know many poisonous herbs, by which means they get rid of all their enemies in a short while. Sometimes we see, with astonishment, that twenty or thirty slaves on a plantation have perished almost at the same time. The cause is looked for, and it is found to be a wretched black who has poisoned them all. Last year, one of our richest planters lost more than sixty who were killed by poisoning. The guilty party was found, and died in chains as if he were possessed by the devil. His corpse and his cabin were burned in the presence of the rest of the workforce, and his ashes were scattered in the wind. This rogue, if God had not prevented him from it, had planned to do away with all the slaves of his master, who has nearly four hundred of them. It is typical enough for the poisoner to go and hang himself, if he sees that he is under suspicion.

See what the diabolical malice of a bad slave is like from the following story. One of our planters, seeing many of his slaves languish away and die, suspected that there was poison involved, and his suspicions fell on an old slave from among his own. It was indeed this hellish monster who, for a reason I do not know, gave slow-acting poison to his comrades. The master could not be certain of this, but thought that he had to act as if he had full proof of the facts. He threatened the slave with having him burned alive, if he did not restore the health of two of his best slaves who were withering away, as it was plain to see. The slave promised that he would, and said to his master that, to do this, he would need the two who were sick to go with him into the forest where there were the right herbs, which had to be given to them on the spot. The master

---

[17] Popular treatments for venereal disease.

forêt, précédés de leur guide, qui leur dit [25ʳ] que pour être plus sûrement et plus promptement guéris il fallait qu'ils se laissassent lier chacun à un arbre. Ils le permirent; mais à peine le traître les vit-il hors d'état de pouvoir se défendre, qu'il tira de sa poche un couteau, et le leur plongea dans le cœur. Pour achever la scène, il se pendit à une branche d'arbre au-dessus des deux victimes de son insatiable fureur. On ne s'en aperçut que trois jours après. Le maître ne voyant pas revenir ses nègres, les envoya chercher dans le bois, où on les trouva tous les trois dans l'état que je viens de vous dire.

La manière la plus usitée de châtier les nègres, c'est le fouet; mais quel fouet? Vous allez frémir à ce récit, représentez-vous donc un de ces fouets, dont se servent nos charbonniers d'Issoudun pour conduire leurs chevaux, c'est à peu près le fouet dont on régale ici les nègres. L'ordonnance du roi défend expressément qu'on donne plus de quarante coups de fouet à un esclave, mais nos habitants qui se moquent des lois les plus respectables excèdent de beaucoup ce nombre. Voici donc comment ils s'y prennent pour châtier un nègre coupable. Ils le font coucher nu, le ventre à terre, et lui lient les mains et les pieds à quatre piquets. Cela fait un des plus robustes nègres de l'habitation, c'est ordinairement le nègre commandeur [25ᵛ] prend le fouet en main, se tenant à huit ou dix pas du coupable, afin de pouvoir donner jeu à son fouet. Il allonge à tours de bras des coups dont l'air retentit à plus de demi-lieue au loin. De la première touche souvent il enlève la peau, le fouet entre dans les chairs, et fait couler du sang en abondance.

Il n'est pas nécessaire qu'un nègre ait commis de grands crimes pour subir ce terrible châtiment. Il est des habitants, et surtout des femmes créoles qui pour un rien font <u>tailler</u> leurs nègres, c'est le terme dont elles se servent pour dire fouetter, et en cela elles s'expriment naturellement car un nègre qui sort de dessous le fouet, a les fesses taillées, comme avec un rasoir. Encore si l'on n'excédait pas de beaucoup, l'ordonnance du roi, mais ce qui ferait horreur à des barbares, n'en fait point à nos habitants. Ce sont des cent, deux cents, trois et même quatre et cinq cents coups de fouet qu'ils font donner en même temps à leurs nègres. Jugez des cris et des hurlements horribles que poussent ces misérables au milieu de leur supplice. Ils sont comme des chiens enragés, et cherchent quelquefois à s'étouffer ne pouvant plus supporter les coups, mais que font [26ʳ] nos Nérons pour l'empêcher? Ils tiennent un tison ardent sous le nez du nègre, afin qu'il n'ait pas le moyen de se couper la respiration: sont-ce des Gètes ou des Sarmates qui exercent ces sortes de cruautés? Non, ce sont des Français, eux-mêmes souvent plus dignes de ce traitement que leurs esclaves. Enfin avant que de délier le nègre qu'on vient de tailler, pour tout appareil on lui frotte ses plaies avec une saumure composée de jus de citron, de sel et de vinaigre. C'est une sauce des plus piquantes, mais nécessaire pour entretenir les chairs dans leur fraîcheur naturelle. Le nègre après cette expédition demeure étendu sur sa cabane, sans pouvoir se remuer quelquefois des mois entiers.

agreed to everything. The two slaves went deep into the forest with their guide leading the way. He said to them that, to be more surely and promptly cured, each of them had to allow himself to be tied to a tree. They allowed this to be done, but no sooner did the scoundrel see that they were unable to defend themselves than he took a knife out of his bag, and plunged it into their hearts. To complete the scene, he hung himself from the branch of a tree above the two victims of his insatiable fury. It was only discovered three days afterwards. The master, seeing that his slaves had not returned, sent to look for them in the forest, where the three of them were found in the state I have just related to you.

The most typical manner of punishing the slaves is with a whip — but what a whip. You will shudder at this story. Imagine one of the whips that our coalmen from Issoudun use to drive their horses — this is much like the whip that our slaves are treated to here. The king's ordinance expressly forbids giving more than forty whiplashes to a slave, but our planters, who scoff at the most respectable laws, go far beyond this number. This is how they go about punishing a guilty slave. They make him lie down naked on his stomach, and tie his hands and his feet to four stakes. Once this is done, one of the most robust slaves in the plantation — it is usually the foreman — takes the whip in his hand, keeping himself eight or ten paces from the guilty party so that he has the space he needs for his whip. He vigorously lands the strokes on him, and the air resounds for more than a half league away. The skin is often taken off with the first lash, the whip gets right into the flesh, and blood flows abundantly.

A slave does not have to have committed a serious crime to suffer this terrible punishment. There are planters, and especially Creole women, who for nothing have their slaves *cut*, which is the term they use for a whipping. Their expression is very appropriate, because a slave, after a whipping, has his buttocks sliced as if he had been under a razor. That would be if they did not go much beyond the king's ordinance, but what would horrify even savages does not trouble our planters. They have one hundred, two hundred, three, and even four or five hundred lashes given to their slaves all at once. Imagine the horrible cries and screams of these wretches while they are being tortured. They are like mad dogs, and sometimes they try to smother themselves because they can no longer tolerate the lashes. Yet what do our Neros[18] do to prevent this? They hold a burning ember under the slave's nose, so there is no way he can stop himself from breathing. Is it the Getes or Sarmates who exert such cruelties?[19] No, these are French people, themselves often more deserving of this treatment than their slaves. Then, before untying the slave who has just been *cut*, they give him for his dressing a brine made of lemon juice, salt, and vinegar. It is an extremely spicy sauce, but necessary to keep the flesh in its natural freshness. After this treatment, the slave is stretched out in his cabin without being able to budge, sometimes for entire months.

[18] Reference to the Roman emperor Nero (*c.* AD 37–68).
[19] Getes and Sarmates: peoples inhabiting Central Asia in Antiquity.

Il est des habitants qui portent beaucoup plus loin la fureur. C'est peu pour eux de tailler leurs nègres avec le fouet, ils les font tailler avec le rasoir ailleurs que sur les fesses, pour leur ôter l'envie et le moyen de courir la négresse. D'autres font mourir leurs nègres sous les coups; ou par quelque autre genre de supplice plus cruel encore, dans la persuasion où ils sont qu'ils ont droit [26^v] de vie et de mort sur leurs esclaves, ce qui est directement contraire à toutes les lois divines et humaines. Mais la fureur connaît-elle des lois? Je sais des habitants qui pour des fautes de peu de conséquence ont fait passer leurs nègres au moulin comme un paquet de cannes, quelques autres les ont fait brûler à petit feu, et nommément une dame fort riche qui était nonchalamment assise dans un fauteuil, la pipe à la bouche tandis qu'on rôtissait à ses yeux un esclave qui avait eu le malheur de déplaire à Madame.

Un autre petit habitant s'étant mis en tête qu'une jeune négresse avec laquelle il avait commerce, lui avait manqué de fidélité, lui enfonça un fer rouge dans la matrice. Le même peu de temps après pour punir un nègre de je ne sais quelle faute, il l'enferma tout nu dans un tonneau hérissé de pointes de fer en dedans, et le laissa mourir de rage. Tous ces tyrans sanguinaires vivent heureux dans la colonie, sans qu'on les ait inquiétés tant soit peu sur leurs cruautés. On s'en est plaint en cour, et le ministre a fait donner des ordres [27^r] qu'on recherchât ces bourreaux de nègres, mais soit indolence, soit prévarication de la part de ceux qui gouvernaient alors, ou enfin faute de preuves suffisantes, car les nègres ne sont point reçus en témoignage contre les blancs, le crime est demeuré impuni. Cela seul ne prouve-t-il évidemment la nécessité d'un jugement universel à la fin des siècles?

Mais Dieu n'attend pas quelquefois le grand jour des révélations pour punir d'aussi monstrueux excès. Toute la colonie a été témoin du fait que je vais vous rapporter, un habitant avait massacré de sa propre main presque tous les nègres les uns après les autres. Il ne lui en restait plus que deux qu'il eut la barbarie de châtrer lui-même. Ces pauvres esclaves, dans la crainte que tôt ou tard on ne les achevât comme les autres, s'enfuirent dans les bois et y périrent de misère. La femme de l'habitant avait aussi trempé quoique bien moins dans le carnage qu'avait fait son mari, aussi en porta-t-elle la peine avec lui. Un beau jour ils devinrent fous et furieux l'un et l'autre, et presque à la même heure, de telle sorte que quittant tout ce qu'ils avaient d'habits sur le corps, ils couraient nus les grands chemins comme des énergumènes. En ce pitoyable [27^v] état ils arrivèrent dans une habitation, c'était chez le commandant du quartier qui les fit mettre séparément aux fers. C'est là où je les ai vus moi-même plusieurs fois. Le mari faisait publiquement sa confession d'une infinité de crimes et de sacrilèges qu'il avait commis dans sa vie. Bref il mourut frénétique ne parlant que des diables d'enfer, et des justes jugements de Dieu. L'épouse que Dieu n'a pas voulu perdre, comme étant plus innocente est entièrement revenue de

There are planters who take their fury much further. For them it is a little thing to *cut* their slaves with the whip. They cut them with a razor — but not on their buttocks — so as to take from them not just the desire, but also the means, of going *a-chasing* female slaves. Others cause their slaves' death from violent blows, or by some other still more cruel torture, persuaded as they are that they have the right of life and death over their slaves, which is directly contrary to all human and divine laws. But does fury respect the laws? I know of planters who, for minor misdeeds, have had their slaves drawn through the sugar mill like a bundle of cane, while others had them slowly burned. I know of one very rich lady in particular who was sitting nonchalantly in an armchair, her pipe in her mouth, while a slave who had the misfortune to displease *Her Ladyship* was being roasted before her eyes.

Another minor planter got it into his head that a young girl slave with whom he was having a liaison had been unfaithful to him, and plunged a red-hot iron right into her womb. A little afterwards, the same one punished a slave — for which misdeed I do not know — by locking him naked in a barrel lined with iron spikes, and left him there to die mad. All these bloodthirsty tyrants are living happily in the colony, without anyone troubling them at all about their cruel acts. Complaints were made at court and the minister gave orders that these torturers were to be sought out but, whether through dereliction of duty or indifference on the part of those who were governing at that time, or lack of sufficient proof — for slaves cannot testify against whites — the crime remained unpunished. Does this alone not clearly prove the need for the judgement of all at the end of time?

However, sometimes God does not wait for the great day of revelations to punish such monstrous excesses. The whole colony was witness to the event that I am going to relate to you. A planter, having massacred by his own hand nearly all the slaves one after the other, had only two left that he had the savagery to himself emasculate. These poor slaves, fearing that sooner or later they would be finished off like the others, fled into the woods where they perished from hardship. The planter's wife had also taken part, although to a much lesser degree, in her husband's bloodshed, and she shared his sentence. One fine day both of them went raging mad, and almost at the same time, so that, casting off all the clothes they had on them, they took to roaming around naked as if they were possessed. In this pitiful state they arrived in a plantation; it was the residence of the commandant of the area who had them put in irons separately from one another. It was there where I myself saw them many times. The husband publicly confessed an infinite number of crimes and sacrileges that he had committed in his life. In short, he died in a frenzy, and all he would talk about was the devils in Hell and the just judgements of God. The wife, whom God did not wish to damn as she was more innocent, entirely recovered

sa folie, et vit encore aujourd'hui, mais avec une édification dont on est aussi charmé qu'on avait été scandalisé de ses emportements.

Quand un nègre se sent coupable, pour éviter le châtiment il ne prend que trop souvent la fuite, et va se cacher dans les bois. Cela s'appelle aller en marronage ou être marron.[21] Ces nègres fugitifs s'attroupent quelquefois comme une bande de voleurs, et vont pendant la nuit piller les habitations voisines. On leur donne la chasse comme à des bandits. S'ils viennent à se défendre contre ceux qui les poursuivent à main armée, et qu'ils soient pris, ils sont pendus sans miséricorde. Se rendent-ils de bonne grâce? On les mène au corps de garde le plus proche, où ils restent jusqu'à ce que le [28^r] maître à qui ils appartiennent, les réclame. S'ils refusent d'arrêter, quand ils en sont requis il est permis à quiconque de les tuer, et celui qui a fait le coup obtient une récompense réglée par le roi, en apportant la tête et l'étampe du nègre marron. Je dis l'*étampe*, afin qu'on sache à qui appartient le nègre; car vous saurez que tous les nègres esclaves ainsi que toutes les bêtes de la colonie sont marqués sur la peau avec un fer chaud de la marque de leurs maîtres.

Un Français qui voit son nègre marron, va le huitième jour de sa fuite, le déclarer au bureau du greffe. La raison de cela, c'est que si son nègre est tué dans le marronage, après la déclaration faite, on le lui paie 500 livres par la déclaration du roi, ne paraissant pas juste qu'un maître, à cause des intérêts du public, vienne à perdre tous ses nègres. On lui donne donc la moitié de ce que vaut communément un nègre. La même somme est payée à ceux dont les esclaves sont exécutés par sentence de justice. Cela s'appelle ici les droits des suppliciés. On les lève chaque année sur les habitants chacun payant une somme par chaque tête de nègre qu'il a dans son atelier. [28^v] Ceux des nègres marrons qui de leur plein gré veulent retourner à leur maître, vont trouver quelque blanc de leur connaissance et le prient de vouloir bien s'entremettre pour obtenir leur grâce. Ce sont le plus ordinairement les bons pères missionnaires qui sont chargés de ces sortes de commissions, et nous y réussissons presque toujours. On n'oserait guère nous refuser, moins par respect peut-être pour nos personnes, que par crainte qu'en cas de refus nous ne leur parlerions plus en faveur de leurs esclaves, et que ce serait ôter par là à ces malheureux fugitifs, la seule voie du retour.

Entre autres bonnes qualités des nègres, ils sont courageux comme des lions. Leur bravoure est à l'épreuve des plus affreux dangers. Ils ont même des sentiments d'honneur que nous admirerions dans les peuples les mieux civilisés. Témoin un nègre qu'on avait condamné à la potence. On lui offrit de lui sauver la vie, s'il voulait accepter l'emploi de bourreau, dans une juridiction voisine. Quelques remontrances qu'on pût lui faire à ce sujet, jamais il ne fut possible de tirer autre chose de lui que ces paroles Moi aimer mieux aller voir

---

[21] Breban uses the spellings *maronage* and *maron*.

from her madness and is still alive today, but in a state of edification which is as enchanting as her rage was a source of scandal.

When a slave knows he is guilty of some wrongdoing, he will only too often take flight and hide away in the woods. This is called going *en marronage*, or being a maroon. These fugitive slaves sometimes gather together like a band of thieves and go about at night pillaging the neighbouring plantations. They are hunted like bandits are. If they try to defend themselves from those who pursue them with arms, and they are taken, then they are hung without mercy. If they surrender willingly they are brought to the nearest barracks where they remain until the master to whom they belong claims them. If they refuse to stop when they are requested to do so, anybody at all is allowed to kill them, and he who actually does so obtains a reward, specified by the king, by bringing the head and the brand of the maroon slave. I say *brand*, as this shows to whom the slave belongs: for, you see, all the black slaves, as with all the animals in the colony, have their master's brand marked on their skin with a hot iron.

A Frenchman who sees that his slave has absconded goes to declare it to the registry office on the eighth day. The reason for this is that, if his slave is killed while a maroon, after the declaration has been made he is paid 500 *livres* according to the king's declaration, as it was not thought just that a master should lose all his slaves because of the public interest. He is as such given half of what a slave is usually worth. The same sum is paid to those whose slaves are executed by a judicial sentence. Here, this is called 'the dues for the executed'. They are levied each year on the planters, with each one paying a sum per head on each slave he has in his workforce. Those among the maroon slaves who want to return to their master of their own free will go and find some white they know and ask him to kindly intervene to obtain their pardon. It is usually the good missionary Fathers who are given this sort of assignment and we nearly always succeed. We are hardly ever refused, perhaps less through respect for our person than through the fear that, in case of refusal, we would no longer speak in favour of their slaves, and that this would mean taking away from these wretched fugitives the only way back that they have.

Amongst the other good qualities of the blacks is that they are as courageous as lions. Their bravery withstands the most terrible dangers. They even have sentiments of honour that we would admire in the most civilized of peoples. One slave, who had been sentenced to the gallows, illustrates this. An offer was made to him to spare his life, if he would accept the function of executioner in a neighbouring jurisdiction. However much they tried to change his mind, the only thing anyone could get him to say was, 'Me prefer go see good God than

bon Dieu, que tuer monde. Les vieux Romains auraient sauvé la vie à l'esclave, en faveur de sa grandeur d'âme, d'autant plus qu'il ne méritait guère [29ʳ] la corde: mais il y a longtemps qu'il n'y a plus de Romains. L'arrêt fut exécuté, et le nègre mourut en héros.

Je ne sache qu'un point où les mœurs de notre colonie sympathisent avec les mœurs de l'ancienne Rome, c'est de donner la liberté à quelques esclaves en récompense de leurs services et de leur zèle. Nous avons ici quantité de nègres affranchis. Ils jouissent paisiblement de tous nos privilèges, à cette loi près qu'il ne leur est pas plus permis qu'aux esclaves de lever la main sur un blanc. Ils sont bons citoyens et bons soldats. L'élite de ces nègres libres compose un corps d'infanterie qui pour la valeur et pour la fidélité ne le cèdent en rien à nos meilleures troupes de France. Ils ont des maisons, des terres, et des esclaves à l'égard desquels ils sont encore plus sévères que les blancs, et là-dessus un me disait qu'il connaissait mieux que nous la nation nègre et que qui voulait s'en faire servir, il ne devait leur rien passer.

Il ne me reste plus qu'à vous dire un mot de l'habillement des nègres. Tous les esclaves, sans en excepter aucun, marchent nu-pieds. Ils y sont accoutumés dès l'enfance, et dans un pays chaud [29ᵛ] comme le nôtre cela est moins dur que commode. Nos petits habitants eux-mêmes sont rarement chaussés dans leurs maisons. Les nègres de la place, sont les plus malpropres. Ils n'ont guère hommes et femmes qu'une chemise sur le corps, en travaillant, et jamais la tête couverte quelque chaleur qu'il fasse. Ce serait un prodige de voir un nègre frappé d'un coup de soleil comme s'en serait [sic] un autre qu'un blanc n'en fût pas atteint quand il n'a pas un soin particulier de sa tête.

Les nègres valets de la chambre se tiennent plus propres que les autres. Ils ont un mouchoir de toile des Indes sur la tête, un autre en guise d'écharpe ou de ceinturon, un troisième à la jambe gauche en forme de brodequin. C'est la belle grâce parmi eux et au fond cela leur sied assez bien. Ils portent le chapeau, lorsqu'ils sont à cheval. Les négresses domestiques ont aussi pour coiffure le mouchoir des Indes ou de Perse, la chemise fine et le jupon de couleur. Elles ne savent ce que c'est que de porter le corset, on voit quantité de ces négresses faire étalage du plus beau linge, et des plus riches dentelles d'Europe. [30ʳ] Mais vous devinez assez à quel jeu les donzelles gagnent de quoi nourrir leur sotte et ridicule vanité. Les nègres et négresses libres sont tous chaussés. Les hommes portent la manchette²² au côté, c'est une espèce de sabre fort large. Les femmes se coiffent à la mode des Françaises mais il n'y a rien qui les défigure davantage, le blanc de leur coiffure ne servant qu'à faire étaler davantage la noirceur et la grossièreté de leur visage.

---

²² *Manchette*: *machete* is defined as a 'gros couteau dont les boucaniers se servent pour fendre les cochons et les bœufs sauvages' in Furetière (1727), III, entry 'Maschette, ou machete', non-paginated.

kill someone.' The ancient Romans would have spared the slave's life because of his nobility of soul, all the more because he hardly deserved the rope; but there have been no Romans for a long time now. The sentence was carried out, and the slave died a hero.

I only know of one area in which the ways of our colony resemble the ways of Ancient Rome, and it is in the freeing of some slaves as a reward for their service and their zeal. We have a good number of freed slaves here. They peacefully enjoy all the same privileges as us, except for the rule that it is no more permitted them, than it is the slaves, to raise their hand against a white. They are good citizens and good soldiers. The elite of these free blacks makes up an infantry corps that, with regard to their valour and fidelity, are in no way inferior to the best of our French troops. They have houses and land, and slaves towards whom they are even more severe than the whites are, and on this subject one used to say to me that he knew the black people better than we do and that whosoever wanted to make use of them should let them get away with nothing.

All that is left is for me to say a word about the clothing of the slaves. All of the slaves, with no exception, walk barefoot. They are used to it since childhood, and, in a hot country like ours, it is comfortable rather than a hardship. Our more modest planters themselves rarely have anything on their feet when in their houses. The slaves who work in the fields are the shabbiest. Man or woman, they have hardly anything else on them but a shirt, while at labour, and their heads are uncovered, however hot it may be. It would be a wonder to see a black with sunburn, as it would be another one for a white not to suffer from it if he does not take particular care of his head.

The slaves who are chamber valets look after themselves with more care than the others. They have a kerchief of India cloth[20] on their head, another in the place of a scarf or belt, and another on their left leg in the manner of a buskin. They think it is graceful and, in fact, it suits them quite well. They wear a hat when they are on horseback. The female domestic servants also have on their heads an Indian or Persian kerchief, a fine blouse and a coloured skirt. They know not what it is to wear a corset. Many of these women can be seen showing off the finest fabric, and the richest lace from Europe. But you may well guess with which pursuit these damsels earn what feeds their foolish and ridiculous vanity. The free blacks, male and female, all wear shoes. The men wear the *machete* by their side; it is a sort of sabre which is very wide. The women dress their hair in the fashion of Frenchwomen, but there is nothing more ruinous to their appearance, as the white colouring does nothing but bring out the blackness and ugliness of their faces.

---

[20] *India cloth*: calico.

Voilà mon très cher frère, le véritable portrait de nos nègres. Je ne sais s'il aura de quoi vous plaire; mais je n'ai rien épargné pour le rendre parfait. Quoi qu'il en soit convenez avec moi que nos missionnaires ont de quoi exercer leur zèle parmi plus de cinquante mille de ces hommes barbares, après tout nous leur devons cette justice, qu'ils nous donnent, à beaucoup près, moins de peine que les blancs qui n'ont pour la plupart, aucuns sentiments de religion. Leur unique et souveraine loi, c'est leur plaisir, et l'argent leur tient lieu de divinité. [30^v] Je me recommande à vos saints sacrifices, et je suis avec toute l'amitié possible

Mon très cher frère

Votre très humble et très obéissant serviteur et frère C. Breban missionnaire de la Comp. de Jésus.

This, my dearest brother, is the true portrait of our blacks. I do not know if it will be pleasing to you, but I have spared nothing to make it perfect. In any case, you will agree with me that our missionaries have what may exercise their zeal, amongst more than fifty thousand of these barbaric men. After all, we must do them this justice that they give us much less trouble than the whites who, for the most part, have no sentiments of religion at all. Their unique and sovereign law is their pleasure, and money is their divinity. I recommend myself to your holy sacrifices, and am, with all the affection possible,

My dearest brother,

Your most humble and most obedient servant and brother C. Breban missionary of the Society of Jesus.

BIBLIOGRAPHY

Manuscripts

BREBAN (Bréban), Claude, Letter [to Breban's brother] from Cap-Français, Saint-Domingue, 19 January 1732, Bourges, Archives départementales du Cher [AdC], 2F 788. Repr./partly repr. in Nicole Dyonet, 'Le Père Bréban, missionnaire berrichon à Saint-Domingue: lettre inédite de janvier 1732', *Bulletin du Centre d'histoire des espaces atlantiques*, 8 (1997), 103–30

LE PERS, JEAN-BAPTISTE, *Le Portrait ou miroir de Saint-Domingue*, Vanves, Archives françaises de la Compagnie de Jésus (Societas Iesu) [AFSI], Fonds Brotier [GBro] 188 (1726? see fol. 22^r), later ed. and modified by Pierre-François-Xavier de Charlevoix, in *Histoire de l'isle Espagnole ou de Saint-Domingue*, 2 vols (Paris: Jacques Guerin, 1730–31)

Mémoire sur l'establissement d'un évesché aux isles d'Amérique, 19 May 1685, Aix-en-Provence, Archives nationales d'outre-mer, C8 B1 (63)

MONGIN, JEAN, *Copie de la lettre du R. P. Jean Mongin, écritte au R. P. Antoine Pagez provincial de la Compagnie de Jésus en la province de Toulouse, de l'isle de la Martinique le 10e may 1679*, Paris, Bibliothèque Mazarine [BM], Ant MS 9, fols 23^r–39^v, repr. in *L'Évangélisation des esclaves au XVIIe siècle*, ed. by Marcel Chatillon, *Bulletin de la Société d'histoire de la Guadeloupe*, 61–62 (3rd and 4th trimesters 1984), pp. 49–72

——*Copie de la lettre du père Jean Mongin missionnaire de l'Amérique, à une personne de condition de Languedoc, écrite de l'isle de Sainct Christophle au mois de may 1682*, Vanves, Archives françaises de la Compagnie de Jésus (Societas Iesu) [AFSI], Fonds Brotier [GBro] 185, fols 1^r–49^v, partly repr. [?] in *L'Évangélisation des esclaves au XVIIe siècle*, ed. by Marcel Chatillon, *Bulletin de la Société d'histoire de la Guadeloupe*, 61–62 (3rd and 4th trimesters 1984), pp. 127–36

——*Copie de la lettre du P. Jean Mongin, missionnaire de l'Amérique, à une personne de condition de Languedoc, écrite de l'île de St Christophle, au mois de mai 1682*, Vanves, Archives françaises de la Compagnie de Jésus (Societas Iesu) [AFSI], Fonds Brotier [GBro] 102, paginated pp. 39–105

——Letter to Giovanni Paolo Oliva, 20 August 1662, Rome, Archivum Romanum Societatis Iesu [ARSI], *Indipetae*, XXVI, no. 59

——(signed by/attributed to Mongin) Copies of letters (1676–82), Carcassonne, Collections of Médiathèque de Carcassonne Agglo/Bibliothèque Intercommunale de Conservation de Carcassonne Agglo [MdC], MS 73 [former code Ma 82] (inv. 2459-47), fols 1–119 as follows:

Fols 1^r–31^r: Letter, untitled [referred to as *Journal*], 15 July 1676, signed *J. Mongin*, incomplete; repr. by Jacques Petitjean-Roget as Jean Mangin [*sic*], 'Journal d'un voyage à la Martinique en 1676', *Annales des Antilles*, 10 (1962), 35–58

Fols 32^r–41^r: Letter from Martinique, September 1676, signed *Mongin*, repr. in *L'Évangélisation des esclaves au XVIIe siècle*, ed. by Marcel Chatillon, *Bulletin de la Société d'histoire de la Guadeloupe*, 61–62 (3rd and 4th trimesters 1984), pp. 37–48

Fols 43^r–49^v [title page, fol. 43^r; letter begins fol. 44^r], *Troisième lettre à un gentilhomme du Languedoc contenant l'attaque et l'embrasement des vaisseaux holandois à l'isle de Tabac faite par Mr le Comte d'Estrée*, 26 March 1677, no signature/signature unclear

Fols 51^r–68^r [title page, fol. 51^r; letter begins fol. 52^r]: *Quatrième lettre au R. P. provincial des jésuites de la province de Thoulouse contenant la relation de la mission de la Martinique*, 29 December 1678, no signature

Fols 71^r–73^v: Letter to an unnamed gentleman, 15 January 1679, apparently no signature

Fols 75^r–78^v [title page, fol. 75^r; letter begins fol. 76^r]: *Sixième lettre au R. Père de Fontenai professeur de matématique au Collège de Clairmont à Paris; observations de la comète de 1681 et 82 faites dans l'isle de St Cristofe* [modified to *St Christofle*], 3 March 1681, no signature

Fols 79^r–119^v [title page, fol. 79^r; letter begins fol. 80^r]: *Septième lettre à un gentilhomme du Languedoc contenant la relation de la mission des nègres, de l'isle Saint Cristofe*, incomplete, repr. with modifications in *L'Évangélisation des esclaves au XVIIe siècle*, ed. by Marcel Chatillon, *Bulletin de la Société d'histoire de la Guadeloupe*, 61–62 (3rd and 4th trimesters 1984), pp. 73–125

Translations of the Bible

The Holy Bible Faithfully Translated into English out of the Authentical Latin [Old Testament], 2nd edn, 2 vols (Rouen: J. Cousturier, 1635)

The New Testament of Jesus Christ, Translated Faithfully into English (Rheims: J. Fogny, 1582)

Works Printed Pre-1800/Editions of Pre-1800 Works

ACOSTA, JOSÉ DE, *De natura Novi Orbis libri duo, et De promulgatione Evangelii apud barbaros, sive De procuranda Indorum salute libri sex* (Salamanca: apud Gillelmum Foquel, 1589 [1588])

—— *De procuranda Indorum salute* (1588), bilingual Latin–Spanish edn, ed. by L. Pereña and others, 2 vols (Madrid: Consejo Superior de Investigaciones Cientificas, 1984–87)

AESOP, *Fables*, bilingual French–Greek edn, ed. by Émile Chambry (Paris: Société d'édition Les Belles Lettres, 1927)

ARISTOTLE, *Politics*, bilingual Greek–English edn, trans. by H. Rackham (Cambridge, MA: Harvard University Press, 1959)

BARTOLI, DANIELLO, *Dell'historia della compagnia di Gesù: l'Asia descritta*, I

(Genoa: Benedetto Guasco, 1656), partly trans. into French by Ignace-Gaston Pardies, published as *Les Miracles de S. François-Xavier, apostre des Indes* (Paris: Michel Le Petit, 1673)

BEDE, *Venerabilis Bedae Historia ecclesiastica gentis anglorum*, ed. by Joseph Stevenson (London: English Historical Society, 1838)

BIET, ANTOINE, *Voyage de la France équinoxiale en l'isle de Cayenne* (Paris: François Clouzier, 1664)

BOUTON, JACQUES, *Relation de l'establissement des François depuis l'an 1635 en l'isle de la Martinique* (Paris: Sébastien Cramoisy, 1640)

BREBAN (Bréban), Claude, *Hymenaei de amore triumphus*, in *In regales nuptias Ludovici XV et Mariae Leczinskiae festi Plausus editi in Regio Ludovici Magni Collegio Societatis Jesu* (Paris: S. Langlois, 1725)

——*Ludovicus XV jurans ad aras, elegeia* in *Ludovico XV Christianissimo regi ob susceptam remis coelestem unctionem obtulere musae parisienses in regio Ludovici magni Collegio Societatis Jesu* (Paris: Louis Sevestre, 1722)

BUONANNI, FILIPPO [?], *Catalogus provinciarum Societatis Iesu* (Rome: Typis Ignatii de Lazariis, 1679)

CALMET, AUGUSTIN, *Commentaire littéral, historique et moral sur la règle de Saint Benoît*, 2 vols (Paris: Emery, 1734)

CAUSSIN, NICOLAS, *La Cour sainte; ou, l'institution chrestienne des grands* (Paris: S. Chappelet, 1624)

Le Code Noir; ou, édit du roy servant de règlement pour le gouvernement et l'administration de justice et la police des isles françoises de l'Amérique, & pour la discipline et le commerce des nègres et esclaves dans ledit pays, donné à Versailles au mois de mars 1685 (Paris: Veuve Saugrain, 1718)

Constitutiones Societatis Iesu (Rome: 1558), repr. and trans. into English (London: J. G. and F. Rivington, 1838)

The Constitutions of the Society of Jesus and their Complementary Norms, trans. by Carl J. Moell et al. (Saint Louis, MO: Institute of Jesuit Sources, 1996)

CYPRIANUS, THASCIUS CAECILIUS (Cyprian of Carthage), *S. Thasci Caecili Cypriani opera omnia*, ed. by Wilhelm von Hartel, 3 vols (Vienna: apud C. Geroldi filium Bibliopolam Academiae, 1868)

DAUBENTON, GUILLAUME, *La Vie du bienheureux Jean-François Régis* (Paris: Nicolas Le Clerc, 1716)

D'AVITY, PIERRE, *Description générale de l'Afrique* (Paris: C. Sonnius, 1637)

DIANA, ANTONINO, *Summa Diana* (Antwerp: apud Hieronymum & Ioannem Bapt. Verdussen, 1656)

DU JARRIC, PIERRE, *Histoire des choses plus mémorables advenues tant ez Indes orientales, que autres païs de la descouverte des Portugais*, 3 vols (Bordeaux: Simon Millanges, 1608–14)

DU TERTRE, JEAN-BAPTISTE, *Histoire générale des isles de Saint-Christophe, de la Guadeloupe, de la Martinique et autres dans l'Amérique* (Paris: Jacques and Emmanuel Langlois, 1654); 2nd edn published as *Histoire générale des Antilles habitées par les François*, 4 vols (Paris: Thomas Jolly, 1667–71)

FROMAGEAU, GERMAIN, and ADRIEN-AUGUSTIN DE BUSSY DE LAMET, *Le Dictionnaire des cas de conscience*, 2 vols (Paris: J.-B. Coignard, 1733)

FURETIÈRE, ANTOINE, *Dictionnaire universel*, 3 vols (The Hague: A. and R. Leers,

1690); repr. ed. by Henri Basnage de Beauval and others, 4 vols (The Hague: Pierre Husson and others, 1727)

GODWYN, MORGAN, *The Negro's and Indian's Advocate: Suing for their Admission to the Church* (London: Printed for the author, 1680)

HAKLUYT, RICHARD, ed., *The Principal Navigations, Voyages, Traffiques and Discoveries of the English Nation*, 12 vols (Glasgow: James MacLehose, 1903–05)

HINGERLE, AUGUSTINO, *Catalogus provinciarum, collegiorum, residentiarum, seminariorum, et missionum, universae Societatis Iesu anni 1750* (Tyrnava: Society of Jesus, 1750)

IGNATIUS OF LOYOLA, *Écrits*, trans. and ed. by Maurice Giuliani (Paris: Desclée de Brouwer, 1991)

—— *Exercitia spiritualia S. P. Ignatii Loyolae, cum sensu eoremdem explanato, a P. Ignatio Diertins S. I. Editio quinta* (Antwerp: Henrici Thieullier, 1696)

Institutes [usual translation]: *D. Justiniani Institutionum libri quatuor*, bilingual Latin–English edn, trans. by George Harris as *The Four Books of Justinian's Institutions*, 3rd edn (Oxford: Collingwood, Newman and Baxter, 1811)

JEROME, *Opus epistolarum divi Hieronymi Stridonensis* (Paris: apud Carolum Guillard, 1546)

JOHN CHRYSOSTOM, *Opera omnia*, ed. by Bernard de Montfaucon,13 vols (Paris: apud Gaume Fratres, 1834–39)

LABAT, JEAN-BAPTISTE, *Nouveau voyage aux isles de l'Amérique*, 6 vols (Paris: Guillaume Cavelier and P.-F. Giffard, 1722)

LA MOUSSE, JEAN DE, *Les Indiens de la Sinnamary: journal du père Jean de La Mousse en Guyane (1684-1691)*, ed. by Gérard Collomb (Paris: Chandeigne, 2006)

LEO I, *S. Leonis Magni Papae Primi opera omnia*, ed. by P.-T. Cacciari, 2 vols (Rome: Apud Josephum Collini, 1753–55)

LESCLACHE, LOUIS DE, *La Philosophie, expliquée en tables*, 5 vols (Paris: [n. pub.], 1651–56)

Lettres édifiantes et curieuses, 34 vols (Paris: Nicolas Le Clerc, 1703–76)

LUCANUS, M. ANNAEUS, *De bello civili*, trans. by J. D. Duff (Cambridge, MA: Harvard University Press; London: Heinemann, 1988)

MARGAT DE TILLY, JEAN-BAPTISTE, LETTER OF 20 JULY 1743, IN *Lettres édifiantes et curieuses*, VII (Paris: J.-G. Merigot le jeune, 1781), pp. 185–255

Mercure de France (Paris: G. Cavalier; Veuve Pissot; J. de Nully, March 1728)

MOLINA, LUIS DE, *De iusticia, tomus primus* (Venice: apud Minimam Societam, 1594)

—— *De iustitia et iure*, 6 vols (Mainz: Nicolaus Heyll, sumptibus Haered. Joh. Godefredi Schönwederi, 1659)

MOREAU DE SAINT-MÉRY, LOUIS-ÉLIE, *Description topographique, physique, civile, politique et historique de la partie française de l'isle Saint-Domingue*, 2 vols (Philadelphia: Chez l'auteur, 1797–98)

—— *Loix et constitutions des colonies françoises de l'Amérique sous le vent*, 6 vols (Paris: Quillau; Lambert, 1784–90)

NADAL, JERÓNIMO, *Evangelicae historiae imagenes ex ordine Evangeliorum* (Antwerp: [n. pub.], 1593)

NICOLE, PIERRE, *Préjugez légitimes contre les calvinistes* (Paris: Veuve de C. Savreux, 1671)

OEXMELIN (Exquemelin), Alexandre, *Histoire des avanturiers*, 2 vols (Paris: Jacques Le Febvre, 1686), repr. as *Histoire des avanturiers flibustiers*, 2 vols (Paris: Jacques Le Febvre, 1699)

Ordonnance de Louis XIV donnée à Saint-Germain-en-Laye (Paris: Chez les associés, 1667)

PASCAL, BLAISE, *Les Provinciales* (Cologne: Pierre de la Vallée, 1657)

PELLEPRAT, PIERRE, *Relation des missions des pères de la Compagnie de Jésus* (Paris: Sébastien Cramoisy, 1655)

PIATTI, GIROLAMO, *De bono status religiosi libri III* (Rome: apud Jacobum Tornerium, 1589)

PIGAFETTA, FILIPPO, *Relatione del reame di Congo* (Rome: Bartolomeo Grassi, 1591?)

Ratio studiorum (1599), bilingual French–Latin edn, ed. by Adrien Demoustier and others (Paris: Belin, 1997)

RIBADENEIRA, PETRUS DE, and OTHERS, *Bibliotheca scriptorum Societatis Iesu* (Rome: J. A. de Lazzaris Varesii, 1676)

ROCHEFORT, CHARLES DE, *Histoire naturelle et morale des îles Antilles de l'Amérique* (Rotterdam: A. Leers, 1658); 2nd edn (Rotterdam: A. Leers, 1665)

SÁNCHEZ, TOMAS, *Compendium totius tractatis de sancto matrimonii sacramento* (Seville: Antonio de Toro, 1623)

——*Consilia; seu, Opuscula moralia* (Cologne: Sumptibus Stephani Breyelii & Haered. Bernardi Gualteri, 1640)

——*Consilia; seu, Opuscula moralia, tomi duo* (Parma: ex. Typographia Pauli Monti, 1723)

SANDOVAL, ALONSO DE, *De instauranda Aethiopum salute* (Seville: Francisco de Lira, 1627), repr. as *De instauranda Aethiopum salute: el mundo de la esclavitud negra en America*, ed. by Angel Valtierra (Bogotá: Empresa nacional de publicaciones, 1956)

SOTO, DOMINGO DE, *De iustitia et iure libri decem* (Salamanca: [n. pub.], 1556), in bilingual Latin–Spanish facsimile edn, ed. by Venancio Diego Carro, trans. by Marcelino González Ordóñez, 5 vols (Madrid: Instituto de Estudios políticos, 1968)

SOUSA, ANTÓNIO CAETANO DA, *Historia genealogica da Casa real portugueza*, 13 vols (Lisbon: da Sylva, 1745)

SURIUS, LAURENTIUS, *Historiae sanctorum omnium nationum*, 13 vols (Turin: Eq. Petri Marietti, 1875–80)

THOMPSON, RAYMOND H., *A Jesuit Missionary in Eighteenth-Century Sonora: The Family Correspondence of Philipp Segesser* (Albuquerque: University of New Mexico Press, 2014)

VIRGIL, *Eclogues, Georgics, Aeneid: Books 1–6*, bilingual Latin–English edn, trans. by H. Rushton Fairclough, rev. by G. P. Goold (Cambridge, MA: Harvard University Press, 1999)

VOLTAIRE (François-Marie Arouet), *Romans et contes*, ed. by René Groos (Paris: Gallimard, 1954)

Printed Works, Post-1800

ALDEN, DAURIL, *The Making of an Enterprise: The Society of Jesus in Portugal, its Empire, and Beyond 1540–1750* (Stanford, CA: Stanford University Press, 1996)

AÑOVEROS, JESÚS MARÍA GARCÍA, 'Luis de Molina y la esclavitud de los negros africanos en el siglo XVI. Principios doctrinales y conclusiones', *Revista de Indias*, 60.219 (2000), 307–29

AVRIL, JOSEPH-TOUSSAINT, *Dictionnaire provençal-français* (Apt: Edouard Cartier, 1839)

BARBOSA CANAES DE FIGUERIDO CASTELLO-BRANCO, JOSÉ, *Estudos biographicos, ou noticia das pessoas retratadas nos quadros historicos pertencentes a Bibliotheca nacional de Lisboa* (Lisbon: F. A. da Silva, 1854)

BLACKBURN, CAROLE, *Harvest of Souls: The Jesuit Missions and Colonialism in North America, 1632–1650* (Montreal and Kingston: McGill-Queen's University Press, 2000)

BOUCHER, PHILIP P., *France and the American Tropics to 1700: Tropics of Discontent?* (Baltimore, MD: Johns Hopkins University Press, 2008)

BURNARD, TREVOR, and JOHN GARRIGUS, *The Plantation Machine: Atlantic Capitalism in French Saint-Domingue and British Jamaica* (Philadelphia: University of Pennsylvania Press, 2016)

Catalogue général des manuscrits des bibliothèques publiques de France, XIII (Paris: Plon, Nourrit et Cⁱᵉ, 1891)

CHAPEAU, ANDRÉ, and CHARLES N. BRANSOM, 'Franciscan Bishops', *Franciscan Studies*, 47 (1987), 287–372

CHAUDENSON, ROBERT, *Des îles, des hommes, des langues: essai sur la créolisation linguistique et culturelle* (Paris: L'Harmattan, 1992), revised with Salikoko S. Mufwene, trans. by Sheri Pargman et al. as *Creolization of Language and Culture* (London: Routledge, 2001).

CHEMIN-DUPONSTÈS, PAUL, *Les Compagnies de colonisation en Afrique occidentale sous Colbert* (Paris: Augustin Challamel, 1903)

CHEVALIER, FRANÇOIS, ed., *Instrucciones a los hermanos jesuitas administradores de haciendas: manuscrito mexicano del siglo XVIII* (Mexico: Instituto de Historia, 1950)

CLASSEN, ALBRECHT, 'A Global Epistolary Network: Eighteenth-Century Jesuit Missionaries Write Home with an Emphasis on Philipp Segesser's Correspondence from Sonora/Mexico', *Studia Neophilologica*, 86 (2014), 79–94

CLOSSEY, LUKE, *Salvation and Globalization in the Early Jesuit Missions* (Cambridge: Cambridge University Press, 2008)

COSTELLO, FRANK BARTHOLEMEW, *The Political Philosophy of Luis de Molina, S. J. (1535–1600)* (Rome: Institutum Historicum; Spokane, WA: Gonzaga University Press, 1974)

CURTIN, PHILIP D., *The Rise and Fall of the Plantation Complex: Essays in Atlantic History*, 2nd edn (Cambridge: Cambridge University Press, 1998)

DAL LAGO, ENRICO, and CONSTANTINA KATSARI, eds, *Slave Systems: Ancient and Modern* (Cambridge: Cambridge University Press, 2008)

DAVID, BERNARD, *Dictionnaire biographique de la Martinique (1635–1848)*, 3 vols (Fort-de-France: Société d'histoire de la Martinique, 1984)

DAVIS, DAVID BRION, *The Problem of Slavery in Western Culture* (Ithaca, NY: Cornell University Press, 1966)

DEMELEMESTRE, GAËLLE, 'Des relations entre les doctrines dominicaine et jésuite au XVIᵉ siècle', *Laval théologique et philosophique*, 73.2 (June 2017), 181–207

DE MOURA RIBEIRO ZERON, CARLOS ALBERTO, *Ligne de foi: la Compagnie de Jésus et l'esclavage dans le processus de formation de la société coloniale en Amérique portugaise (XVIᵉ–XVIIᵉ siècles)* (Paris: Honoré Champion, 2009)

DESSALLES, ADRIEN, *Histoire générale des Antilles*, 5 vols [vol. 3 written by Pierre Régis Dessalles] (Paris: France, 1847)

DOBIE, MADELEINE, *Trading Places: Colonization and Slavery in Eighteenth-Century French Culture* (Ithaca, NY; London: Cornell University Press, 2010)

DOMPNIER, BERNARD, 'Un aspect de la dévotion eucharistique dans la France du XVIIᵉ siècle: les prières des Quarante heures', *Revue d'histoire de l'Église de France*, 178 (1981), 5–31

DOURSTHER, HORACE, *Dictionnaire universel des poids et mesures anciens et modernes* (Brussels: Hayet, 1840)

DUCOEURJOLY, S. J., *Manuel des habitans de Saint-Domingue*, 2 vols (Paris: Lenoir, 1802)

DUSSEL, ENRIQUE, *A History of the Church in Latin America*, trans. by Alan Neely (Grand Rapids, MI: Eerdmans, 1981)

FORRESTAL, ALISON, and SEÁN ALEXANDER SMITH, *The Frontiers of Mission: Perspectives on Early Modern Missionary Catholicism* (Leiden; Boston: Brill, 2016)

GALIBERT, NIVOELISOA, ed., *À l'angle de la Grande Maison: les lazaristes de Madagascar: correspondance avec Vincent de Paul (1648–1661)* (Paris: Presses de l'Université de Paris-Sorbonne, 2007)

GARRAWAY, DORIS L., *The Libertine Colony: Creolization in the Early French Caribbean* (Durham, NC; London: Duke University Press, 2005)

GARRIGUS, JOHN D., *Before Haiti: Race and Citizenship in French Saint-Domingue* (New York; Basingstoke: Palgrave Macmillan, 2006)

GRAMATOWSKI, WIKTOR, *Jesuit Glossary*, trans. by Camilla Russell (Rome: ARSI, 1992)

HALL, GWENDOLYN MIDLO, *Slavery and African Ethnicities in the Americas: Restoring the Links* (Chapel Hill: University of North Carolina Press, 2005)

HARRIGAN, MICHAEL, *Frontiers of Servitude: Slavery in Narratives of the Early French Atlantic* (Manchester: Manchester University Press, 2018)

—— 'Métissage and Crossing Boundaries in the Seventeenth-Century Travel Narrative to the Indian Ocean Basin', *Cahiers du dix-septième: An Interdisciplinary Journal*, 15 (2013), 19–45

HÖPFL, HARRO, *Jesuit Political Thought: The Society of Jesus and the State* (Cambridge: Cambridge University Press, 2004)

HSIA, R. PO-CHIA, *A Companion to Early Modern Catholic Global Missions* (Leiden: Brill, 2018)

—— *The World of Catholic Renewal 1540–1770*, 2nd edn (Cambridge: Cambridge University Press, 2005)

HURBON, LAËNNEC, 'Église et esclavage au XVIIIᵉ siècle à Saint-Domingue', in *Les Abolitions de l'esclavage de L. F. Sonthonax à V. Schoelcher*, ed. by Marcel Dorigny

(Saint-Denis: Presses universitaires de Vincennes; Paris: UNESCO, 1995), pp. 87–100

JAMESON, RUSSELL PARSONS, *Montesquieu et l'esclavage* (Paris: Hachette, 1911)

JAN, JEAN-MARIE, *Les Congrégations religieuses à Saint-Domingue 1681–1793* (Port-au-Prince: Henri Deschamps, 1951)

KING, STEWART R., *Blue Coat or Powdered Wig: Free People of Color in Pre-Revolutionary Saint Domingue* (Athens, GA; London: University of Georgia Press, 2001)

KRUMENACKER, YVES, ed., *Entre calvinistes et catholiques: les relations religieuses entre la France et les Pays-Bas du Nord (XVIe–XVIIIe siècles)* (Rennes: Presses universitaires de Rennes, 2010)

LAFLEUR, GÉRARD, 'Les Hollandais et les Antilles françaises', in *Entre calvinistes et catholiques: les relations religieuses entre la France et les Pays-Bas du Nord (XVIe–XVIIIe siècles)*, ed. by Yves Krumenacker (Rennes: Presses universitaires de Rennes, 2010), pp. 113–33

LAPAIRE, HUGUES, *Le Patois berrichon*, 2nd edn (Paris: J. Gamber, 1925)

LEFEBVRE, CLAIRE, *Creole Genesis and the Acquisition of Grammar: The Case of Haitian Creole* (Cambridge: Cambridge University Press, 1998)

LENIK, STEPHAN, 'Mission Plantations, Space, and Social Control: Jesuits as Planters in French Caribbean Colonies and Frontiers', *Journal of Social Archaeology*, 12.1 (2012), 51–71

MICHARD, LOUIS, and GEORGES COUTON, 'Les Livres d'états des âmes: une source à collecter et à exploiter', *Revue d'histoire de l'Église de France*, 67.179 (1981), 261–75

Mission de Cayenne et de la Guyane française (Paris: Julien, Lanier, Cosnard, 1857)

MOLINA, J. MICHELLE, *To Overcome Oneself: The Jesuit Ethic and Spirit of Global Expansion, 1520–1767* (Berkeley: University of California Press, 2013)

NOONAN, JOHN T., JR, *A Church that Can and Cannot Change: The Development of Catholic Moral Teaching* (Notre Dame, IN: University of Notre Dame Press, 2005)

O'MALLEY, JOHN W., *The First Jesuits* (Cambridge, MA: Harvard University Press, 1993)

—— *Saints or Devils Incarnate? Studies in Jesuit History* (Leiden; Boston: Brill, 2013)

—— AND OTHERS, eds, *The Jesuits: Cultures, Sciences, and the Arts 1540–1773*, 2 vols (Toronto: University of Toronto Press, 2000; 2006)

PATON, DIANA, 'Witchcraft, Poison, Law, and Atlantic Slavery', *William and Mary Quarterly*, 69.2 (2012), 235–64

PEABODY, SUE, ' "A Dangerous Zeal": Catholic Missions to Slaves in the French Antilles, 1635–1800', *French Historical Studies*, 25.1 (winter 2002), 53–90

PETITJEAN-ROGET, JACQUES, 'Les Protestants à la Martinique sous l'ancien régime', *Revue d'histoire des colonies*, 42.147 (1955), 220–65

—— *La Société d'habitation à la Martinique: un demi siècle de formation 1635–1685*, 2 vols (Lille: Université de Lille, 1980)

PEYTREAUD, LUCIEN, *L'Esclavage aux Antilles françaises avant 1789* (Paris: Hachette, 1897)

PIZZORUSSO, GIOVANNI, 'Le Choix indifférent: mentalités et attentes des jésuites aspirants missionnaires dans l'Amérique latine française au XVIIe siècle', *Mélanges de l'École française de Rome*, 109.2 (1997), 881–94

—— *Roma nei Caraibi: l'organizzazione delle missioni cattoliche nelle Antille e in Guyana (1635–1675)* (Rome: École française de Rome, 1995)

PRITCHARD, JAMES, *In Search of Empire: The French in the Americas, 1670–1730* (Cambridge: Cambridge University Press, 2004)

REY FAJARDO, JOSÉ DEL, 'Antoine Boislevert (1618–1669): Fundador de los llanos de Casanere', *Boletin de la Academia Nacional de la Historia*, 77.308 (1994), 81–104

RIBAULT, JEAN-YVES, 'Témoins de l'esclavage à Saint-Domingue: les lettres de deux jésuites berrichons, les PP. Margat et Bréban', *Cahiers d'archéologie et d'histoire du Berry*, 143 (September 2000), 27–36

ROCHEMONTRIX, CAMILLE DE, *Le Père Antoine Lavalette à la Martinique d'après beaucoup de documents inédits* (Paris: Alphonse Picard et fils, 1907)

ROPER, L. H., and B. VAN RUYMBEKE, *Constructing Early Modern Empires: Proprietary Ventures in the Atlantic World, 1500–1750* (Leiden: Brill, 2007)

SCELLE, GEORGES, *La Traite négrière aux Indes de Castille: contrats et traités d'assiento*, 2 vols (Paris: Librairie de la Société du Recueil J.-B. Sirey et du Journal du Palais, L. Larose & L. Tenin, 1906)

SLUHOVSKY, MOSHE, *Believe not Every Spirit: Possession, Mysticism, and Discernment in Early Modern Catholicism* (Chicago: University of Chicago Press, 2007)

SOMMERVOGEL, CARLOS, *Bibliothèque de la Compagnie de Jésus*, 3rd edn, 11 vols (Brussels: Oscar Schepens; Paris: Alphonse Picard, 1890–1932)

STERCKX, ENGELBERT, *Le Catéchisme de Malines* (Malines: Van Velsen, 1851)

SUE, MARIE JOSEPH EUGÈNE, *Histoire de la Marine française*, 5 vols (Paris: Félix Bonnaire, 1835–37)

SWEET, DAVID G., 'Black Robes and "Black Destiny": Jesuit Views of African Slavery in 17th-Century Latin America', *Revista de Historia de América*, 86 (July–December 1978), 87–133

VANTARD, AMÉLIE, 'Les Vocations missionnaires chez les jésuites français aux XVIIe–XVIIIe siècles', *Annales de Bretagne et des pays de l'Ouest*, 116:3 (2009), 9–22

—— 'Les Vocations pour les missions *ad gentes* (France 1650–1750)' (doctoral thesis, Université du Maine, 2010)

WEAVER, KAROL K., *Medical Revolutionaries: The Enslaved Healers of Eighteenth-Century Saint-Domingue* (Urbana; Chicago: University of Illinois Press, 2006)

WHEAT, DAVID, *Atlantic Africa and the Spanish Caribbean 1570–1640* (Chapel Hill: University of North Carolina Press, 2016)

WILSON, SAMUEL MEREDITH, ed., *The Indigenous People of the Caribbean* (Gainesville: University of Florida Press, 1997)

WORCESTER, THOMAS, *The Cambridge Companion to the Jesuits* (Cambridge: Cambridge University Press, 2008)

www.ingramcontent.com/pod-product-compliance
Lightning Source LLC
Chambersburg PA
CBHW070218030726
47505CB00006B/1724